Emperor Leo III the Isaurian

To Mum

Emperor Leo III the Isaurian

Imperial Saviour, Christian Icon Breaker?

Peter Crawford

Pen & Sword
MILITARY

First published in Great Britain in 2024 by
Pen & Sword History
An imprint of Pen & Sword Books Limited
Yorkshire – Philadelphia

ISBN 978 1 39907 283 0

A CIP catalogue record for this book is available from the British Library

Typeset by Mac Style
Printed in the UK by CPI Group (UK) Ltd, Croydon, CR0 4YY.

Pen & Sword Books Limited incorporates the imprints of After the Battle, Atlas, Archaeology, Aviation, Discovery, Family History, Fiction, History, Maritime, Military, Military Classics, Politics, Select, Transport, True Crime, Air World, Frontline Publishing, Leo Cooper, Remember When, Seaforth Publishing, The Praetorian Press, Wharncliffe Local History, Wharncliffe Transport, Wharncliffe True Crime and White Owl.

For a complete list of Pen & Sword titles please contact

PEN & SWORD BOOKS LIMITED
47 Church Street, Barnsley, South Yorkshire, S70 2AS, England
E-mail: enquiries@pen-and-sword.co.uk
Website: www.pen-and-sword.co.uk
or
PEN AND SWORD BOOKS
1950 Lawrence Road, Havertown, PA 19083, USA
E-mail: uspen-and-sword@casematepublishers.com
Website: www.penandswordbooks.com

Contents

Capital saviour
An Isaurian lion
Smasher of Icons?

@haiku_history

'History is a discipline widely cultivated among nations and races. It is eagerly sought after. The man in the street, the ordinary people, aspire to know it. Kings and leaders vie for it. Both the learned and the ignorant are able to understand it. For on the surface history is no more than information about political events, dynasties and occurrences of the remote past, elegantly presented and spiced with proverbs...

...the inner meaning of history, on the other hand, involves speculation and an attempt to get at the truth, the subtle explanation of the causes and origins of existing things, and deep knowledge of the how and why of events.'

Ibn Khaldūn, *Muqaddimah*
foreword (Rosenthal, F. translation, 1958)

Acknowledgements

I would like to give thanks to the established team of contributors who have played some part in the production and publication of this book.

To Phil Sidnell and Pen & Sword for continuing to allow me to write about what is surely now 'not' Ancient History …

To my sister, Faye Beedle, for making sense of my vague instructions and outlines to present such excellent maps and diagrams …

To Noble Numismatics, for once again granting me access to their excellent archive of images.

To the historians, writers, artists and photographers whose work has been consulted, digested, detailed and cited within. My apologies.

To Matt Jones and his team who turned this gather-up of text, photographs, diagrams, maps and drawings into this colourful tome.

I continue to blame John Curran …

To the *Classical Association in Northern Ireland* for providing me with useful distractions.

To all the staff, past and present, at Queen's University, Belfast and Dalriada School, Ballymoney …

And to Mum … I could promise not to buy any more books, but we both know that that would be a lie …

gratias vobis ago

Introduction

Overlaps and Transfers

As this latest literary outing is basically a direct sequel to my previous *Pen & Sword* book on *Justinian II*, it has largely the same origin story: an unpublished tweet about a noseless emperor, and a piece of serendipitous book shopping. As there is some chronological overlap between the lives of Justinian (668–711) and Leo (c.685–741), this means that we will be re-treading over some material covered in *Justinian II.* This will be particularly evident in the sections on the background of the Roman Empire and its neighbours at the time of Leo's birth, his early life, entering imperial service, and mission to the Caucasus, a career he owed to the patronage of Justinian himself. Of course, we will delve more deeply into Leo's background, asking questions such as 'why did Leo and the dynasty he founded come to be known as 'Isaurian' despite neither he nor his family seemingly being from Isauria'?

A more limited re-treading comes for the period 711–717, a period of great political turmoil for the empire, where it was ruled by five different men. I had originally planned to take *Justinian II* up to the accession of Leo in 717; however, so big was my Justinian manuscript that I removed the chapter I had written on the 6-year period between Justinian's murder and Leo's accession, with the idea already germinating that I would use it in a full work on Leo III. Not only is the period 711–717 part of Leo's lifetime, rather than Justinian's, he was also heavily active during that period in military and political terms, leading the Roman response to increasing Arab pressure in Anatolia and then taking up the imperial mantle himself.

It should also be noted that while they did not rule for any prolonged period, the other men to rule during that period – Philippikos Bardanes, Anastasius II and Theodosius III – all had some effect on the Roman Empire, whether it be religious, military or political. Because of that, the chapter on the period does not just focus on the increasing role of Leo, but also the policies and actions of these three short-lived emperors.

The most important single event during Leo III's reign began mere weeks after his accession: the year-long Arab Siege of Constantinople between 717 and 718. Make no mistake: perhaps like no other time in its history to that point, this was an existential threat to the Roman Empire. Such was the infiltration of its remaining provinces and the centralised importance of the capital that had its defences failed, the empire was likely to have fragmented, quite possibly to never come together again. Leo's ability to take advantage of the preparation of his predecessors, Arab miscalculations, a harsh winter, foreign aid, the Theodosian Walls and the imperial navy would secure his status as an 'imperial saviour'.

Despite this status, Leo III is not as well-treated by the sources. This is because the other great development of the age – the initiation of iconoclasm – sharply divided opinion. This 'breaking of icons' was of long-lasting, even epochal importance to the religious and social fabric of the Roman Empire, and Leo's initiating of it forever tainted his reputation in the eyes of the ultimately victorious iconodule – 'lover of icons' – sources. The background to and influences on this immense change in imperial religious policy must be looked at in detail, including the question of whether or not Leo III really was the orchestrator of iconoclasm. Furthermore, his opposition to icons was not the only religious policy attached to Leo III, with actions toward Jews, Montanists and Paulicians also to be investigated.

While much of the focus falls on the Siege of Constantinople and iconoclasm (reflected in the title of this book!), there are various other significant developments and events that take place during Leo's reign. His 24-year tenure on the throne is credited with bringing stability to the empire, but this was not achieved without some internal trouble. He faced rebellions in Sicily, the Aegean, Ravenna, Italy, and from a previously deposed, Bulgar-backed emperor. Were such rebellions part and parcel of an on-going 'military anarchy' and poor army discipline or were they sparked by imperial circumstances and/or the policies of Leo himself?

Leo also faced external trouble. His dealings with the Umayyads did not end with the Siege of Constantinople. Leo's forces reclaimed territory along the Syrian border and launched naval raids against Arab territory in Syria and even Egypt, but Arab raids continued to strike into the Roman eastern provinces, although punctuated by the successful defence of Nicaea in 727 and culminating in the Roman victory at the Battle of Akroinon in 740. It will also be important to look at the consequences of the siege of Constantinople on the Umayyad caliphate and its burgeoning internal problems by the time of Leo's death. The Arab-Khazar war of the 720s and 730s also impacted the empire, leading to a diplomatic détente that saw Leo marry his eldest son to the daughter of the Khazar khagan.

While there was something of a peace with the Bulgar khanate throughout most of Leo's reign, Thrace, Macedonia and Greece were still coming under pressure from Slavs and other Bulgars, with little evidence of a renewed presence in imperial territory largely lost over a century previously. A better recorded erosion of imperial power took place in Italy in the face of Arab raids on Sicily, a weakening exarchate, the rise in independence of the papacy, and a persistent threat from the Lombard kings and dukes.

Bringing stability to an empire racked by almost a century of military defeat did not just take military resistance. Various aspects of imperial administration required attention, with Leo overseeing reforms of financial governance, coinage, provincial infrastructure, military organisation and law codes. The concluding chapter will then look at the immediate and longer-term legacy of Leo III in terms of his impact on the empire and the Roman world as a whole – was it positive militarily, politically, administratively, and even socially, but religiously divisive? An epilogue will look briefly at the continued religious division and the immediate civil war upon Leo's death in 741.

Sources

For the life and reign of Leo III, the historian is faced with a dual problem – a lack of a surviving contemporary secular history and the anti-iconoclast bias of most of the remaining material. There had been a decline in the production of secular history throughout the seventh century, which was 'a result of the transformations in urban culture and in the structure and nature of elite society at this time.'[1] The pressure on the Roman Empire from Persians, Slavs, Bulgars and Arabs saw a change in literary priorities, with more focus on religion, and iconoclasm an extension of this need for dogmatic reason and explanation of on-going negative events. However, the lack of a strong contemporary historian does not preclude the reconstruction of a workable chronology; indeed, the excellent dual volume by Leslie Brubaker and John Haldon on the sources (2001) and history (2011) of iconoclasm demonstrates the amount of material that is available, even if it has to be treated with care.

Iconoclasm itself saw literary sources become weapons in the theological and cultural debates, highlighting and exacerbating the 'very sharp ideological conflict'[2] that developed between the two sides. The debate and its integral part of Roman society perhaps furthered the 'religifying' of the empire's literary output, in terms of who was writing, what kind of source was being written, and recasting certain genres like hagiography and even history itself. This in itself is potentially not a massive issue; indeed, fuelling the production of various types of source could have seen iconoclasm produce a richer and more varied record than many other eras; however, such was the depth of disdain felt by both sides of the debate that it was almost inevitable that the victor would try to eliminate the source material of the vanquished.

And this is what came to pass after the 'Triumph of [Iconodule] Orthodoxy' in 843. Virtually all iconoclast writing was destroyed, while other material was reworked. This often makes the reworked material say more about post-843 attitudes and what the people involved thought and did during the debates, rather than preserve what the original writer thought. This means that the surviving material is all from iconodules and can be highly polemical and prone to rhetorical exaggeration, particularly when it comes to dealing with prominent supporters of iconoclasm. It must be said that some such material can be so obvious in their bias that that is useful, and while our major sources are from iconodules, they failed to completely hide how they used iconoclast sources. Perhaps the most obvious example of this is arch-iconodule Theophanes calling Leo III 'pious', despite considering him an horrendous heretic. Clearly, Theophanes has been careless in his copying of his source.

For Leo III, the surviving textual evidence is largely sufficient for a general look at his rise to power and early reign. This would seem to be due to the work of a contemporary chronicle – the so-called '*History to 720*', which traces events from the late-seventh century, possibly as early as the assassination of Constans II in 668, through to 720.[3] Traditionally seen as an anonymous work, this '*History to 720*' has been attributed by some to a certain Trajan the Patrician. The tenth-century *Suda* records Trajan as the author of a chronicle during the time of Justinian II, which could be the '*History to 720*', while there is some suggestion that whoever wrote this chronicle was a close associate of Leo III.[4] Trajan or not, whoever wrote the '*History to 720*' seems to have been prominent enough in Leo's government or court to present the emperor in a positive light. This, of course, makes it somewhat skewed in its information, lacking in analysis and detail, although skewed in a way – pro-Leo – that is distinctly different from the rest of the iconodule sources.

While the '*History to 720*' might be the ultimate source for much of what we know of Leo's early reign, it is not the *actual* source.[5] This is because it does not survive as a separate work, but is considered a significant source for the late-seventh and early-eighth century in other later works, most importantly the *Breviarum* of Nikephoros, Patriarch of Constantinople (806–815), and the *Chronographia* of Theophanes the Confessor.

Born into an iconodule, Constantinopolitan family, Nikephoros served as a secretary under the Isaurian dynasty and as a commissioner at the Second Council of Nicaea in 787. He then resided at a cloister along the east coast of the Bosphorus before being suddenly chosen as patriarch of Constantinople on 12 April 806. Despite being a layman, rendering his accession uncanonical, imperial support saw Nikephoros sit on the patriarchal throne until the restoration of iconoclasm by Leo V in 814. In monastic exile, Nikephoros continued writing until his death in 828. The most important part of his work is the short historical survey of the period 602 to 769. It was possibly written in c.780 during his time serving as an imperial secretary, although there are arguments for an early-ninth century date.[6] The *Breviarum* lives up to its name in places by being more concise than we would like, while the lack of dates and critique reduces its overall usefulness. It may be somewhat 'less determined in its presentation by iconophile propaganda,'[7] but it is still heavily biased against iconoclasts such as Leo III. With those warnings, the work of Nikephoros remains 'an extremely valuable source of information.'[8]

Theophanes the Confessor was of a similar background to Nikephoros – born in Constantinople to an iconodule family and served in the iconoclast Isaurian court. Theophanes then lived a monastic life, before becoming abbot of an abbey near Cyzicus. This position allowed him to attend the Second Council of Nicaea in 787. Under Leo V, he was imprisoned and tortured for refusing to accept iconoclasm, dying in exile on Samothrace in c.817. Between c.810 and 814, Theophanes wrote a *Chronographia* covering the period from Diocletian to Michael I (284–813). It was a continuation of the chronicle of George Syncellus and used a significant amount of research already done by George. This not only gave Theophanes access to material, particularly of the Middle East where George had lived for a time, that other chronicles did not have, it raises the question of just how much of the *Chronographia* was the work of George instead of Theophanes. Could it even be that Theophanes was merely a copyist rather than the author?[9] The *Chronographia* should be seen as a collaboration, with George having gathered significant amounts of material, while Theophanes brought it together in a coherent work, as well as adding in his own research.

Due to their shared usage of the *'History to 720'*, a query may be raised over what can Theophanes tell us that Nikephoros does not (and vice versa). They provide a similar chronological order, specific information and vocabulary, but 'each historian copied some parts of their common source that the other did not'[10] through personal and stylistic choices. Despite both using the same source, there are differences in Theophanes and Nikephoros that go beyond personal and stylistic usage of the *'History to 720'*/Trajan the Patrician. Indeed, at times, Theophanes is sufficiently more vehement in his attacks on Justinian II than Nikephoros for the possibility of them using different sources to be raised, with the latter using a so-called '713 Chronicle' instead of the *'History to 720'*. Even if this is the case, the chronicles to 713 and 720 do not appear to be all that significantly different.[11]

They do, however, demonstrate that despite the iconodule opposition to him, Leo III had significant influence on the source record. The *'History to 720'* and any

'713 chronicle' may be the origins of much of the poor reception of Justinian II. It was necessary for the Isaurian dynasty to present a legitimate reason for the overthrow of the Heraclians – Justinian II being a 'blood-thirsty and almost mad emperor'[12] certainly fit the bill. This necessity may have been exacerbated by reports of pretenders claiming to be Justinian's son Tiberios.[13] Leo may also have had Justinian targeted due to his championing of orthodoxy, which included support for icons; however, this idea relies on Leo being the fervent iconoclast he is traditionally depicted as and Justinian making more out of image worship than he probably did. It could just be that Leo held a personal dislike for his erstwhile imperial mentor as there were rumours that Justinian had attempted to have Leo killed during his mission in the Caucasus. Whatever the reason, that Leo III, the supposed instigator of iconoclasm, could direct the depiction of an emperor shows that for all the rewriting of literature post-iconoclasm, it could not erase the influence of contemporary sources completely.

It is likely that Theophanes (and George Syncellus) had more sources than Nikephoros.[14] For example, when dealing with Umayyad Syria, Theophanes not only had the work and knowledge of George Syncellus but also a mid-eighth century Syriac source, usually attributed to Theophilius of Edessa, a source also used by Agapios of Hierapolis, Michael the Syrian and the *Chronicle of 1234*. Theophanes used other Latin and Greek sources, likely including an iconodule chronicler for the reign of Leo III after the *'History to 720.'*[15]

However, there is one source that Theophanes does not seem to have used – Nikephoros. Indeed, despite their shared backgrounds, careers, outlooks and usage of the *'History to 720'*, Nikephoros and Theophanes were seemingly unaware of each other's work. It could be that Nikephoros' *Breviarium* was written in c.820 after Theophanes' *Chronographia*, but then why is there no textual evidence that Nikephoros used Theophanes? While the date of the *Breviarium* is debated, either its c.780 or c.820 date raises the question of why did one not use the other as a source? A possible reason that these two prominent historians 'ignored' one another is that iconoclasm may have seen their works go unpublished until not only after their deaths but also the final defeat of iconoclasm in 843.[16]

There are errors in Theophanes' text of various types. As well as inconsistencies of presentation, such as calling the iconoclast Leo 'pious', there are some much more careless mistakes such as in AM6216, which covers the years 723–724, where Theophanes presents the story of pope Stephen II, who did not become pope until 752. To be clear, Theophanes does on occasion stray from his year-by-year account, such as with Leo III's mission to the Caucasus which is recorded in AM6209 (716–717) despite taking place during the second reign of Justinian II (705–711), but with Stephen II there is no such intentional chronological diversion. There are also potentially some other dating issues, stemming from the various calendars in operation at the time, the lag between events and recording, and perhaps just simple error. Such issues likely arise due to the genre of historical writing Theophanes is operating in. Rather than a blended history, he has produced a year-by-year chronicle stitched together from various and sometimes contradictory sources. While this can create issues, the more rudimentary 'stitching together' can allow for some useful disentangling of the sources used by Theophanes.[17]

While there is room for caution about Theophanes' own usage of material, either through error or intentional distortion, there is another avenue that requires judiciousness in certain aspects of the *Chronographia*. Much like many other works of the mid-ninth century, there have been some additions to the *Chronographia*. A clear example comes in AM6177 (685–686), where the text shows knowledge of patriarchs who reigned after Theophanes' death. Indeed, this very alteration can be dated to 840 as it claims that John VII had only been patriarch for six years, yet we know he reigned from 834 to 843. Due to such inherent biases, a lack of critical insight and the way its author presents material, Theophanes' *Chronographia* must be used with care, but with that said, it remains 'the fullest and most useful account of Roman history'[18] for the reign of Leo III.

There is some useful information on Leo III recorded in other more minor and fragmentary chronicles; for example, a certain Agathon writing in 713, but preserved in the Acts of the Second Council of Nicaea in 787, presents some information on events preceding Leo's accession, such as the deposition of Justinian II and the Monothelite policy of Bardanes. Petrus Siculus, writing in the mid-ninth century, provides information on Paulician beliefs and history, although it was written to present them as heretics so care must be taken on what they supposedly believed or actions they took. There are other historiographic traditions beyond those produced within imperial territory that can provide useful information. Various Latin texts highlight western affairs, which still involved imperial forces and interests and were frequently ignored by the Roman sources in the east. They can show attitudes to the empire, both ceremonial and practical. While some information can come from Frankish sources like the anonymous *Liber historiae Francorum*, it is the Italian sources that provide the most cogent material – the *Liber Pontificalis*, Agnellus's *Liber pontificalis ecclesiae Ravennatis* and the *Historia Langobardorum* of Paul the Deacon. Somewhat fortunately, this trio of sources provides some of the viewpoints of three of the main players in the Italian peninsula – the papal side from the 'civil servants' behind the *Liber Pontificalis*,[19] the Ravennate/anti-papalism of Agnellus and the Lombards. Together they provide plenty of information, but as will be seen, little of it involved Leo III. Even iconoclasm can be somewhat hidden, with

Agnellus not mentioning it directly, probably due to his anti-papalism;[20] that said, the *Liber Pontificalis* sees descriptions of icons and images increasing as the eighth century progresses. There are also several local chronicles to also provide occasional insight on certain aspects of Italian politics and views on the empire. Another source from the Latin-speaking western Mediterranean is mid-eighth century Spain. The *Chronicle of 741* and the *Chronicle of 754* can give insights into developments not just in Spain but occasionally abroad too, with the former using a similar Syriac source to Theophanes, possibly Theophilus of Edessa, or the original Greek source that Theophilus might have used.[21]

The eastern lands bordering the Roman Empire are home to numerous literary traditions, which can give us different views of the Roman Empire and Umayyad caliphate in cultural, religious and political terms, as well as their own local developments. Perhaps the largest grouping is the Syriac tradition. Under that umbrella are the Jacobite (western), Nestorian (eastern) and Maronite traditions. These can have their own styles and forms, such as being either annalistic or hagiographical. Initially identified as the work of Dionysius of Tel-Mahre, but really compiled by an anonymous monk at the Zuqnin monastery, the eighth-century *Zuqnin Chronicle* encompasses events from the Creation to c.775 in four separate parts. Its fourth part details Christian communities under Umayyad control in the Middle East. The actual *Chronicle* of Dionysius of Tel-Mahre, Jacobite patriarch of Antioch from 818 to 845, is a little later in date and covers the period 582–842; however, it only survives in sections copied by Michael the Syrian, patriarch of Antioch (1166–1199), who also used excerpts from other sources. The *Chronicle to 1234*, written in thirteenth-century Edessa, used similar sources to Michael the Syrian, but independently of him and therefore somewhat corroboratory. Several of the Nestorian chronicles end in the seventh century, such as that of Elias of Nisibis (975–1046), which preserves useful information on Sassanid Persia, but little on the eighth century. Syriac also provides a series of other anonymous chronicles (to 724, 813, 819 and 846) which preserve additional as well as corroborative and some contemporary material.[22]

Not only is the Syriac tradition separable into several sub-groups, the entire eastern tradition itself can be divided into several linguistic classifications; however, there is something 'artificial' about some of these divisions, such as the 'common tradition, style and subject matter of Syriac and Christian Arabic historiography.'[23] This Christian Arabic tradition is best represented by Agapios of Hierapolis/Mabboug and Eutychios. While such sources might rely on Maronite chronicles or share a lot in common with Greek and Syriac writers, by being bilingual, they may preserve information otherwise not available to the other traditions, particularly with Roman interaction with the Arabs.[24]

Armenian sources like Ghevond's *History of Armenia* and Stephen of Taron's *Universal History* can be very localised, focusing on Armenian regions/families and religious issues, a focus that increases in the eighth century as Roman power receded in eastern Anatolia and the Caucasus. They can still provide some useful third-party material on the Romans and Umayyads, as well as additional information about the frontier zone between the two states.

Muslim historiography is a very different beast to the more well-established literary traditions of the Eastern Mediterranean. In its earliest days, the genre had a very limited chronological framework, focusing more on tribal, familial and personal achievements/concerns. Indeed, at times, some of its works could be considered little more than compendiums of 'oral traditions'. Such a basis has Muslim sources providing contradictory information about the same events or persons, leading to much of Muslim historiography being long thought of as being of limited use; however, considerable currency was put into the 'chain of transmission' by recording witnesses and the (assumed) reliability of the sources. This 'chain of transmission' makes many Muslim sources superior to others of much longer established traditions at identifying where they got their information from. Roman sources use pre-existing material, but rarely record what that pre-existing material is. These ideas, both bad and good, survive in some form in more mature Muslim historiography. Some older reports may be disregarded in favour of new 'invented and validated'[25] reports that fit the required/demanded framework. There are also numerous repeated *topoi*, with formulaic comments on army sizes, battles, capture of settlements etc., material that can appear useful but can be difficult to verify due to the involvement of legend and vested interests. However, we must be careful in claiming this as a deliberate rewriting of history; it is more the consequences of a series of choices.

Specifically, for the period of the life and reign of Leo III, Muslim historiography relies on material compiled from various sources – historical, poetic, oral or religious – in the ninth and tenth centuries. This raises the issue of the material not being contemporary with the events they are describing, but this is no different than having to rely on Nikephoros or Theophanes as 'primary' sources. So while there is dispute over the usefulness of Muslim sources for the eighth century, leaving the reader to tread carefully, it should by no means disqualify the entire genre as a source of information on not only developments in the Umayyad caliphate but also in the Roman Empire.[26]

The most prominent Muslim source for Leo III is Tabari, a ninth/tenth century Iranian polymath, who wrote history, poetry, lexicography, grammar, ethics, mathematics, medicine and Qur'anic commentary. It is his *Tarikh al-Rusul wa al-Muluk – History of the Prophets and Kings* – that is most of interest here. Other histories and minor chronicles can fill in gaps in Tabari's record or serve as a control on some of his information. Al-Baladhuri's ninth-century *Kitab Futuh al-Buldan – Book of the Conquest of the Countries* – focuses mostly on the seventh century but provides useful information on later periods, while al-Ya'qubi's *World History* provides some information on the Roman Empire; unfortunately, his history of the empire itself is lost. The anonymous '*Book of Sources*' preserves a detailed account of the Siege of Constantinople 717–718 and subsequent Arab raids.

The literary genre of hagiography becomes particularly important during the eighth century. The lives of saints and martyrs, panegyrics, homilies and stories about relics and miracles 'reflect popular and unofficial views and attitudes'[27] in belief, society and culture. There are ideological issues, with hagiographic sources presenting the subject and their beliefs in the best (but not always historically accurate) light. Iconoclasm era hagiography was frequently presented in a social context – work of the peasant, soldiers' duties, priests' actions, with such a focus on the deeds of individuals potentially raising the usefulness of the hagiography. Many of these works were written much later, despite claims to being contemporary. Some faced significant reworking over the decades and centuries, making their original content impossible to recover. Some were even largely invented. This does not make hagiography entirely worthless, but much more complex and anachronistic. These issues are more acute in the iconoclast era as that dispute became so formative and key to Roman societal and political life. A prime example of these potential issues is the *Vita Germani archiepiscopi Constantinopolitani*, which professes to tell the life of a prominent character in the earliest years of iconoclasm – patriarch Germanos, but appears to have been radically rewritten or even wholly composed in the twelfth century. The *Vita Stephani iunioris* has similar issues, although lacking the severe chronological detachment. It may have come from the iconoclast era and involved some possible invention, but it may have been constructed to put forward patriarchal propaganda regarding Germanos' role in opposing Leo III's initiating of iconoclasm.

Another important religious source of information on iconoclasm comes from the Acts of the Council of 787, which not only presents iconodule beliefs but also preserves many of the arguments put forward by the iconoclast Council of Hieria in 754, as well as some material written during the reign of Leo III. However, the Acts reflect the iconoclasm of Constantine V rather than that of Leo, with the former and his *Peusis* having been a driving force in the development of iconoclast philosophy.

Insights into policies and developments during a certain reign can come from legal material propagated during it; however, the 150 years after the death of Justinian I was a period of decreasing legal material. The Roman government had other more important priorities than promulgating new laws in the maelstrom of the seventh century. That is not to say that the Heraclian emperors did not issue laws, but it was seemingly not until the reign of Leo III that a more extensive look at Roman legislation could take place. This was in the form of the *Ekloga*, which was a selection of key parts of Roman legislation aiming to make law more accessible and comprehensible. The focus and inspirations of this law code can give insights into the aims and outlooks of the Roman people and state in the aftermath of one of its most harrowing centuries. There are also other collections of legislation – the *Nomos Mosaikos*, Farmers Law, Rhodian Sea Law and Military Law/Mutiny Act – which could form something of a body of secular law for the early-eighth century. Some of these laws share a style and presentation with the *Ekloga*, but it is not unanimously agreed that they are from the late-seventh/early-eighth century.

The tenth-century emperor Constantine VII wrote or had commissioned numerous works during his reign, with some proving useful from the study of the empire of previous centuries: *De Caeremoniis* – '*On Ceremonies*' – describes well-established imperial court ceremonies; *De Administrando Imperio* – '*On the Administration of the Empire*' – provides advice on running the empire and how to deal with its various foes, while *De Thematibus* gives information on recent events in the provinces. Useful political, administrative and military information relevant to the eighth century can be gleaned with these works, but care must be taken as they are all tinged by their tenth century production.

Other historical information comes from a genre of what might be seen as tourist guides of Constantinople. The late-eighth/early-ninth century *Parastaseis syntomoi chronikai* – '*Brief Historical Notes*' – presents some interesting, but shallow, information on monuments and sites within the city. This *Parastaseis* also makes up part of a tenth-century collection of such guides called the *Scriptores originum Constantinopolitarum* ('*Writers on the origins of Constantinople*'), also known as the *Patria of Constantinople.* Even with their presenting of legendary and mythical material, such guides can be invaluable for the record of early Constantinople and its monuments.

The period encapsulated by iconoclasm saw the development of much of the art and architecture, particularly religious, that was to help shape the Medieval Roman 'Byzantine' state; however, there are considerable issues with identifying material to associate with Leo III specifically. This is due to a lack of secure dating for much of the surviving material, so some of the material classed as either 'Isaurian' or accredited to predecessors or successors could well belong to Leo III. The limited visual imagery from the period was not only due to the existential threat to the empire diverting energies elsewhere but also due to the nature of iconoclasm and the reaction to it erasing a lot of the evidence that came before or during it.[28] The *Parastaseis* recorded a statue in the Neorion harbour attributed to Leo III, while patriarch Germanos claimed that Leo had a statue of the apostles and prophets erected in front of the imperial palace in Constantinople.

While art and architecture from the era was affected by contemporary politico-religious choices, archaeological evidence for the iconoclast period has been greatly impacted by more modern decisions. Archaeological investigation of the Late Antique/Early Medieval east lags behind other geographical and chronological periods, leaving 'Byzantine' archaeology a relatively young subject. That said, strides are being made to address that. Such as it is, archaeological evidence can provide insights into various facets of Roman life, being particularly important for the social aspects which get little or no attention from the written sources. It can present us with a more complex urban picture; goods production and movement can enlighten the transfer of populations; new fortifications and repairs to the walls of Constantinople can highlight the resetting of imperial defences in the wake of Arab conquests, and the focus on certain areas and cities can show the attempts to 'systemise' the themes. However, even with these potential benefits, caution must still be advised on the extent of what archaeology can tell us. Not only are virtually all excavations limited in scope, they also only present a small snapshot of time and place.

Epigraphy as a genre straddles the boundary between written and archaeological. Changing priorities and cultural values amongst the governing and elite classes and perhaps the reduction in urban culture saw a marked decline in the field throughout the fifth, sixth and seventh centuries. This means that there is very limited epigraphical material from the entire iconoclast period, although examples survive such as the inscription on the walls of Nicaea commemorating the successful defence of the city in 727.[29]

Coins and their circulation can demonstrate the reach of the empire or a specific emperor, militarily and economically. They can also provide insight into the aims of revolts during the reign of Leo III – was its leader looking to claim imperial power and therefore minted coins bearing their image? Some significant numismatic change occurred under Leo III. His gold coins (*solidi/nomismata*) depicted his son Constantine on the reverse from 729 instead of the usual 'cross on steps' motif, an innovation that continued throughout the eighth and on into the ninth century. Initially, Leonid copper coins followed this *nomismata* innovation, only to revert to the formula of both emperors on the obverse and a value mark on the reverse in the 730s. Perhaps most poignantly, Leo also re-introduced the silver *miliaresion* that took influences from previous Roman silver issues, but also took significant cues from the new Islamic silver dirham, demonstrating a momentous shift in numismatic trend-setting. One other significant development with numismatics under Leo is that his eastern coins no longer sport mintmarks, presumably because Constantinople was the only eastern mint in operation. That said, western mints in Sicily, Naples, Rome and Ravenna continued to issue, although their coins were debased during Leo's reign.[30] Much of the imperial propaganda employed by Leo on his coins is repeated in the seals issued during his reign, with the styles Leo followed being used continually through much of the eighth century. Unlike coins, which under Leo saw the date replaced by a purely decorative formula, seals frequently carry the indiction and so there are many dated seals from this period. Something which can hinder the dating of certain coins and seals is that under the Isaurian dynasty it became a more common practice to depict emperors long after their deaths. Indeed, Leo III continued to appear on the issues of his successors perhaps up to the Second Council of Nicaea in 787.[31]

The iconoclast era has drawn an immense amount of scholarship, with the attached bibliography only scratching the surface. Because of this, it is difficult to pick out just a few. I have already mentioned the extensive dual volume on the sources (2001) and history (2011) of the period by Leslie Brubaker and John Haldon, with both of these authors publishing useful articles and books on various aspects of religion, military and empire as well. Of particular note is Brubaker's 2012 work raising questions on Leo III's actual role in the initiating of iconoclasm. More generally, there are the subject-shaping works by the likes of George Ostrogorsky and Alexander Vasiliev; the numerous publications of E.W. Brooks, Averil Cameron, Walter Kaegi and Warren Treadgold on aspects of the Roman Empire in the era of Iconoclasm; Hugh Kennedy on aspects of the Umayyad caliphate; the twin works by Stephen Gero on iconoclasm during the reigns of Leo III and Constantine V, while I found Thomas Noble's 1984 work on the development of the 'Papal State' of particular use in deciphering the maelstrom of early-eighth century Italy.

Spelling Conventions and Nomenclature

Given the various languages involved in the eighth century and its recording – Latin, Greek, Armenian, Syriac, Arabic, Germanic, Avar, Slavic, Bulgar, Khazar Turkic, Berber – some spelling conventions are required. Lacking real knowledge about any of these languages, I have aimed for consistency rather than any overriding linguistic principle. That said, direct quotation from various sources will see some different spellings used.

In general, Anglicised versions of personal names will be used over Latin or Greek, so for the most part we will be in the realms of Leo and Constantine rather than Leon and Constantinus; however, on occasion, due to the number of individuals sharing the same name, different spellings may be employed to differentiate them, such as 'Artabasdus' and 'Artabasdos.' The neighbours of the Roman Empire present trickier linguistic issues as names incur different spellings in their transliterations into Latin/Greek and then English. For example, the name of the founder of the Umayyad dynasty is rendered Muawiyah, Mu'awiya, Muawiya, Mauias to list a few. There can be similar problems with Bulgar, Slavic and Turkic names.

The Anglicised ancient name of an existing town, city or region prevails in the text, such as Constantinople over Istanbul, Antioch over Antakya or Anatolia over central Turkey. Roman-era provincial names are preferred, although on occasion, lesser-known place names will be accompanied by more famous modern names to aid in its identification. As for the empire as a whole, some trace the beginning of the 'Byzantine Empire' to the reign of Constantine I, using the 'Byzantine' label that inhabitants of Constantinople had come to refer to themselves as, which in turn came to be applied to the whole empire in the sixteenth century. However, I view this as something of an historiographical creation of a new, but essentially fictitious state in the form of the 'Byzantine Empire'. For me, the state based on Constantinople was recognisably and lineally the 'Roman Empire' until at least 1204, if not all the way to 1453. Therefore, aside from in quotations from other historians, throughout this work, the realm of Leo III will be referred to as the 'Roman Empire' and its inhabitants as 'Romans.' The only significant deviation comes when delving into events in Italy, where the duchy and people of Rome are an active factor – in this case, the Roman Empire will be referred to as 'imperial' and its agents as 'imperials'. As for its neighbours, 'Umayyad' and 'Arab' are used largely interchangeably, while the proto-states of the Lower Danube and the northern Caucasus are referred to respectively as the 'Bulgar Khanate', with their ruler known as the 'khan' and the 'Khazar Khaganate', with its ruler the 'khagan'.

Dating Issues

By the eighth century, the Romans were using a combination of *Anno Mundi* – 'World Year' measured from the Creation based on the Septuagint text of the Bible and a 15-year indiction cycle, which saw the year begin on 1 September. This causes some issues when attempting to translate it to the modern Gregorian calendar. The year of Leo III's accession is AM6209, which began on 1 September 716 and ended on 31 August 717, so if we were only told that he attained the throne in AM6209, we could only posit 1 September 716 to 31 August 717; however, as we are told it occurred on 25 March of AM6209, we can say Leo acceded to the throne on 25 March 717. An example of the problem that can arise comes in the birthdate of Justinian II. Theophanes records it taking place in AM6160: 1 September 668 to 31 August 669. Without any outside help on a specific date, month or season, we are left with a Gregorian date of 668/669. A similar problem arises when using Muslim sources. The Islamic calendar is usually denoted as 'AH' – *Anno Hegirae*: 'in the year of the Hegira', starting in 622 and is based on the lunar cycle. This means that it is always considerably out of sync with Roman and modern calendars. Therefore, the Roman indiction/ *Anno Mundi* and Islamic Hijri calendars can date the same events months, even years apart. However, it seems that the long-held idea that virtually every major event of the late-seventh/early-eighth century was 'systematically misdated'[32] is not correct. Theophanes in particular seems much more accurate in his dating than was usually thought, and while there are still some individual mistakes these likely show that, rather that some systemic issues, 'Theophanes like the rest of us had trouble converting eastern sources' years of the Hegira into ordinary solar years.'[33]

Any errors in continuity and consistency remain my own.

Lists of Office Holders

Roman Emperors

Constantine IV	15 September 668–14 September 685
Justinian II	14 September 685–695
Leontios	695–15 February 698
Tiberius III	15 February 698–21 August 705
Justinian II	21 August 705–4 November/11 December 711
Philippikos Bardanes	4 November/11 December 711–3 June 713
Anastasius II	3 June 713–November 715
Theodosius III	May 715–25 March 717
Leo III the Isaurian	25 March 717–18 June 741
Constantine V	18 June 741–14 September 775
Artabasdos	June 741–November 743
Leo IV the Khazar	14 September 775–8 September 780
Constantine VI	8 September 780–19 August 797
Irene	19 August 797–31 October 802

Umayyad Caliphs

Abd al-Malik b. Marwan	12 April/7 May 685–9 October 705
Al-Walid I	9 October 705–25 January/11 March 715
Sulayman b. Abd al-Malik	25 January/11 March 715–24 September 717
Umar II	24 September 717–4 February 720
Yazid II	4 February 720–26 January 724
Hisham	26 January 724–6 February 743

Popes

Benedict II	26 June 684–8 May 685
John V	23 July 685–2 August 686
Conon	21 October 686–21 September 687
Sergius I	15 December 687–8 September 701
John VI	30 October 701–11 January 705
John VII	1 March 705–18 October 707
Sisinnius	15 January 708–4 February 708

Constantine	25 March 708–9 April 715
Gregory II	19 May 715–11 February 731
Gregory III	18 March 731–28 November 741

Patriarchs of Constantinople

George I	679–January/February 686
Paul III	687–693
Kallinikos I	693–705
Cyrus	705–early 712
John VI	Early 712–715
Germanos I	715–730
Anastastios	730–754

Lombard Kings

Perctarit (second reign)	671–688
Alahis	688–689
Cunincpert	688–700
Liutpert	700–701
Raginpert	701
Aripert II	701–712
Ansprand	712
Liutprand	712–744

Lombard Dukes of Benevento

Transamund I	665–703
Faroald II	703–724
Transamund II (first reign)	724–739
Hilderic	739–740
Transamund II (second reign)	740–742

Lombard Dukes of Benevento

Romuald I	662–687
Grimoald II	687–689
Gisulf I	689–706
Romuald II	706–730
Audelais	730–732
Gregory	733–739
Godescalc	739–742

List of Illustrations and Maps

All Maps, Plans and Diagrams were drawn by Faye Beedle

Stemmata

Maps and Diagrams

List of Plates

Coins

ABD AL-MALIK: gold aniconic dinar, issued in AH80 (699–700) from the Damascus mint. *Courtesy of Noble Numismatics* (http://www.noble.com.au/)

JUSTINIAN II: (second reign, 705–711): gold *solidus*, issued in 705 from the Constantinople mint. Obverse: facing bust of Christ, with cross behind head, curly hair and close beard, wears pallium and colobium, raising hand in benediction, dN IhS ChS REX REGNANTIUM. Reverse: crowned facing bust of Justinian, wearing loros and holding crosses, DN IUSTINIA NUS MULTUS A, PAX. *Courtesy of Classical Numismatic Group, Inc.* (http://www.cngcoins.com)

LIUTPRAND: gold *tremissis* issued during his reign (712–744) from the Pavia mint. Obverse: bust looking right, DN LI TPRAN; P in right field. Reverse: St Michael standing left, SCS MIHHIL, holding long cross and shield. *Courtesy of Classical Numismatic Group, Inc.* (http://www.cngcoins.com)

Al-WALID I: gold aniconic dinar, issued in AH94–95 (713) from the Damascus mint. *Courtesy of Noble Numismatics* (http://www.noble.com.au/)

PHILIPPIKOS BARDANES: gold *solidus*, issued between 711 and 713 from the Constantinople mint. Obverse: facing and crowned bust of Philippikos, DN FILIPICЧS MЧL TЧS [AN], wearing loros, holding cross globe and eagle-tipped sceptre. Reverse: cross on steps, VICTORIA AЧGЧ Z/CONOB. *Courtesy of Classical Numismatic Group, Inc.* (http://www.cngcoins.com)

ANASTASIUS II: gold *solidus*, issued between 713 and 715 from the Constantinople mint. Obverse: facing, crowned and draped bust of Anastasius, ∂ N APTЄMIЧS A NASTASIЧS MЧL, holding cross globe and akakia. Reverse: cross on steps, VICTORIA AЧGЧ ΘΘ/CONOB. *Courtesy of Classical Numismatic Group, Inc.* (http://www.cngcoins.com)

THEODOSIUS III: gold *solidus*, issued between 715 and 717 from the Constantinople mint. Obverse: facing crowned bust, ∂ N TһЄO∂O SIЧS MЧL A, wearing loros, and holding akakia and cross globus. Reverse: cross on steps, VICTORIA AЧGЧ H/CONOB. (© *Otto Nickl*)

SULAYMAN: gold aniconic dinar, issued in AH97 (715–716) from the Damascus mint. *Courtesy of Classical Numismatic Group, Inc.* (http://www.cngcoins.com)

LEO III: gold *solidus*, issued between 717–720 from the Constantinople mint. Obverse: facing crowned and draped bust, ∂ N D LEO N PA MЧL, holding cross globe and akakia. Reverse: cross on steps, VICTOR[IA AVGЧ Δ/CONOB. *Courtesy of Noble Numismatics* (http://www.noble.com.au/)

LEO III and CONSTANTINE V: gold *solidus*, issued between 737–741 from the Constantinople mint. Obverse: facing crowned bust of Leo, ∂ N D LEO N PA MЧL N, wearing chlamys and holding cross globe and akakia. Reverse: facing crowned bust of Constantine, ∂ N CONS TANTINЧ Θ, wearing chlamys and holding cross globe and akakia. *Courtesy of Classical Numismatic Group, Inc.* (http://www.cngcoins.com)

LEO III and CONSTANTINE V: silver *miliaresion*, issued between 720 and 741 from the Constantinople mint. Obverse: cross on steps, IhSUS XRISTЧS NICA. Reverse: LEON/ S CONST/ANTINE E/ C**QEЧ bA/ SILIS. *Courtesy of Noble Numismatics* (http://www.noble.com.au/)

UMAR II: gold aniconic dinar, issued in AH101 (719–720) from Damascus mint. *Courtesy of MANTIS* (http://numismatics.org/collection/1971.49.297)

YAZID II: silver aniconic dirham, issued in AH103 (721–722) from Damascus mint. *Courtesy of Classical Numismatic Group, Inc.* (http://www.cngcoins.com)

TIBERIUS PETASIUS: gold *solidus* issued in 728 or 730–731 from a mint in Blera or Naples. Obverse: facing, crowned bust, ∂ N TIЧERIЧS MЧLTЧS A, wearing chlamys and holding cross globe and akakia. Reverse: cross on steps, VICTOR IVTGTA(?)/CONOB. *Courtesy of Classical Numismatic Group, Inc.* (http://www.cngcoins.com)

HISHAM: gold aniconic dinar, issued in AH119 (737) from the Damascus mint. *Courtesy of MANTIS* (http://numismatics.org/collection/1917.215.3401)

GODESCALC: gold *solidus*, issued between 739 and 742 from the Benevento mint. Obverse: facing, crowned and draped bust, D N I-INЧS P P, holding cross globe. Reverse: cross globe on steps, VICTORI IVGVSTO, D-G across fields/ CONOB. *Courtesy of Classical Numismatic Group, Inc.* (http://www.cngcoins.com)

CONSTANTINE V and LEO IV: gold *solidus* issued between 751 and 757 from the Constantinople mint. Obverse: facing crowned busts of Constantine V and Leo IV, CONSTANTINOIS S LEON O NEOS, wearing chlamys, cross above. Reverse: facing bust of Leo III, ∂ LE ON PA MЧL, holding cross potent. *Courtesy of Noble Numismatics* (http://www.noble.com.au/)

ARTABASDOS: gold *solidus*, issued between 742 and 743 from Constantinople mint. Obverse: facing, crowned and draped bust of Artabasdos, ∂ APTAЧA-SDOS MЧLT, holding patriarchal cross. Reverse: facing, crowned and draped bust of Nikephoros, ∂ NIChFORЧS MЧLTЧM, holding patriarchal cross. *Courtesy of Classical Numismatic Group, Inc.* (http://www.cngcoins.com)

Pictures

All in the public domain, unless stated otherwise

Tervel the Bulgar as St Trivelius.

Pope Constantine, *Nuremburg Chronicle,* 1493.

Pope Gregory II, *Nuremburg Chronicle,* 1493.

Detail of Chludov Psalter, ninth century, depicting an act of iconoclasm.

'Charles Martel divides the realm between Pepin and Carloman', *Grandes Chroniques de France*, Bibliothèque Nationale, Ms. fr. 2615, fol. 72.

Pope Gregory III, eighth century papal medallion. (© *ASKI*)

Patriarch Germanos.

'Argument about icons', *Codex Skylitzes Matritensis*, fol. 50vb.

'The fleet of the Romans setting ablaze the fleet of the enemies', *Codex Skylitzes Matritensis*, fol. 34vb.

'The Arabs attacking Constantinople during the reign of emperor Leo III', Constantine Manasses, *Chronicle*, miniature 47.

Inscription commemorating the successful defence of Nicaea and the restoration of its walls.

ISAURIAN DYNASTY

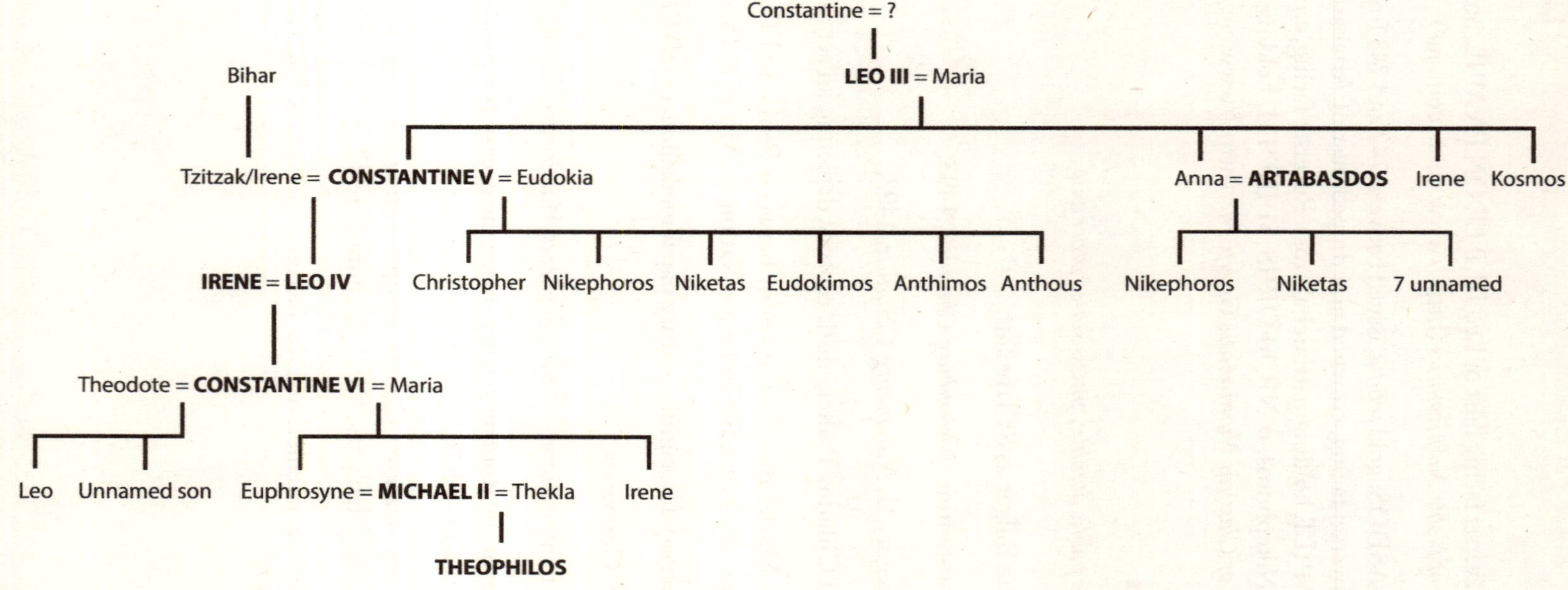

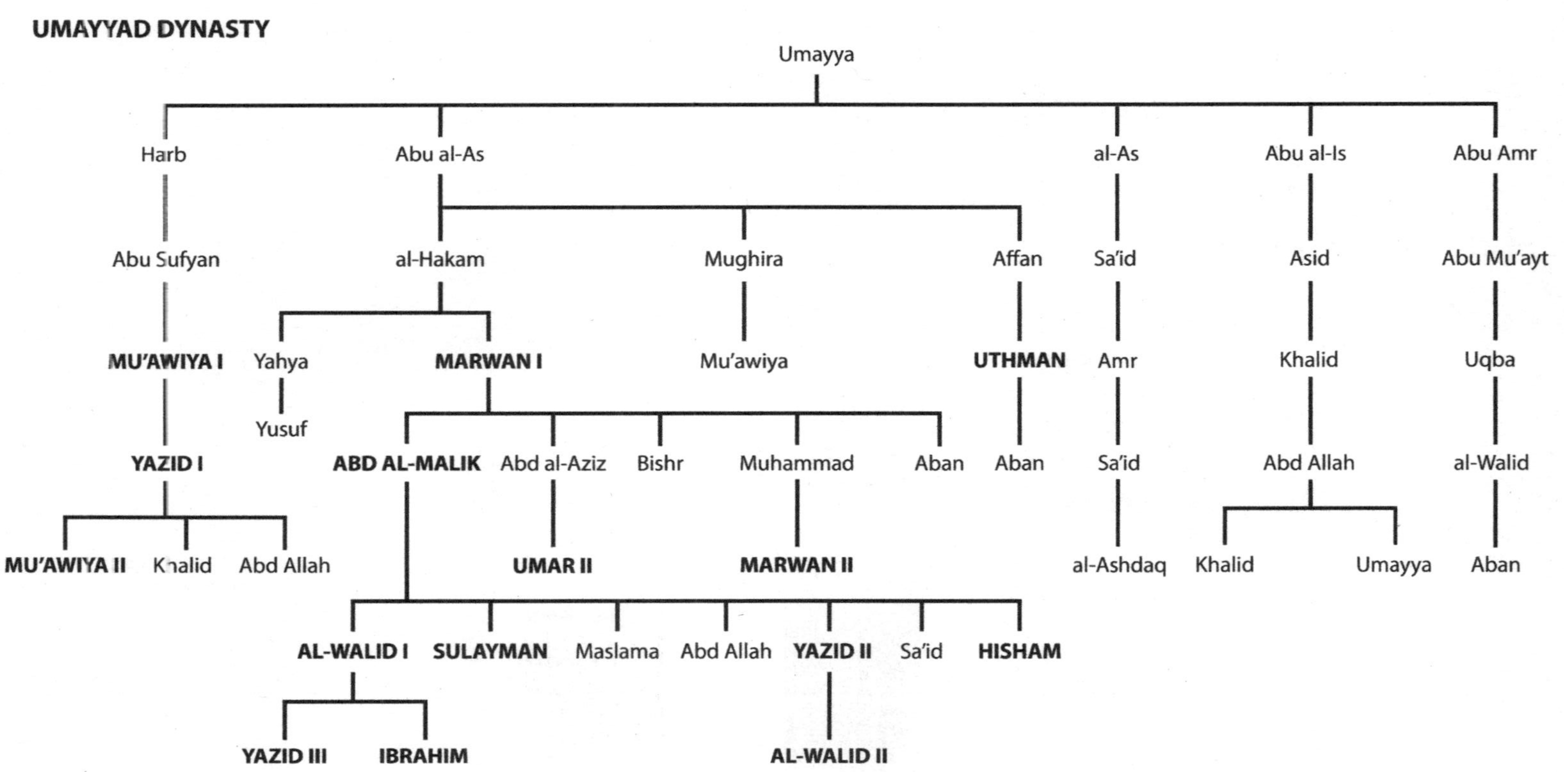
UMAYYAD DYNASTY
Umayya
Harb
Abu al-As
al-As
Abu al-Is
Abu Amr
Abu Sufyan
al-Hakam
Mughira
Affan
Sa'id
Asid
Abu Mu'ayt
MU'AWIYA I
Yahya
MARWAN I
Mu'awiya
UTHMAN
Amr
Khalid
Uqba
Yusuf
YAZID I
ABD AL-MALIK
Abd al-Aziz
Bishr
Muhammad
Aban
Aban
Sa'id
Abd Allah
al-Walid
MU'AWIYA II
Khalid
Abd Allah
UMAR II
MARWAN II
al-Ashdaq
Khalid
Umayya
Aban
AL-WALID I
SULAYMAN
Maslama
Abd Allah
YAZID II
Sa'id
HISHAM
YAZID III
IBRAHIM
AL-WALID II

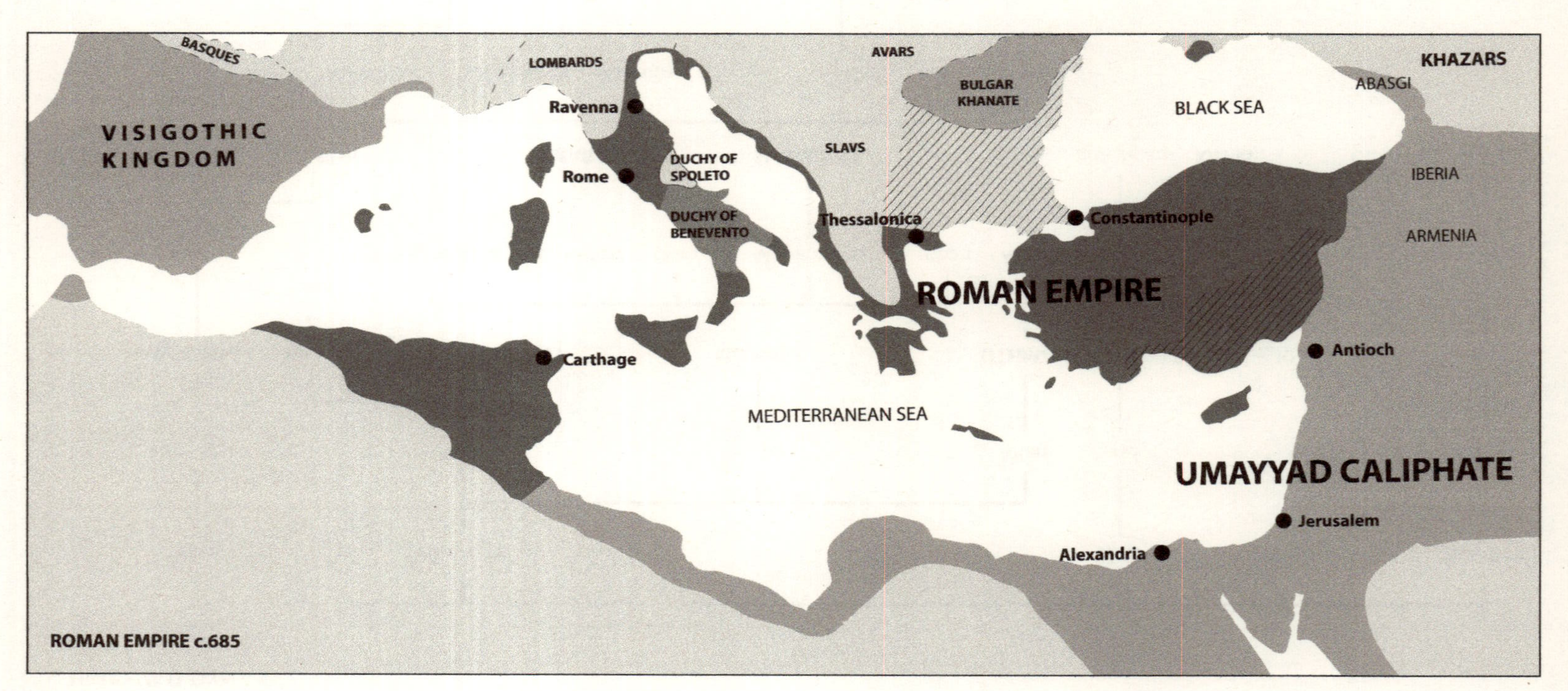
BASQUES
LOMBARDS
AVARS
KHAZARS
ABASGI
BULGAR KHANATE
BLACK SEA
Ravenna
VISIGOTHIC KINGDOM
DUCHY OF SPOLETO
Rome
SLAVS
IBERIA
DUCHY OF BENEVENTO
Thessalonica
Constantinople
ARMENIA
ROMAN EMPIRE
Antioch
Carthage
MEDITERRANEAN SEA
UMAYYAD CALIPHATE
Jerusalem
Alexandria
ROMAN EMPIRE c.685

Chapter 1

From Heraclian Stability to Military Anarchy – The Roman Empire of 685

'Victory at all costs, victory in spite of all terror, victory however long and hard the road may be; for without victory, there is no survival.'

Sir Winston Churchill

Unexpected Survival

It is something of a surprise that the Roman Empire survived the seventh century. The Persians and Avars had come close to extinguishing it in the 620s, while the armies of emergent Islam had altered the Roman landscape forever through the 630s and 640s. However, the decisive and perhaps expected hammer blow had not come on either occasion. The Avaro-Persian siege of Constantinople in 626 made little impression, while internal strife prevented the Arabs from launching an all-out assault on the Roman capital – the so-called 'First' Arab Siege of Constantinople of the 670s seems much less a full-blown siege and more a half-hearted blockade and raiding of Constantinopolitan waters.[1] That said, while the weakness of imperial opponents in the face of the Land Walls of Constantinople had saved the Roman Empire, the Mediterranean world of 685 looked significantly different than it had in 600. Egypt, Libya, Palestine, Syria, Mesopotamia, Armenia and virtually the entire Balkans had been lost to the Romans, with Anatolia facing annual raids. Many of these losses would be permanent.

It was not just through the strength of the Constantinopolitan defences that the Roman state persevered through decades of haemorrhaging territory and resources. When faced with such an existential threat, even though militarily exhausted, the Roman people and imperial infrastructures proved resilient. They were aided by the fortune of coming under the leadership of a dynasty of skilled military and political commanders – the Heraclians. The founder of the dynasty, Heraclius won the war against the Persians by leading an invasion himself and led a somewhat orderly retreat from the Levant to defensible positions in Anatolia in the face of the Arab advance. Constans II used the somewhat solid base provided by his grandfather to achieve limited success, winning a favourable treaty from the Umayyads, defeating some Slavs in the Balkans and making some initial strides against the Lombards in Italy. Constantine IV stood up to two usurpers and led the resistance to whatever actually constituted the 'First' Arab Siege of Constantinople, while Justinian II won victories over the Arabs, Slavs and Ravennate rebels.

The successes of the Heraclians in steadying the ship, on top of the pre-eminent position it had enjoyed before the troubles of the seventh century, meant that despite the substantial losses of territory, the Roman Empire of 685 still encompassed enough land to continue to defend itself and go on the offensive on various frontiers. That Roman resilience, inherent and inspired by the Heraclians, would be needed, as through the early life of our subject, Leo III, the empire would continue to lose territory, facing the definitive loss of Africa, further erosion of its position in Italy and more grinding warfare against the Umayyads in eastern Anatolia and the Caucasus.

The continued external pressures on the Roman state and the internal ructions it caused meant that overseeing the survival of the empire on their watch did not immunise the Heraclians from violent scrutiny: Heraclius faced a coup from within his own family; Heraklonas was deposed in a bout of familial infighting; Constans II was assassinated by his chamberlain; Constantine IV faced a plot centred on his brothers; and Justinian II was deposed not once but twice. And this does not take into account the other members of the Heraclian family and others done away with by various emperors for the sake of the succession and/or perceived internal security. It was this increasing 'Military Anarchy' that brought down the Heraclian dynasty and was to provide the setting for Leo III's accession to the imperial throne.

Inside the Walls

One of, if not *the*, most significant factors in the survival of the Roman Empire in the seventh century was the position and defences of the imperial capital, Constantinople. Being founded only in 330, on the surface, this 'city of Constantine' was a veritable urban youngster when compared to various cities still within the empire at the time – Thessalonica was founded in 315 BC, Rome traditionally in 753 BC, while Athens had been continuously occupied since 3000 BC.[2] However, the 'founding' of Constantinople in 330 was in fact a second (or even third) urban *re-founding* on the site.

The settlement that would eventually become modern Istanbul was traditionally founded in 667 BC, reputedly by the Megarian king Byzas, although it may be that that name was instead of Thracian origin.[3] This seeming eponym gave the city the name Βυζάντιον/*Byzantion*. That said, there were at least two other settlements recorded in what is now Istanbul that may predate the foundation

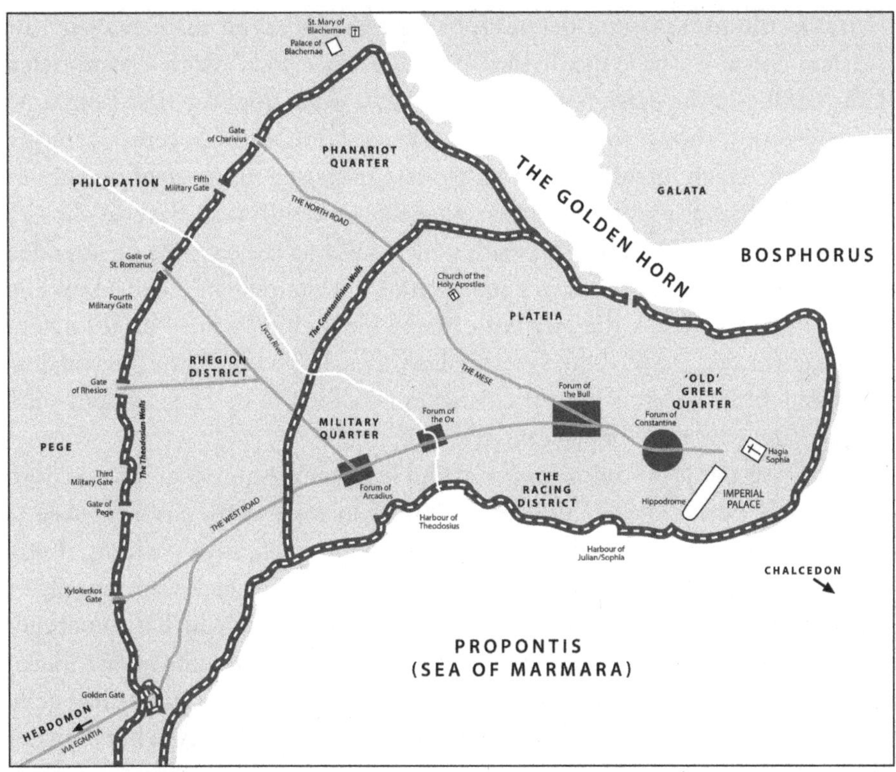

of Byzantion. Pliny the Elder records that Byzantium was 'formerly called Lygos', which seems to have been focused on the Sarayburnu/Seraglio Point, while the second-century geographer Dionysius of Byzantium lists another settlement at the head of the Golden Horn called Semystra, after a nymph of the same name, which almost became the site of the Greek colonisation but for poor omens.[4] It would seem that both of these pre-'Byzantine' settlements were founded by local Thracians. Furthermore, recent archaeological finds in European Istanbul would seem to predate not only these historical settlements but also the millennia-old Copper Age occupations – 5500–3500 BC – on the Asian side of the Bosphorus by up to 1,200 years.

The potential for Byzantion having been 'refounded' already before it became the 'city of Constantine' comes in the second century AD. During the civil war that erupted upon the assassinations of Commodus and Pertinax in 193, Byzantium sided with one of the opponents of the eventual winner, Septimius Severus, and faced siege and sack at his hands. The damage was so extensive that when Severus undertook the rebuilding of the city, it was given a Romanised plan and briefly renamed *Augusta Antonina* after his son, Caracalla (Marcus Aurelius Antoninus).

It was the site's natural defences, being surrounded on three sides by the sea, and position astride the divide between Europe and Asia that so attracted Constantine in the early-fourth century. He was far from the first Roman to recognise this, shown by Cassius Dio's strong criticism of Severus' razing of Byzantion, which he called 'a strong Roman outpost and a base of operations against the barbarians from Pontus and Asia'[5] (and of course, Severus showed that he recognised its strategic position by rebuilding the city). As he intended for Constantinople to be his imperial capital, Constantine initiated a building programme to bedeck the city with incredible architecture – the forums of Constantine and the Ox, the Great Palace, the Hippodrome, the Augustaion, the Church of the Holy Apostles, later to be added to by Hagia Sophia and Hagia Eirene to name but a scant few.

But it was not just sublime imperial and holy architecture that was to adorn the 'city of Constantine'. While the geographic location of the city offered east-west trading routes, natural harbours and a strong defensive position, it was not without its drawbacks. Chief amongst them was the site's water supply or lack thereof. It only had a few small springs and the Lycus, which is sometimes called a 'river', was really just a stream. This led the fourth-century rhetorician Themistius to comment that even though the Constantinian dynasty had gone to great lengths to beautify Constantinople, it was 'girdled by gold but dying of thirst.'[6] So for it to become the immense imperial capital Constantine envisaged, Constantinople would need nearly 500 km of channels and aqueducts to bring water from the Belgard Forest in Thrace.[7] And once that water entered the city limits, it had to be sent to various vast open-air reservoirs and dozens of subterranean cisterns for distribution to the population.

Another of the drawbacks was its sheer size – as it grew, Constantinople quickly outstripped the capabilities of its hinterland to provide for it. It was fortunate then that Constantinople had an empire to feed it. Its coastline allowed for numerous harbours to facilitate the importation of those resources, with none more important than the grain fleet that came from Egypt. Constantinople not only consumed the products of empire, its harbours and numerous warehouses made it a major trading hub, playing a significant role in redistributing the wares of the world. This immense logistical enterprise enabled Constantinople to grow from a sparsely populated but impressively endowed settlement in the mid-fourth century to overtaking Rome as the largest city in the Mediterranean within a century, possibly reaching over 600,000 inhabitants, if not more.[8]

A third drawback stems more from the success the Romans made of Constantinople rather than the site of the city itself. Indeed, it is more of a general issue for large concentrations of people in the ancient world. It could well be that refugees from the territorial losses and raids suffered by the Roman Empire during the seventh century actually saw the population of Constantinople increase at a time when the breadbasket of the capital – Egypt – had been permanently lost. Even in normal times, a large, compacted and undernourished population is dangerous; however, since 541, the late-antique world had been wracked by an immense plague cycle. It being a trading hub and centre of naval, military and political power opened Constantinople up to infection from various corners of the empire and beyond. There would be at least two major outbreaks during the Isaurian dynasty, one during Leo III's lifetime, but it must be remembered that such focus on major outbreaks hides the fact that plague was likely a constant companion for the inhabitants of not just Constantinople or the Roman Empire as a whole, but to the entire Mediterranean world, including Rome's tribal, barbarian and Muslim opponents.

Its central position between Europe and Asia enabled Constantinople to become, not just a trading hub, but a nerve centre of imperial rule the like of which the Roman world had perhaps not seen since before the crisis of the third century. Constantinople could be seen as almost an island city-state supported by and administering its provinces, power emanating from the imperial seat, which the emperor rarely left for any length of time. This concentration of power in Constantinople increased the resilience of the Roman state as a whole, for as much damage that could be done to the provinces, the capital could still emanate that power and represent a focus of imperial continuity. Gradually, it could be said that Constantinople became not just the empire's capital, but the empire itself.

However, such a concentration of imperial, administrative, cultural and religious power and influence made Constantinople itself a very appealing target for an invader. Being the main bastion of the Roman Empire meant that Constantinople needed to be well-defended. And it was. The rapid expansion in population meant that even by the end of the fourth century, the defences built by the Constantinians were already too small for the city. Their replacements have become known as the Theodosian Walls, as they were usually considered to have been begun during the reign of Theodosius II under the direction of the praetorian prefect Anthemius; however, there is some evidence that the walls were begun in around 405/406 and were therefore planned and begun under Theodosius' father, Arcadius.[9]

Once completed, the scale and scope of the Theodosian Walls were truly epic. They encompassed an area that doubled the size of Constantinople, which was already not a small settlement. And in terms of defence, these were not just ordinary run-of-the-mill fortifications – the Theodosian Walls were the greatest fortifications of the ancient and medieval world. Approaching from the west, an enemy attack faced a 20m wide, 10m deep moat and then a 20m killing zone just to reach the outer wall. That first circumvallation was 8.5m high and 2m thick, with 96 towers placed at 55m intervals.[10] If the attacker got to and over this first line, he was then faced with another 20m terraced killing zone before reaching the main inner wall, which was 12m high, 5m thick and also crowned by 96 towers.

While not as comprehensive as the Theodosian land walls, Constantinople also boasted significant upgrades to the original seaward defences of Byzantion. It was initially thought that these upgrades came at the same time as Constantine's refounding of the city, but there is no surviving reference to them before 439, when Cyrus of Panopolis, the urban prefect of Constantinople, was ordered to repair the city walls and complete them down to the sea. But even this appears to be an error repeated by various later sources such as Theophanes and the *Chronicon Paschale.* Some significant repairs to the land walls were carried out by the praetorian prefect, Constantine, after an earthquake in 447 and he is accredited by *Patria* I.73 as connecting the sea walls to the Theodosian land walls. Indeed, the very existence of any substantial seaward defences in the same order of magnitude as the land walls before the seventh century has been doubted. The lack of mention of seaward defences during the siege of 626 has been noted, although the supremacy of the Roman navy in the face of the Avars and Persians might negate the need of such mention. There are also very limited fifth-century finds of associated sea wall brick work. There is perhaps no extant contemporary mention of the sea walls until the turn of the eighth century.[11]

Whenever they were completed, the sea walls were similar to the land walls in terms of appearance but were much less intricate. They were made of a single wall, which was not as tall as the land walls. Only in the various harbours dotted around the coast was there a second circuit. Part of the reason for the sea walls not needing to be as formidable as the landward defences were the strong currents around the city, which made it extremely difficult to make an orderly attack, particularly on the southern and eastern sides, while the northern approaches were defended by the Golden Horn, an inlet that provided a magnificent natural harbour, the entrance to which was itself guarded by sizeable towers both from within Constantinople itself and the satellite city of Galata on its northern side. On top of that was the strength of the Roman navy and its own 'secret weapon' in the form of 'Greek fire'. Furthermore, the seaward defences would see major refurbishment and an important upgrade in the early-eighth century; an upgrade that was to have a significant impact on the reign of Leo III.

This combination of vast land and sea fortifications posed a conundrum for any and all attackers. Between their construction and the breaching of the sea walls in 1204 by the Fourth Crusade, the only successful attempts to capture the city were undertaken by Romans during times of civil war, and none of those overcame the defences through force – they relied on betrayal from those within or sneaking into the city due to local knowledge. Indeed, the land walls would only be rendered vulnerable by the invention of the cannon a millennium after their construction. And even then, large sections of the Theodosian Walls still stand today.

Outside the Walls – Themes

The defences of Constantinople might have provided the Roman Empire with a bastion of incredible strength, durability and resilience, but that does not mean that the empire itself had not changed significantly. A quick glance at a map will show that, but not all of these changes were enforced by the cataclysmic events of the seventh century. The most obvious cartographic revelations would be the loss, reclamation and then gradual loss again of the western provinces of the empire since the fifth century. However, digging down a layer further than purely territorial, there had also been some important administrative developments in reaction to pressures faced by the empire in the sixth century.

The first of these major changes came in the west. Distracted by the Avars in the Balkans and the Persians in the east, the emperor Mauricius (582–602) felt that the administrative and military problems faced by Roman Italy required the creation of a new provincial organisation: the exarchate. This saw Italy divided into a series of duchies and placed under the regional command of the exarch of Ravenna, who held civilian and military authority. A similar administrative arrangement followed in Roman North Africa and the islands of the western Mediterranean (apart from Sicily), which were aggregated under the command of the exarch of Africa from Carthage.

The idea was for the exarch to be able to administer the western regions without having to look to Constantinople for leadership. However, there were issues with this. Such a dissemination of authority relied on the exarch being able to impose his imperially-invested power – in Italy, the interjection of the Lombards made that difficult. And as the authority and territory of the exarchate shrank, the various provincial *duces* began to act independently. Furthermore, the concentration of civil and military power in the role of the exarch coupled with the geographic separation from the emperor meant that the exarch would not always act in accordance with imperial wishes – Ravennate exarchs are seen siding with the papacy against the emperor and with the Ravennate archbishop against the papacy and the emperor, while the African exarchate hosted two separate usurpations against Constantinople. And this is just a small snapshot of the exarchs who died in post either fighting for or against the empire.[12]

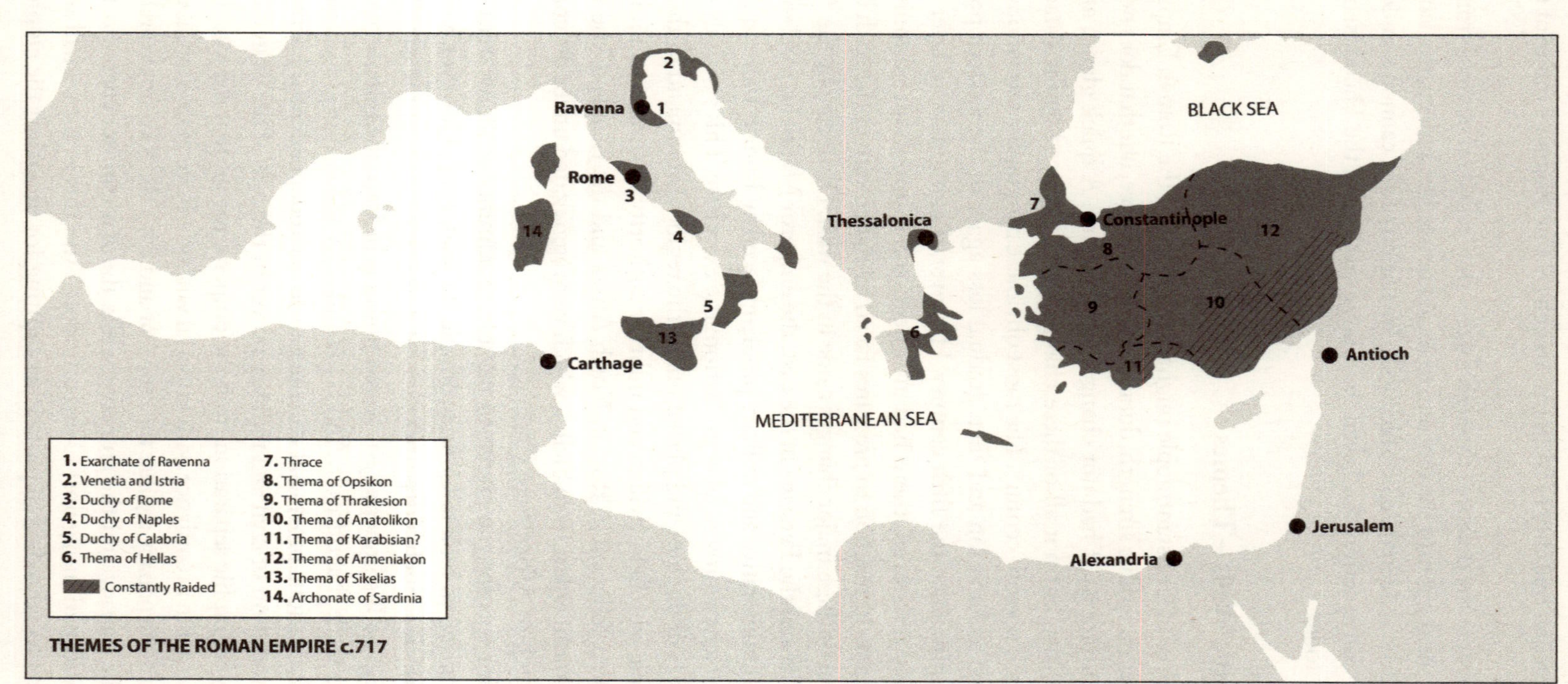

THEMES OF THE ROMAN EMPIRE c.717

The African exarchate was much less troubled than that of Italy. While Carthage did have to deal with the occasional raids of the Berbers and internal issues regarding pay, the Ravennate exarch had similar financial troubles, but also the Lombard kings and dukes, intransigent bishops and increasingly independent underlings gnawing away at his power and territory. And yet, by the turn of the eighth century, it was the African exarchate that had disappeared, swept away by Arab invasion. That is not to say that the Ravennate exarchate was in much better shape. The exarch was in the process of being relegated in importance in Italy.

While these exarchates offered well over a century of imperial service, it is difficult to determine if they really provided any substantial benefit to the empire, beyond allowing the central government to effectively ignore its western outliers as wasteful burdens rather than useful assets. That the emperors would continue to accept an abrogation of direct control over imperial territory is very telling. However, even if the exarchates and their dissemination of power were of little real use and/or a blemish on the sovereignty of the emperor, the social, political, religious and military problems that had initiated their creation had not abated; they had only become worse and worse. The collapse of the Danube frontier and the loss of the eastern provinces forced the Heraclians to follow a similar exarchate policy at the core of the empire. This would become known as the 'theme system'.

Unfortunately, the development of this thematic reorganisation received little focus from the sources. And even material we do have from the likes of Theophanes may be tarnished by him filling gaps in the record with the provincial layout of his period a century later. What can be gleaned from the surviving material suggests that the transformation from the previous Roman provincial set up into the 'theme system' was a gradual one, rather than the result of the choices of a single emperor such as Heraclius or Constans II.[13] And even this 'gradual transformation' containing notions of planning seems out of place. The 'evolution' of this new provincial layout was uneven and haphazard, to the point that the very name 'theme system' is a misnomer. There was nothing 'systematic' about the 'theme system'.

The basis for these new provincial units was the retreating imperial field armies. This is reflected in the usage of the word 'theme' (θέμα/*thema*, pl. Θέματα/*themata*) to describe these new entities. Although its exact etymology is uncertain, 'theme' had been used to mean either a military unit or army, including these retreating field armies. And as these military occupations became a lot less temporary, the geographic regions made up of several former provinces that had been attached to these armies in order to support them took on the name of the army that was stationed there[14] – the Anatolic theme (Θέμα Ἀνατολικῶν/

Thema Anatolikōn) was born out of the eastern field army of the *magister militum per Orientem*; the Armeniac theme (Θέμα Ἀρμενιάκων/*Thema Armeniakōn*) out of that of the *magister militum per Armeniae*; and the Thrakesian theme (Θέμα Θρᾳκησίων/*Thema Thrakēsiōn*) out of that of the *magister militum per Thracias*. The four earliest themes were rounded out by the Opsikon theme (Θέμα Ὀψικίου/*Thema Opsikiou*), which was formed from the *Obsequium*, the imperial retinue of the emperor on campaign.

The commanders of these new thematic armies were the *strategoi* – 'generals' – who held similar civil and military authority to the exarchs.[15] The Opsikon theme was slightly different in having a *comes* as its commander. The soldiers of these 'thematic' armies were likely paid initially in cash, only to then be allotted land to live on and to farm to support their families and the army. Such allotments likely allowed the empire to reduce a soldier's pay while also giving him a vested interest in defending his new home. Service in the thematic armies was to be hereditary, which also reduced the need for expensive military bounties and unpopular conscription.[16] This combination of powerful *strategoi* and local land allotments helped make soldiers more self-sufficient and better looked after by the authorities through the reduction of some bureaucratic delay, expenditure and abuses.[17] There are some questions about the exact nature of service within the thematic armies. Could it be that the Opsikon was something of a standing army centred on the emperor or the position of the capital, while the other thematic armies involved slightly less permanent service, perhaps only mustered for specific actions? Certainly, being decommissioned when not on campaign would explain the seeming lack of complaint over reduced pay and rations.[18]

The size of these thematic armies is difficult to gauge, mainly because the sources record virtually nothing about the size of the Roman army of the seventh or eighth century. The only potential number given for the thematic army as a whole comes in 773, when Theophanes records that Constantine V 'gathered the soldiers of the *themata* and the Thrakesians and joined the Optimatoi to the *tagmata* to a total of 80,000.'[19] It is impossible that Constantine V congregated *all* thematic forces for a Bulgar expedition, stripping the Asian themes bare; however, this figure might represent the size of the entire Roman army, with Theophanes mistakenly associating it with Constantine's expeditionary force.[20] A deduction from pay roll figures has suggested that the Roman army of 641 was around 109,000,[21] from which would have to be deducted the 15,000 of the seemingly lost army of Africa, along with further losses against various imperial enemies, to come to a total close to 80,000. Perhaps the only other numerical inference that can be made, beyond references to thematic detachments, comes in the origin of the thematic armies amongst the regional field armies, which we know the sizes for.

Field Army[22]	Size in 559	Theme	Size in 773?
Praesental	40,000	Opsikon *et al.*[23]	34,000[24]
East	20,000	Anatolic	18,000
Armenia	15,000	Armeniac	14,000
Thrace	20,000	Thrakesian	8,000
Illyria	15,000	Kibyrrhaeot/Hellas	4,000
Italy	20,000	Sicily	2,000

Such is the mess of the source material that it is impossible to give definite dates for the creation of the individual themes, although that did not stop some from trying. The appearance of 'lands of the themes'[25] in Theophanes saw some posit the existence of the 'theme system' as early as 622; however, this overlooks the pre-existing meaning of 'theme' as an army or military unit, rather than a geographic district, not to mention any anachronistic terminological use by Theophanes.

In dating the formation of the 'theme system', we are really left with inferences and the dates individual thematic armies are first recorded, some of which are much later than might be imagined. The Armeniac theme, taking in Pontus, Armenia Minor, eastern Paphlagonia and northern Cappadocia from its capital at Amaseia, is the earliest attested in 667. Its partner in the defence against the Umayyad Arabs was the Anatolic theme. It is first mentioned in 669, centred on Amorion and covering lands in Lycaonia, Pisidia, Isauria and much of Phrygia. Despite its central position in Bithynia, western Paphlagonia and parts of Galatia and its headquarters in Nicaea, the Opsikon theme is not mentioned until 680.[26]

However, it is the fourth of the earliest themes – the Thrakesian theme – that highlights some of the major issues with dating and even situating parts of the 'theme system'. It would seem logical to think that it was stationed in Thrace, much like the Anatolic and Armeniac themes covered parts of Anatolia and Armenia respectively; however, while the 'Thrakesian' theme took its name from the Thracian field army, it was *not* stationed in Thrace, a disconnect that hinders its identification. It is not mentioned in the sources until 711, when the Thrakesian *tourmarches*, Christopher, was sent to Cherson by Justinian II.[27] This saw it thought that the provinces of Ionia, Lydia and Caria that made up the Thrakesian theme were part of a larger Anatolic theme until being established as a theme of their own in the early-eighth century. However, the *Thracianus exercitus* recorded in the *iussio* of Justinian II in 687 is now thought to reference the Thrakesian thematic army, rather than the forces of geographical

Thrace, which were instead attached to the Opsikon.[28] It is likely then that the Thrakesian theme was created at around the same time as the Anatolic, Armeniac and Opsikon themes.[29]

Of course, exactly when that was is impossible to know. A more general suggestion for the dating of the themes is that the field armies were probably situated in the regions that form the thematic provinces around them in the last years of Heraclius' reign (610–641),[30] but little in the way of official establishment occurred until that of Constans II (641–668) or later. It could be that lulls in Romano-Arab conflict, such as that which came with the First Fitna (656–661), allowed the empire to give form to its ad hoc provincial and military arrangements. Indeed, Justinian II founded the Hellas theme (θέμα Ἑλλάδος/*Thema Hellados*) in 688–689 during the lull that came with the Second Fitna (680–692). It must be said that this Helladic foundation date is something of an extrapolation from a lack of direct source attestation. When the soon-to-be emperor Leontios was made *strategos* of Hellas in 695, this was the first mention of the Hellas theme, with it assumed that Justinian founded it while he was in the region in late 688.

For some added confusion, the Hellas theme was not actually called a 'theme' in the sources for another century. The term used for it was a στρατηγία/*strategia*, suggesting that it was under the command of a *strategos*, but it is unknown if there was any difference between a *strategia* and a theme. Could a *strategia* reflect the lack of strong Roman presence in parts of the territory of this new Hellenic province, with its *strategos* only having military authority? Could it be something of a stepping stone to a full theme? Or does it just highlight a lack of clarity of thematic terminology, with Hellas established as a theme in c.688 and the sources failing to mention/define it properly? There is also a lack of clarity on the land incorporated in the Hellas *strategia*/theme, but Boeotia, Attica, Megara, Euboea, Corinthia and the Argolid seem to have been part of it, with its capital at either Athens or Thebes.

As an addendum to the Hellas *strategia*, it is not clear what Justinian II did with the lands in Thessaly, Macedonia and around the Strymon that his campaign in 688–689 had helped secure. They would become themes in their own right over a century later after more Greek territory was reclaimed, but were they in any way attached to the new Hellas *strategia*? Were they something of a proto-theme or an even more ill-defined region under the command of the Thessalonian eparch? This would seem to be further evidence of the lack of clear 'thematic' organisation even by the late-eighth century.

Justinian II also seems to have extended the use of themes further west as well. Seals from his first reign[31] record a certain Salventios serving as *strategos*, with the Sicilian theme being the only theme of comparable time frame. Arab sources also seem to back the presence of a *strategos* on the island between 687 and 695.[32] Its capital was at Syracuse, with the Sicilian *strategos* having some control over the Italian duchies of Calabria, Naples, Gaeta and Amalfi.[33] The establishing of a Sicilian theme may have been Justinian mistrusting the exarchs at Carthage and Ravenna politically, militarily and/or religiously, as well as thinking that the position of Sicily would allow a strong garrison force there to intervene in Africa and Italy. Justinian II or his immediate successors also appear to have organised Sardinia as something like a theme, but with the slightly lesser status of *archontate*. This is likely to have happened after the final demise of the Africa exarchate in 698, but suggests an added level of hierarchy to the 'theme system' by the eighth century.

There is another pair of 'thematic' provinces that appeared in the late-seventh and early-eighth centuries – the Karabisiani (Καραβησιάνοι/*Karabēsianoi*) and the Kibyrrhaeots (Κιβυρραιῶται/*Kibyrrhaiōtai*). Both these establishments seem to be naval in nature, with the Kibyrrhaeots called a 'nautical theme' (θέμα ναυτικόν/*thema nautikon*) and the Karabisiani perhaps providing something of a prototype for it. However, the source material is unclear about their origins, organisation and even general make-up. The first definitive mention of the Karabisiani – the name derives from the Greek κάραβις, meaning 'ship' – comes in c.680 during a Slav attack on Thessalonica, but its formation could be linked to the growing Arab threat at sea, possibly after the Arab penetration of the Sea of Marmara in the 670s or even the aftermath of the Roman defeat at the Battle of the Masts in 655.[34]

The lack of clarity in the sources also provides considerable trouble in defining what the Karabisiani really was. Was it a provincial fleet stationed in the Aegean or a name for much if not all of the Roman navy, with bases in virtually every maritime province?[35] There might have been some initial focus in the Aegean and southern Asia Minor, with a capital at Attaleia,[36] with Justinian II seen settling Mardaites in southern Asia Minor as naval manpower. But this is by no means definite. Indeed, while it is sometimes named as the 'Karabisiani theme', this is incorrect. Whatever the Karabisiani was, it does not fit any of the admittedly nebulous 'thematic' organisation, lacking territorial divisions, land forces and civilian authority, remaining a purely naval organisation.[37]

The role of the Karabisiani is further muddied by the appearance of the Kibyrrhaeots. The first record of these 'men of Cibyrrha' comes with their involvement in the 697/698 expedition to Africa.[38] Such a role in a high-profile expedition would suggest that the Kibyrrhaeot district was well-established by this date. Its location in either Caria or Pamphylia, in or near the initial Karabisian heartland, possibly makes the Kibyrrhaeots a core *droungos* subdivision of the Karabisiani. That their *droungarios*, Apsimar, could become the emperor

Tiberius III may also hint at firm foundations and prominence.[39] Justinian II's bolstering of southern Asia Minor with Mardaite naval recruits could have formed the basis of an expansion of the Kibyrrhaeot *droungos*, seeing it promoted to a status lofty enough to even supersede the perhaps more unwieldy Karabisiani.[40] However, if there was any such supplanting, it was more gradual than a single imperial directive. There is evidence for continued Karabisian activity on into the eighth century and possibly significant naval developments during the reign of Leo III. There would also be more themes added to the roster, but they were all from the later years of the Isaurian dynasty and beyond.[41]

'Thematic' Revolt?

Its continued expansion on into the eighth century would suggest that, despite its haphazard beginnings, the 'theme system' was an unmitigated success. Far from it. The improvised reorganisation might have helped restore some integrity to imperial territory, but it did not sweep away the empire's internal or external problems: they helped put the brakes on collapse rather than reversing it. Externally, while some successful campaigning beyond the frontiers was facilitated, Slavs, Bulgars and Arabs continued to raid Roman territory with impunity, the thematic armies being largely incapable of stopping them. Even with the limited stability the 'theme system' brought, the empire still faced considerable internal problems – disgruntlement, revolt and sedition amongst the soldiery remained close to the surface, as it had done since the late-fifth century.[42] Not even the reconquests of Justinian I had broken this trend of military unrest; indeed, his over-stretching of imperial resources exacerbated it.

Military revolt helped spark the first phase of the seventh-century crises, with Phocas leading the Danube army to overthrow Mauricius, while the Heraclian dynasty overthrew Phocas with the forces of the African exarchate. And while it was to rule the empire for a century, every emperor of the Heraclian dynasty faced some kind of unrest. Heraclius faced military opposition from supporters of Phocas, while there were suggestions of revolt amongst the army that was to be defeated at Yarmuk.[43] The familial drama between Heraclius, Constantine III and Martina/Heraklonas was only ended by military intervention. Constans II faced usurpations in Constantinople and Africa. Even when thematic armies start to appear, there was no drop off in military unrest, with Constantine IV facing usurpation in Sicily, revolt from the Armeniac *strategos*, 'protest' from the Anatolic army, and undisciplined rout against the Bulgars. Justinian II was deposed not once, but twice by military revolt, either side of Leontios being deposed by a rebelling African expedition and Tiberius III being overthrown by a Bulgar-backed Justinian. In many ways, the seventh-century Roman Empire contained all the ingredients for the cascade of military revolt it played host to: repeated military failure and impotence, reduction in land and resources, and religious strife, all on top of a pre-existing tendency towards unrest. As will be seen, this period of military unrest, punctuated by revolt against the ruling emperor, was not going to disappear with the Heraclian dynasty.

But perhaps somewhat against expectation, while seemingly rife with opportunity to escalate such military unrest, the thematic armies and their powerful *strategoi* had little effect on the frequency of revolt.[44] They did become focal points, but this was because they were the army and its leaders, which had been the centre of unrest for centuries, rather than any inherent issue with its specific organisation.[45] There was also still military revolt from outside the thematic system. Aspects of the thematic system might provoke unrest, but many of them were also potential benefits as well. The contraction of the empire brought these armies closer to the centres of power, politicising them, but also bringing them closer to the influence of the emperor. It also brought the armies closer to each other, acting as each others' deterrents, while alliances between *strategoi* could be a benefit and a threat to the empire. A *strategos* might be a powerful problem, but the concentration of authority in a single civilian/military governor could tighten imperial control if the *strategos* was loyal; hence the appointment of family members by Tiberius III and Leo III and the reuse of men of proven loyalty (and ability).[46] Some care would have to be taken in such appointments, for while meritocratic competition could provide a small but effective and controlled leadership group, it could also promote in-fighting, resentment and paranoia both within and without.

Despite the power of these positions, it is difficult to gauge how much influence the *strategoi* had on imperial policy. As will be seen with Leo III during his time as Anatolic *strategos*, circumstances might dictate that a general in the field would have to act without reference to the reigning emperor. However, while the exarchs, *strategoi* and other officers would usually become the focal point of revolt, the influence of the ordinary soldiery should not be overlooked. Along with the clergy, they became increasingly prominent in presenting provincial opinion.[47] Leo III would codify this 'centrality of soldiers to both society at large and to the emperors'[48] in the *Ekloga*, singling out the rank and file for more of a share in spoils.

While it may not have exacerbated it, the theme system did not eliminate military unrest. It was easy to blame unpopular emperors like Constans II or Justinian II for the revolts that they faced, but this does not account for the indiscipline and unrest faced by a popular and successful emperor like Constantine IV, or why the Heraclians in general continued to face problems in spite of being considered disciplinarians, without necessarily becoming unpopular for it.[49] There were likely more systemic issues in play, reappearing even after sustained periods of military calm and success. But even with this continued undercurrent of unrest and the lack of clarity about what it was and who initiated it, it must be said that this 'theme system' worked better than could be imagined for an improvised reorganisation for a state clinging on for grim death.

Land Reform, Law and Language

The achievements of the themes and the Heraclian emperors in stemming destruction allowed for some further imperial administrative and legal reform. The expansion of the theme system had required land redistribution to the soldiers. While the extent to which this saw the thematic armies based on 'soldier-farmers' might be overplayed in favour of professional recruits from rural backgrounds, there would still seem to be significant land given to soldiers upon their retirement, aiding them to raise families and provide supplies and future recruits for the empire.[50] And even if it is not directly connected to the theme system, the number of small landowners did increase during the seventh century. Territorial losses and the retreating of various military and civilian populations likely increased the population density of much of the empire. Providing land for these people saw the necessity of breaking up large holdings into smaller units, a policy which will have involved confiscations or the recognition of refugee occupations as legitimate. Such policies incurred the wrath of the land-owning aristocracy, who were losing out on some of their land to these new small landowners.

This presented emperors with a new avenue of popularity by supporting these small landowners in the face of greedy aristocrats. By doing so, the emperor was also preserving the expanded tax base and limiting the power of the super-rich to resist his control. The swing towards the small landowners may be seen in the *Nomos Georgikos*. Whether attributable to Justinian II or not,[51] 'the Farmer's Law' reflects regional and/or imperial interest in protecting the rights, customs and practices of small landholders in the eighth century.[52] It provided mechanisms for dealing with 'boundary disputes, property exchanges, leases, trespassing, hired labour, losses of livestock, theft, and related matters.'[53]

Another major land policy affecting the empire during this period was the organised movement of peoples. Population transfer was a long-standing imperial policy, with virtually every emperor involved in settling significant numbers of non-Romans on imperial territory.[54] It could bring land back into circulation, build up the tax base and provide new recruits for the army in the regions where the settlers were planted, all the while diluting the strength of extramural enemies. For centuries, the empire had proven extremely capable in integrating such foreign settlers, and while this ability had faded somewhat, it had not gone completely. Internal transfers such as Armenians and Syrians being used to repopulate Thrace were an important development for the life of Leo III. The last decades of the seventh century alone saw large numbers of Cypriots, Mardaites and Slavs[55] settled in different parts of the empire. While the Cypriot resettlement seems more about bringing land back into use, the Mardaite and Slav transfers were closer to military colonies, stationing populations in positions to provide military and naval recruits. Whatever they were, they proved of extended duration,[56] although the possibility of further annoyance of Roman citizen landowners who had to accommodate these foreign settlers must have existed.[57]

These immense changes to Roman provincial organisation and land distribution may have necessitated a wide-ranging reform of the tax system.[58] It would not be surprising that the pre-existing system of the *capitatio* (head tax) and the *iugatio* (land tax) would need to be replaced by the late-seventh/early-eighth century, given that it was over 400 years old by this point. There are issues with the sources about when these reforms were introduced. By the early-ninth century, the tax system was comprised of a hearth tax levied on families (*to kapnikon*) and a separate land tax (*he synone*). The references to the *to kapnikon*/*he synone* taxes under Nikephoros I (802–811) infer that they were well-established by that time, with some hint of them already existing under Leo III and possibly before.[59]

Such land and tax policies were not radical, born out of necessity or being the next logical steps in imperial development, but they were not necessarily good for the reputation of any emperor enacting such policies. This was because expanding the small landowner class and modernising the tax system required depriving others of some of their land and wealth. This raised opposition from urban dwellers and in particular the landed aristocracy; opposition that the biased sources claim that Justinian II met with imprisonment, confiscations, and even physical coercion.[60] Such a concerted attack on the elite seems unlikely, but imperial bolstering of the small landowning class and protecting them from land-hungry aristocrats was a major policy of the emperor and perhaps not fully effective until the eleventh century.

Another important imperial development highlighted in the *Nomos Georgikos* was one of language – it was composed in Greek rather than Latin. Greek language and culture had always been prominent in the eastern provinces of the Roman Empire, but as the centre of imperial gravity had shifted from Rome to Constantinople, the prevalence of Greek had gradually increased. However, while the western provinces had been largely lost, there was no definitive break with the Latin heart of the empire. Latin influences on the vocabulary of the army and on imperial coins can still be seen in the eighth century. Indeed, what is claimed by some to be the new 'Byzantine' Empire was not a purely Greek state. It was instead an amalgam of Roman, Greek, oriental and Christian civilisation. This fusion of various civilisation traits may not have been complete by the Heraclian dynasty, but it was already clear that whatever this 'Byzantine' identity was going to look like in its final medieval form, it was going to permeate large sections of Roman society.

And this included right at the very top where the Roman emperor was no longer known by the title of *Augustus* but rather by the Greek βασιλευς (*basileus*). And yet, while this might seem a strong indication of the Hellenising of a Roman title, there is more cultural merging going on here than immediately meets the eye. Because *basileus* predated the title of *Augustus*, it had something of a different meaning, such as 'hereditary ruler' or 'king'. It also had been used in a specific way – without a definite article – to refer to a Persian despot. So *basileus* was being used to describe a position beyond its original definition, with Roman and oriental influences altering its meaning. The Roman emperor was not suddenly just to be seen as a 'king'; he was still an emperor – a 'king of kings' – only with a new/old name.

'Byzantine' Religion

While there was some dissemination of power to exarchs and *strategoi*, the 'emperor of the Romans' remained a paragon of absolute monarchy;[61] however, there was a slight change in the reach of that absolutism. Virtually since its inception, the Roman imperial position had had a significant religious dimension, with the office being combined with that of *pontifex maximus* – 'chief priest' – and tied up with numerous other pagan beliefs and practices, not least the deification of emperors after their death. This became impractical following the Christianisation of the empire in the fourth century, necessitating the reinvention of the emperor's position within the religious hierarchy of the empire.[62] But this reinvention did not happen overnight and was not without pitfalls. By the time it was embraced by Constantine I, the Christian Church had already had over 300 years of hierarchical development behind it and inserting the emperor into or on top of that hierarchy caused significant friction. From the very outset, there were cries of 'what has the emperor to do with the church?'[63] and these would still ring true at the turn of the eighth century. This was despite the religiosity of the imperial position only increasing in the intervening years. From the mid-fifth century onwards, new emperors would be crowned by the patriarch of Constantinople, involvement in church councils increased, and religious ceremony incorporated into court life and the very person of the emperor. This culminated in the Heraclian portrait of the Roman emperor as God's representative on earth.

But it was not just the imperial position itself that was becoming more Christianised. In response to the breaking of the Romano-Christian stranglehold on the Mediterranean world, rather than lose faith, large sections of the population saw the plight of the empire as a divine punishment for their sins; something to be fixed by a redoubling of their faith. This enabled the Christianity of the Roman Empire to become even more of a unifying factor in the face of pagan Avars, Slavs, Bulgars and Turks and the Islamic caliphate. However, the importance of religion at every stratum of Roman society could see any attempted change considered against 'orthodoxy' met with significant opposition. And under Leo III, such a challenge seems to have come against the prevalence of icons in virtually every household. The resultant iconoclasm would alter the fabric of the Roman Empire.

Such doctrinal division was hardly new. Throughout its history, Christianity had never been a united faith. And, if anything, this only increased when it became the faith of the empire. The 'imperial orthodoxy' expressed by the creeds endorsed by the Councils of Nicaea (325), Constantinople (381) and Chalcedon (451) were not accepted by all Christians, both without and within Roman territory. The seeming pedantry of some of the disagreements – the nature of the Trinity, the divine, human or mixed nature of Jesus – might seem strange today, but in the ancient world, these were of vital importance to the spiritual well-being of church, state and individual. They could see entire sections of the empire out of communion with each other for extended periods.

The major division faced by the Heraclian dynasty had its roots in the Council of Chalcedon two centuries earlier. Its elevation of the Constantinopolitan patriarch to a level second only to the pope in Rome was taken by the latter as a challenge to papal supremacy, while large sections of the eastern provinces rejected Chalcedon altogether. Even an emperor, Anastasius I (491–518), had rejected it and was therefore to be considered a heretic by the standards of church orthodoxy. He would not be the last … Attempts at fixing this Chalcedonian dispute had led to a generation of schism between Rome and Constantinople. Such examples of doctrinal compromise either being rejected or causing a slightly different but no less divisive disagreement were not uncommon.

And this growing divide between east and west was only exacerbated by further imperial efforts to heal the divisions of Chalcedon, even by the most prominent emperors – Justinian I's anathematising of three controversial writings while they were received relatively well by eastern non-Chalcedonians, raised considerable opposition from the papacy, while Heraclius' championing of Christ's singular 'energy' – Monoenergism – as a possible avenue of agreement between pro- and anti-Chalcedonians was considered to be inadvertently providing justification for Monophysitism – the non-Chalcedonian doctrine of Christ's single nature.

In the face of this initial failure, Heraclius and his allies doubled down, by issuing the *Ecthesis*, which promoted Christ's dual nature and single divine will, and forbade debate over His 'energy.' Constans II even issued an imperial edict – the *Type of Constans* – making such discussion illegal. As can be imagined, this latest compromise – Monothelitism – and its imperial enforcement did little to bring about unity. Pope Martin I openly rejected this 'doctrine of one will', the *Ecthesis* and the *Type*, which led Constans to take the drastic step of arresting and exiling the pontiff. Other opponents of Monothelitism faced exile, torture, and even physical maiming in attempts to silence them.

The loss of Egypt, Syria and Armenia, the main centres of opposition to Chalcedon, removed the main reason for Monothelitism, although it, the *Ecthesis* and the *Type* remained imperial policy for a decade after Constans II's murder in 668, possibly pragmatically in the face of military problems. And when Constantine did turn his attention to religious policy in 680, he not only abandoned the interventionist approach of his father, he abandoned imperial support for Monothelitism; a *volte face* that was officially confirmed at the Sixth Ecumenical Council at Constantinople in 680/681. Monothelitism and Monoenergism were condemned as heresy for diminishing Christ's humanity – the imperial orthodoxy had it that Christ had 'two natural wills and two natural energies, without division, alteration, separation and confusion.'[64] Half a century of Heraclian heresy was gone almost overnight. Constantine built on the good relations with the papacy this *volte face* engendered, removing the need of imperial approval of a papal election, undertaking a symbolic 'adoption' of his sons by the pope[65] and granting the papacy tax breaks in Sicily, Calabria and on the sale of grain.[66]

Justinian II sought to follow in his father's orthodox footsteps, championing the Sixth Ecumenical Council, maintaining good relations with the papacy, extending its tax breaks to Bruttium and Lucania[67] and targeting the heretical Paulicians.[68] However, in wanting to display his orthodoxy more grandly, Justinian picked a fight with the pope. The emperor found that neither the Fifth nor Sixth Ecumenical Councils had published disciplinary canons – fixing that oversight gave him a reason to call his own council, known as the Quinisext Council in 691/692.[69] The result was 102 canons 'designed to upgrade the moral standards and practices of orthodox Christians, both clergy and laity;'[70] however, in choosing to base those standards of clerical uniformity on Greek customs,

Justinian and his allies were providing an avenue of significant opposition from the 'barbaric' Latin West.

Pope Sergius I refused to sign the Quinisext canons, claiming that they contained 'new errors.'[71] It is not clear what these were, but some rulings on clerical marriage (Canons 3, 13) and the forbidding of the depiction of Christ as a lamb (Canon 82)[72] may be seen as novel. Justinian was furious at this rejection, arresting prominent allies of Sergius and then ordering the arrest of the pope himself.[73] This move met with significant opposition in Italy, with the imperial officer sent to carry out the arrest reputedly forced to hide under the papal bed before being ejected from Rome.[74] While this was not some large-scale rejection of imperial rule in Roman Italy, Justinian likely saw imperial and religious adherence as indistinguishable, such was the success of the sanctifying of the imperial position.

Various religious and legal texts from the late-seventh/early-eight century – Justinian's *iussio* of 687, the opening address of the Quinisext Council, the preamble of the *Ekloga* – 'imply an emperor who was both the divinely appointed and divinely guided ruler as well as the shepherd and defender of the Christian flock under God's divine protection.'[75] The emperor was now more than 'just' the leading lay person on the planet. Furthermore, the pronouncements of Quinisext take orthodoxy, the church, the civilised world and the Roman Empire as one and the same.[76] In such circumstances, it could well be imagined that Sergius was readying himself for another expression of imperial outrage; however, Justinian's first deposition and exile in 695 halted any immediate repercussions, but upon his restoration a decade later, Quinisext was quickly back on the imperial-papal agenda.[77]

By then, Justinian had matured enough to seek accommodation with the papacy rather than confrontation. But even in this air of compromise and concession, the new pope John VII did not capitulate over Quinisext.[78] He died soon after, but there was no suggestion of foul play, nor was there over the rapid death of his successor, Sisinnius.[79] The next pope was Constantine, another man of eastern extraction and possibly even known personally to Justinian.[80] Before he could raise Quinisext with the new pontiff, the emperor showed his want of better relations with the papacy by siding with Constantine against a recalcitrant archbishop of Ravenna, going as far as to sack the city itself for its religious and political rebellion.[81] There then followed a peculiar episode where the new exarch, after meeting with Pope Constantine in Naples, marched to Rome and executed several members of the papal court.[82] The exarch is unlikely to have acted so violently without the consent of either the emperor or the pope, with there being some suggestion of financial impropriety or opposition to the burgeoning rapprochement between Justinian and Constantine.[83]

Any worries that Pope Constantine would capitulate over Quinisext were ill-founded, for the new pontiff proved 'a distinctly skilled politician.'[84] Even when he accepted an 'invitation' to Constantinople to meet personally with Justinian,[85] he refused to be cowed. Justinian 'renewed all the church's privileges'[86] – likely restating the primacy of Rome, its authority over Ravenna and tax exemptions, although exactly what arrangement was arrived at over Quinisext is unclear. It is likely that Justinian released the papacy from adherence to the canons it found objectionable,[87] which would be a significant climb down. The *Liber Pontificalis* gives a significant role in the formulating of whatever compromise was reached to a member of Constantine's entourage, the future Pope Gregory II,[88] who would face an even more momentous doctrinal dispute with Leo III.

A more cynical view would be that there was no compromise, with the emperor and pope merely agreeing to disagree over the offending canons. Certainly, the doctrinal and practical variances at the centre of Quinisext were to continue, with vague compromises over the succeeding centuries growing into definitive schism between east and west. While being willing to compromise with the pope might reflect well on an emperor with a poor reputation, that Justinian felt the need demonstrates a decline of imperial power and influence in Italy. Despite the sacralising of the empire and its emperor, several popes had been able to reject Quinisext and resist pressure from Constantinople. This also shows that the Romano-Christian world remained ripe for doctrinal and/or practical dissension. Anything that could be portrayed as a major change to the 'orthodoxy' of the Church was likely to cause significant division. But this was not something that seemed to discourage Leo III; he would face ferocious opposition to his doctrinal 'innovation', and not just from the papacy.

Even with the frontiers settling down somewhat after the previous 50 years of retreat, the Roman Empire of 685 was still trying to understand its place in the new reality of the end of Late Antiquity, while not completely giving up on turning back the clock against these 'ephemeral' conquests. Under the Heraclians, it had proven itself resilient in the face of battlefield and territorial losses of a scale that would have (and in the case of Persia had) overthrown other states, able to reshape its provincial and military infrastructure on the fly. And having achieved some semblance of equilibrium, it undertook to reshape its laws and tax system to reflect new political realities, which in the process began the moulding of the Roman Empire into something a little different. As of 685, that final transition from the Late Antique Roman Empire to the Early Medieval 'Byzantine' Empire had yet to make contact with its major catalyst – the religious, social and cultural transformation that was iconoclasm… However, even before the Romans had the opportunity to entertain/reject that epochal shift, they would have to face not only a bout of 'Military Anarchy', but a concerted attempt against the very heart of the Roman world … An existential threat in perhaps the truest form that the Roman Empire had not faced in a millennium.

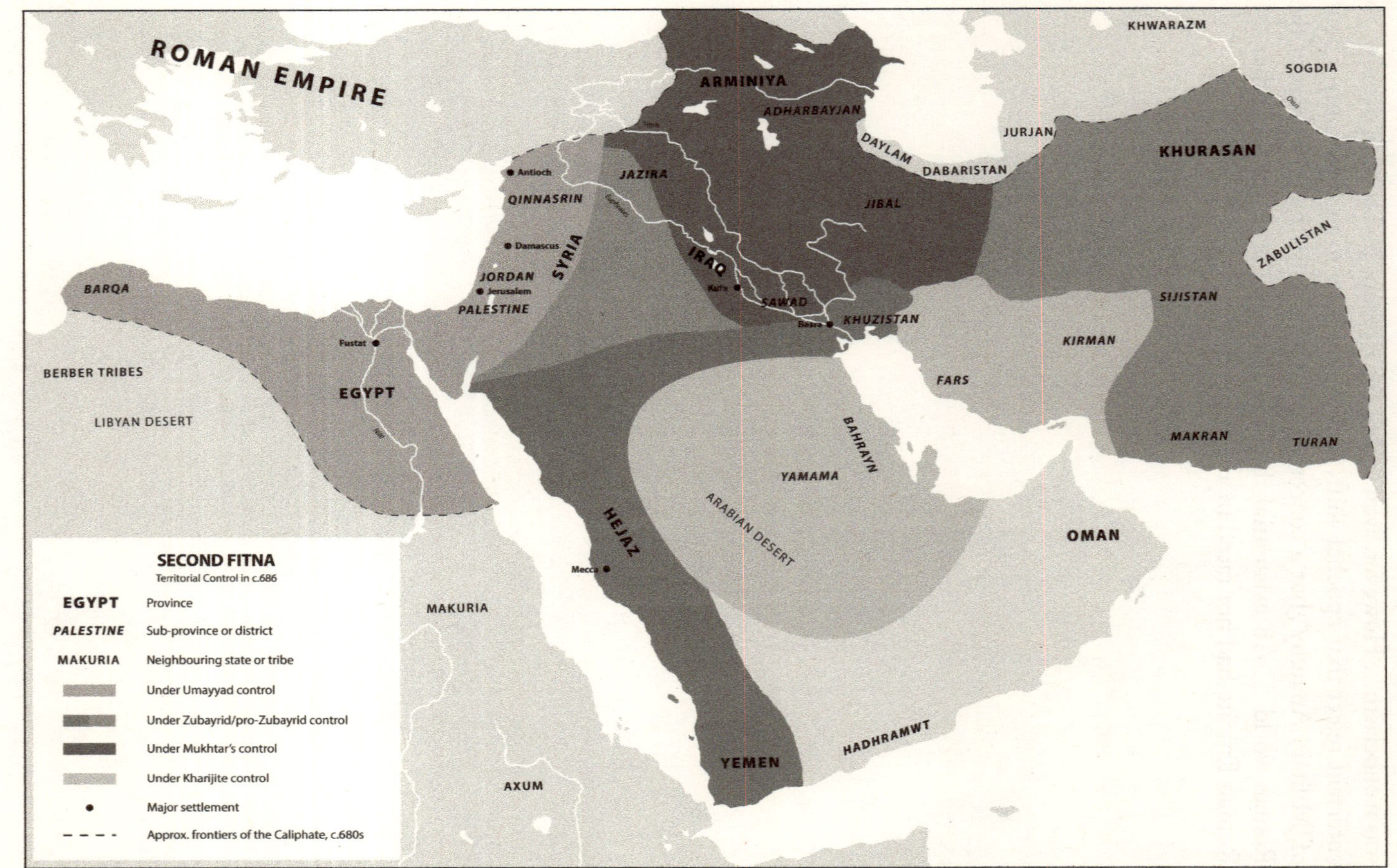
ROMAN EMPIRE
KHWARAZM
SOGDIA
ARMINIYA
ADHARBAYJAN
JURJAN
DAYLAM
DABARISTAN
KHURASAN
Antioch
JAZIRA
QINNASRIN
JIBAL
Damascus
SYRIA
IRAQ
ZABULISTAN
JORDAN
Jerusalem
BARQA
Kufa
SAWAD
SIJISTAN
PALESTINE
Basra
KHUZISTAN
Fustat
KIRMAN
BERBER TRIBES
FARS
EGYPT
LIBYAN DESERT
BAHRAYN
MAKRAN
TURAN
YAMAMA
ARABIAN DESERT
HEJAZ
OMAN
Mecca
MAKURIA
YEMEN
HADHRAMWT
AXUM
SECOND FITNA
Territorial Control in c.686
EGYPT Province
PALESTINE Sub-province or district
MAKURIA Neighbouring state or tribe
Under Umayyad control
Under Zubayrid/pro-Zubayrid control
Under Mukhtar's control
Under Kharijite control
Major settlement
Approx. frontiers of the Caliphate, c.680s

Chapter 2

The Enemies of the Empire

'Enemies of the Imperium, hear me. You have come here to die. The Immortal Emperor is with us and we are invincible. His soldiers will strike you down. His war machines will crush you under their treads. His mighty guns will bring the very sky crashing down upon you. You cannot win. The Emperor has given us his greatest weapon to wield. So make yourselves ready...'

Governor-Militant Lukas Alexander
(*Warhammer 40K: Dawn of War: Dark Crusade*)

External and Internal 'Struggles' – The Umayyad Caliphate

While the Roman Empire might have survived the seventh century, it was still faced with dangerous opposition. Indeed, perhaps the most significant reasons behind its survival took place not within the empire itself, but beyond its frontiers within the Arab caliphate. On two separate occasions, when it looked to be about to deliver the decisive hammer blow to the Roman Empire, the caliphate had almost torn itself apart with internal conflicts – the First Fitna (656–661) and the Second Fitna (680–692). The main spark of complaint behind these two Muslim civil wars was the succession to the Prophet Muhammad as the temporal and spiritual leader of the Arab caliphate.[1] The death of each of the first four caliphs had revealed the lack of consensus on how the next ruler was to be chosen – Abu Bakr's appointment faced opposition from those who had expected Muhammad's nephew and son-in-law, Ali b. Abi Talib, would become caliph; Umar was merely appointed caliph by Abu Bakr; Uthman was chosen by a somewhat contrived six-man committee appointed by Umar, while Ali was elected by the people of Medina and those responsible for the assassination of Uthman. This lack of a clear succession process led to deep divisions within Islam between those who favoured election by representatives of the community and those who championed the hereditary succession of Ali and his descendants.

For all this internal strife, the Arab caliphate had continued to make spectacular territorial gains – Abu Bakr had overseen the conquest of Arabia and initiated the attacks on the Roman and Persian empires, while the lands claimed under Umar had enabled him to divide the caliphate into 13 provinces stretching from the Eastern Sahara to the mountains of Afghanistan. Umar also made great strides in providing good governance to the nascent Arab caliphate through provincial subdivision and appointment of officials to oversee the collecting of taxes and the dispensing of justice. Under Uthman came the final defeat of the Persian Empire, the suppression of several revolts, repelling of Roman counter-attacks and the pressing on into Pakistan, Anatolia and the Mediterranean.

While Uthman used his background as a merchant and the administrative achievements of Umar to bring economic prosperity to the caliphate, which in turn expanded its military capabilities, he also sowed the seeds of his own demise. This was because, despite the beautifying of holy sites and centralising of Muslim worship through the production of hundreds of Qur'ans, the most immediate impact of Uthman's reign came in his empowering of his own relatives of the *Banu Umayya* as provincial governors, planting the seeds of dynastic succession. By 649, Egypt, Kufa, Basra and Syria were under the control of Umayyads, with the most important of these being the governor of Syria, Muawiyah b. Abi Sufyan. The empowering of Muawiyah by Uthman had some basis in necessity as Arab Syria was the vanguard in the war with the Romans, defending Arab territory, striking into Anatolia and launching the first Arab naval campaigns. The problem going forward for the caliphate was that however necessary it was deemed, Muawiyah's prolonged Syrian tenure allowed him to build a strong, disciplined Syrian army that owed its loyalty more to him than the caliphate. When Uthman's increasing acquisitiveness and 'doting love for a corrupt and rapacious kin'[2] saw him assassinated in 656, it sparked a contest – the First Fitna – that was to change the face of caliphal rule.

The subsequent election of Ali should have been an opportunity to unify the elective and Alid views of caliphal succession, but Uthman's nepotism saw to it that Muawiyah could refuse to step down as Syrian governor when Ali demanded it. And when Ali doubled down by threatening Muawiyah with military force, civil war erupted. The divisions caused by this eruption were so significant that they were to become schisms within the Muslim faith, forming the Sunni, Shia and Kharijite denominations. Despite essentially winning the three major battles of the war, Ali and his officials were outmanoeuvred by Muawiyah politically, while the sheer fact that Ali had entered negotiations with the Syrian rebel saw the hardliners in his camp form their own rebel cause as the Kharijites. And in early 661, Ali was assassinated by one of their number. The Alids attempted to fight on but Muawiyah was now militarily supreme, and their caliphal candidate, Ali's son al-Hasan, was soon capitulating on the promise that Muawiyah would not attempt to establish an Umayyad dynasty.

It was not a promise that Muawiyah kept. While his near 20-year reign may have maintained caliphal integrity through diplomatic decentralisation rather than military might and saw the continued advance of the armies of Islam in Africa and Anatolia, it only kept a lid on the factionalism revealed by the First Fitna rather than doing away with it. And once he selected his son, Yazid, as his successor,[3] instead of the promised election, another civil war was inevitable.

When it erupted in 680,[4] opposition to the Umayyads centred on Abd Allah b. al-Zubayr, son of a companion of Muhammad, and Husayn b. Ali, the younger son of caliph Ali, while the Kharijites remained a threat. Husayn was quickly dealt with at the Battle of Karbala on 10 October 680, but the massacre of him and his supporters only galvanised opposition to Yazid's regime. Another Umayyad victory in 685 over an Alid remnant, calling themselves the Tawwabin, meaning 'penitents', focused Alid support on Mukhtar al-Thaqafi, who took control of Kufa in late 685.[5] Meanwhile, al-Zubayr established himself in Mecca, taking control of much of the Hejaz, only for Umayyad forces to seize Medina in late 683 and lay siege to Mecca. It was perhaps only the sudden death of Yazid before the year was out that saved the Zubayrid cause. The succession of Yazid's inexperienced teenage son, Muawiyah II, further undermined Umayyad authority in Arab lands, reducing Umayyad territory to just parts of Syria. Much of the rest of the Arab world transferred its loyalty to al-Zubayr.

Fortunately for the Umayyads, disease carried off Muawiyah II within months of his accession. Not wanting to trust in the dead caliph's younger brothers, the Umayyads turned to an experienced cavalry commander, a cousin of Uthman and Muawiyah I, Marwan b. al-Hakam. Together with the loyal Iraqi governor, Marwan rallied enough support to forestall a pro-Zubayrid takeover of Syria at the Battle of Marj Rahit in August 684. While there were some setbacks in Iraq and the Hejaz, Marwan was then able to reclaim Egypt and thwart another Zubayrid invasion of Palestine in early 685.

But before Marwan could capitalise on these successes, he too was carried off by disease after a reign of just nine months. This saw Marwan's eldest son, Abd al-Malik, become Umayyad caliph in early summer 685. He was able to build on the stability established by his father, using the resources of Syria and Egypt to take the fight to al-Zubayr and Mukhtar, although success was far from assured. Abd al-Malik's first two attacks on Alid Kufa came to grief; however, Mukhtar's violent dealing with internal opposition sparked a much more successful attack on Kufa from Zubayrid Basra. By April 687, the Second Fitna was a straight fight between the Umayyads and Zubayrids.

Both sides showed some reticence to initiate a final confrontation in the late 680s due to disorder within their own ranks,[6] with two abortive Umayyad campaigns in Iraq. It was not until autumn 691 that Abd al-Malik made the decisive breakthrough. Taking advantage of dissension in the Zubayrid ranks and their distraction with the Kharijites, the caliph squared up to the Zubayrid army at Maskin. The resultant battle was in the balance, with the Zubayrids in a position to launch a potentially decisive cavalry strike. However, it was here that Umayyad machinations and Zubayrid dissension came into play – right when it should have launched a battle-winning attack on Abd al-Malik's flank, the Zubayrid cavalry deserted. And when the Zubayrid reserve followed suit, refusing to throw away their lives in a futile gesture,[7] the Umayyads seized a victory that brought them control of Iraq, Kufa, Basra and all the Arab eastern provinces.

Abd al-Malik could now turn to deal with al-Zubayr himself in Mecca, who had spent most of the 680s having considerable trouble with a Kharijite statelet in Yamama. Things had gotten so bad that al-Zubayr's territory had been limited to the Hejaz and sometimes not even there, as the Kharijites proved able to approach Medina, capture Ta'if and make the Hajj pilgrimage to Mecca. Therefore, when the Umayyads arrived to contest the region, they found that the Zubayrids offered little in the way of battlefield opposition, while Abd al-Malik made judicious use of diplomatic contact to undermine the Kharijites. This did not mean that resistance collapsed immediately. It required a damaging eight-month siege of Mecca to finally defeat al-Zubayr, while the combined armies of Basra and Kufa were needed to defeat the Kharijites;[8] however, this was all achieved by 693 – the whole Arab caliphate was back under the command of the Umayyads.

Abd al-Malik was now able to reform aspects of the caliphate – he oversaw the recentralisation of caliphal government, the professionalising of the army and the Arabization of the administration, which included the introduction of Islamic coinage. However, while the end of the Second Fitna ushered in something of a Golden Age for the Umayyads, Abd al-Malik and his immediate successors did not fix all of the caliphate's woes – the sectarian divisions within Islam were now well on their way to becoming denominational, while inter-tribal tensions were on the rise and would play a significant role in the Third Fitna and the Abbasid Revolution (744–750).

While in the two decades between these two Islamic civil wars Muawiyah had been able to raid into Roman territory on an annual basis, have his navy penetrate into the Aegean and undertake whatever constituted the 'First' Siege of Constantinople,[9] the two periods of Muslim 'Struggle' presented an opportunity for the Roman Empire. Muawiyah himself had agreed a truce with Constans II in 657/658, which allowed the emperor to bring some organisation to the administrative chaos that was Roman Anatolia, re-establish Armenia in the imperial fold, and conduct his own raids on Umayyad territory. It also allowed

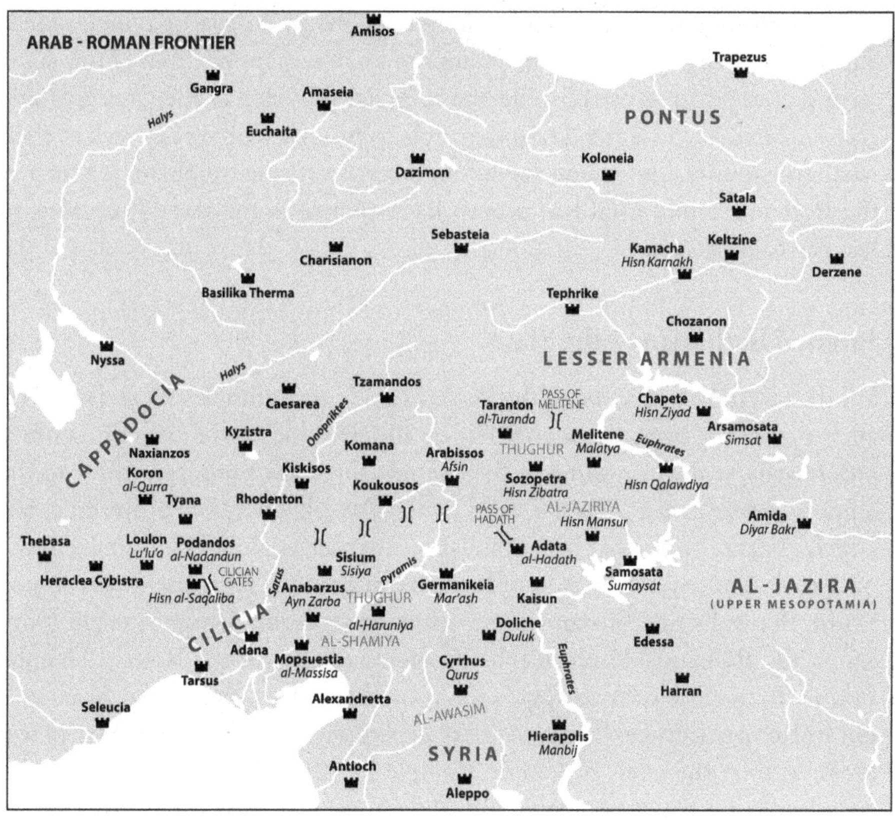

Constans to inflict some sort of defeat on the Slavs and plan his extended Italian campaign.

Had the Roman Empire been in slightly better shape in the early 680s and not faced the emergent Bulgar khanate along the Danube and Slav trouble in Greece, it could well have made more significant use of the Second Fitna. Even as it was, Constantine IV launched counteroffensives into Cilicia, reclaimed cities like Germanikeia and Pisidian Antioch, and raided the Umayyad Levant with the imperial fleet and the Mardaites, while Justinian II's forces struck deeply into Umayyad territory, possibly reaching northern Iran. This demonstrated that the empire was still capable of dealing damage to the caliphate. A Roman Empire unencumbered by other external distractions might well have established a more secure position in Armenia and Caucasia, reclaimed some of the lost islands and further undermined Arab control of Syria.

That said, the caliphal ability to survive two such ructions should have put paid to any continued Roman thought that the Arab conquests were merely ephemeral. With the reforms of Umar, Uthman, Muawiyah I and then Abd al-Malik, the caliphate became less a collection of conquered territories and more a well-organised state that would not dissolve in the face of a single defeat. Therefore, while on the surface, the campaigns of Constantine IV and Justinian II were successful in re-establishing the imperial presence in the Caucasus and eastern Anatolia, once the Arabs were able to turn their attention back to their northern frontier, 'the region tended to revert to … the caliphate.'[10] Much as the Roman Empire itself had proven its resilience in the seventh century, so had the caliphate.

Internal Barbarians – the Slavs

While the Arabs had replaced the Persians as Constantinople's most dangerous enemy, another imperial enemy fell by the wayside as the seventh century progressed. At the beginning of the century, the main European threat to the empire's interests came in the form of the Avar khanate,[11] a polyethnic, but largely Asiatic, group that had established themselves along the Danube in the mid-sixth century. At the nadir of Roman fortunes, the Avar army was camped before the walls of Constantinople, while its underlings were spreading out across the Balkans. However, the complete collapse of the Roman Danube frontier in the face of Avar aggression proved as devastating to the Avars as it did to Roman Europe. It is somewhat hyperbolic to suggest that Avar power broke against the walls of Constantinople in 626 – Mauricius' invasions of Avar territory a generation previous had done significant damage to the already under-developed Avar infrastructure, but in the aftermath of their failed siege, the Avars lost control of many of the constituent tribes of their coalition. The combination of the loss of manpower and various territories shaking off their suzerainty geographically detached the Avars from the Romans. So, while it was not until the turn of the eighth century that the Avars were completely wiped from the map, they disappear from the Roman source record and from their political and military considerations.

While the Romans might have been happy to see the back of the Avars, it was their misfortune that their northern threat was replaced by two different ones. The underlings that the Avars lost control of in the aftermath of the siege of Constantinople were one of these different threats: these were the Slavs. Unfortunately, we are reliant on very scant non-Slavic sources for their early history and much of their initial southern movement is obscured by Avar overlordship. There was an attempt by the sixth-century Gothic historian, Jordanes, to link the Slavs back to Baltic peoples recorded by the likes of Tacitus, Pliny the Elder and Ptolemy, which is far from clear.[12] Indeed, the lack of historiographic clarity on who these people were increases the difficulty in identifying proto-Slavs in the archaeological record. And due to the significant area they expanded into and their ability to assimilate with various cultures, it is very difficult to connect them with any one cultural origin archaeologically.[13] Although not necessarily those recorded by Tacitus,[14] there may be some linguistic connection between the Slavs and earlier Balts, possibly a shared ancestor.[15]

This lack of clarity on their origins has enabled 'nationalist rivalries ... rooted in the demands of contemporary politics'[16] to greatly expand the proposed homeland of the Slavs and attempt to give them much deeper roots as a hidden majority than was the case.[17] However, attempts to suggest that the proto-Slavs were a creation of contact with the Roman world of the Lower Danube seems to go too far the other way.[18] A middle ground between these two might be in order – a centuries-long migration through various regions, being influenced by them so as to somewhat hide their presence, with limited Romanisation along the Danube sparking a population growth that allowed the Slavs to roam so far after escaping Avar suzerainty.[19]

It must be noted that whoever these Slavs were, they were not one large group. There were a considerable number of tribes that came under the Slav umbrella, which is perhaps demonstrated in the different names recorded for them in the sources. Some Western sources called them 'Venethi/Veneti,' or 'Sclavi/Sclavus'; others record certain groups as 'Wenden/Winden' or 'Windische.'[20] By the late-seventh century, eastern Roman sources have moved beyond the more generic 'Sclaveni' or 'Antae' to record specific subtribes, some of which reflect where these Slavs had settled such as the 'Strymonitai' around the river Strymon in Macedonia.[21]

The Romans knew enough about the Slavs by the late-sixth century to make some generalisations about them and their military capabilities. Despite being 'undisciplined and disorganised,'[22] the *Strategikon* considered Slavs to be 'populous and hardy, bearing readily heat, cold, rain, nakedness, and scarcity of provisions.'[23] This made them well-suited to raiding and guerrilla warfare,[24] which contributed greatly to the Roman inability to make any substantial headway in reclaiming the mountainous Balkans from them. The decentralised and disparate nature of these Slavic tribes also added to that difficulty as it hindered the Roman ability to either destroy or co-opt them as there was little in the way of governmental infrastructure to negotiate with and the Romans increasingly lacked the overwhelming power needed to subdue entire tribal groups.[25]

While there is a mention of a Slavic people as early as the late-fourth century,[26] the earliest definitive record of them comes in the form of the Antae raid of the Balkans during the reign of Justin I (518–527).[27] There were various other Slavic raids on Roman territory through the remainder of the sixth century, driving deeply into the Balkans, reaching Thessalonica and even Constantinople at one point.[28] The Romans did have some success against various Slavic tribes during their campaigns against the Avar khanate, eliminating Slavic settlement south of the Danube in the late-sixth century.[29] However, after recovering from these defeats and while the Avars themselves focused on Constantinople, the Slavs were able to surge south and fan out far and wide across the Balkans. Cities such as Naissus, Serdica and Salona were taken, while Thessalonica came under repeated attack and some Slavic tribes penetrated into the Peloponnese. The depleted and distracted Roman forces in the region could do little or nothing.

After a brief reset, Constans II did win some sort of victory against Slavs, and Constantine IV probably fought against some of them as part of his Bulgar campaign, but it is Justinian II who led the first well-recorded attack on Slavs in northern Greece, specifically against those pressurising Thessalonica. That Justinian had to fight his way through Thrace and Macedonia to reach the second city of the empire 'reflects the practical realities'[30] of the extent of the Slav incursion and the collapse of Roman authority so far south of the Danube. Justinian's subsequent victory in Macedonia in 688 saw Thessalonica 'no longer harassed or raided by the neighbouring Slavs;'[31] indeed, the victory may have been sizeable enough to allow the formation of the new Hellas theme and, along with enough incentives, to persuade thousands of Slavs to accept settlement in Anatolia in return for military service.

While this was a useful boon at the outset of Justinian's reign, it was but a minor advance in the face of the immense swathe of territory that was the increasingly Slavicised Balkans between the Danube and the Haemus Mountains, Macedonia, Thrace, Thessaly, along the Strymon river to Thessalonica, the Peloponnese and parts of Greece. And Justinian's Macedonian success was not the beginning of some great push to reconquer those territories. It would be another century before any significant Roman progress would be made against the Slavs under Nikephoros I (802–811) and another 300 years before the entire peninsula was restored to the Roman Empire through the victories of Basil II (976–1025).

Masters of the Lower Danube – The Bulgars

While the Slavs had spread out across the Balkans almost en masse, the second of the new threats to Roman territory in the wake of the contraction of the Avar khanate was somewhat more localised; however, because of that concentration along the Lower Danube, it was even more of a threat. Similar to the Avars and the Slavs, the lack of clear historiographic, archaeological or etymological evidence renders the origins of these other Danubian newcomers unclear. To make matters worse, it could well be that their name – Bulgar – either predates

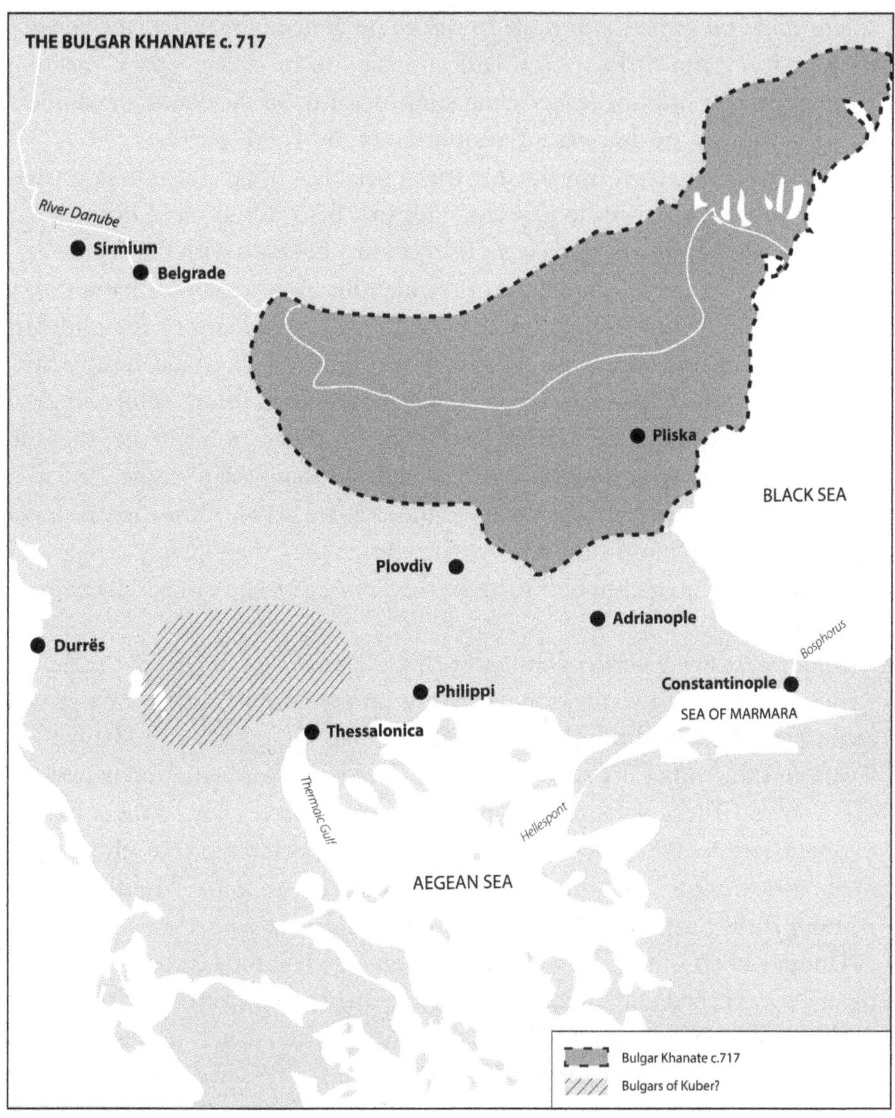

the people that it became more closely associated with or is used anachronistically for past peoples to create a non-existent connection.[32]

Chinese sources record possibly Turkic peoples called the Buluoji or the Pugu, whom they describe as 'troublemakers', which may fit in with the Turkic word *bulğha*, meaning 'mix' or 'disturb.' This has raised the idea that the Bulgars were a Turkic or mixed confederacy originating on the western boundaries of China, before migrating across the Central Asian steppe to arrive on the fringes of Europe.[33] Roman sources may present some backing to the idea of a mixed confederacy, as they are varyingly associated with Turkic and Hunnic peoples.[34]

There could be some Latin roots to the name 'Bulgar': '*burgaroi,*' mercenaries stationed in *burgi* forts; a Germanic translation of *homo pugnax*, meaning 'combative man' or from *vulgaris*, meaning 'usual' or 'of the common people'.[35] It could also be that this was a Latinisation of the Turkic *bulğha*.

In terms of an actual timeline for the appearance of the Bulgars in western affairs, there are attempts to give the 'Vulgares' Biblical roots and historians of the Armenians and Lombards posit fifth century conflicts with the 'Vulgares.'[36] This all looks either anachronistic or misidentification. Priscus of Panium, one of the best-informed sources on Transdanubian barbaricum in the mid-fifth century, makes no mention of 'Bulgars' or anything similar in his dealings with the peoples of the Ukrainian steppe. In 480, it is claimed that the emperor Zeno paid 'Bulgars' to attack the Goths,[37] but there is wariness over whether these are the same Bulgars who would establish a khanate along the Danube. And even though there are frequent mentions of the Bulgars between this first recorded appearance in 480 up to the mid-sixth century, they then largely disappear.[38] Indeed, there is no mention of them in the *Strategikon* as an imperial enemy to be prepared for.

If they were living north of either the Black Sea or Caspian Gate,[39] the Bulgars were in the path of two major new arrivals on the Ponto-Caspian Steppe who could have subsumed the Bulgars to make them disappear so suddenly – the Avars and the Turks.[40] The Bulgars may have been fortunate to live between the Avar and Turkic spheres of control. This might have allowed them to form a confederation of their own, which was then in a position to take advantage of the power vacuum when the Avars moved further west to the Middle Danube and the Turks turned their focus back to Central Asia.

Under Kubrat of the Dulo clan,[41] what emerged on the Ukrainian steppe in the 630s was called Old Great Bulgaria, covering the area from the Sea of Azov to the northern Caucasus.[42] While sometimes referred to as a 'proto-state' with a capital at either Phanagoria or Poltava, there is little evidence that Kubrat was able to establish anything beyond a loose tribal confederation. Indeed, under internal and external pressures,[43] Old Great Bulgaria essentially collapsed on Kubrat's death probably during the last years of the reign of Constans II, breaking into at least five separate groups, each led by a son of the dead khan. The eldest son, Batbayan, made some attempt to maintain the confederation, only to be seemingly defeated and subjugated by the Khazars by 668.[44] The second son, Kotrag, led a group north along the Volga, founding a statelet that would convert to Islam and survive until the Mongol conquests.[45] The fourth son, Kuber, initially led a mixed coalition in vassalage to the Avars, only to escape to Macedonia in the late-670s/early-680s.[46] From there he, along with local Slavs, threatened Thessalonica.[47] The youngest son, Alcek, also fell under and escaped Avar domination, except his escape led him to Italy, settling near Ravenna or further south in the Lombard duchy of Benevento, where they were still a recognisable group by the late-eighth century.[48]

However, it was the middle son, Asparukh, who was to cause the Roman Empire the most trouble. The group he led from the Ukrainian steppe was likely made up of Bulgars, Slavs, Huns, Turks, Germans, Roman provincials and others. Settling in the Oglos, seemingly an angle of land formed by the Danube delta or its tributaries,[49] Asparukh found a location that could be easily defended from attack.[50] And so it was to prove when Constantine IV attacked. Possibly spurred on by raids by Asparukh's Bulgars on Danubian lands[51] (or seeing them as an easy target), in 680, Constantine IV gathered 'all the thematic armies'[52] and marched on the Danube, shadowed by an imperial fleet. However, when the Bulgars refused to fight, the Romans were forced into an ineffective blockade of the Oglos. A decline in the emperor's health further undermined imperial attempts to force a victory. And when Constantine had to withdraw for treatment, the Roman position collapsed. Asparukh then launched a counterattack, turning the disorderly Roman withdrawal into a rout.[53] Such was the scale of the Roman defeat that Constantine had to sign a treaty with Asparukh that provided the Bulgars with annual tribute and imperial recognition of their ownership of the Danube delta. This saw 680/681 become the traditional foundation date of the Bulgar khanate that was to survive for over 300 years.[54]

Perhaps demonstrating their bias against him, the sources present the prelude to Justinian's march to Thessalonica as involving the doing away with his father's treaty with the Danube Bulgars. This accusation presumes that Justinian was going to fight the Bulgar khan, but instead he moved west to fight the Slavs around Thessalonica. Part of that mission meant forging safe passage along the *Via Egnatia* in the face of 'groups of Bulgars.'[55] It is unlikely that this involved khanate Bulgars, but rather one of the other groups who had migrated from the steppe into the Balkans, possibly those of Kuber. While Justinian forced his way through whatever mountainous defences these Bulgars had,[56] on his return journey to Constantinople, the young emperor blundered into an ambush set by these same Bulgars. Justinian's army escaped only after taking heavy casualties.[57] Romano-Bulgar relations are somewhat quiet for much of the next decade, with perhaps only Tiberius III winning some sort of victory over an unidentified group.

In late 704, the focus of the Roman world fell definitively upon the court of the Bulgar khan Tervel when he received a rather distinguished visitor – the deposed emperor Justinian II himself. Through various promises of reward,[58] the emperor and khan marched on Constantinople in 705 (a march that would see the advent of a certain Konon into the historical record). This culminated in

Justinian II regaining the imperial throne before the year was out. And how did the re-enthroned *Basileus* reward his Bulgar ally? Well, aside from 'many gifts,'[59] the title of *Caesar* and the (unfulfilled) promise of marriage to his daughter,[60] Justinian seemingly rewarded Tervel with war.

In perhaps 708, Justinian II marched against the Bulgars. It is depicted in the sources as very much a Roman treaty-breaking betrayal of Tervel.[61] Or at least by Theophanes, as Nikephoros does not mention Tervel at all during Justinian's Bulgar campaign of 708. It could be that Theophanes is projecting the political outlook of his time a century later when the Bulgar khan was in control of the northern reaches of Thrace back onto 708, when their control there was much more doubtful. Tentatively, this Romano-Bulgar conflict seems to have centred on lands to the south of Tervel's khanate, making it possible that Tervel was the aggressor or that Tervel was not actually involved at all. Justinian and Tervel are recorded as being on cordial terms just three years later,[62] so it could be that Justinian was targeting another Bulgar group to reinstate Roman control of the Black Sea coast, possibly even with the tacit approval of the khan.

Whoever the target was, the 'great army'[63] gathered by Justinian marched and sailed to northern Thrace … and disaster. Despite capturing the stronghold of Anchialus, the Romans neglected to scout the surrounding uplands, which would have revealed the presence of a force of Bulgars. An attack on Roman foraging parties left them shorn of most of their cavalry,[64] allowing the Bulgars to blockade Anchialus. Justinian had to endure ignominious retreat back to Constantinople.[65] Rather than avenge his father's debacle at Oglos, Justinian had basically replayed it, once again proving that Bulgars, of the khanate or not, were a significant threat. Of course, the reign of Justinian II had also proven that the Bulgars could be useful allies as well, something that was going to be of immense importance during the first year of Leo III's time on the throne.

Providing Princes of the Line: Khazar Turks

While the Umayyads, Slavs and Bulgars posed threats to the core of the Roman Empire, it also faced trouble on its extremities. To the east, one such problem had already had direct contact with the empire and an influence on the other tribes the Romans were dealing with in the late-seventh century: the Turks. They had founded their own extensive khaganate across the Central Asian Steppe throughout the mid-sixth century, with their drive west pushing the Avars to the Danube. Only civil war in this enormous Turkic Khaganate may have prevented it from more direct interference in Europe. But as it withdrew back east, the khaganate left some Turkic tribes behind. This might have included some of the constituents of the Bulgar confederation, but definitely included the tribe

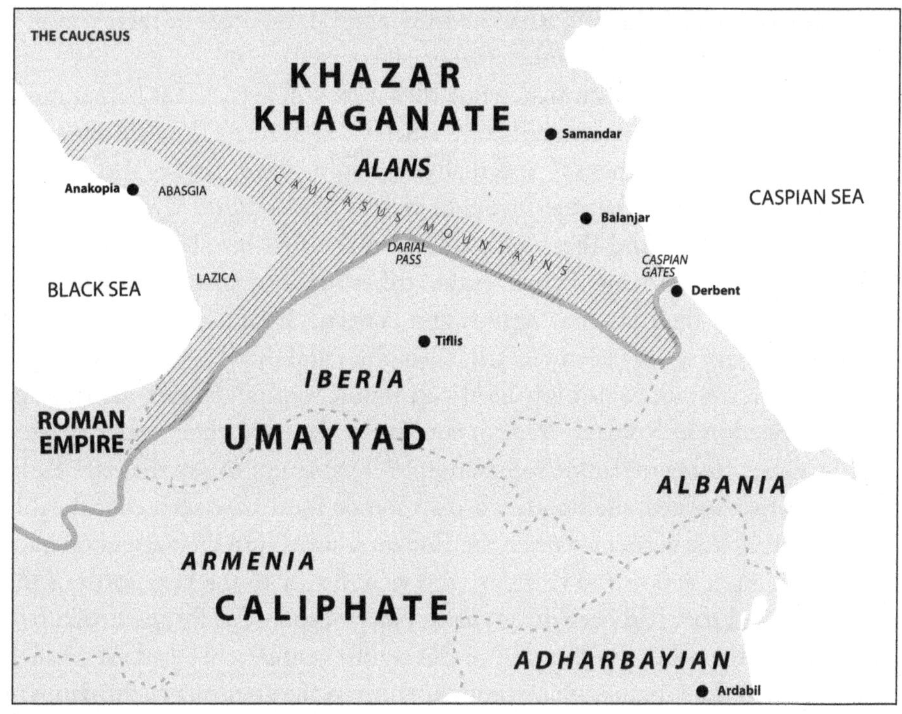

that was left in control of the lands north of the Caucasus: the Khazars. The lack of clarity in the origin of this name – Turkic, Chinese or Middle Persian via Latin[66] – may demonstrate how the Khazar Khaganate was a polyethnic and polylingual conglomeration; a Khazar-led group of Huns, Bulgars, Alans, Caucasians, Turks and other Asiatics, rather than a purely Turkic ethno-state.[67] This may also explain how descriptions of 'Khazars' can vary from distinctly Asiatic to more Indo-European.[68]

As befitting its tribal and nomadic origins, the Khazar Khaganate made only gradual progress in shifting to a more sedentary existence and therefore solid governmental foundations. However, it was enough to give the khaganate longevity – it was still predominant in the northern Caucasus in the mid-tenth century. Indeed, even by the late-seventh century, there are suggestions of infrastructural development, including a time-limited dual kingship, providing religious and political leadership, complete with its own traditions and rituals.[69] While evidence for them is much later, there were likely mechanisms in place to provide a sizeable army from tribal, subject and allied groups around a royal core,[70] with subordinate officers called *tarkhans* and administrative officials called *tudun*, possibly governors or diplomats. These administrative developments, along with the relative peace their rule brought, allowed the Khazars to exploit their position along the Silk Road and the natural resources of their region – pastoralism, fishing, local manufacturing, slaves etc.[71]

This development meant that, while they were still regarded as barbarians – there were reports of human sacrifice[72] – when Constantine VII would advise his son to 'never marry a Khazar'[73] it actually highlights the occasions that Roman emperors *did* marry Khazars: Justinian II and Constantine V, with Leo IV being half-Khazar. And these were not even the first instances of proposed Romano-Turkic marriage. When Turkic tribesmen had been useful allies for the Romans in their last war against the Persians, it had seen an unfulfilled promise of marriage between Heraclius' daughter and the khagan (or his son).[74]

However, despite such high-level communication and agreements, after this interjection in Romano-Persian conflict in the 620s, there was a 50-year lull in direct Romano-Turkic interactions.[75] This is not to say that the Turks were inactive; indeed, the Ponto-Caspian steppe must have seen considerable action during this period for when the Roman sources turn their attention back to the region, it is now the Khazars who were firmly to the fore north of the Caucasus and they had been at very least partly responsible for the breakup of Old Great Bulgaria.[76] By the turn of the eighth century, they had established a foothold in the Crimea, which brought them to the attention of the deposed Justinian II, who turned to the Khazar khagan, Busir, for help in achieving his restoration.[77] This initial agreement led to Justinian's marriage to the khagan's sister or daughter, a union which saw the birth of a half-Khazar heir to the Roman imperial throne, Tiberios.[78]

Despite this union, Busir was quick to betray Justinian when imperial authorities wanted the deposed emperor dead. And once he was back on the throne, Justinian did not forget this betrayal. When he sent to Khazaria for his wife and son, the imperial fleet he despatched initially was of considerable size. If this was an attempted demonstration that Khazaria was within the reach of Roman forces, it went badly as poor weather severely damaged the fleet, with Busir issuing a disdainful rebuke. The khagan would not withhold the emperor's wife and child from him, but he held little fear of Roman arms.

Justinian's weak position in the aftermath of his restoration saw him willing to reach out to those who had wronged him; thus, the next time Busir is mentioned, he is visiting Constantinople.[79] And yet, any patching up of the relationship between the emperor and the khagan engendered in this visit did not last long. By 710, perhaps looking to build on the Khazar foothold in the Crimea, Busir had sent a *tudun* to Cherson. It is here that the meaning of *tudun* becomes most important – if it was meant for a 'diplomat' then this is to be expected in a border territory between two states; but if it was a 'governor' then this is something much more intrusive. Any such intrusion was at least part of the reason why Justinian sent a large expeditionary force to Crimea.[80] This in turn led Busir to double down in subverting Roman officials and locals, sending troops to Cherson, hosting the usurper Bardanes and helping him build a following that was able to overthrow Justinian II in 711. Much like the Bulgar khan, at the outset of the eighth century, the Khazar khagan had been partly responsible for putting a Roman emperor on the imperial throne.

With such highly consequential Romano-Khazar interaction, it should not be forgotten that the Khazars had other non-Roman contacts. We have already seen the Turkic ability to strike through the Caucasian passes as allies of Heraclius. And during the 50-year lull in direct Romano-Turkic relations, the Khazars were not solely focused on establishing their own predominance north of the Caucasus and at the expense of some of the Bulgars. As early as 642, Arab armies were probing the Caucasian passes and by 652 they had launched an attack on the Khazar capital at Balanjar, only to suffer a heavy defeat. A second Arab incursion was also defeated three years later. The Khazars would respond by striking south of the Caucasus when the Arabs were distracted by their own internal struggles and may even have imposed some suzerainty on Albania,[81] before a much larger Khazar raid swept through the Caucasian passes in 683/685, defeating and killing Georgian and Armenian leaders. Once the Umayyads had firmly re-established their rule of the caliphate, a 'Second Arab-Khazar War' was not too far away.

Kings and Dukes: The Lombards

The western-most threat faced by the Roman Empire had been one partially of its own making. When the Avars had arrived along the Danube in the mid-sixth century, Justinian I had followed the tried and tested policy of employing one group of barbarians to attack another; however, not only had this helped build up the strength of the Avars, it sent one of the tribal targets cascading into Roman Italy. Like many Germanic tribes, these Langobards, Anglicised as 'Lombards',[82] are attributed a south Scandinavian origin, before migrating to the Baltic coast and down the Elbe to reach the Middle Danube over the course of the first 500 years AD. Even by their earliest appearances in Roman sources, the Lombards had attained a reputation for savagery in spite of their insignificant numbers.[83] It could be that such thoughts were based on direct military contact as the Lombards may have been situated along the Elbe when the Roman legions were active there.[84] Unsurprisingly, as the legions withdrew from Germania, information about the Lombards declined steeply, relying on limited archaeology to say anything about them for the next century.[85] When

they do reappear, as part of a defeated raid on Roman Pannonia in 166,[86] it is all too brief.

The Lombards remained far enough away from Roman territory or largely subsumed by some of the various tribal confederations to arise in the third to fifth centuries – Suebi, Saxons, Goths and even Huns – to escape notice from the source material.[87] Beyond the 'regal historical fiction' of the eighth-century Lombard historian, Paul the Deacon, the Lombards came more clearly into view with the Roman defeat of the Gothic kingdom of Italy in the 530s. This allowed the Lombards to not only secure themselves along the Middle Danube but to also occupy parts of the former Roman provinces of Noricum and Pannonia. This might seem like a move to enrage the empire, but the Romans allied with the Lombards, employing them against the resurgent Goths in Italy[88] and the troublesome Gepids on the Danube.

By the mid-560s, Paul the Deacon records the Lombards under Alboin winning a devastating victory over the Gepids and then 'choosing' Italy as a new home for his people.[89] While the Lombards were likely involved in the Gepid defeat, it was much more the work of the Avars, and while it was something of a choice for Alboin to lead his people away from the Middle Danube, it was a choice between Avar subjugation and flight than a victorious march to a new home. Such a migration will not have been limited to the Lombards themselves. Alboin no doubt brought significant numbers of various other groups looking to escape the Avars – Gepids, Huns, Sarmatians, Bavarians, Rugians and Roman provincials.[90]

After 30 years of almost unbroken warfare with the Goths, Roman Italy was in no state to resist this Lombard migration: its countryside devastated, its cities decaying, its military exhausted, its finances in ruin, its population low. Within five years of their arrival, the Lombards had not only found land for themselves, but they were also carving out a fully independent kingdom, incorporating major cities like Milan and Pavia.[91] Indeed, they were only thwarted from taking over the entire peninsula through Roman control of the seas allowing coastal cities to resist and an ill-timed breakdown in their own leadership. Upon his assassination in 572, Alboin had been succeeded by Cleph, whose ruthlessness made him unpopular enough for him to be assassinated in 574.[92] This led to a collapse in Lombard central authority, with no king recognised for the next decade as the various Lombard dukes fought amongst themselves. It might be expected that the chaotic 'Rule of the Dukes' would see Lombard conquests rolled back somewhat; however, if anything, the multiplication of Lombard leaders caused more trouble for the Romans rather than less. Dukes looking to build their position sought out opportunities to attack imperial territory, with two independent Lombard duchies – Spoleto and Benevento – set up in central and southern Italy.

However, the anarchy at the heart of Lombard politics eventually saw the dukes elect a new king, Cleph's son, Authari. This was not enough to prevent another ducal revolt in 626, but by then Authari and his successor Agilulf had given some stability and resilience to the central Lombard authority. Therefore, even when it was faced with internal issues, the Lombards proved capable of at very least resisting any Roman attempts to reclaim formerly imperial territory. Indeed, it was usually Lombards grinding out more of Roman Italy for themselves than losing land. This meant that by the mid-seventh century the Lombard kings and dukes controlled the Po Valley, Tuscany and Liguria, and most of central and southern Italy. And while the Roman navy maintained the imperial presence in the western islands, coastal fortresses, the major cities of Ravenna, Rome and Naples and their hinterlands, as well as the heel and toe of Italy, that Lombard grind continued on into the eighth century.

The Lombard threat itself, regardless of the strength of its kingship, was not monocephalic. The duchies of Spoleto and Benevento frequently followed their own agendas, which could be equally anti-Lombard as they were anti-imperial. Even certain dukes within the Lombard kingdom were not beyond acting on their own against what was left of Roman Italy. That fragmentation of Italy also provided opponents for the empire in the form of rebel Ravennate exarchs and *duces*, while the decline of imperial authority in the peninsula saw the papacy become increasingly independent. Indeed, the religious divides between Rome and Constantinople during Leo III's life – first Justinian II and Quinisext and then iconoclasm – only furthered the political divisions between Italian lands loyal to the pope and loyal to the emperor.

Throughout the eighth century, there would be various alliances between the papacy, Lombard, and Roman duchies, against various opponents and to various ends. Ultimately though, the most important alliance going forward for Italy was that between the papacy and the Frankish kingdom. The real fruit of this alliance would not come until after the reign of Leo III, but the looming presence of the Franks is something to be wary of. Imperial territory in Italy will also have faced external pressure from Slavs and Bavarians in the north, while perhaps the most powerful Roman imperial official in the west, the Sicilian *strategos* faced Arab raids on his territory from newly-conquered Umayyad Africa.

Such were the extent of these alliances and imperial distractions (and infirmities) that the Roman Empire was increasingly relegated to a bit part player in what was supposed to be imperial territory. When he remained loyal, the Ravennate exarch had fallen down the list of powerful individuals in the peninsula, behind Frankish mayors, Lombard kings and dukes, Sicilian *strategoi*, Roman popes and even some imperial/Roman *duces*. And so limited was the trust he had in his remaining officials in Italy, both in terms of loyalty and power, that the emperor would have to send his own eastern representatives to deal with aspects of Italy.

The Roman Empire of c.685 was clearly under considerable pressure on all fronts; it was being ground out in the west, swamped in the centre and under existential threat from the east. It needed to take advantage of every opportunity offered by its various opponents to improve its own position: internal divisions amongst the Lombards and Umayyads; the scattered nature of the Slavs; good relations with the young Bulgar khanate, and geographical separation from the Khazars. How much progress, if any, would the empire make in the lifetime and reign of Leo III? After the disastrous seventh century, could the Roman Empire strike back?

Chapter 3

The Origins and Early Career of Leo III

'A king's time as ruler rises and falls like the sun. One day Simba, the sun will set on my time here and will rise with you as the new king.'

Mufasa, *The Lion King*

Leonid Identity Crisis?

Sometime in the last-quarter of the seventh century, the man who was to lead the Roman Empire through its existential crisis and found the Isaurian dynasty was born, presumably either in Isauria or at the very least of Isaurian descent. However, before even getting into the events of his life, the subject of this book suffers from an identity crisis in the sources: none of the three parts of the name he is known by – 'Leo III Isaurian' – is correct. His original name was *not* Leo; he was *not* the third emperor to reign under that name; and he was *not* an Isaurian. He was born in around 685 with the given name Konon, which Leo revealed to the patriarch Germanos when the latter claimed that there was a prophecy that the icons would be condemned during the reign of an emperor Konon, rather than an emperor Leo.[1] This regnal name does not seem to have been something he chose for himself at his accession, but was perhaps instead a nickname that Konon was known as to his family and friends because he was as 'brave as a lion'. The error in regnal number (a modern issue rather than an ancient one) stems from the overlooking of the emperor who ruled from 695 to 698. His name was Leontios, but perhaps because the only previous imperial 'Leontios' had been a usurper in 484–488, it was an ill-omened name for a man who had just overthrown the reigning emperor. In search of much less tainted imperial pedigree, upon his accession, Leontios took 'Leo' as his official imperial name, appearing as such on his coins and in western sources. So, this Leontios should be remembered as 'Leo III', while the main subject of this book was really 'Leo IV'.

Perhaps the most egregious 'eponymous' error associated with Leo III is his being known as 'the Isaurian' and the founder of the 'Isaurian dynasty'. He was born in Germanikeia (modern Kahramanmaraş in Turkey) and therefore rather a Syrian. While not necessarily its originator, Theophanes Confessor has much to do with propagating this mistake. He describes Leo as being 'derived from Germanikeia, but actually from Isauria.'[2] This is not necessarily a contradiction as being 'derived from Germanikeia' – and therefore a 'Syrian' – could be a geographic label rather than an ethnic one, reflecting Leo's living in Syrian Germanikeia rather than it being his heritage. Later in his *Chronographia*,[3] Theophanes refers to Leo as solely 'the Syrian' – *paranomotatou Syrou* – without any similar insertion of ἐχ της'Ισαυρίος. This is by no means conclusive evidence, but it could highlight the problems with the patchwork nature of Theophanes' work. Indeed, the mention of Isauria in Leo's heritage by Theophanes could be entirely secondary,[4] with the troublesome ἐχ της'Ισαυρίος appearing 'tacked on'.

A potential reason for any such 'tacking on' in the text of Theophanes could be further confusion between Leo III and the emperor Leontios.[5] As already seen, Leontios ruled as 'Leo' and both he and Leo III served as Anatolic *strategos* before ascending the throne. Most importantly, Leontios is recorded as being from Isauria.[6] It would not be surprising for there to be confusion between two emperors from the eastern frontier called Leo, who ruled not all that far apart. More confusion regarding Isaurian imperial 'Leos' could come from the statistic that of the previous four emperors to be called Leo or Leontios before Leo III, three had Isaurian blood – along with the late-seventh century emperor Leontios, Leo II (473–474) was half-Isaurian and the fifth century usurper Leontios was from Dalisandus in Isauria.[7] Might Theophanes, George Syncellus, or even one of his copyists have inserted the qualifying phrase having come across mention of an emperor Leo from Isauria? A later insertion could explain why the troublesome phrase is missing from the ninth-century Latin translation of Theophanes' work by Anastasius Bibliothecarius, who referred to Leo as '*ex Germanicensibus dirivatus, genere Syrus*' and made no mention of Isaurian origins. Similarly, in the early-ninth century, the *Vita Stephani iunioris* refers to Leo as a 'Syrian by birth'; however, the *Parastaseis syntomoi chronikai*, which was at least partly written in the eighth century, refers to Leo as Isaurian,[8] suggesting that even if it is incorrect, it was an early designation, possibly earlier than Theophanes.

Another possible explanation for the Syrian/Isaurian origin mix-up is that it is the Syrian attribution that is incorrect, with Theophanes making a geographic error, recording Leo's birthplace as being Germanikeia when it was instead Germanikopolis in Isauria. The sources that follow Theophanes and their copyists then compounded this error by repeating it.[9] Such a geographic mishap has been doubted by modern sources.[10] In the last years of the eighth century, surely not long after Konon's family was transplanted to Thrace, Germanikeia fell to the Arabs. One might wonder if Justinian II orchestrated the removal of some of its population because he recognised that imperial forces were not going to be able to defend Germanikeia much longer.[11] It would be reclaimed by Constantine V in 746, who transferred the kinsmen of his mother, the empress Maria, to Roman territory.[12] Pointedly, there is no mention of transplanting the kin of his father. Does that mean they had already moved west? Or does it mean that there never had been any kinsmen of Leo around Germanikeia because he and his immediate family were already migrants to that area? The transplanting of populations and settling of refugees was a well-established Roman policy and the maelstrom that was seventh-century Asia Minor could have seen Isaurians moving to Syrian Germanikeia. It must also be said that even though the name of his dynasty – 'Isaurian' or 'Syrian' – might reflect his origins, neither would definitively characterise the dynastic bloodline, with Khazar and Athenian blood injected into it through the marriages of Constantine V and Leo IV respectively.[13]

Leo's reputed knowledge of Arabic likely puts his origins closer to the Romano-Arab border in Syria, although Isauria is hardly that far removed from Arab territory. Strangely, Leo's ability to speak Arabic is a tradition in Arabic sources such as al-Mubarrad's *al-Kamil* and the *Kitab al Uyun*,[14] with no Roman/Greek/Syriac sources mentioning it or showing interest in how the emperor might have been able to read the letters that caliph Umar II reputedly sent to him.[15] Theophanes did call Leo 'Saracen-minded,'[16] while the inhabitants of Amorion are said to have called Leo 'a Nabataean Arab', which could reflect knowledge of any Leonid bilingualism. However, Theophanes was instead reflecting the perceived Islamic basis to what was considered Leo's iconoclastic heresy, while the complaints of the Amorions are recorded by the *Kitab al Uyun*, which is three centuries detached chronologically and likely represents Arab or Syriac thoughts on Leo rather than Roman.

Not only did his early life along the Romano-Arab frontier seemingly see him learn Arabic, it perhaps also saw Leo raised as a non-Chalcedonian Jacobite Christian. In his recording of Constantine V's transplanting of his maternal relatives from Germanikeia in 746, Theophanes mentions that that emperor also transferred 'Syrian monophysitic heretics … [and] most of these have lived in Thrace until the present day.'[17] This may hint at similar leanings for Leo and his parents. Leo would then have converted to Chalcedonian orthodoxy upon his entry into imperial service. Any such religious conversion might also be tied to his name change. Officially becoming 'Leo' in place of 'Konon' could be part of his attempt 'to minimise his Syrian ancestry and choose a name that emphasised his adherence to Chalcedonian orthodoxy.'[18] 'Leo' was a name not only with imperial pedigree and popularity amongst eastern Romans, but also with orthodox and papal groups – there had been a Pope Leo II (682–683) in the years immediately preceding Leo's birth. The *Kitab al Uyun* suggests that

Leo was not forgotten in his Syrian home, for over three hundred years later there was 'a celebrated church called after him.'[19]

We might also ask if there was anything 'Isaurian' about the name Konon. Of the 11 men listed in *PLRE* with the name 'Conon', possibly 4 were of Isaurian extraction; however, of the 16 Konons listed in the *PmbZ*, which deals with the period surrounding the time covered by this work, none are identified as Isaurian (if Leo III is excluded). This does little to dismiss or promote an Isaurian penchant for naming their sons Konon and does not mean that some of them were not Isaurian, as the defeat of the Isaurian rebellion of the late-fifth century and the Arab conquests will have seen Isaurians scattered throughout imperial territory. But it must be said that even if there was some Isaurian preference for the name, Konon was already a Greek name of long-standing, taking in a fifth/fourth-century BC Athenian general, an Augustan-Age mythographer, a third-century Pamphylian martyr saint, and a late-seventh century pope, who was born in Sicily but whose father had been an officer in the Thrakesian theme.[20]

All of this proves that attempting to cut through the 'Theophanic' fog that surrounds Leo's ethnic/geographic origins can perhaps only make things more unclear. The likelihood (although not certainty) is that the man who would become 'Leo III the Isaurian' and found the 'Isaurian' dynasty (717–802) was born in Germanikeia, part of the ancient region of Commagene in Roman Syria. While there is some room for potential Isaurian roots, he (and therefore his dynasty) should *probably* be seen as 'Syrian' rather than 'Isaurian'.[21]

Early Life and Imperial Encounter

This fog extends to information regarding Leo's early life. No exact date or even year of birth is recorded for him, although it is usually thought that he was born in around 685, the same year that the man who would put him on the fast track to political power, Justinian II, ascended the throne. Virtually nothing is known of Leo's parents, save for the aforementioned idea that kinsmen of his mother remained in Germanikeia as of 746, the implication that they might have been Jacobite Christians, and a suggestion from the *Kitab al Uyun* that his father's name was Constantine.[22] And even this suggestion seems based on merely an inference garnered from what became a family tradition once in power – naming the first born son after his imperial grandfather: hence the imperial Isaurian line consisted of Leos and Constantines. The *Kitab al Uyun* repeats this inference by stating that the father of the emperor Leo V the Armenian (813–820) was called Constantine, despite it being recorded as Bardas by *Theophanes Continuatus*.[23] Furthermore, such an imperial tradition is not evidence of a pre-existing family convention. There was no such tradition with regard to female members of the family – i.e. Constantine V did not name his first born daughter after his mother Maria, so there is little backing for Leo III's mother being named Anna, as his first daughter was.

The *Kitab al Uyun* records a prophecy that Maria had a dream about Leo, where 'a cock spreading his wings in her court, and all the cocks of the Romans answered him. And he said to her, 'Keep this vision secret and let no one hear of it."[24] Such oneiromancy was a long-standing practice in the ancient world and continued to be so despite the Christianisation of the Graeco-Roman world, possibly because it was prominent in the Bible.[25] Leo would have told Maria not to mention such an imperially prophetic dream because it would have caused trouble with the authorities, as will be seen with Philippikos Bardanes. Of course, such a story is laced with hindsight reporting, but it does infer that Leo and Maria were married *before* being transplanted from Germanikeia to Mesembria. This would not seem to be the case if Leo was born in around 685 and was transplanted to Thrace before 695,[26] making him not even a teenager at the latest date of his time in Germanikeia, but then his birth year of 685 is by no means certain and could possibly be brought forward enough to make him of marriageable age before the family moved to Mesembria. Or the inference of Leo and Maria being married while in Syria is incorrect.

The *Kitab al Uyun* records Leo's transfer to Thrace (it speaks incorrectly about Constantinople) as taking place 'during the time of civil war', which it does not specify. And as the period of 695 to 717 is referred to as the 'Twenty Years' Anarchy', when seven consecutive changes of emperor were facilitated through violence or threat, there is no real way to narrow it down. E.W. Brooks suggests that Leo came to Thrace in 698, which would make the period of civil war that between Leontios and the soon-to-be crowned Tiberius III.[27] However, this would require the rejection of Theophanes, who specifically states that Leo migrated from Germanikeia to Thracian Mesembria during the first reign of Justinian II from 685 to 695.[28] While Theophanes is capable of mistakes, at this point of his *Chronographia*, he or George Synkellus had access to a source with considerable information about the early imperial service of Leo III. Indeed, so detailed is this source that it has been suggested that it was notes taken from or even by Leo himself.[29]

There has even been some attempt to question the whole notion of a transplanting, although this has been considered needless,[30] and we do find Leo in Thracian Mesembria in 705, rather than his recorded home in Germanikeia. The transplanting of populations and settling of refugees was not just a long-standing Roman policy, it was one of significant recent history with Constans II and Justinian II settling large numbers of Slavs in Bithynia and Cappadocia as sources of military manpower, perhaps as 'a clear indication of the damage inflicted by almost constant warfare on the indigenous populations.'[31] Such devastation is summed up by the *Zuqnin Chronicle*:

> 'the regions of Asia and Cappadocia ... as far as Melitene and by the river Arsanias as far as Inner Armenia ... had been graced by the inhabitants of a numerous population and thickly planted with vineyards and grain and every kind of fruitful tree; but since that time (they have) been deserted and ... have not been resettled.'[32]

The repopulating of core provinces through transplantation was likely taking priority amongst Roman imperial authorities. Such was the state of the empire in the late-seventh/early-eighth century that being uprooted and moved from the eastern frontier for the western frontier may have seen Leo and his family merely exchanging the raids of Arabs for those of Bulgars. And if there is any kernel of truth to his supposed Isaurian background, this move to Thracian Mesembria may not have been the first transplanting the family of Leo had faced.

When settled in the Thracian foothills of the Haemus (Balkan) Mountains, Leo became a shepherd tending a sizeable flock of at least 500 sheep. The *Kitab al Uyun* refers to him as a winemaker, which is not completely out of the question as Thrace was a hotbed of viticulture. While the record of Theophanes is to be preferred over the *Book of Springs*, it is not necessarily an 'either/or' – Leo and his family could have kept sheep and cultivated grapes. In 705, the day-to-day routine of the young shepherd was shattered by the arrival of a Bulgar army. Given that his home in Mesembria was not exactly on the doorstep of Constantinople, being some 250km up the coast of the Black Sea and perhaps 100km closer to the Danube than the capital, the presence of Slav and Bulgar raiders was likely not unheard of even in the brief period of time Leo and his family had been in Thrace. There had been imperial campaigns against Slavs and Bulgars in the last quarter of the seventh century.[33]

However, there were some significant differences about this Bulgar army when compared to previous raiders. Firstly, it was led by the Bulgar khan, the formidable and successful Tervel; secondly, due to the khan's presence, it was a force of significant size, being made up of at least 5,000 Bulgars and Slavs[34] and quite possibly many more, with the recorded 5,000 men being Tervel's royal guard around which were thousands more Bulgars, Slavs, Germans, Huns and ex-Roman provincials; thirdly, and most strikingly, this Bulgar force was not only led by the khan: standing beside him was the deposed Roman emperor Justinian II.

His career requires a full work to elucidate on,[35] but in short, Justinian II became the sixth emperor of the Heraclian dynasty when he ascended the throne at the age of just 16 upon the unexpected death of his father, Constantine IV. In attempting to live up to the illustrious name he had been given, Justinian's reign began well. Within months of his accession, he had launched a successful campaign against the Umayyad caliphate, taking advantage of the distraction of the Second Fitna to extract a beneficial treaty. In 688, he personally led a campaign west out of the imperial capital to relieve Thessalonica from Slavic pressure. He also oversaw considerable numismatic, financial, administrative and legislative reform; however, in the process of this reforming, despite many being to the great benefit of the empire, Justinian made powerful enemies. By shifting at least some of the burdens of state onto the wealthier classes in order to build up a small landowner base, Justinian alienated the most powerful groups immediately around him. And when these were added to a religious dispute with the papacy (which included an attempt to arrest the pope) and perhaps most damagingly a serious military defeat at the hands of Abd al-Malik's Arabs at Sebastopolis in 692, Justinian's reign was in trouble. In 695, a rebellion in Constantinople saw Justinian deposed and replaced by the imprisoned general, Leontios. Justinian was exiled to the Crimea, but not before suffering the horrors of *rhinokopia* and *glosstomia* – the cutting off of the nose and tongue, which was supposed to remove him from candidacy for imperial power.

But Justinian was not going to let deposition, exile and disfigurement prevent him from his imperial birth right. While in Crimean exile, he negotiated a marriage alliance with the Khazar khagan as the core of a campaign to reclaim the throne. And when he was betrayed by his new ally, Justinian was still not to be denied, killing two would-be assassins with his bare hands and making the long, perilous journey around the Black Sea to the mouth of the Danube. Here, he met with Tervel, who jumped at the chance to help restore a Roman emperor to the throne. And so, in the spring of 705, a Bulgar army led by the Bulgar khan and a deposed Roman emperor marched south from the Danube towards Constantinople.

In the face of this vast army marching through his home in the Haemus foothills, the young Leo approached Tervel and Justinian and presented them with his flock of 500 sheep as a gift. What the *Kitab al Uyun* calls Leo's 'admirable courage'[36] was certainly a pragmatic and opportunistic move, for there was a good chance that Leo's flock would have been appropriated without recompense by the passing army anyway. Presenting them as a gift saw Leo make the very best of what could have been a bad job. So impressed was Justinian with this gift and with Leo personally that he appointed him as a *spatharios*, something of a bodyguard/aide-de-camp. A brave and clever Roman bodyguard will have been welcome, but this rapid promotion, taking Leo away from his possibly boring and even dangerous life in rural Thrace, reflects more on how Justinian will have had very few followers after a decade in exile. He likely felt that being responsible for the promotion of Leo will have made his new *spatharios* more personally loyal and willing to protect him. Leo's ability to speak Arabic may well have helped bring about his commission.

With Leo in tow, this Bulgar army continued on to Constantinople, bypassing the imperial army stationed at Apollonia Pontica (modern Sozopol in Bulgaria) and then camping at the northern section of the city walls before the Gate of Charisus and the Blachernae. When the city did not capitulate after three days, with Justinian's entreaties met with insults, the emperor took advantage of some local knowledge and stole into the city through perhaps the Aqueduct of Valens, which had been cut during the Avar siege of the city in 626.[37] As he had been commissioned as a *spatharios*, is recorded as serving bravely during civil conflict[38] and had been judged by Justinian as 'a true friend,'[39] it is attractive, although unprovable, to place Leo in the small group who infiltrated the city through the cut aqueduct and helped Justinian take control of the Blachernae region and then Constantinople as a whole. Such service would certainly encourage the recording of Leo as a 'a true friend' of the now restored emperor. And it would appear that Leo almost immediately needed that friendship.

Imperial Censure and Caucasian Service

The rapid promotion of Leo roused jealousy amongst his fellow officers, some of whom might have been with Justinian in exile. These individuals were so envious of Leo that they contrived to have him accused of seeking the crown.[40] If the sources are taken at their word, such an accusation – whether it was true or not, or based on knowledge of Maria's prophetic dream – would have proven fatal to Leo, for Justinian II's restored reign is depicted as being drenched in blood, driven by paranoia and revenge. However, this depiction of Justinian is very much reliant on a source record that is 'distorted and unfair,'[41] with many modern historians becoming 'so preoccupied with the chroniclers' gruesome tales of the disfigured emperor, driven by frantic desire for vengeance, that they have made no real attempt to consider it in a more balanced light.'[42]

Certainly, his restoration had been accompanied with some bloodshed: Justinian's imperial predecessors (usurpers in his mind), Leontios and Tiberius III, were publicly humiliated, mutilated and then beheaded; Tiberius' brother, Herakelios, and other military officers were hanged from the walls of Constantinople, while various high-ranking officials and nobles who had sided with Leontios and Tiberius were also executed.[43] But the various methods of execution recorded by hostile sources like Nikephoros and Theophanes[44] – luring them to banquets, thrown into the sea in sacks – as well as the sheer 'uncountable' extent claimed[45] would appear to stem from the 'black legend' that grew up around Justinian II. He also did not execute some of his most prominent opponents. The patriarch Kallinikos, who had crowned both Leontios and Tiberius III, may have been blinded (reputedly by being forced to stare into a bowl of boiling vinegar) but he was allowed to live out his life in exile in Rome.[46] Another rather striking survivor of this supposed Justinianic purge, suggesting that there was really no such thing, was 'one of the most potentially dangerous persons of the Empire: Theodosius, the son of Tiberius [III] Apsimar,'[47] a figure we will meet later as an iconoclastic ally of Leo III. Further evidence that this paranoiac monster is largely a fiction is demonstrated in the treatment of Leo upon this accusation of imperial pretension reaching Justinian. While he did not dismiss it out of hand, the emperor called his 'true friend' to attend an inquiry, which found no evidence against Leo. The accusers were 'shamefully exposed as slanderers,'[48] and suddenly found themselves in need of a less arbitrary Justinian than the sources depict.

Not long after his acquittal, Leo was selected by Justinian for a dangerous mission into the lands north of the Caucasus. He was to contact the Alans, an Iranian tribe, and use the diplomatic and financial clout of Constantinople to persuade them to attack the Abasgians in the north-eastern corner of the Black Sea (modern day disputed territory of Abkhazia in north-western Georgia). The Abasgians looked to be about to switch their allegiance from the empire to the Umayyads, and sparking a local conflict in Abasgia with non-imperial forces might have dragged in some Arab forces, relieving some pressure on Roman forces in Anatolia. Such Arab campaigning in the region might also encourage resistance from the Christian peoples in the area, something which had been lacking in recent years, with the likes of Lazica going over to the Umayyads in the last years of the seventh century.[49] It might be asked why Leo was charged with such a dangerous task – was it an admission of his skills and indeed the trust Justinian had in him, or was it evidence of Justinian's wariness of his *spatharios* in the aftermath of the accusations made against him? Again, the hostility of sources like Theophanes towards Justinian will suggest the ulterior motive of getting rid of Leo – 'if, indeed, Justinian did not wish to harm Leo openly, he did begin to feel anger towards him',[50] while the likelihood is that the emperor needed someone who he could trust to do the job.

The exact date for the resultant Caucasian adventure of Leo amongst the Alans and Abasgians is not clear. This is because we are reliant on Theophanes for the detail on this episode and he places it in his entry for the year 716–717 when recounting Leo's early career in the build up to his ascension of the imperial throne.[51] Of course, the involvement of Justinian II and Leo in the episode places it during Justinian's second reign between 705 and 711, with the likelihood (although not certainty) being that it took place in the middle or towards the end of that period. Whenever it took place, Leo was sent off to the Caucasus with a significant sum of money with which to buy Alan interference. It seems that Leo was to operate as secretly as possible and therefore probably travelled with very few companions. This made carrying the funds he had been given impractical, so he deposited them in the city of Phasis (modern Poti in Georgia). As Phasis was in Umayyad-aligned Lazica, this might raise some concerns about the veracity of some aspects of this story or at least the totality of Arab control of the region. It may instead be a testament to any lingering Roman support in Phasis or Leo's success in remaining incognito. As he is recorded 'taking a few natives with him,'[52] it would also seem that Leo used some of the imperial cash to buy safe passage through Lazica and a group of bodyguard/guides. We could also propose that he might have used any ability to speak Arabic and his likely Syrian heritage to keep himself from any suspicion.

With his guides, Leo crossed into neighbouring Apsilia, made it through the Caucasus Mountains and into the territory of the Alans. He was welcomed there with all the honour due to a Roman diplomat, and through the combination of diplomacy, financial promises and maybe hints of Roman military aid, Leo succeeded in persuading the Alans to strike at Abasgia. Theophanes even claims that the Alans captured Abasgia as a whole, but this appears to be an error.[53] After this positive start, Leo's position in Alania began to unravel. The leader of the Abasgians sent a message to the Alans, telling them that Leo had been sent to rouse them against their neighbours on false promises, claiming that Justinian had had the money stored in Phasis removed. He offered to ransom Leo from the Alans for 3,000 gold pieces to preserve peace.[54] Theophanes presents this rumour of the removal of the funds from Phasis as a fact, with the motive being to bring about the demise of Leo, either at the hands of the short-changed Alans or the angered Abasgians, due to the imperial belief that Leo *had* been plotting to seize the throne. Theophanes even has Leo himself believing that this was Justinian's plan.[55]

There are serious issues with this whole story. At the very least, the report stems from the one man who had the most to gain by foiling the Roman embassy to the Alans – the Abasgian leader. A query may be raised about how the Abasgian leader might have known about Leo's presence amongst the Alans, his aim there and the depositing of funds in Phasis. Betrayal would seem the most logical avenue of explanation, but before jumping to the conclusion of *imperial* betrayal, there are various others who might have informed the Abasgians – whomever Leo left the funds with in Phasis, whomever he hired (or failed to hire) as guides through Apsilia and the Caucasus, other Lazicans, Apsilians and even Alans he encountered on his journey, or even Leo's jealous fellow officers. If he was so set upon getting rid of Leo, Justinian would have just used the enquiry into his reputed imperial pretension to achieve it or simply 'disappeared' him, rather than employ such a 'byzantine' ambuscade of large amounts of money and the tribes of the Caucasus. 'Such indirect methods of ridding himself of a foe are strikingly unlike Justinian's usual course of action against his enemies.'[56]

Given the bias of the sources, it is impossible to ascertain the extent of the trouble that Leo may now have faced in Alania, but any combination of his inability to pay the Alans, the forewarning of the Abasgians, their attempted bribery of the Alans and any opposition of the emperor was highly problematic. He had an almost literal 'sword of Damocles' hovering above his head, which could strike at any time. Perhaps somewhat unexpectedly, the Alans stayed true to the agreement they had come to with Leo, even in the face of him potentially not being able to fulfil his financial promises and the Abasgian bribe. They reputedly responded to the Abasgian leader that they had not made common cause with Leo on account of the money he offered them 'but because of our friendship with the emperor.'[57] The Abasgian leader could have taken such a statement as an indictment of his own turning his back on his allegiance to the Roman Empire, but instead he upped his bribe to 6,000 *nomismata* for the handing over of Leo and the maintaining of the peace. The Alans confided in Leo of this increased offer for his life and together they conceived of a gambit…

> 'As you can see, the road leading to the Roman country is closed, and you have no means of going on your way. Let us rather deceive them by agreeing to surrender you, and we shall send some of our men to accompany them. Thus, we shall gain a knowledge of their mountain passes so as to raid and destroy their country and perform what is pleasing to you.'[58]

With the agreement of Leo, the Alan sent emissaries to the Abasgians agreeing to their terms. The Abasgian leader then sent emissaries of his own to take custody of Leo. The plan was that after the *spatharios* was surrendered, the Alans would follow, kill the Abasgian emissaries and take Leo to the safety of their army in preparation for their stealthy invasion through the Caucasian passes. Leo was taking a significant risk in going along with any such plan, although stuck in the midst of the Alans, he had little choice. If he refused, his hosts might just sell him to the Abasgians. And even if the Alans stayed true to their word, who was to say that the Abasgians would not just kill him once he was in their custody? They might have thought to ransom him on to the Arabs or back to Constantinople, but killing him would have been less immediate hassle and worthy of reward from either the caliph or the emperor (if the latter wanted Leo dead). As it was, the Alans stayed true to their word, handing over Leo and his companions to the Abasgian emissaries, but then their leader Itaxes[59] overtook the column, killed the Abasgians and freed Leo. An Alan army then struck into Abasgia, where it took 'many captives and caused much destruction.'[60]

When word of Leo's success in instigating this Alan attack on Abasgia reached Constantinople, Justinian now looked for a way to extricate Leo from the Caucasus. He sent to the Abasgians, telling them that 'if you escort our *spatharios* and let him pass through your country without harm, we shall forgive you all your transgressions.'[61] Theophanes' tone would have it that this was the emperor's latest attempt to do away with Leo, but more likely Justinian was looking to use Leo's presence and his rapport with the Alans for further diplomatic gain. Essentially, should the Abasgians help Leo to return to Roman territory and return to their imperial allegiance, the emperor would call off any subsequent Alan raids of their territory. The Abasgians were happy to agree to such an arrangement and sent to the Alans once more, offering hostages and safe passage to Leo through their territory. However, Leo refused, not trusting the Abasgians or the emperor.

This refusal left the Abasgians in a poor position – they were unable to openly demonstrate their acceptance of Justinian's offer and as time went on with no word of Leo's return to imperial territory, the emperor may have begun to think that the Abasgians had rejected his offer and even that something untoward had happened to his diplomat. This could be reflected in the sudden appearance (at least in historiographical terms) of 'an army of Romans and Armenians'[62] besieging the Lazican city of Archaiopolis (modern Nokalakevi in Georgia). This was not just some border town on the immediate doorstep of Roman territory – it was situated north of Phasis, so this army, perhaps part of the Armeniac field army, had struck well beyond the Romano-Lazican border into territory that ostensibly owned its allegiance to the Umayyad caliphate. Even though Theophanes states that it happened 'some time later',[63] this armed intervention against Lazica was surely part of the same imperial plan that saw Leo negotiating with the Alans to strike at Abasgia. Part of Leo's ability to persuade the Alans to act against the Abasgians likely involved the promise of Roman military action in the region. Justinian's committal of forces to Lazica would also suggest that the whole affair, at least from its outset, was not a convoluted plan to get rid of Leo.

The Alans of Itaxes soon brought word to Leo that a column of Roman soldiers were operating in Apsilia and the Caucasian mountains. Encouraged, Leo set out with an escort of 50 Alans across the mountains in snowshoes to meet this Armeniac 'vanguard'. What he found was a raiding/foraging detachment of 200 men, but when he enquired about the rest of the army, he did not receive a positive answer: 'It returned to the Roman country when the Saracens attacked.

As for us, being unable to depart to the Roman country, we were making our way to Alania.'[64] The Armeniac army appears to have either taken too long to subdue Archaiopolis or the Umayyad response was quicker than expected. Receiving word that an Arab army was on its way to Lazica, they lifted their siege and retreated to imperial territory. Far from being a vanguard, these 200 men operating in Apsilia were looters or foragers who had been left behind by the alacrity of the Armeniac retreat and were now stranded in Apsilia by the Arab presence in Lazica, eking out an existence through brigandage.

Not only was Leo still trapped in the Caucasian foothills with no obvious route back to Roman territory, he was also now much more conspicuous in the presence of 250 Armeniacs and Alans. However, it was this increased military strength that provided Leo with another potential escape route. During their raiding of Apsilia, the Armeniacs had come into contact with Pharasmanios, warden of the Apsilian fort of Sideron (possibly modern Tzibile in Abkhazia). While an Arab subject, he had made some sort of compact with the Armeniac brigands, possibly allowing them to use his land in return for not raiding it. Leo looked to use these good relations as an avenue to cross his territory to the Black Sea coast. He contacted Pharasmanios and asked him to extend the peaceful relations he had with the Armeniacs to the Roman Empire in general and aid Leo and his small army to take ship for Trebizond. When the warden refused, Leo resorted to military action. He sent some of the Armeniacs and Alans to raid the fields around Sideron, which caused enough panic to present an opportunity to seize the gates of the fortress. Pharasmanios still held most of the fort, which was strong enough to resist Leo's initial attempts to capture it, first diplomatically and then militarily.

At the height of this stand-off, another army appeared at Sideron. Fortunately for Leo, it was not the Arab army, but a 300-man escort of Marinus, leader of Apsilians. He had thought that the attack on Sideron was the vanguard of a major Roman push in the region, hoping either to offer submission or prevent a large-scale conflict. When Marinus found the more limited size of the Romano-Alan force, he entered diplomatic negotiations with both Leo and Pharasmanios. The Apsilian leader offered to escort Leo and his men to the coast, with the Sideron warden now more willing to accept imperial overlordship and even to offer his son as a hostage.

Taking advantage of his bolstered position, Leo demanded that Pharasmanios allow him entry into the fortress as a show of his re-established Roman allegiance. The warden only agreed to do so on the promise that Leo would only enter Sideron with 30 men and not do harm to Pharasmanios himself. Despite this agreement, either Leo, Pharasmanios or both broke its terms,[65] leading to the *spatharios* ordering his 30 men to facilitate the capture of Sideron by taking possession of the citadel gates. As a warning and to prevent revenge attacks, Leo had the fortress burned to the ground, its walls flattened, and its inhabitants scattered. Leo and his men then joined up with the escort of Marinus and marched across Apsilia, where he was well-received. Upon reaching the Black Sea coast, he was able to take ship back to imperial territory.

This brought an end to Leo's Caucasian adventure. While the sources are keen to depict it with the anti-Justinian slant of being a convoluted plot to rid himself of a *spatharios* whose loyalty he doubted, it was instead an imperial attempt to open a new front in the war with the Umayyads. Specifically, Leo's expedition to the Alans was part of a wider scheme in the western Caucasus – Justinian would not have contributed manpower and funds merely to the instigating of a low-level raid of Abasgia. The aim may have been at the very least to bring all of Lazica, Abasgia, Apsilia and the Alans to a pro-Roman stance. It was therefore quite probable that Leo was not the only diplomat sent to the region at this time. His ability to deposit funds in Phasis and the Armeniac army's move through Lazica to Archaiopolis might suggest that the way had been paved for them by others.

Leo had been successful in proving himself a capable diplomat in buying Alan allegiance to the empire and directing them against the Abasgians. He also then proved himself decisive, even ruthless, in the capture of Sideron and negotiating any pro-Roman stance on the part of some Abasgians and Apsilians, which may well have been an added bonus for the expedition, as was the repatriating of the 200 Armeniac brigands. However, as a whole, the scheme to open up a new front was largely ineffective. While Abasgia's allegiance to the caliphate would be extremely loose, to the point where it would give allegiance to the Roman Empire under Leo III, the rest of the western Caucasian lands remained more firmly under Arab sway. This failure was due to the lack of success by the Armeniac army that had been tasked with the invasion of Lazica, through poor performance, poor planning and/or poor estimation of Lazican resistance and Arab response times.

The full extent of the ineffectiveness of the imperial scheme for the region would take time to reveal itself, so when Leo left Caucasia, he did so with a successful expedition behind him. However, the detailed section of Theophanes' account of Leo's early career in AM6209 breaks off upon his return to Roman territory. This leaves us with something of a gap in our knowledge of Leo's movements and interactions. As the date and length of Leo's Caucasian adventure is unknown, that gap could cover almost the entire period between Leo's joining of Justinian II in 705 and Leo's reappearance as Anatolic *strategos* in 716/717. And even if it is decided that the Caucasian episode did not begin until near the end of Justinian's second reign, that still gives at least five years of Leo's career that are not sufficiently illuminated by the sources. But then the sources had much more important things to focus on during the years 711–716 than the career of a young and largely insignificant *spatharios* …

The Roman Empire was in the process of trying to tear itself apart…

Chapter 4

'Only' Six Years Anarchy? Imperial Crisis at the Dawn of the Eighth Century

'But what do we have left, once we abandon the lie?' Varys replied. 'Chaos? A gaping pit waiting to swallow us all.'

'Chaos isn't a pit … **Chaos is a ladder.** Many who try to climb it fail and never get to try again. The fall breaks them.'

Varys and Petyr 'Littlefinger' Baelish,
Game of Thrones S03E06 'The Climb'

19 Months: The Reign of Philippikos Bardanes

Even before the chaotic period that eventually brought that lowly *spatharios* to the imperial throne, the Roman Empire had already gone through a period of political instability. The first reign of Justinian II (685–695) had raised enough opposition amongst the wrong people to see him deposed and replaced by one of his generals, Leontios. But then Leontios himself had only reigned for just shy of three years – 695 to 698 – before being overthrown by Apsimar, a naval commander whose forces had rebelled out of fear for imperial retribution for their failure to recover Carthage from the Arabs.[1] While the period 695 to 717 is usually characterised as the 'Twenty Years Anarchy', this overlooks the fact that Apsimar reigned (as Tiberius III) for seven years and was then followed by the six years of Justinian II's second reign. It could be argued that the *real* anarchy did not begin until the second deposition of Justinian, with the period 711–717 seeing five men sit on the imperial throne.

Sources such as Nikephoros, Theophanes and Agnellus would have it that the outset of this 'hot-potatoing' of the imperial crown was the 'vengeful reign of terror'[2] that Justinian II embarked upon in 705. While such a depiction is 'distorted and unfair,'[3] one leg of that supposed 'vengeance tour' sparked the revolt that was to permanently end his imperial tenure – the Crimean city and place of his exile, Cherson. Aside from any want of vengeance for his treatment by the Chersonites, there might be one other very good reason for Justinian involving himself militarily in the Crimea late in his second reign. It may be that since Justinian escaped from the Khazar assassins, the Khazar khagan (likely his brother-in-law) had installed a Khazar official – a *tudun* – in Cherson.[4] If this represents a Khazar encroachment on Roman territory, a vehement imperial response would not only be understandable, it would be expected.

With a 'manifestly absurd'[5] order to exterminate all Chersonites, a large expeditionary force was dispatched to the Crimea in early 711. As the expedition was also to target the Khazar-held city of Bosporus, Justinian either suspected or had evidence of a Chersonite-Khazar alliance. The initial campaigning met with some success, prompting the hostile sources to focus on reputed mass drownings, and roasting alive and imprisoning of Chersonites. Upon returning to Constantinople, the imperial fleet was wrecked by a massive storm. These losses, exaggerated in the sources as they were, may have encouraged the Chersonites and Khazars to continue their struggle against imperial forces. The appearance of a Khazar army in the Roman Crimea not only persuaded Justinian to plan a second expedition, they persuaded the new Chersonite governor, Helias, and whatever troops he had under his command to defect. The Chersonites, Khazars and imperial defectors then passed the point of no return in executing imperial envoys and elevating one of their own as a challenger to the throne of Justinian II. Their choice fell upon an officer called Bardanes.

This latest imperial usurper is recorded as the son of a patrician called Nicephorus, who was born in an Armenian colony in Pergamum, with a proposed connection to the Mamikonian family.[6] However, there has been some more recent dissent from this attributing of Armenian heritage to both Bardanes and Nicephorus.[7] While they would have little to say about Bardanes and even less of it good, the sources do commend him for his 'eloquent and prudent'[8] discourse. There is one story told about Bardanes' earlier life that was used to explain his lowly position when he appears in the historical narrative. Bardanes met a heretical, clairvoyant monk in the monastery of Kallistratos.[9] That Bardanes would know such a monk not only hints at his own religious leanings, but also that he was in Constantinople in the last quarter of the seventh century. It could also highlight, along with his father being a patrician, that Bardanes was somewhat active in Constantinopolitan politics or administration. In their meeting, the monk informed Bardanes that 'You are destined for the empire.' Bardanes was troubled by this pronouncement, recognising the danger such a prediction placed him in, only for the monk to retort 'if God so commands, why do you contradict him?'[10] When Leontios succeeded Justinian in 695, Bardanes sought out the monk, who told him 'Do not hurry; it is yet to come.'[11] And when Leontios was deposed and succeeded by Tiberius III, Bardanes made a similar complaint and received a similar response.

Bardanes made the mistake of confiding in one of his friends about this monastic prediction. Possibly keen to win the appreciation of the latest new emperor, this 'friend' told Tiberius III. Bardanes was arrested, flogged, tonsured and exiled in chains to Kephalonia. Theophanes has Bardanes recalled from exile on the restoration of Justinian, perhaps as part of a general amnesty; however, Nikephoros suggests that rather than a recall, Bardanes' presence in the Chersonite expedition was his being transferred to the Crimea in a continuation of his exile.[12] Such a predictive story may demonstrate the religious origin of much of the surviving source material but perhaps also how the claims of individuals like Bardanes and Leo III to the imperial title were so tenuous and their accession so unlikely as to be worthy of monastic or oneiric 'predictions'.

Would being an exile and therefore an opponent of Justinian II be enough for the Chersonites to choose Bardanes as their emperor? On top of also being the son of a patrician, he must have had a leadership role within the Chersonite expedition. Bardanes may even have been the most well-connected and appropriate of the leaders within the Cherson fleet to claim the imperial title. The commanders of the expedition, Mauros and Stephen Askemitos, had already returned to Constantinople, meaning that Bardanes only had to outrank the *spatharios* Helias, who had been sent to the Crimea to become governor of Cherson, a role which in itself might highlight Helias' low rank.

News that the local revolt had escalated into an imperial usurpation saw Justinian abandon any thoughts of a negotiated settlement and dispatch a second expedition under Mauros with orders to destroy Cherson. After making some headway against its walls, Mauros' assault was thwarted by the arrival of a Khazar army at the city. At this relief, Bardanes fled to the court of the khagan, only soon to be recalled to Cherson when the forces of Mauros, fearful of Justinian's response to their failure, also acclaimed him emperor. Wary of subterfuge, the khagan extracted a promise and a gold coin from each man in the defecting army. Under the regnal name Philippikos, Bardanes returned to Cherson to press his claim on the imperial throne.

Guessing that the extended quiet from his second Cherson expedition signified an expansion of the rebellion, Justinian took to the field; however, he made the peculiar choice to leave the imperial capital and move east along the south coast of the Black Sea. While he did gain confirmation of the defection of Mauros at Sinope, Justinian had critically misjudged the aims of Philippikos Bardanes. Rather than wait in the Crimea or move against the Asian themes, the forces of Philippikos struck directly at Constantinople, and, despite charging headlong back towards his capital, Justinian was too late. The usurping army had taken control of Constantinople, killed Justinian's son and the *comes Opsikon* and were now moving against Justinian himself. In offering amnesty, Helias secured the neutrality of the emperor's army and at a subsequent parley made sure that Justinian was not going to come back from his second deposition by cutting his head off. Even if it does not leave a particularly good taste, the unedifying story of the butchering of Justinian's 6-year-old son, Tiberios,[13] and various other supporters and officials of Justinian were part and parcel of a violent regime change. The sending of Justinian's severed head around the empire as proof of his demise might also turn the stomach a little, but how else could people be persuaded that the former emperor was now definitely dead? However, if Philippikos Bardanes and his supporters thought that removing the Heraclian dynasty would solve the Roman Empire's woes, they were to be sorely mistaken. If anything, it made things worse.

Militarily, the one potentially offensive action attributed to the reign of Bardanes focused on Armenia. Theophanes proclaims in 712/713 that 'Philippikos drove the Armenians out of his country and obliged them to settle in Melitene and the Fourth Armenia.'[14] There is some issue with this record as it is unclear exactly who these Armenians were and why Bardanes might have been targeting them. A revolt in the region might explain why Justinian II had patriarch Cyrus anathematize the Armenians and also why the emperor headed so far east when faced with usurpation to the north in 711 – perhaps he thought that Bardanes had reached out to his countrymen.[15] Michael the Syrian suggests that various Armenians were expelled from the empire under Bardanes, with the Arabs settling them in Melitene and Fourth Armenia.[16] But even this is not completely satisfactory, as so unclear is the Romano-Umayyad frontier that ownership of Melitene at this point is uncertain. It may have been in Roman hands in 712, before falling to Maslamah b. Abd al-Malik in 714. However, Theophanes has Maslamah active in Armenia not only during the reign of Bardanes, but seemingly in connection with Bardanes' Armenian action. The Arab general even sacked the Armeniac capital at Amaesia around this time. Such an Umayyad presence may explain the imperial response, with Bardanes thinking that a move to secure part of his father's Armenian homeland would be a good start to his reign. The ejection of some Armenians from imperial territory could either be the removal of opponents of Bardanes/supporters of Justinian or Maslamah taking large numbers of prisoners during his raid.

It is uncertain if Bardanes took part personally in any imperial action in Armenia – in his previous entry, Theophanes proclaimed that the new emperor was content to stay in the imperial palaces when confronted with opposition.[17] The chances are that so early in his reign, Bardanes will not have looked to repeat Justinian's mistake of leaving the capital at a time of upheaval. Any Roman campaign in Armenia, either against Arab incursion or Armenian rebellion, was likely to have been undertaken by the Armeniac *strategos*. These were not the only Arab attacks on Roman territory to take place during the brief reign of Bardanes. The frontier town of Sision was abandoned in around 711, along with a series of fortresses near Melitene, while Misthia and Pisidian Antioch were sacked in 712/713.[18]

But any plans Bardanes might have had to confront the Arab attacks on the eastern provinces in greater force were quickly scuppered by a second front opening right on his doorstep as the Bulgars advanced into Roman territory. Tervel had aided Justinian II in his restoration in 705 and been suitably rewarded with 'many gifts,'[19] and if the Battle of Anchialus had been against a separate Bulgar group,[20] the alliance between Tervel and Justinian may have provided a *raison de guerre* for the Bulgar khan. There is also some suggestion that the Bulgar attack in 712 was caused by the failure to pay an annual tribute to the khan,[21] which would make it Bardanes who had, inadvertently or intentionally, broken any Romano-Bulgar treaty. One could well understand if the new regime had overlooked such a payment in the chaos of its enthronement.

Whatever his motives, Tervel's army struck deeply into Roman Thrace, approaching the Bosphorus by way of Philea. So sudden was their attack that many were caught out in the open celebrating weddings and hosting dinners, enabling the Bulgars to take many captives and spoils, while killing others. The invaders then made a demonstration against the walls of Constantinople, approaching the Golden Gate. Without any opposition, the Bulgars then returned home, further devastating Thrace and removing 'innumerable cattle.'[22] The lack of imperial threat to this Bulgar incursion may hint at the weakness of the empire's Thracian and/or Constantinopolitan forces. Bardanes responded to this by transferring the Opsikon army from Asia Minor into the Balkans. This action facilitated the end of Bardanes' reign in mid-713, but while it highlights part of the immediate military failure of the new regime, it was not the real catalyst in its removal. For that, we must look elsewhere.

In the reputed character of Bardanes, we find several flaws recorded by Theophanes and Nikephoros. He was considered profligate with imperial funds, for having 'found a lot of money and expensive property collected by the previous emperors … through confiscations and various pretexts, and senselessly and vainly squandered it.'[23] Nikephoros also records Bardanes banqueting with his friends and then sleeping until midday, although this was in celebration of the anniversary of the re-dedication of Constantinople on 11 May, so it cannot be taken as a general reflection of the emperor's conduct,[24] yet sleeping at an important time would help bring about Bardanes' downfall. Theophanes also describes him as incompetent, disreputable, and adulterous, while Nikephoros regarded him as administering the empire 'in an indecorous and negligent manner.'[25] However, such ill-judgements of character and ability must be treated with caution, for they were almost all negatively coloured by one specific religious policy of Bardanes.

We have already seen how Bardanes' rise to imperial power had been supposedly predicted by the monk from the Kallistratos monastery; however, there was another aspect to the divine deal he proposed for Bardanes – in order to have a 'mighty and long' reign on the throne, Bardanes had to agree, under oath, to cast down the 'wrongly enacted' Sixth Ecumenical Council.[26] This marked the monk and Bardanes himself as followers of Monothelitism. This was a sizeable obstacle to the perceived legitimacy of Bardanes amongst the orthodox inhabitants of the empire. Heterodox emperors had ruled successfully in the past, so long as they were moderate in their religious dealings. Immediately upon his accession at a time of military instability, Bardanes would have been best suited to follow such a moderate path. He did not …

Within weeks of his accession, Bardanes made his Monothelitism central to his regime. The orthodox patriarch, Cyrus, was deposed, which in itself is not a sign of religious realignment. Cyrus had been a close partisan of Justinian II so deposition and confinement to the Chora monastery could have been seen as part of the excising of the previous regime. However, Cyrus was replaced as patriarch by John VI, a committed Monothelite. This appointment might meet with some opposition, particularly when it came to the new patriarch's profession of faith, but it was still potentially survivable. However, Bardanes then set about keeping his oath to the Kallistratos monk by convening 'a false assembly of bishops to cast out the holy ecumenical council.'[27] Theophanes somewhat gives the impression that this attempted restoration of Monothelitism was the work of a small cadre of churchmen, along with Bardanes – patriarch John VI, Germanos of Cyzicus, Andrew of Crete, Nicholas the *quaestor*, the deacon Elpidios, Antiochos the *chartophylax* and 'other men of the same ilk.'[28] However, even though the Arab conquests had removed the Monothelite areas from the empire, Nikephoros suggests that there was pro-Monothelite feeling in Constantinople, stating that Bardanes had the support of 'other priests and many senators' in his rejection of the imperial orthodoxy of the 'two wills and two energies'. Certainly, Bardanes would not have anathematised the Sixth Ecumenical Council on personal belief, the pronouncement of a single monk or a small cadre of supporters, even if it was part of a divine bargain. This suggests that there was Monothelite support within the political and military elites.[29] There was likely a political aspect to this restoration of Monothelitism. As it had been a doctrine promulgated under the emperor Heraclius, Bardanes may have been looking to harken back to past glories to solidify his position,[30] although looking to recall Heraclian achievements might not have been the best thing to do given how Bardanes' usurpation had seen the end of that dynasty.

As we are relying on Theophanes and Nikephoros' interpretation of whatever sources they were using, we are not entirely certain of the contemporary reaction to the restoration of Monothelitism. The support of the future patriarch Germanos and Andrew of Crete suggests that there was some level of support from the clergy, but even that is not necessarily the case as they were under duress from the threat of imperial reprisals. The rapidity of the restoration of the pronouncements of the Sixth Ecumenical Council after Bardanes' deposition would suggest that the reception of Monothelitism had been lukewarm in the east. However, in Italy, the reception was openly divisive. Upon receiving the declaration of the imperial faith, Pope Constantine brought it before a council in Rome, which rejected it as heresy. Bardanes' name was excluded from prayers, papal documents and coins, and his faith declaration and imperial portrait were sent back to Constantinople. The people of Rome reputedly even installed a *cibotarea*[31] in St Peter's, a Latinisation of the Greek κιβωτός, meaning 'chest' and used most prominently for the Ark of the Covenant, suggesting a similar 'ark' containing copies of the Acts of the Six Ecumenical Councils was displayed to portray their sacredness.[32]

But this papal rejection of Bardanes was not the end of the affair. At this time, the duchy of Rome had become vacant, and a certain Peter saw an opportunity for advancement. He is recorded sending to Ravenna for confirmation of his ducal elevation – this hints at it being the Ravennate exarch who appointed the Roman *dux*, but there are some issues with this. The historical record regarding the Roman *dux* is poor – indeed, Peter is the first known holder of the office, which could have it that the *dux Romae* was a relatively new position. Furthermore, at the time that Peter sent to Ravenna for confirmation of his elevation, there was no sitting exarch – the position had been vacant since the death of John III Rizocopos in 711 and is not recorded as being filled until the appointment of Scholasticus in 713.

Peter did receive imperial verification of his promotion to *dux Romae*;[33] however, 'once it became known that Peter had obtained his promotion in the name of the heretic emperor, the majority of the Roman people ... determined not to accept him as duke.'[34] It is here that the *Liber Pontificalis* makes mention of a certain Christopher being a 'former duke', which given its vicinity to the story of Peter's accession as Roman *dux* may suggest that that accession had been at the expense of a papal-supporting/anti-Monothelite Christopher. Alongside Agatho and supporters, Christopher confronted Peter on the *Via Sacra*, sparking a 'civil war' (i.e. a riot). There had been over 60 deaths, with Peter's faction having the worst of it, before Pope Constantine intervened to stop the fighting.[35] Despite this defeat and what was surely the continued opposition of Christopher's faction, Peter remained Roman *dux* until 725, suggesting that his faction was more 'imperial', imposing Constantinople's writ rather than being out-and-out 'defenders of the heretic'[36] and that neither the pope nor Christopher had enough power to oust him.

For imperial politics, this was an early demonstration that the papacy and its allies were taking the first steps to filling the void left by the crumbling exarchate of Ravenna. But in 712, it demonstrated that Bardanes' religious policy was not going to receive the full support of the provinces. The question could be asked as to what accelerative effects a prolonged Monothelite emperor might have had on the decline of imperial Roman Italy. The very hint of a heretic-supporting Roman *dux* had caused a 'civil war', so at the very least we might have expected more conflict between imperial and papal forces. Perhaps fortunately for Roman Italy or even the papacy, this is a question that did not need to be asked …

This was because the reign of Philippikos Bardanes fell apart after just 19 months. There is no definitive reasoning presented in the sources for the plot that deposed him. Even religiously orthodox men such as Theophanes and Nikephoros do not refer to Bardanes' heresy in their recording of his deposition in May 713. They instead focus on the military men who carried out the plot, giving no reason for their action. Bardanes' reign had not begun well militarily, with seeming Armenian revolt, continued Arab raids, armed discontent in Italy, and Bulgar attacks on Thrace and even the capital. There could have been some opposition within the military to Bardanes' Monothelitism, although Christian doctrinal issues do not seem to have affected the army to any great degree yet. The Opsikons, who were the perpetrators of the deposition, may have resented their transfer from Asia to Europe to deal with Tervel's raiders and/or their seeming loss of influence upon the overthrow of Justinian II.[37] They might even have seen an opportunity 'to establish themselves in an emperor-making or permanently 'praetorianist' role'[38] slipping away, with their transfer to Thrace taken as evidence of them being treated like any other thematic army.

Whatever its background, by the first days of June 713, the patrician Theodore Myakios had persuaded the *comes Opsikon*, George Bouraphos, to send troops into Constantinople to remove Bardanes. The job was given to Rufus, the Opsikon *protostrator*, who led a small force of thematic soldiers to the capital. Entering through the Golden Gate, Rufus and his men made their way to the imperial palace where they found the emperor sleeping, having spent the Saturday before Pentecost enjoying an equestrian contest, bathing in the Bath of Zeuxippos and lunching with his aristocratic friends. The Opsikon plotters seized Bardanes and took him to a quiet place in the Hippodrome, where they blinded him. The fact that Rufus and his followers could take hold of the emperor in the imperial palace, spirit him away to the Hippodrome and then blind him without opposition suggests that there was little support for this Monothelite emperor of Armenian extraction who had overthrown the Heraclian dynasty. Bardanes was not executed, but not only were his 19 months as emperor up, he died before the year 713 was out, suggesting that his blinding had done for him either through its messiness, shock, or infection.[39]

A Slight Improvement: The 27-Month Reign of Anastasius II

It is difficult to ascertain from the sources whether or not the plot of George, Rufus and Theodore involved a plan for the succession. The rapidity of the following accession – the next day according to both Nikephoros and Theophanes – could suggest that a plan had been in place, with their imperial candidate, Artemios, in on the plot from the start. And given that Artemios held the position of *protoasecretis* – a senior bureaucrat responsible for writing up imperial legislation – could suggest that the plot to remove Bardanes was not purely military in origin. But these are only suggestions and not very solid ones. It could easily be almost the exact opposite: the plot was spur-of-the-moment, based entirely on an impulsive military hierarchy, with the choice of Artemios as the new emperor made because he just happened to be in the right place at the right time.

Aside from his name and bureaucratic position, nothing is known about the man who was acclaimed emperor in succession to Bardanes in Hagia Sophia on 4 June 713, the Feast of Pentecost. Even his lofty position in the imperial bureaucracy says little about him as such high office does not necessarily reflect ability, although to have made it so high without ability would suggest good connections, familial or personal. But again, this is entirely speculative. Rather than a well-connected, ruthless opportunist, Artemios could quite easily have been a conscientious and skilled bureaucrat whose skills were recognised by more than one imperial regime, allowing him to rise through the ranks and then be in and around the imperial palace on the night the plotters struck.

What we do know is that when Artemios was crowned emperor, he took the regnal name of Anastasius. There could be several reasons why he chose such a name. While he had been a Miaphysite heretic, Anastasius I was a court bureaucrat who had given the empire 27 years of solid (and in financial terms, spectacular) rule. This choice of name may also contain some reaction to the reputed squandering of the imperial treasury by Bardanes. It should also be said that 'Anastasius' can also mean 'resurrection', something that the empire desperately needed in 713. As Anastasius II's acclamation took place in the Hagia Sophia, he was almost certainly publicly crowned by the patriarch of Constantinople, who was still John VI, despite his Monothelitism. Indeed, he would remain patriarch for another two years, suggesting that the plot against the regime of Bardanes was not necessarily a violent insurrection against his restoration of Monothelite heresy.

Perhaps John VI had had a change of heart? He would not have been the only one. The man who would succeed him as patriarch in 715, Germanos, bishop of Cyzicus, had given overt support to the Monothelite restoration of Bardanes. And yet, by the time of his elevation to patriarch, Germanos received the support of not just the emperor, but also the church, Senate and people of Constantinople, numerous other bishops and priests, and the papal legate.[40] The turnaround must have been convincing. And it may have been quicker than usually proposed, for it has been suggested that Germanos became patriarch in 714, with Theophanes recording the appointment happening on 11 August of the second year of Anastasius' reign, and that by August 715, the emperor was in Nicaea and the capital was under siege by a rebel fleet.[41] The naval actions of that period may not equate to a full blockade or siege, so a physical translation in August 715 would not have been impossible. Unfortunately, the record is lacking on why John VI needed to be replaced – had he died or had he been deposed, possibly because he had been unable to fully turn away from Monothelitism or at least shake that association? Even his proposed tenure of three years does not help the chronology, for if he became patriarch in 711, counting inclusively would see his patriarchate end in 713, rather than 714 or 715.

The year-long delay in replacing John VI does not mean that Anastasius was in any way slow 'to restore Chalcedon orthodoxy and rehabilitate the sixth council.'[42] In the first few months of his reign, Anastasius interjected in Italian politics, where his declaration of orthodoxy was met with 'great exultation, while the day of darkness came down on all the heretics.'[43] With his reign the product of a military revolt, Anastasius II will have needed as much legitimacy and support as he could get and the acceptance of his declaration of orthodoxy by the pope will have been much welcomed. Anastasius also appointed a new exarch – the imperial chamberlain and patrician, Scholasticus. One could well imagine that during his visit to Rome – it was he who delivered Anastasius' declaration of orthodoxy – Scholasticus consulted the pope over the position of Peter and perhaps in a reflection of his pro-imperial rather than pro-Monothelite stance, Peter was kept on as *dux Romae* on the proviso that 'he would not attempt to create any opposition.'[44]

Anastasius II was also quick to stamp his political authority. Within a fortnight he targeted the men he owed his new position to. Both Theodore Myakios and George Bouraphos were blinded and exiled to Thessalonica. It is not recorded whether Rufus was similarly punished or if he was at the side of Anastasius II during this cull. He was in a position to inform the emperor of who had ordered the removal of Bardanes (if Anastasius had not already been in on the plot). If he had shown loyalty and support for the new emperor, Rufus could have been promoted, possibly even replacing his former commander as *comes Opsikon*. But it is just as likely that because Anastasius was removing those who had been powerful enough to plot successfully against his imperial predecessor, Rufus faced a similar fate to George and Theodore. Owing his throne to the military leaders around the capital could have been a double-edged sword for Anastasius – it could have brought strong support from the Opsikon, but it could also have brought overweening military influence on imperial policies. Eliminating those responsible for the removal of Bardanes would have been seen as making Anastasius' position stronger and safer by removing this undue military influence and discouraging future rebellion. At least that might have been the aim ... Anastasius may also have been attempting to clear himself 'of any popular stigma for the mutilation of his predecessor.'[45]

According to the shared source of Theophanes and Nikephoros, Anastasius did a good job in choosing his officials and *strategoi*, including possibly a certain Leo as Anatolic *strategos*. The empire needed its best men in position due to what the Umayyad caliphate was planning for the next few years. The annual Arab raids had continued, with 713/714 seeing Maslamah leading a devastating raid on Galatia,[46] but something more was in the offing and Anastasius' intelligence sources told him he needed to find out more. Therefore, he dispatched an embassy under the patrician and urban prefect, Daniel of Sinope, to caliph al-Walid I in Syria 'on the pretext of negotiating peace,'[47] but really to investigate the size and strength of the expedition that was being planned. When Daniel returned, he was able to inform the emperor that the Umayyads were planning a massive strike not just into Roman territory, but a targeted attack on Constantinople itself by land and sea. Anastasius took significant steps towards the preparation of the city and the empire. He ordered that anyone who could not provide three-years' worth of food should leave Constantinople, while also building up its stores. He also set about making significant repairs to the imperial fleet, both in terms of smaller and larger ships, and to the land, sea, and machine defences of the capital.[48] The significance of these actions should not be forgotten.

Anastasius did not just rely on diplomatic and defensive measures to disrupt Umayyad preparations for their expedition (which were already facing some disruption through the death of al-Walid and dispute between his son Abd al-Aziz and his brother Suleiman). He also looked to go on the offensive. Some encouragement may have been given to the Anatolic and Armeniac *strategoi* to put pressure on the Arab raiding columns and even Umayyad territory, but the largest counter-offensive came with his rebuilt imperial fleet. Reports arrived of the Alexandrian fleet moving north to Phoenix (likely that on Rhodes rather than in Lycia or Phoenicia) with the aim of collecting cypress wood for repairs and shipbuilding. Anastasius took this opportunity to send a squadron of the imperial navy, loaded with some Opsikon regiments, to join with other ships at Rhodes (probably from the naval forces in southern Anatolia – either Karabisiani or Kibyrrhaeots). He gave command of the expedition to 'a prudent and experienced man'[49] John the Deacon, the grand *logothete*. Upon assembling at Rhodes, John called a council with his officers on the plan to attack the Arab fleet at Phoenix. 'While everyone else readily obeyed,'[50] there was a section of the expedition – called 'evildoers' by Theophanes – who not only rejected this plan, but openly rebelled against John and the regime of Anastasius II – the Opsikons.

With this one act of mutiny, what was a strong and decisive start to the reign of Anastasius II came crashing down within months. And the catalyst was one of the reign's earliest actions. The attempt to impose discipline and unshackle himself from the influence of the military, particularly the Opsikons, through the removal of George Bouraphos and Theodore Myakios, had the opposite effect. Rankling under strict disciplinary measures and angry at the perceived imperial ingratitude, the Opsikons were likely waiting for the opportunity to vent that dissatisfaction with Anastasius. And their dispatching from the capital to take part on the planned raid on the Arab fleet at Phoenix was just such an opportunity. John the Deacon was murdered and the fleet broke up. However, the mutinous Opsikon regiments could not simply return to the capital. Instead, they headed for their thematic bases in north-western Asia Minor to gather further support. By the time they reached Adramyttium (part of the Thrakesian theme), they had decided to elevate their mutiny to a usurpation.

Their choice of imperial candidate fell upon a local tax collector called Theodosius. Reputedly, he was 'an idle and ordinary fellow'[51] who had little interest in being thrust into imperial contention, going as far as to flee for the hills around Adramyttium. The Opsikons had to drag him out of hiding and forcibly proclaim him emperor. There could be some truth to this for the end of Theodosius III's reign hardly demonstrated that his heart was in the job, but it could also be said that this reluctance to accept imperial elevation was merely part of the traditional *refutatio imperii*, around in some form since Augustus nearly 750 years previously. Indeed, similar 'reluctance' had reputedly been shown by Heraclius in 610, so it was not completely unheard of by 715.[52]

The sources likely made a little too much of this reluctance. It has been argued that far from being a tax-collector in Adramyttium, Theodosius III was instead the son of Tiberius III, marking him out as a viable contender. Certainly, the Theodosius, bishop of Ephesus, who played a significant role at the iconoclastic Council of Hieria in 754 was listed as 'son of Apsimaros' by Theophanes,[53] but if this bishop was the former emperor, it would surely have been mentioned. This suggestion also requires Theodosius III to survive his deposition by 40 years and for Theophanes to record that the grave of an iconoclastic heretic reputedly performed miracles. The bishop of Ephesus could have had some connection to the deposed Theodosius III (a son perhaps?), but it seems unlikely that the usurper of 715 was connected to Tiberius III.[54]

Upon hearing of this usurpation, Anastasius posted loyal officers around the capital and the fleet, and then crossed the Bosphorus and made for Nicaea. Moving away from the defences of Constantinople was a strange choice and he had the example of Justinian II to learn from. Did Anastasius feel insecure in the capital or was he keen to nip this usurpation in the bud by attacking and defeating it quickly? It must be said that Nicaea was the Opsikon thematic capital, so maybe he thought to cut off the head of the snake; furthermore, moving to Asia Minor would have brought Anastasius into closer contact with two men who would later claim to be firm supporters of his, Leo and Artabasdos, the Anatolic and Armeniac *strategoi*. This denial of the Opsikons some of their home territory and a congregating of loyalist thematic forces in north-western Asia Minor should have been enough to bring matters to a head rather quickly. Instead, the civil war lasted six months, with Leo and Artabasdos offering Anastasius only nominal support. While they were distracted by the Arab advances into Anatolia and Armenia, it seems that neither *strategoi* really cared about keeping Anastasius on the imperial throne. It may even be that they were already planning a move of their own.

Anastasius was left shorn of a major part of his military support, which rendered his bold move to Nicaea the cause for his defeat. Theodosius and his backers rallied much of the Opsikon theme and a force of *Gothograeci*, Hellenised descendants of Goths settled in Bithynia. They were also able to capture some more ships and sail through the Hellespont and the Sea of Marmara to establish themselves at Chrysopolis, on the opposite side of the Bosphorus to Constantinople itself. Without the Anatolics and Armeniacs, Anastasius was unable to make any inroads against Theodosius' position. The conflict descended into a contest for control of the Bosphorus and Constantinople itself. The renovated imperial fleet, operating out of the harbour of St Mamas, was strong enough to repel Theodosius' ships over the next six months. However, when the imperial fleet moved to the urban harbour of Neorion, Theodosius seized the opportunity, quickly ferrying his forces across to Thrace and effectively taking control of the land outside the walls of Constantinople. This move away from blocking the crossing of the Bosphorus was another strategic misstep by Anastasius. Perhaps they were thinking that the fighting was done for the year as it was by now late autumn/early winter 715, but the subsequent admittance of Theodosius' forces into Constantinople through treachery could suggest that some of those 'loyal officers' Anastasius had posted to lead the fleet and the capital in his absence were anything but. Whoever it was who opened the Blachernae gate likely soon regretted that decision because the Opsikons and the *Gothograeci* effectively treated Constantinople like a conquered foreign city as they 'raided by night the houses of the citizens and wrought great havoc without respect for anything.'[55] This reflects disastrously on the control, or lack thereof, that Theodosius had over his own forces; however, this was not the first time in living memory that Constantinople had been treated in such a way – the forces of Tiberius III had plundered the city upon their capture of it from Leontios in 698, although these episodes could represent 'urban-rural hostility as much as the general behaviour of soldiers.'[56]

In the face of the Opsikon-backed usurper, who was now in control of Constantinople, and the failure of his thematic allies to aid him Anastasius may have reached out to the only other army of any size which might be willing and able to intervene on his behalf – that of Maslamah, the commander of the Arab armies charged by the caliph with attacking and capturing the Roman imperial capital ... You could imagine that such treachery would see any support for Anastasius melt away, but then not only was he becoming increasingly desperate, Justinian II and Bardanes had used foreign aid to further their imperial ambitions in recent years. If there was any concerted interaction between the emperor at Nicaea and the advancing Umayyad general, it came to nought. With the imperial capital in his hands and loyalist resistance crumbling away, Theodosius marched upon Nicaea. In the end, little to no fighting was required. When Anastasius saw the hostages in the train of the usurper – pro-Anastasian officers and patriarch Germanos, together with the failure of his land and sea forces, his nerve broke. He made contact with Theodosius, and asked for safe conduct in return for him giving up the imperial title and taking monastic orders. Theodosius agreed, exiling the now ex-emperor to Thessalonica.[57]

The recording of Anastasius' reign throws up some chronological issues. His accession is straightforward, dated to Pentecost – 4 June 713; however, Theophanes attributes him with a reign of only 1 year 3 months; a section in which Theophanes also misdates the reign of Bardanes as lasting 2 years 9 months, rather than 1 year 9 months at most.[58] Demonstrating the chronological tangle that Theophanes has gotten himself into, in recording Germanos' translation to the Constantinopolitan patriarchate, he places it in Anastasius' second year, but then mentions it being in the 13th indiction, which would equate to 715 instead of 714, giving Anastasius a third regnal year he otherwise denies him. A *follis* from Ravenna bearing the legend *ANNO III* suggests that Anastasius did have a third regnal year, and therefore was still emperor after 4 June 715 (if the coin is of Anastasius). Theophanes is not the only one to make a dating error with regard to Anastasius' deposition – the *Chronicon Altinate* puts it on 1 June

715, but has mixed up his deposition date with his execution in 719.[59] It would seem that the twelfth-century *Chronicle* of Michael the Syrian produces the most likely length for the reign for Anastasius II: 2 years 5 months, stretching from 4 June 713 to November 715.[60]

Despite the 'military anarchy', we should not overlook the actual skills of the men who attained the imperial throne, however briefly, with Anastasius II appearing to be a 'highly competent [emperor] … who took a firm grip on fiscal and military administration and prepared Constantinople for the coming Arab siege.'[61] Perhaps partly due to this competence and Theodosius' lenience in not enforcing any sort of physical mutilation, this was not the last we will hear of Anastasius II.

Was He Bovvered?: The 22-Month Reign of Theodosius III

Assigning the man who reigned as Theodosius III a 22-month reign is being a little generous, for while he was acclaimed in around May 715, he was not firmly on the throne, figuratively or literally, until his entrance into Constantinople possibly at late as November 715. It was possibly more of a 16-month reign, but even with this brevity and the lack of detail in the sources, Theodosius' time on the throne saw important developments. The focus of much of the attention for the reign of Theodosius was the developing situation in Anatolia with the advance of the Arab expedition targeting Constantinople. Part of that situation was the fact that the civil war between Theodosius and Anastasius did not technically end with the surrender, abdication and exile of the latter. While they had provided little aid to Anastasius, the *strategoi* Leo and Artabasdos refused to capitulate to Theodosius, claiming to be continuing to resist in the name of the now-deposed emperor.

While his forces had been brutal towards parts of Constantinople, Theodosius III proved moderate in the face of his opponents, pardoning patriarch Germanos and then following his advice in allowing Anastasius II to live in monastic exile. He also quickly demonstrated his religious orthodoxy, restoring an image of the Sixth Ecumenical Council removed by Bardanes, while also removing images of the heretic emperor and his Monothelite patriarch. Somewhat optimistically, in recording this action, the *Liber Pontificalis* claims 'that by the fervour of [Theodosius'] faith all dispute in the church ended.'[62] This would also suggest that Theodosius sent a profession of his orthodoxy to the pope to further elicit such a positive reaction in Rome. However, this appears to be the height of Theodosius' involvement in Italy, highlighting the increasing impotence of imperial authority on the peninsula.

The event from Theodosius' reign with perhaps the most important legacy for the future of the Roman Empire, beyond the approaching storm in Anatolia, came in relations with the Bulgars. There had been Romano-Bulgar conflict of some sort since the Roman defeat at Anchialus in 708, and even if these Bulgars raiding Thrace were not from the khanate, the possible failure to pay pre-existing tribute payments under Bardanes led to a Bulgar khanate raid of Thrace in 712. It could be that skirmishing continued post-712, especially if Bardanes, Anastasius and Theodosius either refused to or could not pay the tribute. Continued raids would certainly provide a reason for the newly-enthroned Theodosius to look to negotiate a cessation of the conflict. Unfortunately, the exact circumstances of the so-called 'Treaty of 716' are not recorded and we are only informed of its terms due to the khan Krum seeking a re-establishing of it in his negotiations with the emperor Michael I in early 813. Strangely, Theophanes records the treaty and its terms for his entry of 812/813, but not for that of 716.

> The terms in question established the boundary at Meleones in Thrace, [a tribute] of vestments and [dyed] red hides to the value of 30 lbs. of gold; furthermore, that refugees from either side should be returned to their respective homes even if they had plotted against their own rulers, and that those who traded in both countries should be certified by means of diplomas and seals: (anyone not having seals would lose) his assets which would be confiscated by the Treasury.[63]

These terms represent a Roman recognition of the Bulgar ownership in the Zagora region, and while the boundary marker of Meleones cannot be identified, it could be a geographic term, suggested as being a mountain peak in north-eastern Thrace, possibly the summit of the Manastir Heights. While the Romans paying any sort of annual tribute to the Bulgars might seem strange, this was a reaffirmation of previous tribute arrangements conceded by both Justinian II in 705 and his father Constantine IV in 681. The Bulgars were also granted access to Constantinopolitan markets, although it was not unfettered with imports and exports requiring state seals and documents.

We might ask if Theodosius' willingness to make peace with the Bulgars, ceding territory and promising further tribute payments to them, reflects not only the growing unease regarding the approaching Umayyad expedition against the imperial capital but also some rumours about the rebel *strategoi* Leo and Artabasdos coming to some arrangement with Maslamah. Indeed, the specific term regarding the exchange of refugees charged with conspiracy may not only be looking back to Bulgar involvement in the restoration of Justinian II and his failed repelling of the usurpation of Bardanes, but also the possibility of them aiding in any attempted overthrow of Theodosius III. Such Bulgar interference in Roman imperial politics had not only been seen before, it would be seen again in the very near future. And yet, even with that aspect of failure in the 'Treaty of 716', it would prove to be very advantageous for the Roman Empire. This was perhaps because the treaty not only shut down a frontier for the Romans to allow them to focus more of their military strength on the defence of Constantinople, it may have restored the alliance between Tervel and Justinian II. And the Roman Empire was soon going to need any friends it could get.

One other aside about the 'Treaty of 716' is a question over who was the Bulgar khan that Theodosius was negotiating with. It is usually considered to have still been Tervel, but there is discussion over the dates of his reign, with suggestions that it ended in 715, 718 or 721: this has the Romano-Bulgar treaty of 716 come under the aegises of Tervel or his successor Kormesiy.[64] Our sources introduce further issues with what seems like a misidentification. When recalling the terms of the treaty, Theophanes records Kormesios as 'the then lord of Bulgaria,'[65] which is a definite error as Kormesios was the Bulgar khan during the early reign of Constantine V, around 753–756. The similarity between 'Kormesiy' and 'Kormesios' would make for an understandable error on the part of Theophanes or his source. There have been some attempts to rectify this inconsistency beyond it just being a misidentification, such as there being another Romano-Bulgar treaty between Constantine V and Kormesios which also used the 'Treaty of 716' and was being referred to by Krum in his negotiations with Michael, or even suggesting that Kormesios was long enough lived to have been a joint ruler with Tervel.[66] There could have been some overlap between Tervel and Kormesiy, but it seems more likely that Tervel remained the Bulgar khan throughout the 710s, negotiating the 'Treaty of 716' with Theodosius III and then initiating the Bulgar involvement in the Arab siege of Constantinople, either through treaty obligations or other reasons.

If Theodosius had been thinking about peace with the Bulgars to facilitate a refocusing of more of his attention on Anatolia, it either came too late or he did not take full advantage of it. In early 717, an army appeared before the walls of Nicomedia, but it was neither the native thematic army of the Opsikon nor the vanguard of the Arab land expedition against Constantinople. Instead, it was the Anatolic army under the command of Leo the Isaurian, who had gone from 'supporter' of the previous emperor to a usurper claiming the throne for himself. Fortuitously, in taking control of Nicomedia, Leo captured Theodosius' son. He then pressed on to Chrysopolis and entered into negotiations with the emperor. Faced with this Anatolic, Armeniac and even Arab-backed usurper on his doorstep, who also held his son as a hostage, Theodosius seems to have offered little in the way of resistance.

Again, we must be cautious regarding notions of Theodosius' general reluctance to wield imperial power – it may be borne out of an historiographical misreading of the traditional *refutatio imperii*, his short reign, and his own recognition of the hopelessness of his situation in early 717. Not only was Leo ready to cross the Bosphorus and lay siege to Constantinople, with Maslamah's expedition looming on the horizon, but both the Senate and patriarch Germanos showed little support for Theodosius continuing as emperor, urging his abdication in return for being allowed to return to private life.[67]

Furthermore, there is one other important player in this confrontation who is rather conspicuous by their absence. While Nikephoros suggests that military as well as civilian dignitaries were part of the pressure put on Theodosius to abdicate due to his 'lack of experience and his incapacity of offering resistance to the enemy,'[68] neither he nor Theophanes mention the involvement of the Opsikon. As they were the reason that Theodosius was on the throne, it might be expected that they would fight to keep him in power. A new emperor raised by another theme might move to diminish their position, as they felt Anastasius had done. Did the alliance of the Anatolics, Armeniacs and Arabs scare the Opsikon into non-resistance? Had Leo managed to circumvent their loyalty to the Theodosian regime? Or had they, much like the Senate and patriarch, decided that continuing to back Theodosius was to back a losing cause? We can only speculate.

Any support that Theodosius had managed to garner in his overthrow of Anastasius II and its aftermath very quickly melted away and under 'a promise of his immunity from Leo'[69] given by Germanos, Theodosius III abdicated. Theophanes suggests that Theodosius merely handed over the empire to Leo, although Nikephoros has Leo elected emperor by Constantinopolitan authorities with no mention that the Anatolic *strategos* was in revolt against the emperor at the time – as if the 'military and civil dignitaries' chose Leo because of his official position rather than because he was effectively holding a knife to the empire's throat.[70] The *Vita Stephani iunioris* infers that Theodosius III abdicated to avoid further Christian bloodshed.[71] The *Zuqnin Chronicle* presents a more melodramatic resignation by Theodosius, possibly influenced by the idea that he had been reluctant to take up imperial power in the first place.

> When the Emperor (Theodosius Constantine) saw that a host was marching against him and that his military commander, Leo by name, had negotiated with them, his heart quaked and his hands shook. He resigned the empire, put down the crown and shaved his head. For there is a custom

> among Roman emperors, if one of them resigns the empire, he shaves his head and stays in his house, having from that time on no entourage. This one acted likewise. Even when Leo, the military commander, sent him a message, saying: 'Strengthen yourself and fear not!' he was not persuaded, and firmly resigned the empire.[72]

Having abdicated, Theodosius was allowed to live out his life in the church. While the sources are more explicit on his confinement to a monastery, the deposed emperor may have become the bishop of Ephesus. This would not be unprecedented, as not only had several emperors who lost or gave up their throne taken monastic orders, including Anastasius II, two fifth century examples – Avitus and Glycerius – had been forcibly appointed as bishops. It is more likely that it was his son, who was allowed to follow him into ecclesiastical exile in 717, that re-emerged on the imperial stage as the iconoclastic bishop of Ephesus in c.729, took a leading role in the Council of Hieria and then died on 24 July 754 to be buried in the Church of St Philip in Ephesus.

It must also be remembered that now that Theodosius III had given up the throne, there was a leadership decision to be made amongst the victorious party. The opposition of Leo and Artabasdos to Theodosius had reputedly begun as support for Anastasius II and it is difficult to nail down when this reputedly 'loyalist' revolt became a usurpation intending to see Leo the Isaurian installed on the imperial throne, rather than the restoration of Anastasius II. Whenever it took place, it was a full-blown conversion, as there was no suggestion of Anastasius emerging from his monastic confinement to retake the throne, even though he had suffered no form of dynastic mutilation that would have disqualified him from the position. We could infer numerous things about this – that Leo and Artabasdos never had any intention of really supporting Anastasius beyond as a legitimising aspect to their opposition to Theodosius; that Anastasius II was not sufficiently popular enough with the right people for there to be any clamour for his restoration; that the army and Senate wanted someone with more proven military and political leadership in charge with the approaching Arab storm; or that being tonsured removed Anastasius from leadership consideration in the eyes of many. As already said though, this was not the last we would hear of Anastasius II and his imperial pretensions.

Accepted as emperor by all the major players in Constantinople, Leo the Isaurian crossed the Bosphorus and 'according to imperial custom, he was received in procession as he entered Byzantium through the Golden Gate and, having come to the Great Church, was invested with the imperial crown'[73] on 25 March 717 by patriarch Germanos. The reign of Leo III is usually considered the end of the 'Twenty Years of Anarchy,' but such a designation only came about with the fullness of time. His eventual 24 years on the throne brought political stability to the Roman Empire, but in the immediate aftermath of his accession, Leo's fledgling reign nearly ended just after it had begun. 'Within weeks the capital of the east Roman state was once more blockaded and under siege.'[74] And opening the gates to the latest besieger would not mean the replacing of one emperor with another, but the possible extinguishing of the Roman Empire altogether.

And even after successfully resisting this existential threat, Leo III would face several rebellions and usurpations, suggesting that rather than less than a 'Twenty Years Anarchy', as suggested earlier in this chapter, we may instead be looking at more than 20 years of imperial instability. And this is even before you delve a little deeper into the military unrest that was present in some form under the Heraclian dynasty. That unrest was perhaps only kept under control by the empire's good fortune to be led by a line of strong military leaders in Heraclius, Constans II, Constantine IV and even Justinian II and Tiberius III, before it happened upon Leo III. Had it not, the more than a century of military tension and unrest might have burst out into a more prolonged period of military and political anarchy of the kind seen after the demise of the Heraclian dynasty, when the imperial legitimacy gap saw the unrest bubbling just under the surface burst forth – summed up statistically as seven emperors in sixteen years.

But even in that chaotic period, there were periods of calm – Tiberius III ruled for seven years – and valuable diplomatic, military, naval, logistical, and structural preparations made by Justinian, Anastasius and Theodosius, all of which Leo III (and the Roman Empire in general) was to benefit from significantly in the first year of his reign. As we shall see in the next chapter, Leo himself played a significant role in providing Anastasius and Theodosius with time to carry out their repairs, upgrades, and negotiations when proving how he was 'an effective military commander as well as an accomplished politician and diplomat'[75] in his dealings with the various Arab commanders of the Umayyad expedition marching towards Constantinople.

But when we last left him, Leo the Isaurian was departing Caucasia with a largely successful expedition to the Alans behind him, but under a possible cloud of mutual suspicion between him and Justinian II. Just how did Leo the Isaurian extricate himself from such a position in order to rise to be a challenger for the imperial throne in 717?

Chapter 5

A Game of Cat and Mouse in Anatolia

'Playing **cat and mouse** is generally only fun for the cat.'

Jim Butcher

Return or Not to Return?

Having managed to rouse the Alans against the Abasgians, destroyed the fortress at Sideron and then been escorted through hostile territory by the leader of Apsilians, Leo had a significant decision to make – to return to Constantinople or not? This might seem peculiar for having successfully fulfilled his remit in the north-western Caucasus and more on top of that in possibly bringing some Abasgians and Apsilians into a pro-Roman stance, would Leo not expect reward from the emperor in Constantinople? In actual fact, Leo may have been operating under the assumption that Justinian II wished him harm. Ideas of a convoluted plot to rid himself of Leo seem fanciful, but Justinian's willingness to listen to accusations against Leo from his fellow officers, even if they were proven false, and then rumours from the Abasgians that Leo's funds for the Caucasian adventure had been removed on imperial orders, may have convinced Leo that returning to the capital was not a good idea. Even reputed imperial efforts to help Leo escape Caucasia and return to Constantinople were treated with scepticism. Did Justinian wish to get him back to Constantinople to reward him for his success or to punish him for whatever had soured the emperor?

The surviving sources are not clear on whether Leo returned to Constantinople or not. And those who suggest he did, do not agree on when. This is also not helped by the lack of dates for Leo's Caucasian expedition. While a problematic passage in Theophanes claims that, upon extricating himself from Abasgia, Leo 'went to Justinian,'[1] his journey to Alania could have begun late enough in Justinian's reign that by the time Leo returned to imperial territory, Justinian II might already have been dead. There has been some suggestion that this was the case, with Leo not arriving back in Constantinople until 713.[2] The twelfth-century epitomiser Zonaras categorically states that Leo did not return during Justinian's reign, which is peculiar because he uses Theophanes as his source for this period.[3] He could have altered the story somewhat because it did not fit in with the dark reputation of Justinian, for if Leo did arrive back in Constantinople during Justinian's last years, he was not the target of the kind of horrific action that that emperor was supposedly meting out to his enemies. It may have suited Zonaras' narrative to remove Leo from Justinian's vicinity, although in the process he possibly provides indirect evidence that the idea that Justinian wanted Leo dead was incorrect.

In historiographical terms, perhaps what is more important here is that Leo *thought* Justinian was out to get him, even if he was not. This not only impacted Leo's actions during and after the Caucasian expedition, it may also have had considerable ramifications for Justinian's historical reputation once Leo ascended the throne. This is because a significant amount of the material used by the likes of Theophanes and Nikephoros to compose their histories was written during the reign of Leo III, raising the tenuous and speculative possibility that latent Leonid anger over his perceived poor treatment by Justinian played a role, portraying that emperor as a vengeful, paranoid monster. Leo's reign also faced reports of individuals claiming to be Justinian's son, Tiberios,[4] providing a dynastic slant to any Leonid attempts to destroy the reputation of Justinian and the Heraclians.[5]

Similar speculation and tenuous sources are all we have for Leo's imperial service between his Caucasian adventure and appearance as Anatolic *strategos*, a period of five years or more. When Anastasius II 'bestowed care on military affairs and appointed capable commanders to take charge of them,'[6] there is little reason to doubt that Leo was amongst them. His tenure in the Anatolic theme would certainly bear this out. That Anastasius would appoint Leo to such an important position could suggest that either Leo did return to Constantinople pre-711 and was therefore not targeted for personal destruction by Justinian, or that Leo did not return to the capital until after Justinian's demise, either by design or due to the time his embassy to the Alans took place. His success in the Caucasus could help explain his promotion to *strategos*, with his report to the emperor proving his abilities, although it might be asked why he became Anatolic *strategos* and not Armeniac *strategos* if his Caucasian adventure had been so pivotal in his promotion. The answer comes in his origins, whether they be Syrian or Isaurian. These connections to the Romano-Umayyad frontier and the attendant ability to speak Arabic, combined with the initiative, ruthlessness, and success he had shown amongst the Alans, Abasgians and Apsilians, likely saw Leo appointed to the Anatolic theme sometime between 713 and 715.

While there is little in the written sources about Leo's ascent from *spatharios* to *strategos*, there could be some information about him to be harvested from lead seals. Two different seals of the late-seventh/early-eighth century[7] record a

Konon separately as a *tourmarches* and a *patrikios*. While it is by no means certain, these could be the seals of the same person as he ascended through the Roman hierarchy. And as Leo III was born Konon, it is attractive, if unprovable, to think that not only are Konon the *tourmarches* and Konon the *patrikios* the same person, but that they are also both the future emperor Leo III. It would certainly not be surprising for Leo III to have been a *tourmarches* – a division commander under a *strategos* – before his elevation to *patrikios* and Anatolic *strategos*.

There is one other (dubious) tradition about Leo's career prior to his becoming Roman emperor. The *Letter of the Three Patriarchs*, reputedly a collaborative effort by the patriarchs of Alexandria, Antioch and Jerusalem to defend icons to the emperor Theophilos in 836, records Leo being an artisan by trade and signing up for military service under the Anatolic *strategos*, Sissinios the patrician. His good service saw Leo promoted, coming to the attention of Theodosius III, who appointed him as a *spatharios*. This conflicts with Theophanes, who says Justinian II appointed Leo to such a position, although it could be argued that Theodosius *re-appointed* Leo as a *spatharios*, possibly with the original appointment being taken away or not surviving the end of Justinian's reign. This story then provides the intriguing notion that Leo was charged with leading an expedition to Italy to combat a foreign invader – the Lombards – in Campania, Amalfi, and Naples. In this narrative, it is Leo's success against the Lombards, rather than in Anatolia, that allows him to return to Constantinople, be proclaimed emperor by the army, and accept the imperial crown from a thankful Theodosius.[8]

There is potentially time for Leo to have taken part in another campaign between that in the Caucasus and his appearance as Anatolic *strategos*, but this epistolary tradition is not backed up by any independent sources – George Monachus records something similar, but he is using the patriarchal letter to Theophilos as his source. Our main sources for this period do not mention any such imperial expedition to Italy at this time, particularly the likes of Theophanes who had access to records of Leo's pre-imperial career. As will be seen later, Leo did plan and even launch an Italian expedition during his reign, while the literary tradition of Theodosius being an unwilling emperor is also called upon, so the *Letter of the Three Patriarchs* is not completely detached from a historiographical basis.

But however intriguing its story is and however much we might like to fill the void in Leo's career chronology between the Caucasian adventure and his appearance in Anatolia, we do not have anything trustworthy to fill that void. Perhaps the only other suggestion we have is how the *Kitab al-Uyun* has Leo, after he came to imperial attention and showed his energy and courage in conflicts, holding other positions between his appointments as *spatharios* and as Anatolic *strategos*, having been 'advanced from post to post,'[9] but without any suggestion of what those roles might have been. All we can really do is set the scene for what Leo was about to face in Anatolia once his personal narrative starts up again with him already the Anatolic *strategos*.[10]

Into the Lion's Mouth – Roman Anatolia upon Leo's Arrival

The Arab conquest of the Middle East in the 630s and 640s had culminated in initial attempts to extend those conquests into the interior of Asia Minor; however, stiffening Roman resistance and Arab distraction with the Persian conquest and internal ructions saw the Taurus Mountains established as the Romano-Arab frontier. It remained porous enough to allow raids in either direction, with the Arabs doing more damage but lacking any definitive conquest on that front throughout much of the remainder of the seventh century. The military activities of Constantine IV and Justinian II were even able to extract favourable treaties from the Umayyad caliphate in the 670s and 680s; however, developments in the last decade of the century suggest that the Roman ability to extract such favourable treaties was less about returning Roman strength and more about Umayyad preoccupation with the Second Fitna.

In 692, an overconfident Justinian II found this out to his cost when he orchestrated a confrontation over aspects of the most recent treaty. The subsequent Battle of Sebastopolis was a disaster for the Romans, with mass defection leading to the imperial army being heavily defeated. This led to the Umayyads restoring their control over much of Armenia and Caucasia and reinitiating their annual raids of Roman territory. The Arabs did not have it all their own way. Herakleios, brother of Tiberius III, achieved several successes early in the eighth century – a large-scale strike into Syria in 700/701, a victory (or two?) in Cilicia between 703–705 and another success at Sision in 704/705. There was also an Armenian rebellion in 703/704 that had to be dealt with.[11]

However, these Roman successes engendered an increasingly competent Umayyad response, first under Muhammad b. Marwan and then Maslamah b. Abd al-Malik. While a caliphal son, Maslamah was removed from the succession due to his mother being a low-born concubine, but this did not stop him from becoming an increasingly prominent general. Possibly active a few years earlier, the first appearance of Maslamah in the Roman sources comes in the aftermath of a Roman victory in Cilicia by a general called Marianos. This defeat had seen a friend of Maslamah's, Maimun the Mardaite, killed, leading to Maslamah swearing revenge. He set his sights on Tyana, possibly the site or origin of the victorious army of Marianos. Tyana held an important strategic position as a lynchpin in the Roman defences in the Taurus foothills, controlling the northern routes to Cappadocia and the western routes into Anatolia. Maslamah's campaign against Tyana began in 708, continued through the winter and then culminated in 709. An initial battlefield victory over the Tyanan garrison allowed Maslamah to put the city under siege, but despite the destruction of its walls, Tyana held firm. Soon, the increasingly wintry weather saw many of the Arab besiegers withdraw; however, enough of them remained in the vicinity to defeat a Roman relief force. This defeat broke the spirit of the Tyana garrison, which capitulated. The city was then largely destroyed and deserted, giving the Arabs easier access through the Taurus Mountains to the interior of Asia Minor.

Several Cilician forts were captured to further secure communications through the Taurus, while the main northern road was controlled by the capture of Camacha in 711. This allowed Maslamah and his generals to launch a series of strikes between 712–714, sacking major cities like Amaseia, Tarantum, Mistheia and Pisidian Antioch, with Arab forces reaching the coasts of the Aegean Sea and the Bosphorus. It was surely this wave of repeated Umayyad success, the inability of even the largest Roman armies of the Anatolic and Armeniac themes to do much about them and on-going Roman internal strife[12] that encouraged the caliph and his generals to consider the Roman Empire ripe for the picking.

> On account of the frequent assumptions of imperial power and the prevalence of usurpation, the affairs of the empire and of the City were being neglected and declined; furthermore, education was being destroyed and military organisation crumbled.[13]

Theophanes would have it that what became the Arab expedition to conquer Constantinople in 717–718 was launched in the year 715–716 with the advance forces under Suleiman b. Mu'ad[14] and al-Bakhtari b. al-Hassan[15] on land and Umar b. Hubayra by sea, ahead of the main body under Maslamah. But the scale of the undertaking as will be seen in the next chapter – 'an innumerable host of horse and foot'[16] – suggests that months, if not years, of planning, organisation, recruitment, and gathering of material went into the expedition before its launch. This would mean that rather than be the brainchild of caliph Sulayman, the expedition to conquer Constantinople germinated under his predecessor, al-Walid I (705–715).

The launching of the expedition during the caliphate of Sulayman became laden with prophetic, even apocalyptic meaning. The *Kitab al-Uyun* has Sulayman being informed by various learned men that the caliph to capture Constantinople had to have the same name as a prophet – Sulayman (i.e. Solomon) took this as his destiny and upon returning from his Hajj pilgrimage to Mecca in 715/716, stationed himself at Dabiq in northern Syria, from where he oversaw final preparations for the expedition that was to fulfil that destiny. It will also not have escaped the attention of said learned men or the caliph that the year 100 in the Muslim calendar was fast approaching (it equates to 718–719). While Sulayman is recorded telling Maslamah that once he had approached Constantinople and put it under siege he was 'to stay there until he either conquered the city or received Sulayman's order to return,'[17] the caliph also reportedly stated that 'I shall not cease from the struggle with Constantinople until either I force my way into it, or I bring about the destruction of the entire dominions of the Arabs.'[18] This may reflect just how tied up in these apocalyptic prophecies the caliph had become – it seemed that to him, this war between the Roman Empire and the Umayyad caliphate was now a fight to the death, with the crescendo quickly honing into view. Although it should be noted that he was not so caught up in prophetic notions as to lead the expedition in person. Ill-health, which was soon to put paid to Sulayman, saw the caliph remain at Dabiq.

It was perhaps with such existentially-laced orders ringing in his ears that Maslamah launched the vanguard of the expedition to take Constantinople. This was not to be a mad dash across Asia Minor or a rapid advance by sea to blockade the Sea of Marmara, but rather a methodical progression, aiming to neutralise points of Roman resistance, such as the thematic armies and major cities, and to establish lines of supply. This shows that for all of their preparation, the Umayyads were under no illusion of the obstacle that Constantinople, its walls and navy represented. This wariness of continued Roman ability to resist may also be seen in an Umayyad action that appears tied to the preparations or even progression of the expedition.

While the chronology of the sources upon which we rely can be questionable (Tabari mentions the following event happening in two consecutive years (AH97 and 98), so any time between September 715 and August 717), at some point, caliph Sulayman sent his son Dawud to campaign near the Arab-held city of Melitene, where he captured the Hisn al-Mar'a ('the Woman's Fortress').[19] This could possibly be seen as a feint to divert the attention of the Armeniac *strategos* to prevent him from joining up with the Anatolic *strategos* in resisting the overland advance of Maslamah's forces. Certainly, we do know that these two *strategoi*, Leo and Artabasdos, were working closely together – Artabasdos would marry Leo's daughter, Anna. When it is queried why these two *strategoi* did little to help Anastasius II against Theodosius, the answer usually given is that 'they really did not care to aid him, preferring to wait for an opportunity that would benefit themselves;'[20] however, they were faced with the daunting prospect of Maslamah's expeditionary force. It would not be all that surprising for the *strategoi* to have found the situation on the frontiers of more importance to not only their own survival but also that of the empire than the struggle for the throne. Surely, withdrawing their forces from the themes back towards the capital would have been disastrous for the Roman presence in Anatolia.

'The Game's Afoot' – The 'Siege' of Amorion

The surviving sources give little detail of the progression of the Umayyad land expedition through eastern and central Anatolia or on the Roman response to it. It may be an argument from silence, which is always dangerous, but this could suggest that Maslamah's forces, both the main body and the vanguard, were able to make relatively serene, unhindered progress. Any diversionary aim of Dawud's raid on the 'Women's Fortress' may well have prevented Artabasdos from aiding Leo in confronting the Umayyad forces marching west, leaving Leo unable to mount any sort of substantial opposition. This could speak to the comparative weakness of the Anatolic and Armeniac armies in the face of the enormous force of Maslamah. That the capital of the Anatolic theme did not have its own garrison suggests that its thematic army was either dispersed to other positions or was deployed in the field, although as we shall see, it was not under the direct control of the Anatolic *strategos* when he appeared at Amorion in 716.

And it is with the arrival of the Umayyad vanguard of Suleiman and al-Bakhtari outside Amorion that the record of Theophanes about the Arab attempt on Constantinople begins in earnest. It seems from their first recorded interactions that there had already been diplomatic contact between the Umayyad hierarchy and the Anatolic *strategos*. Suleiman and al-Bakhtari not only knew of Amorion's lack of a thematic garrison and its opposition to Leo's support of Anastasius II (the Amorians reputedly did not like Leo because they saw him as a 'Nabataean Arab'),[21] they also immediately put forward the idea of supporting Leo in his own attempt to gain the imperial throne. From this position outside Amorion, they reputedly wrote to Leo, stating that 'We know that the Roman Empire befits you. Come, therefore, to us and let us confer about peace.'[22] Suleiman turned up the pressure further by putting Amorion under blockade, planning to use it as the site of his rendezvous with Maslamah and as an important base for the Umayyad supply lines.[23] He also had his forces proclaim Leo emperor, and urged the Amorions to do the same. Suleiman would surely not have undertaken such a ploy without the involvement of Maslamah and Sulayman. It must have been part of the Umayyad plan to conquer Constantinople and/or in the aftermath of that success, suggesting that they recognised the difficulty of the aim and perhaps the need of some kind of client emperor post-conquest. The likes of Tabari presents the upcoming siege of Constantinople as being something of a backdrop of Maslamah and Sulayman believing that Leo 'would deliver the land of the Byzantines (to the caliph).'[24] The *Kitab al-Uyun* has Maslamah coming to terms with Leo, with the *strategos* receiving some Umayyad protection in return for information and advice on the how to capture Constantinople. The *Chronicle of 1234* claims that Leo 'had made a covenant with the Arabs, who he led to believe that he would help them to capture Constantinople.'[25]

Indeed, the same *Chronicle* makes this 'covenant' between Leo and Maslamah much more central to events around Amorion and interwoven with Suleiman's later advance to Chalcedon. It has Theodosius III acting against Leo upon hearing of his agreement with the Arabs, rounding up the *strategos*' relatives and confining them to Amorion. In response, Leo obtains 6,000 cavalry from Suleiman, who struck at Chalcedon with it, and then marched on Amorion to free his family. However, in speaking to the leaders of Amorion, Leo reassured them 'that his relationship with Maslamah was a pretence, designed to save his territory from destruction.'[26] There is enough different in the record of this *Chronicle*, as well as its chronological detachment (it is late-twelfth/early-thirteenth century, although it does use material from Theophilus of Edessa) to cast doubt. It has Leo win a victory over forces under Theodosius III's son, after which his thematic army acclaimed Leo as emperor, and then in attributing Leo as taking 'every possible precaution to ensure the City's impregnability,'[27] it has him undertake preparations actually made by Anastasius II and Theodosius III.

Other sources make no mention of Leo directly using Arab cavalry to force Amorion's acceptance of him; instead, they have the Umayyad blockade (not supported or enforced by Leo) and the seeming promise of peaceful treatment should they switch their allegiance to their Anatolic *strategos* leading the inhabitants of Amorion to accept Leo. It really had no option, for while its lack of a garrison had enabled Amorion to hold a different political allegiance to its *strategos*, that same lack of military presence made it vulnerable; a vulnerability that Leo, Suleiman and the Amorions themselves recognised. It may still have taken a rousing speech from Leo to bring the Amorians over to his side.

> I will not rule over you except by your commands; but you have heard of my character and my valour and ability, and your affairs are in confusion, and your kingdom is sore, smitten and the civil war is raging, and this Maslamah, the son of Abd al-Malik has come close to your territory, and he will attack you. Therefore, let me in and entrust your government to me; and, if I bear myself in it in accordance with your wishes, well; but if not, turn me out and do with me what you please.[28]

However, if there was any notion that accepting Leo as emperor would see the pressure on Amorion lifted by Suleiman, it did not play out. Nearing Amorion, Leo felt that the city was about to fall to Suleiman and so he sent to the Arab general inquiring 'If you want me to come to you to discuss peace, why are you besieging this town?'[29] Looking to lure Leo in, Suleiman replied that he would withdraw from Amorion if Leo himself would come to his camp. The Anatolic *strategos* agreed, arriving at his thematic capital with just 300 cavalry, reflecting either the paucity of the forces under his command or the necessity of them being elsewhere. While Leo received a respectful welcome from Suleiman's men, he did not camp immediately amongst them, staying half a mile away. That lack of trust might seem to have also extended to Amorion itself, for Leo did not take up residence there, with the city remaining under Arab blockade despite Leo's arrival.

Over the next three days, the *strategos* and Umayyad commander conducted negotiations regarding the lifting of the blockade and some kind of compact. These negotiations went nowhere, with Leo suspecting that Suleiman was intentionally drawing them out as a stall tactic to capture him and Amorion. This suspicion was further aroused when Leo hosted the Arab commanders in his camp for dinner. Suleiman looked to surround the camp with 3,000 men. When informed, Leo confronted the Arab commanders, who claimed that their cavalry was hunting down a slave who had stolen 'a great treasure.'[30] Playing along, Leo offered aid in finding their renegade slave, but at the same time, he sent word to Amorion of this planned Arab betrayal, urging them not to capitulate, even in the face of the approaching Maslamah. The Amorions responded by sending their bishop to Leo, to whom he reiterated his advice.

Upon hearing that Leo had received a messenger from Amorion, Suleiman demanded that the bishop be handed over to him. Leo denied the presence of the bishop, while having him disguised as one of his men and join a foraging party, which allowed the bishop to escape. With Suleiman's representatives sceptical and continuing to make threats, Leo offered to join the Arab commander in riding to meet Maslamah. This placated Suleiman, who thought that the bishop of Amorion paled in significance compared with the opportunity to apprehend the Anatolic *strategos*. They therefore allowed Leo to go out on a hunt with 200 men, and were seemingly unworried about his proposed moving of his camp to some meadows, which they felt was not a good idea and would not accompany him. This was surely Leo's plan, telling his men 'After giving us their word, they wanted to seize us and, through us, to ruin the Christians. But they will not take any of the men or horses that are left to us.'[31] Leo led his men a further 10 miles away and then sent a bodyguard back to Suleiman to complain about his planned abduction – 'you gave me safe conduct, but you want to capture me by treachery. That is why I have withdrawn.'[32]

Suleiman's distraction with Leo and Amorion hindered communications with Maslamah, who he did not know had already reached Cappadocia through Germanikeia, and also spread dissatisfaction amongst his own men, which was further exacerbated by Leo's escape. They complained 'why are we investing the walls instead of raiding?'[33] Left with no choice, Suleiman lifted his blockade of Amorion and departed from the immediate vicinity. Showing that Leo had more troops at his disposal than he initially let on, the *strategos* then sent 800 men into Amorion under the *tourmarches* Nikaias as a garrison. Given the circumstances, Nikaias felt that the city would soon be under attack again and so ordered many of the women and children to leave. In the meantime, Leo withdrew south to Pisidia.

Deal or No Deal? Leo the Isaurian and Maslamah b. Abd al-Malik

As Maslamah entered Cappadocia at the head of his large expeditionary force, he ordered his men not to inflict any damage on the territories loyal to Leo, suggesting that there had been an Umayyad ploy to use Leo to gain control of Constantinople and the empire as a whole. Hearing of these Cappadocian developments, Leo contacted Maslamah, complaining of Suleiman's attempt to capture him and using it as a reason not to meet the Arab general. Maslamah refused to believe much of what Leo's men were telling him, feeling that Leo was lying about the entire Amorion episode as part of the developing political game. At length though, Leo's representative convinced Maslamah of Suleiman's actions and Leo's control of Amorion, its garrisoning with up to 1,000 men and the defensive preparations it was undertaking. This failure by Suleiman angered Maslamah to such a degree that he initially determined to mount an all-out assault on Amorion before the winter. But having then calmed himself, Maslamah again wrote to Leo, looking to re-establish diplomatic relations and whatever 'peace' agreement they might have had between them.

Leo continued to play a shrewd game, recognising that Maslamah's large army, while still advancing west, could not stay in one place for any significant time and in around five days, it would have traversed the provinces loyal to him. Still fearful of being captured, Leo attempted a further delaying tactic. He sent an embassy of two honorary consuls to Maslamah asking that not only his person but also the valuables, resources, and soldiers in his personal force would be vouched safe for by the Arab general. Maslamah saw what Leo was doing, but if he still wanted the *strategos'* cooperation, not to mention an opportunity to capture him, he too had to play along.

As the consular representatives returned to Leo with a written pledge of Maslamah's willingness to undertake the safe conduct of the *strategos* and his thematic army, everything fell into place for Leo. Maslamah's large army was on the move again, arriving at Akroinon. This is the first identifiable location along Maslamah's route after emerging from the Taurus Mountains, possibly through Germanikeia, into Cappadocia. Theophanes does record his presence at Masalaios and Theodosiana, but these are unknown. The position of Akroinon further west of Amorion suggests that the Arab general had given up on attacking the Anatolic thematic capital that year, likely through the agreement with Leo.

Certainly, it was at this point, following this agreement, that Leo detached himself from the Amorion theatre and travelled north to Nicomedia, where his serendipitous capture of Theodosius III's son initiated his rapid acceptance as emperor in Constantinople. It might be expected that Maslamah and his expeditionary force had gone beyond land loyal to the Anatolic *strategos*, but Akroinon is usually thought to be in the Anatolic theme. This could demonstrate the lack of firm definition in thematic provincial boundaries. The western extent of the Anatolic theme was initially thought to reach both the Aegean and Mediterranean coasts of what is now Turkey; however, the Thrakesian theme was in existence by at least 711, if not by 687. And even if Akroinon was part of the Anatolic theme, Maslamah did not rest there long, moving further west into territory more definitively not in the Anatolic theme. He wintered in 'Asia' (the Arab fleet under Umar returned to Cilicia), which could refer to the ancient Roman province of 'Asia Province', which took in lands covered largely by the Thrakesian and western half of the Opsikon themes. And the two places Maslamah is recorded as being active after his dealings with Leo and before his final advance towards Constantinople – Pergamon and Sardis[34] – were in the Thrakesian theme.

The record of Maslamah's dealings and indeed capture of Pergamon in both Theophanes and Nikephoros (it is the only specific event that Nikephoros mentions about Maslamah's advance towards Constantinople) involves one particularly horrific scene. When the Arab army laid siege to Pergamon, the inhabitants became so overwhelmed by despair that they turned to a magician for advice. He had the people of Pergamon cut open a pregnant woman, remove the foetus and boil it in a cooking pot. 'All those who were intending to fight dipped the sleeves of their right arm in this detestable sacrifice.'[35] Rather than aid them in warding off the Arab attack, this hideous act brought down the divine wrath upon Pergamon – 'their hands became incapable of taking up weapons and, in the face of their inactivity, the enemy captured the city without resistance.'[36]

Sardis and Pergamon might be the only named cities that Maslamah personally acted against in the winter of 716/717, but significantly more settlements were targeted by him once his forces moved on from Akroinon.

> As soon at the Arabs had left Leo's territory, they began to do all sorts of mischief and to commit all kinds of outrage in Roman territory, burning down churches and houses, looting, shedding the blood of men and taking children captive. Many cities in the region of Asia fell to them that summer and they ruined them and took captives and looted, slaughtering the men and sending the children and women back as slaves to their own country.[37]

But by far the most important settlement that Maslamah's forces acted against was a clear indicator that his objective had not changed – he dispatched Suleiman with 12,000 men to invest Chalcedon 'to cut off supplies from that approach to Constantinople and to lay waste and pillage Roman territory in general.'[38] Whatever agreement there was between Leo the Isaurian and Maslamah b. Abd al-Malik, it had not seen to the cancelling or even the postponement of the Arab march towards Constantinople.

But just what was the extent of the 'agreement' between Leo and Maslamah? Was Leo always planning to sell out Maslamah and use the agreement to his own benefit? Or did Leo and Artabasdos initially plan to use Arab backing to elevate themselves while subjugating the Roman Empire to the Umayyad caliphate, only for the opportunities offered by Amorion resistance to allow them to manipulate the situation to their own ends? This is ultimately the problem we face with the nature of the Leo/Maslamah deal – we cannot really know the motives of any party, with Leo's actions fitting the mould of imperial traitor *and* loyalist manipulator, while Maslamah can come across as either a calculating manipulator himself or a gullible fool.

There being diplomatic contact between a Roman and Arab general is not surprising, even during war time. We have already seen the Romans sending an embassy to the Umayyads for 'peace talks' but really looking to find out what the caliph had planned, while Anastasius II had seemingly reached out to Maslamah for aid against Theodosius III. Could such contact have been through Leo, initiating what became the agreement between the *strategos* and the Arab general? It is likely that either the Anatolic or Armeniac *strategos* would have been informed about an imperial embassy passing through their territory en route to the Umayyads, particularly if the aim was to allow Arab forces to cross into Roman territory. And even in the unlikelihood that they were left out of the ambassadorial loop, as Anatolic *strategos* and a close ally of the Armeniac *strategos*, Leo would have known earlier than most of the aims and extent of the Arab expedition.

Given how Leo's involvement with iconoclasm was to make him decidedly unpopular with a large section of Roman historiographical output, the very existence of such an agreement might be questioned, with it all being part of iconodule attempts to blacken his name. However, it became a significant part of Arabic and Syriac historiography, such as Tabari, the *Kitab al-Uyun* and the *Chronicle to 1234*, to present Leo as having come to terms with Maslamah and caliph Sulayman. The *Kitab al-Uyun* in particular has Maslamah, in a statement to the people of Constantinople, refer to Leo as his *mawla*,[39] a word that can refer to either side of a patron/client or slave/freedman relationship; it could even just mean 'friend'.

The historical tradition presents an agreement between Leo and Maslamah as not only factual but well enough known or at least rumoured for the Amorians to hold it against Leo. However, all of our sources are non-contemporary and may be reporting from the benefit and even the detriment of hindsight, with the results of the 716/717 campaign and the following year skewing the detail of the events involved. There is a chance that Theophanes had access to more contemporary material and he does have Leo making promises to Maslamah, but all as part of a deception.[40] This, plus the existential threat to the empire and his use of a more pro-Leonid source, might explain why Theophanes, a staunch iconodule, is less judgemental of Leo for coming to an agreement with the Arabs than we might expect.

While it is presented as Arab backing for Leo's usurpation changing Amorion's mind,[41] along with the intendent promise of a lifting of the blockade of the city, the speech reported by the *Kitab al-Uyun* in which Leo talks Amorion around to backing him raises another potential avenue of intrigue. Given his later rejection of Maslamah, which he reputedly forewarned the people of Constantinople about,[42] might part of Leo's talking around of the Amorians have included informing or at least inferring that all of his dealings with the Arabs were based on a ruse? Certainly, in his secret messages to the city and his meeting with its bishop, Leo showed himself not to be acting in the best interests of Suleiman and Maslamah.

It must be said, as the *Kitab al-Uyun* points out, that Maslamah himself likely had very little to lose in backing a side in the Roman civil war – even if Leo failed, it would undermine the empire at a time when the Umayyad expedition was en route to Constantinople. And if Leo was successful, Maslamah had potentially put his client on the Roman throne; however, this 'nothing to lose' notion was only retained if Maslamah did not take actions and decisions to maintain the agreement with Leo that might be detrimental to his own cause. As we shall see in the next chapter, Maslamah may well have put too much faith in Leo, even when those around him and Maslamah himself could see that Leo was stringing him along – 'I see your general is playing with me.'[43]

Despite this potentially poor reflection on Maslamah, his interactions with Leo did facilitate a largely unhindered advance through the Taurus Mountains,

Cappadocia and the Anatolic theme (with some wariness on what is possibly an argument from silence). It also helped his establishing of lines of supply and communication, the seeming neutralisation of Thrakesian forces and the securing of winter quarters in 'Asia' through the raiding of Roman territory, attacking and capturing Roman cities and sending Roman citizens back to the caliphate as slaves.[44] Maslamah's order to his forces to not damage Leo's thematic territory was a potentially successful attempt to manipulate the *strategos*, making it seem that Leo had made an agreement when he had not and leaving him little choice but to acquiesce. Or it was all part and parcel of a pre-existing agreement arrived at through earlier negotiations between *strategos*, Arab general and caliph.

Of course, Leo the Isaurian greatly benefitted from any agreement as well, whether through design or opportunism. He is seen complaining to the Arabs in terms that could be construed as admonishing Maslamah and Suleiman for acting contrary to an agreement, a flashpoint that may only have arisen due to the unexpected opposition of Amorion to Leo's opposition to Theodosius III. But he was able to make the best of a bad situation, using the Umayyad threat to his thematic capital to not only reclaim control of the city but also the freeing of his theme from significant damage and possibly even shaming Maslamah into giving Leo more leeway in his actions in the coming year.

The presence of the various corps of the Arab expedition likely encouraged the unifying of the Asian themes behind Leo and Artabasdos. As we have seen regarding the differing loyalty between the Anatolic *strategos* and his thematic capital, 'Asia Minor was no political monolith. Local opinions and allegiances adjusted to the decisions of the battlefield, and to the anticipated outcome of the civil war.'[45] The elevation of Leo III was a rare case of the Anatolic and Armeniac themes being on the same side in a civil conflict. It would be more usual to see them on opposite sides, such as the war between Constantine V and Artabasdos.[46] This lack of political unity in Asia increased the size of the job presented to Leo in 716 and beyond. The aforementioned civil war between his son and brother-in-law shows that Leo III would not be completely successful in galvanising the themes, but he laid the groundwork, which increases the scale of the Isaurian dynasty's achievement throughout the eighth century. And it seems that part of Leo's groundwork was to accept or at least fake accepting the aid of the Arab expedition, the very *raison d'etre* of which was to conquer Constantinople and subjugate/destroy the Roman Empire. If he had any choice, it was a significant gamble to take.

Even though Maslamah recognised that Leo was taking advantage of their negotiations, he did continue to act in what could be considered Leo's interests. His refusal to move against Amorion and then departing Anatolic lands whilst ordering his men to do no damage appear indicative of an agreement with Leo.

Attacking Nikaias' 1,000-strong garrison might have been time-consuming, but certainly not beyond the abilities of Maslamah's column. That he did not try to take a city that had been thought useful to the expedition might suggest that he had assurances that his lines of communication and supply would not come under threat in Anatolic territory. Might Leo have even promised to provide resources to the Arabs at competitive prices?

There may be further pro-Leonid actions from Maslamah after he bypassed Amorion, for the way was now open to move north across the Anatolic-Opsikon border to put pressure on the very core of the Roman Empire. Such a move would also have put Maslamah in a prime position to oppose Leo's own planned strike north against Theodosius III. However, instead of going north, Maslamah moved west to Akroinon and then into the Thrakesian theme, allowing Leo to move to Nicomedia and then Constantinople. The lack of overt Arab involvement may have been considered as a bolstering of Leo's imperial claim. Of course, Suleiman may have moved to Chalcedon in the winter of 716/717, which would have been hot on the heels of Leo's own presence in the area. The approach of the Arab expeditionary vanguard could have forced the hand of Theodosius III, Germanos and the Constantinopolitan Senate to bring about the change in imperial leadership sooner rather than later – the conspiratorially-minded might suggest that the timing was a little too beneficial for Leo. It would seem that Maslamah still felt he would get something out of the agreement, despite Leo's manipulations, even if that was just disruption at the heart of the Roman world, rather than an emperor who would betray the empire to him.

Maslamah moving west rather than north could have just been for his own military and strategic benefit. Had Maslamah moved north in the winter of 716/717, he might have forced a compact between Leo and Theodosius in defence of the imperial capital, and found himself caught between Opsikon, Anatolic and Thrakesian forces. The Arab expedition was capable of defeating such a conglomeration of Roman forces, but any such victory would have ultimately proven pyrrhic as any casualties would have reduced the effective strength he could bring against the walls of Constantinople. Heading west allowed Maslamah to pick off one of the Roman armies still in the field. Not only was the Thrakesian army weaker than that of the Opsikon, Leo's move to Nicomedia would have distracted said Opsikon forces, permitting Maslamah to deal with the Thrakesians in isolation, inflicting enough damage to reduce or remove them as a threat to his position or lines of supply once he moved against Constantinople.

It should also be remembered that the Arab expedition was not just some mad dash to the Bosphorus. The planning and then steady progress across Anatolia highlight that the Umayyads recognised the obstacle posed by the

Roman capital and so preparations not just before the expedition's departure but also during its overland progress had to be made. By moving into 'Asia' and attacking various cities,[47] Maslamah gave himself the option of naval support, while dealing with the Thrakesian garrisons would provide more security for his lines of supply and communication (or in the worst case, lines of retreat).

Whatever its form or terms, having been able to use it to bolster his own position, Leo now swore to the people of Constantinople he would break his agreement with Maslamah and fight against him, even using the agreement to manipulate Maslamah to the benefit of the empire.[48] And as we shall see with the siege of Constantinople, Maslamah reputedly opened himself to such manipulation by still holding out hope that his compact that had offered some strategic benefit to the Arab expedition and imperial enthronement to Leo could still be used in the midst of what was an existential fight for the future of the Roman Empire.

For all the comment on his military prowess being part of the reason for his being 'chosen' over Theodosius III, it is arguable that at the time of his accession, Leo III had not demonstrated much in the way of military ability. There are likely military roles and actions unrecorded by the sources, both before and during his tenure as *strategos*, but we only have knowledge of his action at Sideron and the likely non-existent Italian venture – his imperial power had been achieved largely through political skill, cunning, and opportunism. And while those skills would again come in useful, within weeks of his accession, the new Roman emperor was now going to have to show himself a capable military leader on the walls and waters around Constantinople.

Chapter 6

Imperial Baptism of Fire: The Great Siege of Constantinople 717–718

'I am not afraid of an army of lions led by a sheep; I am afraid of an army of sheep led by a lion.'

Attributed to Alexander the Great, but possibly Anonymous

Not the First? Or Even the Second?

If Maslamah still felt that his agreement with the newly-enthroned Leo III would bear its intended fruit, he surely made efforts to contact his supposed ally through the winter of 716/717. And the seeming presence of Suleiman and 12,000 Arab soldiers at Chalcedon will have made any such Arab diplomatic entreaties to the new emperor impossible to ignore. Whatever Leo did or did not say or do, on top of the suspicions he had, Maslamah reinitiated his overland march to the coast opposite Constantinople in the spring of 717, fully intent on attacking the Roman imperial capital. Rather than move to join Suleiman at Chalcedon, from where an attempted crossing of the Bosphorus would have been under the constant harassment of the imperial fleet stationed in waters immediately around Constantinople, Maslamah looked to cross the Hellespont, known in modern times as the Dardanelles. He established himself at Abydos and began to gather ships from locals to ferry his army across the strait to Sestus. This Abydos-Sestus route had already played a major role in east-west military history, with it being where the Persian king, Xerxes, had his bridge of boats established for his invasion of Greece in 480 BC.

However, there had been a much more recent non-Roman armed crossing of this aquatic boundary between Europe and Asia. This was because the siege that Constantinople faced in 717–718 is, or at least was, frequently labelled as the 'Second Arab Siege of Constantinople'. It was traditionally thought that Arab forces invested the Roman capital between 674 and 678, which saw the repulsing of the forces of Muawiyah I by those of Constantine IV. That Roman victory, associated counterattacks and Umayyad internal trouble supposedly resulted in the cessation of hostilities through a peace treaty whose terms were advantageous to the Romans.[1]

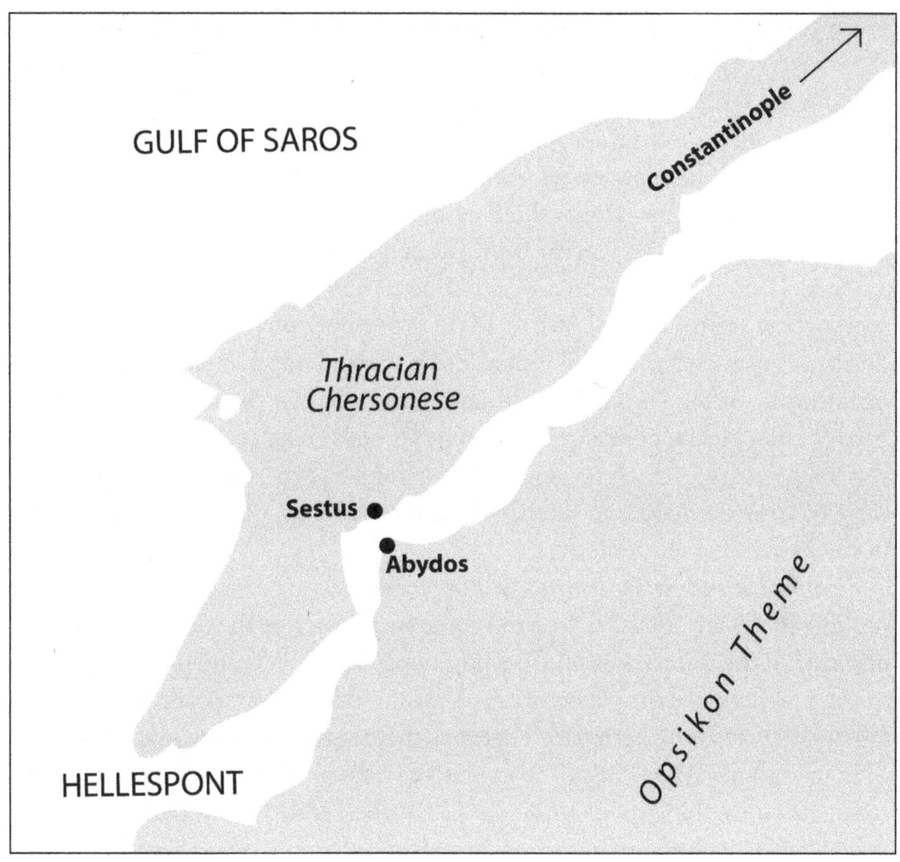

The depiction of Arab movements in the run up to this 'siege' in Theophanes does seem like the strategic preparations for an attempt on Constantinople – land forces penetrating to Chalcedon, the capture of various naval bases in Cilicia, Lycia, Smyrna and Cyzicus, and raids of Anatolia distracting Roman forces to allow for an overland march to the Bosphorus.[2] Theophanes' summer of 674 even has an Arab landing at Hebdomon and Roman repulsing of Arab probes of the Golden Gate.[3] But any such landing would appear to be the apogee of this Arab expedition, with this 'siege' degenerating into a series of naval raids over the succeeding four years. Constantine IV may then have won a decisive naval victory over Yazid b. Shagara, leading to the Arab departure from Cyzicus and the annihilation of their fleet by a storm off Syllaion in Pamphylia, backed up by a Roman land victory.[4]

However, almost every aspect of this supposed 'First Siege' – its date, narrative, extent and even its very existence – have come under scrutiny. The main Roman source for the events is Theophanes, but even his account does not completely fit with the 'accepted' version of this so-called 'First Siege', as he posits it lasting seven years, rather than the usual 674–678. He also does not state which dates these seven years cover – he could be counting inclusively from the start of the expedition in 672 to 678 or from the initial attack in 674 to the final withdrawal of all Arab forces from their forward bases in Anatolia in 680. It has also been suggested that Theophanes has got his dates wrong due to having two separate sources to deal with – 'Trajan the Patrician' and 'Theophilus of Edessa.'[5]

Further dating issues arise from other primary material with patriarch Thomas II's inability to send a synodical letter to Pope Vitalian throughout his patriarchate from 17 April 667 to 14/15 November 669. This was supposedly due to an Arab blockade of Constantinople throughout that period. The source of information on Thomas – a declaration of George the *chartophylax* at the Sixth Ecumenical Council on 28 March 681 – also suggests that this incursion was 'long-lasting', which he may not have done had there been 'an even longer siege of Constantinople in the 670s,'[6] although this is placing too much faith in the patriarchal chronology.[7]

The Arabic and Syriac sources do not record any sort of siege at all, with raids peaking in the late-660s.[8] These too come with issues, as the defeat of whatever occurred in the waters around Constantinople in the 660s and 670s might have made Arabic sources less keen to broadcast the existence of a confrontation that Umayyad forces were bested in. That said, there was enough recorded expansion of Umayyad naval capability and extensive raids on islands and coastal regions to suggest something more ambitious. And when added to overland Arab raids and possible involvement in the revolts of Roman commanders, a grand strategic plan to put pressure on Constantinople during the caliphate of Muawiyah I is not out of the question.[9]

You can see from this combination of different source traditions that the facts behind the 'First Siege' are impossible to reveal. Might the record of Umayyad landings at Hebdomon and probing of the Golden Gate be a later addition by the sources used by Theophanes and Nikephoros, influenced by the Arab siege in 717–718? Or might Theophanes, in melding together two differing accounts to present a 'long' siege of Constantinople throughout most of the 670s, be presenting an event of 'no historical substance'?[10] Perhaps all that is certain is that *something* happened in the waters around Constantinople during the caliphate of Muawiyah I.[11] The Arab occupation of Cyzicus would not have taken place in a vacuum and they will not have done nothing with it, even if the presence of the Roman navy limited them to raiding of the coast and shipping lanes.

There is some basis to posit an even earlier Arab attempt to capture Constantinople. Using the account of the Armenian historian Sebeos, it has been suggested that the forces of Muawiyah sought to attack the Roman capital in the 'thirteenth year of Constans',[12] which would put the attempt in the aftermath of the Arab naval victory at the Battle of Phoenix/Battle of the Masts in 654.[13] 'The king of Ismael [caliph Uthman] ordered all his troops to assemble in the west and to wage war against the Roman empire, so that they might take Constantinople and exterminate that kingdom as well,'[14] only for poor weather to prevent Muawiyah from bringing all of his forces to bear against the walls of Constantinople from his base at Chalcedon.[15]

Sebeos' reputation as an historian is good enough to make dispensing with this idea of an Arab attack on Constantinople in 654 difficult, although it does not necessarily take on the appearance of a siege – more an opportunistic dash to the Bosphorus to take the Roman capital by surprise. The same could be said of whatever Muawiyah's forces undertook in the late-660s/670s, with Cyzicus rather than Chalcedon the focus of naval raids across the Sea of Marmara and the Bosphorus with some thought to strike against Constantinople if the opportunity arose. It could be then that Constantinopolitan waters faced Arab pressure of varying intensity throughout the period of c.654 to 680,[16] with either *both* or *neither* of the Arab expeditions launched by Muawiyah's forces – post-Phoenix and then in the late-660s/670s – to be viewed as a 'siege', with the attempt of Maslamah in 717–718 either the 'First' or the 'Third Arab Siege of Constantinople'.

Another major aspect of the so-called 'First Siege', beyond its date, narrative, extent and even existence, was the reputedly definitive role played by Greek fire[17] in saving the imperial capital. It is surely to have helped the Roman navy, but the Umayyad fleet was not destroyed as it was attacking Crete in 675/676. Indeed, it could be that the real tipping of the scales in Roman favour was instead, after the Theodosian Walls and imperial navy had resisted Arab raids, the return of the forces that had been operating in Italy under Constans II. The naval and military counteroffensives they enabled Constantine IV to launch, along with destruction wrought by the weather and internal Umayyad division, may have been the source of the advantageous treaty for the Romans, rather than the chemical burning of the Arab fleet.

Whatever form the pressure on Constantinople from mid-650s to the late-670s took, it presented evidence of not only the persistence and scale of the threat posed by the Umayyads, but also the importance of the Theodosian Walls, the imperial fleet, and of Constantinople itself as the bastion of the Roman Empire. And even if Muawiyah's forces had not launched an attack on Constantinople, meaning that there had not been an attempted siege of the city in living memory, the geography and fortification of Constantinople meant that Maslamah's strategic plan in 717–718 was going to be straightforward, and hence so was the defensive plan of the Romans.

'They Brought the Wrong Type of Camels' – Preparations for the Siege of Constantinople 717–718

Having gathered enough ships at Abydos, Maslamah commenced the transferring of a large section of his force to Sestus, with the aim of approaching Constantinople from the landward side. He sent word back to Dawud b. Sulayman that the attack was underway and informed him that it was time to bring up the rest of the caliphal army. That Maslamah could undertake this crossing unmolested might demonstrate the strategic importance of the stationing of 12,000 men at Chalcedon, who were now under the command of al-Bakhtari as Suleiman had been put in command of the fleet along with Umar – had the imperial fleet or city garrison moved west to threaten Maslamah's crossing they would have left Constantinople vulnerable to a sneak attack.

That Maslamah could possibly 'spare' 12,000 men hints at the sheer size of the forces he had at his disposal from across the lands of the Umayyad caliphate. In recognising the formidable defences of Constantinople, the Umayyads had brought together a combined naval and land expedition, which required Syrian and Egyptian crews, specialist technicians and the building of an enormous number of ships, not just for combat but also for transportation. The Arabs also needed to be able to feed and water the vast number of men involved in such an expedition. Indeed, it has been argued that Maslamah's strategic focus was on starving the city into submission rather than storming its walls,[18] which would have only further increased the task of Arab logistics to feed the army and navy whilst it tried to throttle Constantinople. Clearly 'the campaign had been carefully planned and involved a complex logistics effort.'[19]

The surviving source material does not give concrete information about the size and make-up of the Arab expeditionary force, providing only snippets or unreliable numbers. For example, perhaps the closest source we have to the siege (beyond those used by Theophanes and Nikephoros), the late-eighth century *Zuqnin Chronicle* merely records that the Arabs were 'great and innumerable.'[20] Theophanes himself does not give a size for the land forces involved, but does mention there being 1,800 ships, while the tenth-century Arab historian al-Mas'udi suggests that there were 120,000 Arab troops. This would be a sizeable force, but not beyond the capabilities of the Umayyad caliphate. By the time we get to the twelfth century, we start to see definite exaggeration, with Michael the Syrian and *Chronicle to 1234* claiming that there were 200,000 men and 5,000 ships thrown against the Roman imperial capital in 717–718.[21] Setting aside such exaggerations, the Arab forces were much bigger than the garrison of Constantinople. It could even be that Maslamah commanded a force greater in size than the entire Roman army.[22]

Despite its size, the expeditionary force of Maslamah did not represent the full might of the Umayyad caliphate. The *diwan* army registers from the Atlantic to India could suggest a total Umayyad manpower in the early-eighth century of between 250,000 and 300,000.[23] Sulayman still had sizeable forces under his direct command at Dabiq, while significant reinforcements would be sent to Maslamah by Umar II. The Umayyads were also still capable of campaigning on the far fringes of their empire – Spain, Gaul, Central Asia and the Indian subcontinent – *and* launch raids of Roman territory: we have already seen Dawud b. Sulayman capturing the 'Women's Fortress' near Melitene in 717, while in 718, Amr b. Qais raided across the Romano-Arab frontier.

In terms of the make-up of Maslamah's force, we do get some information from the sources. The core was likely made of soldiers from Syria and Jazira (Upper Mesopotamia), who had been the centre of Umayyad power. They also had the most experience of fighting against the Romans with the decades of frontier raiding.[24] The expeditionary force also included 3,000 *mutawa* volunteers who hoped for material and spiritual gain from taking part.[25] We also see financiers within the caliphate providing horses in return for a share of the spoils taken from Constantinople, perhaps demonstrating the confidence the Arabs had in Maslamah.[26]

The Arab supply train was reputedly made up of 12,000 men, 6,000 camels and 6,000 donkeys.[27] Stores had been built up for several years, with Tabari stating that Maslamah's cavalrymen each carried a stash of grain to be used during the siege, rather than using it to feed themselves as they traversed Roman territory.[28] The Arab commander also had his men cultivate the land taken in by their extensive camp and beyond into the abandoned fields of Thrace, so that his forces could reap the harvest the following summer, again demonstrating that the Umayyads recognised the task ahead of them. This was also shown in the Arabs building more permanent houses of wood rather than just relying on their tents.[29] The Arabs would also raid the surrounding territory, further building up their stash of grain – 'the soldiers ate what they obtained from raiding and, later, from what they had sown',[30] although these incursions may have had a significant negative affect going forward. There was also a significant number of siege engines and even some stockpiled incendiary materials, such as naphtha, which was to be used on both land and sea.

Maslamah had several sub-commanders under his leadership – we have already seen Suleiman b. Mu'ad in action at Amorion and Chalcedon, with his first officer al-Bakhtari al-Hassan, although the *Kitab al-Uyun* has Abdallah al-Battal in this position, who became a semi-legendary figure as the Turkish hero, Battal Gazi. In most historical sources, al-Battal does not appear until a decade after the siege of Constantinople. Other subcommanders of the Syrian core of the expedition included Abd Allah b. Abi Zakariyya al-Khuza'I, Muhammad b. Jabr and Khalid b. Ma'dan,[31] with the latter promulgating Hadith 4:175 – 'The first army from amongst my followers who conquers the city of Caesar will be forgiven their sins.'[32]

Perhaps the arm of the Umayyad expedition that we might be able to discern the most information about is its navy. It is worth noting that the very foundation of the Arab navy was still within living memory in 717. It had had to be created from scratch in the mid-seventh century, initially depending on captured Roman ships, before later using the shipyards of Egypt, Tyre and Tunis to build their own. However, this development was hampered by the loss of specialist shipbuilders, who either fled to Roman territory in the wake of the Arab advance or refused to serve their new masters. Indeed, there appears to have been a general reluctance of Egyptians to serve in the navy due to the poor conditions and pay. This may be borne out by a series of Greek papyri from Apollonopolis in the decade prior to the siege of Constantinople, with conscription being needed, which came back to haunt the Umayyads during the siege of Constantinople.[33]

And yet, despite these issues, the Umayyad armada that appeared at Constantinople in 717, under the command of Umar b. Hubayra and briefly Suleiman b. Mu'ad, was reputedly of monstrous size, with exaggerations of 1,800 and 5,000 recorded for it. That the sources could think that such numbers *might* be correct would intimate that the Arabs did bring a significant number of ships with them. The same can be said for the reinforcement fleets that would appear during the siege – they were probably not as big as recorded, but of relatively large size. At the core of the Arab fleet were large, heavy warships called the *shalandi*, the early-Arab equivalent of the Roman heavy *dromon* with 250 oarsmen and 150 marines. We have no real notion of how many of these vessels there might have been but when we see a 'mere' 20 ships being destroyed by Leo's forces considered worthy of record, it would suggest that not only were these ships larger warships, but also that 20 was a notable (although not debilitating) percentage of the warships Maslamah had under his command. While this is almost entirely speculative, we should probably be thinking in the realms of about 200–300 warships in the Arab fleet. The majority, however, of the Arab fleet were *katenai*, armed merchant ships used to carry the siege provisions. Their design is largely unknown other than being of considerable size for their type, having to carry donkeys, camels, horses, weapons, grain, clothes, oarsmen, marines, soldiers, and other supplies.

Perhaps somewhat surprising is to find that some of the Arab ships were armed with a form of 'primitive Greek fire' or naphtha, something usually associated with the Romans. However, Arab versions of 'Greek fire' are not just limited to the siege of 717–718; Pseudo-Sebeos has Arab machines launching flammable material during the 'First Siege of Constantinople', while Muhammad b. Qasim used such machines during his invasion of India in 710. Theodosius Grammaticus has Arabs having 'fire-launching biremes' at Constantinople in 717–718, likely a machine (not necessarily the same kind of pump that the Romans had) mounted on *shalandi*.

These ships, their cargoes, and payloads, along with the vast number of men mobilised, demonstrates that the Arabs had made a concerted effort to provide sufficient logistical support to conquer the Roman imperial capital. However, some of these immense logistical efforts backfired on the Arabs; for example, the large, heavily-laden *katenai* were to prove slow-moving, difficult to manoeuvre, and vulnerable to attack. The measures taken to recruit such a large force did not provide the most willing of participants, and plans to gather supplies from the area around Constantinople could raise opposition. Another suggestion made is that the dromedaries that the Arabs brought in large numbers as beasts of burden were the wrong type of camels, as they were not suited to harsh winters, unlike their Bactrian cousins,[34] although the Arabs should be forgiven for not planning for the extreme winter the area around Constantinople was to face in 717–718.

Roman Preparations

Even with their extensive preparations, it still seems that the Arabs had underestimated the task ahead of them. The Constantinopolitan defences, natural and man-made, may even have made any assault essentially 'mission impossible'[35] in the period. The immensity of the Theodosian Walls meant that Constantinople could be well-defended by a force significantly smaller than the attackers, which was certainly the case for the 717–718 siege. Given the exhaustion of the Roman Empire's resources through constant warfare and territorial losses over the course of the previous century, the Roman forces within the capital were likely not larger than 15,000, made up from Leo's personal guard of *domestici*, *excubitores*, *spatharii*, *numeri*, *foederati*, *bucellarii*, *hetaireia*; ceremonial units such as the *scholae* and *candidati*, and possibly some men he trusted from the Anatolic army, as well as detachments from the Opsikon army and Thracian forces. The city itself did not have a permanent militia, but there was a city watch (*kerketon*), while the city guilds, circus factions, and some of the remaining general population could be mobilised to defend the walls.

It may be asked why the empire did not concentrate more men in Constantinople at a time when that great imperial bastion and quite likely the empire was under the gravest threat. The answer lies in logistic and strategic concerns. The Romans faced similar and perhaps more acute resource limitations than the Arabs on having to feed however many soldiers they had stationed in Constantinople, not to mention the civilian population. Furthermore, the Arab ability to continue to strike into eastern Roman Anatolia even when Maslamah was deployed at Constantinople demonstrates that the Romans needed to continue to defend their Asian provinces. Denuding the Thrakesian, Anatolic and Armeniac themes by removing their armies to defend Constantinople would have allowed the Umayyads to conquer large swathes of Roman Asia. The imperial capital might then have been saved, but it would find itself with no empire to rule.

The sheer extent of the Arab preparations for the siege, both in terms of size and duration, gave the Romans time to prepare their manpower, resources, and defences. And as we have seen, while their reigns had not been of substantial length, Anastasius II and Theodosius III had made significant moves to make Constantinople ready to repel the Umayyad attack: both the land and sea walls had been repaired, stores had been built up within the city, those who could not feed themselves were asked to leave, the imperial fleet had been repaired, accords had been made with the Bulgars, all this on top of the garrison being brought together from the empire's armed forces.

A significant addition to the Constantinopolitan sea defences may have been made around this time with a great, linked chain established across the mouth of the Golden Horn from the Tower of Eugenius of the city proper in what is now the modern suburb of Sirkeci to the old, likely Justinianic, *Kastellion* of Galata – *Megalos Pyrgos* – in the northern suburb of Constantinople also known as Sykai, Pera or in modern times, Karaköy. The exact date of this addition is unclear, with both Leo III and Anastasius II being attributed with its creation. It may even have been added earlier still, with its lack of mention during the so-called 'First Siege of Constantinople' possibly presenting something of a *terminus post quem* in the 660s/670s, although the already-mentioned issues with that 'siege' further hinders what is already speculation. While its date might be suspect, what is not is the effectiveness of this Great Chain. In its 700-year Roman history, this Great Chain would only be broken once – by a Venetian ram during the Fourth Crusade. The only other occasions it was circumvented were by the Kievan Rus' in 907 and by the Ottomans in 1453, both of whom towed some of their ships overland from the Bosphorus, around Galata, and then relaunched them in the Golden Horn, behind the chain. The threat it posed would play a significant role in the siege of 717–718.

Another on-sea weapon the Romans had in their arsenal has already been mentioned – the closely guarded state secret that was 'Greek fire'. A brief history and make-up of this substance can be seen in the Appendix, but with regards to the Arab siege of 717–718, it is usually given a starring role in turning back the Umayyad navy; however, much like its reputed role in the 'First Siege', the importance of Greek fire in the contest between Leo III and Maslamah may have been greatly exaggerated.[36] Although that is not to say that the Roman defenders did not make good use of this medieval flamethrower.

The population of Constantinople at the turn of the eighth century is difficult to calculate and that is even before trying to estimate how many inhabitants listened to the order that any who could not feed themselves for three years should leave.[37] The previous 150 years had seen the city repeatedly ravaged by plague, warfare, siege, and disruption to its food supply. Therefore, despite it being a major hub for refugees fleeing the Arab conquests, the population of Constantinople had likely significantly declined from its peak of several hundred thousand. It has even been suggested that it had slumped to 50,000 by the mid-eighth century.[38] Such a drastic decline may explain why the Aqueduct of Valens, cut during the Avar siege of the city in 626, was not repaired until 768, by which time the population of the city was starting to recover. The system of 100 internal collectors and cisterns[39] was considered adequate to water the remaining population. This might present the unexpected benefits of a reduced population in times of siege. While there were fewer potential militia to defend the walls, it allowed for more concentration of resources for use by the soldiery. More generally, there were fewer mouths to feed and water. The reduced population will also have seen sizeable portions of the land encompassed by the walls left uninhabited, providing free space to plant and grow vegetables.[40] Such *intra muros* allotments are unlikely to have made the city self-sufficient, even with its drastically reduced population, but it will have helped relieve some of the pressure caused by the Arab cutting of supply lines.[41] The Great Chain might have also helped in the logistics of the capital. By maintaining control of the Golden Horn, the Romans made it impossible for the Arabs to enforce a complete blockade of Constantinople as a circumvallation of the full length of the Golden Horn and Galata's defences may have been beyond even the vast Umayyad forces. Some supplies may therefore have entered the city from the Black Sea coast through the Golden Horn estuary.

In general, logistical support was going to be vital to both the besieged and the besieger. As it was, due to their preparations and the defences of Constantinople, the Romans would prove more adept and ready for the fight, although the Arabs were by no means arrogant in their assessment of the resources needed for the mammoth task. In the early stages, the logistical planning by the Arabs met with success – their armies crossed Anatolia with its own supplies and a fleet carrying provisions, weapons, and men reached the coastlines around the Roman capital with little difficulty; however, upon arrival at Constantinople, the Arabs faced sterner Roman opposition than they initially thought; the winter weather was going to be substantially worse than planned for and their naval power was going to prove insufficient. But make no mistake, while there may have been some limited relief of the pressures imposed by the siege, the inhabitants and defenders of Constantinople suffered deprivation during the Arab blockade. Indeed, such was the importance of Constantinople, the siege of 717–718 was the Roman Empire's 'ultimate trial'.[42]

That this contest could be viewed as 'mission impossible' and the 'ultimate trial' for each side demonstrates its importance. And beyond logistics, both sides had cause for confidence. The Arabs were buoyed by a century of almost unbroken success and by the substantial victories and conquests achieved by the Marwanid branch of the Umayyad dynasty since the mid-680s. And yet, the Romans could look back at their ability to survive the seventh century calamities through their infrastructural and military organisation, improvisational skills, and their toughness and sheer bloody-mindedness as a people. Lesser nations would have capitulated during the various nadirs of the 600s, but would the Romans crumble under the test from the Umayyad juggernaut?

The Siege Begins – Early Umayyad Setbacks

The scattered information about the siege of 717–718 does not only affect the make-up of the forces involved and their preparations; it also provides issues about its exact date. Again, we face deviations through inclusive counting, the differences between Roman and Muslim calendars, and generally different notions of what constituted the Arab attempt to capture Constantinople – the actual siege itself or the various campaigns that formed its prelude. There may even be some intentional changes to make the dates of the siege seem more symbolic.

Some Arab sources mention the siege lasting two years, but this is either from counting inclusively – even a single day over a year would be considered 'two years' – or counting the 'siege' as involving the entire extended campaign from the overland advance of the Arab vanguard and the activities surrounding Amorion. Such a counting of preliminary operations as part of the 'siege' campaign as a whole makes it difficult to know how far back we should go. A combination of Tabari and Roman hagiography suggests an attack on a Roman island, possibly Crete, in AH97 (5 September 715 – 24 August 716) by Umar b. Hubayra, the Arab admiral for much of the siege campaign, which could see this attack be taken as part of the Arab advance against Constantinople. Do we take in the attempted naval and marine actions of Anastasius II and the Arab preparations they were meant to disrupt? Or possibly even the Arab capture of Tarsus in 712?

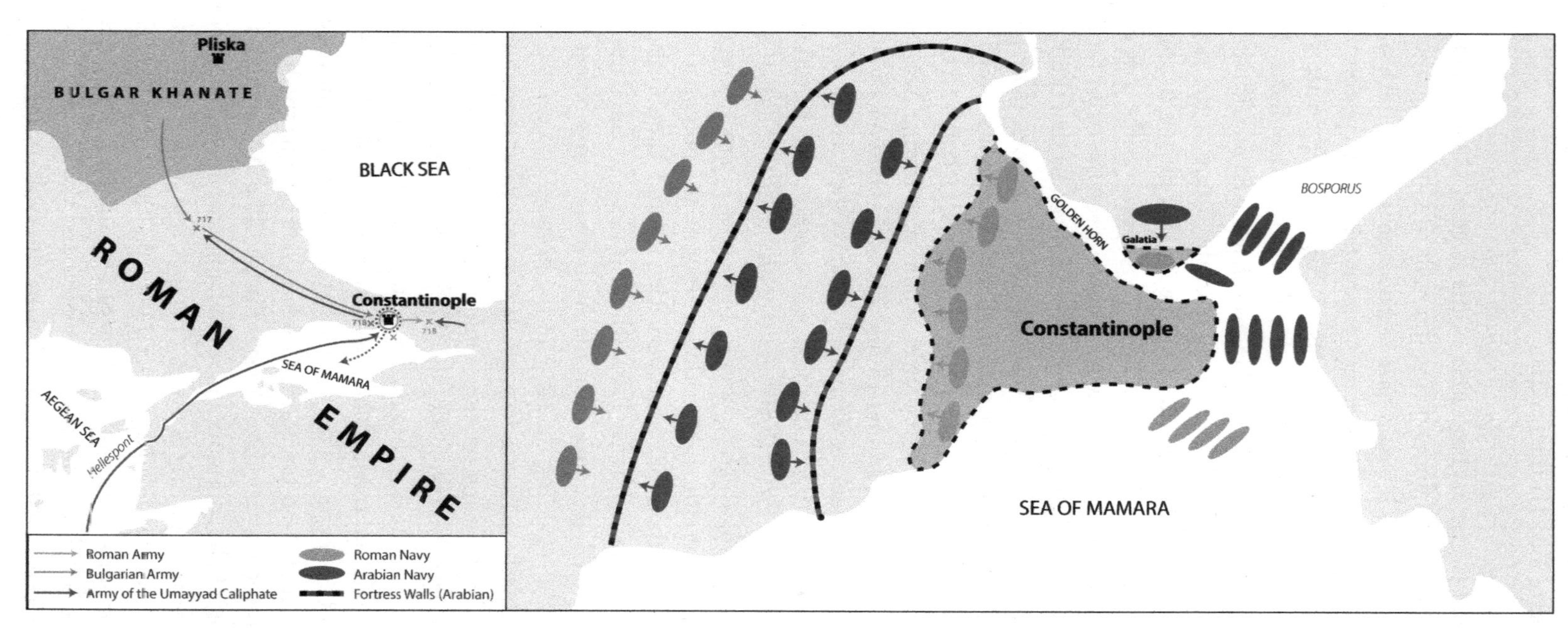
Pliska
BULGAR KHANATE
BLACK SEA
717
ROMAN
Constantinople
718
719
SEA OF MAMARA
AEGEAN SEA
Hellespont
EMPIRE
Roman Army
Bulgarian Army
Army of the Umayyad Caliphate
Roman Navy
Arabian Navy
Fortress Walls (Arabian)
BOSPORUS
GOLDEN HORN
Galatia
Constantinople
SEA OF MAMARA

In terms of the actual beginning of the siege, it is surely to be dated to the arrival of Maslamah's forces before the walls of Constantinople, and maybe a few days after that as it would have taken some time for the Umayyad army to establish a landward blockade of the Constantinopolitan peninsula. Theophanes gives the date of the Arab arrival as 15 August 717,[43] with the *Synaxarium Ecclesiae Constantinopolitanae* probably following Theophanes, but getting its date wrong by saying 16 August.[44] However, when taken with the Arab sources, which have 15 August 718 as the date of the lifting of the siege, this would mean that it had lasted one year to the day in Theophanes' dating, which seems a little too coincidental, particularly as 15 August was the date of the Feast of Dormition to the Virgin Mary, who would be given the credit for the survival of Constantinople in the years to come. It could even be that the Romans altered their own records to have this Marian feast play an even more prominent role than it did.[45] Modern scholars tend to follow Nikephoros over Theophanes on this occasion, with the former stating that the siege lasted 13 months,[46] which when coupled with the Arab sources, would suggest that Maslamah's siege of Constantinople started around 15 July 717 and ended on 15 August 718.[47]

The Arab sources are not completely clear on their dating of the siege either. That it lasted more than a calendar year caused some historiographical and chronological issues for Arab historians, with the likes of Tabari and al-Mas'udi placing it in AH98, which equates to 14 August 716 to 13 August 717, which seems a year early, although would incorporate the potential starting date of Nikephoros. On the other hand, Ibn Khayyat and Ya'qubi place it in AH99 (14 August 717 – 2 August 718), which is close to the dates attributed by Theophanes. Such discrepancy in the Arab sources may reflect the murkiness of information regarding the siege in the decades and centuries after it took place, particularly to its starting date. If that was what these four named Arab historians were focusing on, they could demonstrate a similar divide between them as between Nikephoros (July 717) and Theophanes (August 717).

Whatever date the siege began, the main part of the Arab army arrived outside Constantinople and made Hebdomon, a coastal suburb of Constantinople, its main base of operations. This meant that, as the closest entrance to the main concentration of Arab forces, the Golden Gate became the focus of any Arab attempts to force a way into Constantinople. The Arabs then undertook the surrounding of all Constantinople's land approaches 'with a stockade, digging a great ditch and erecting above it a parapet-like wall of unmortared stone.'[48] These siege walls extended from Hebdomon on the coast of the Sea of Marmara in a crescent north to the northern tip of the Golden Horn and then on to the shore of the Bosphorus to blockade Galata and the Golden Horn. As already mentioned, the coastline and estuary of the Golden Horn was difficult to surround, and it may be that the Roman garrison targeted this area for raids. However, the source for these raids, the *Chronicle to 1234*, speaks of the Arabs having to deal with Roman scouts attempting to disrupt supply lines 'on the opposite coast,'[49] without clarity as to which coast it is talking about – the opposite coast of the Constantinopolitan peninsula and therefore the Golden Horn, or that of the Sea of Marmara and therefore in the Asian lands of the Opsikon. But even if the *Chronicle to 1234* is unclear, it is likely that the Arab presence on *both* of these 'opposite coasts' came under attack from Roman raids throughout the siege.

Rather than challenge Maslamah's crossing or his march east to the capital, Leo resorted to pulling most, if not all of his Thrace-based forces back to defend Constantinople. He also had them undertake a scorched earth policy, stripping the *extra muros* suburbs of the capital and its immediate vicinity of as much materiel and resources as they could.[50] However, this lack of open Roman contesting of the Arab approach to Constantinople does not mean that Maslamah's forces were one-dimensional in that approach or even that they had it all their own way. Maslamah seems not to have made a mad dash to Constantinople from Abydos through Rhegion to Hebdomon. On their arrival in Europe, Theophanes notes the Arabs 'punishing the Thracian fortresses,'[51] which could mean that part of the Umayyad army overcame some Roman forces stationed there. Tabari suggests that the Arabs conquered a 'city of the Slavs'[52] at around this time; and while he does not specify where this was (there were settlements of Slavs in Roman Asia Minor and even Arab Syria), that he mentions it in relation to Maslamah's operations before Constantinople makes it likely that he is talking about a settlement in Thrace.

This Arab 'punishing of Thracian fortresses' may have been a consequence or even a catalyst of another major part of the Umayyad advance towards Constantinople – the movements and near-demise of Maslamah himself. The Arab general may have crossed to Thrace 'six miles below the city'[53] – this could suggest that rather than from Abydos to Sestus, which was some 300 km from Constantinople, Maslamah having crossed directly to Hebdomon once his advance force was established there. However, this does not necessarily fit in with the report that he was in direct command of the Arab rear-guard of 4,000 cavalry, which presumably would have been marching east from Sestus to Hebdomon. It could be that rather than a rear-guard, Maslamah took command of a cavalry force to scout the area that was to be the hinterland of his camp for the foreseeable future. He is also recorded sending out foraging parties, which reputedly brought back mountains of grain,[54] although it is unlikely that Maslamah would partake in such foraging.

Whatever the circumstances for his presence in Thrace at the head of 4,000 cavalry, it almost came to fatal grief for Maslamah. During the night, 'the Bulgar allies of the Romans fell upon him unexpectedly and slaughtered most of the force that was with him. Maslamah [only] escaped by a hair's breadth.'[55] We might enquire why the Bulgars launched such an attack. First and perhaps foremost, the diplomacy of Justinian II and Theodosius III had obtained a treaty and possibly even an alliance with the Bulgar khan. And it is quite possible that Leo III reached out to the khan, no doubt with his agents offering financial inducements, to ensure the continuation of these good relations. The Bulgars and their Slavic subordinates may also have been annoyed by any wide-ranging foraging and capture of the 'city of the Slavs' undertaken by Arab forces.

There is no record of the Umayyads contacting the Bulgars in an attempt to achieve their neutrality or even an alliance against the Roman Empire. Of course, this is an argument from silence, and it does seem like a big enough oversight for it to be difficult to believe. Given the extent of their realm and the prominence of diplomacy in Maslamah's expedition so far, the likelihood is that some sort of Umayyad embassy was sent to the Bulgars. Even if they were approached, the Bulgars stayed true to their agreements with the empire or decided that preserving a weakened Roman Empire was more to their benefit than helping the vigorous Arab caliphate take Constantinople. The potential benefit of capturing some imperial territory in Thrace, Macedonia, and along the Black Sea coast would surely be outweighed by being almost certainly the next target of the rampant forces of Islam, who would be looking to subdue the pagan Bulgars as they moved into the Balkan peninsula. 'Better the devil you know… than the devil you do not…' Any Bulgar rejection of Umayyad overtures might explain some of the more aggressive moves by Maslamah's forces – 'punishing the Thracian fortresses', capturing the 'city of the Slavs', the widespread foraging and possibly whatever operation he was undertaking with the 4,000 cavalry. Perhaps the Umayyads arrived in Thrace knowing that the Bulgars were going to be hostile.

The unclear chronology and gaps in the historical record regarding Bulgaro-Arab relations prior to the siege of Constantinople leaves us uncertain of what was the cause and what was the effect. Were the Bulgar attacks on the Arabs retaliatory or opportunistic first strikes? Were the Arabs attempting to forcefully assert their dominance in eastern Thrace over an already proclaimed Roman ally, reacting to Bulgar raids, or looking to secure the surrounding area without a specific target in mind beyond the Romans? Regardless of its origin, the threat posed by the Bulgars and Slavs to the Arab lines, potentially trapping them against the Theodosian Walls, will certainly have been much more acute after the near-death experience of Maslamah. The recognition of this threat was reflected in the dual aspect of the Arab circumvallation of Constantinople. The combination of stone wall, palisade and trench not only faced towards the immense defences of the imperial capital, but also out into the Thracian hinterland to protect the Arab position from attack.

This might not have been just out of fear or wariness of the Bulgars. We have already seen that the Arab action involved in the 'First Siege' of Constantinople was possibly interrupted by the return of Roman forces from the west in the early years of the reign of Constantine IV. Maslamah may have been wary of a similar episode playing out once more, for given the amount of preparation the Arabs put into this siege, it would be expected that they tried to learn from previous experiences and planned to counter any issues their predecessors had come up against. Even if there was no sizeable Roman force abroad, with the forces of Roman Italy and Hellas either too distracted or not strong enough to inflict any real damage on Maslamah's forces, a seaborne relief force from the Asian themes would almost certainly approach the Arab position through the Aegean Sea and then attempt to march along the *Via Egnatia* to threaten the Arab rear. Because of such considerations, Maslamah's dual aspect camp meant that there was no real 'rear' to the Arab lines, which essentially constituted a fortified camp stretching from Hebdomon, around the Golden Horn to the Bosphorus shore north of Galata. Maslamah also seems to have charged a sizeable detachment of 20,000 men under the command of Sharahil b. Abd with patrolling the western approaches.[56]

With his army in position, the next piece of Maslamah's siege puzzle arrived – his fleet. Under the command of Suleiman, the Arab fleet appeared outside Constantinople on 1 September. This seems a little late compared to the arrival of the army in mid-August or even mid-July, but then the fleet had been overseeing, facilitating, and protecting the crossing from Abydos to Sestus and possibly that of Maslamah to Hebdomon. The Arab commander will also have been wary of bringing up their ships in dribs and drabs as that could have allowed the imperial navy to pick them off one at a time. Suleiman may also have advanced carefully through the Sea of Marmara to flush out any Roman squadrons looking to raid the Arab fleet, coastal positions, and supply lines.

Initially, the Arab fleet anchored 'between the Magnaura and the Kyklobion,'[57] which is essentially along the coast of Hebdomon; however, two days later, with a south wind blowing, the fleet sailed past Constantinople to take up positions along the European and Asian coasts of the Bosphorus and the Sea of Marmara, from Galata to Kleidon in Thrace and Eutropios and Anthemios on the Asian side. Maslamah and Suleiman were either looking to reposition their ships or were forced into it. Might the anchorage off Hebdomon have not provided sufficient protection from either the weather or Roman naval raids? Or might this have been the next move in tightening the blockade of Constantinople by seizing control of the Bosphorus? A tighter blockade would have seen the imperial fleet confined to the Golden Horn – this would have allowed the Arabs to attack the sea walls, which would in turn have forced Leo to detach men from the land walls.

However, the imperial fleet was still free to operate, and this dispersal of Arab ships presented Leo with an opportunity.[58] The large, heavily-laden Arab *katenai* provided a tempting target. The Romans were further aided by a change in the weather. As the Arab rear-guard of 20 ships, with 2,000 marines on board, sailed north past the city, the wind first slackened and then turned from southerly to northerly. This and the current saw the Arab rear-guard pushed back towards Constantinople. Leo and his admirals sent out a squadron of their Greek-fire wielding *dromones*. This attack saw these 20 Arab ships (and maybe some supply ships they were escorting) left as 'blazing wrecks', with some crashing into the sea walls, others sinking, and others scattered along the coast and islands of the Sea of Marmara – Theophanes mentions the islands of Oxeia and Plateia, some 20 miles south of Constantinople.[59]

On the surface, losing 20 ships from a supposed fleet of 1,800 may not seem like much of an issue, but even looking past the exaggeration of Arab ship numbers and the possibility that these 20 ships were a more significant proportion of a core of 200–300 Arab warships, the Roman ability to quickly destroy the Arab rear-guard left lasting psychological effects. It was a reminder to the Romans that their fleet was capable of dealing damage to the Arabs and delivered a general morale boost to the defenders; to the Arabs, it was a lesson in the dangers of the Greek fire-wielding Roman navy and of manoeuvring in the waters around the imperial capital, making them wary of pressing their naval blockade as tightly as they would have liked. Even when the Arab fleet was further reinforced as the siege went on, 'they dared not confront the [Romans] in open waters.'[60]

Leo tried to capitalise on this victory by attempting to lure the Arabs into a trap. Knowing that the Arabs sought to gain control of the Golden Horn, that the recent destruction of their rear-guard might have engendered some desperation in the Arabs, and possibly thinking that Maslamah might have taken this gesture as part of their 'agreement', the emperor had the Great Chain lowered. This would have seen any Arab squadron that took the bait trapped in the Golden Horn, once the chain was raised again, not only against the Roman fleet but also within range of the various missile turrets and artillery in the towers and on the walls of Constantinople and Galata. The Arab ships refused to take this bait and abandoned any plan to anchor at the sea walls, instead removing themselves further north to the bay of Sosthenios, an inlet halfway up the European side of the Bosphorus.[61]

This defeat by Leo's fireships was not the only potential disaster to overtake the Arab siege in its first few months. In late-summer/early-autumn 717,[62] caliph Sulayman fell ill after Friday prayers and died a few days later at Dabiq. The circumstances of his death could signify that Sulayman succumbed to the outbreak of plague in Syria and Iraq known as the *ta'un al-Ashraf* – 'plague of the Notables', as his eldest son Ayyub had done.[63] The trouble that Sulayman's illness and demise might have caused the caliphate is that there had been some trouble surrounding the succession. Even in his short reign of just over two and a half years, Sulayman had lost two designated heirs, first his brother Marwan al-Akbar and then Ayyub. He considered naming another son, Dawud, as heir on his deathbed, but was talked out of it due to Dawud being at Constantinople and possibly already dead. Even if Dawud was still alive, recalling him meant an interregnum and some disruption to the expedition. Sulayman may even have gone as far as to choose another of his sons, possibly Muhammad, in writing, only to change his mind as Muhammad was too young.[64]

The fact that Sulayman was looking to his own sons ahead of his remaining brothers was something of a break with the growing trend, particularly amongst the sons of Abd al-Malik. This raises questions about some inter-family strife and possibly the undue influence of an adviser close to Sulayman, Raja b. Haywah, who was the ultimate source of Tabari's information on the Umayyad succession of 717.[65] It is Raja who is depicted as warning Sulayman against choosing Dawud, and when Sulayman pressed him for his opinion on a cousin called Umar b. Abd al-Aziz, Raja declared him 'a worthy, excellent man and a sincere Muslim.'[66] Sulayman recognised that there would be strife amongst his brothers, who 'will never allow [Umar] to rule over them, unless one of them is put next in succession'[67] – he, therefore, assigned his eldest remaining brother, Yazid, as successor to Umar. Even with this two-generation succession plan, there was still some initial Umayyad opposition. Abd al-Aziz, son of al-Walid I, attempted to claim the caliphate upon Sulayman's death, gaining support in Damascus; however, he submitted to Umar II, his maternal uncle.

Rather than any dislike for his brothers or undue influence from Raja, Sulayman might have shown some preference towards Umar because he was 'most sympathetic to his policies.'[68] One such policy might have been support for the on-going siege of Constantinople. Given the amount of materiel and manpower that had been contributed to this Herculean task, opposition to it within the caliphate would not be surprising. However, Umar II proved determined to continue the siege and would reinforce it in early 718.

Why Need Help? Diplomacy, Duplicity and Disaster at Constantinople

There is more than one reason why Umar would feel the need to send reinforcements to Maslamah. First off, most logically, is that any and all attempts to capture Constantinople had failed. It is one of the peculiarities of the sources for the siege that there is very little record of land attacks by Maslamah's forces, or at least in the main sources. The likes of Theophanes and Nikephoros focus almost entirely on naval operations, to the degree that we might think that that was all there was in terms of fighting. Even a lesser-known record – that of the twelfth-century Islamic scholar, Ibn Asakir, focuses on another naval operation undertaken by the Romans. In his *Tarikh Dimashq – 'History of Damascus'*,[69] – Ibn Asakir records a reputed eye-witness account of two brothers who took part in the siege, Laith(?) and Abu Khurasan. They sailed to the siege with Umar, and partook in an action before the Golden Horn. Laith writes of the Arab fleet becoming wary – even 'afraid' – to approach the harbour and having one of its ships falling victim to a Roman raid, who 'threw on it grapnels with chains and towed it with its crew into Constantinople'. Abu Khurasan then led a counterattack that prevented another ship from being captured.

However, while this story focuses on further naval raiding, it also presents Leo 'the autocrat of Rūm' being more proactive than other sources would have it. And not just with these ship-capturing raids. Upon arriving at Constantinople, Laith and Abu Khurasan witness the immense stand-off between the lines, on land and sea, of the Muslim host – 'I had never seen a longer one' – and the foot soldiers, mangonels and onagers of Leo, showing that even though he was stationed 'on the tower of the [Golden] gate of Constantinople', the emperor was in a position to launch military strikes on the Arabs, as well as resist any that they themselves launched. Indeed, between Laith and Ibn Asakir, the Romans are presented as using cowardly tactics on land and sea, which are more likely to be feigned flight, hit-and-run actions, quite possibly in attempts to draw the Arabs into range of their artillery. Again, this shows Leo being more proactive than usually thought, willing to launch attacks on Arab forces, rather than just hide behind the walls.

It must also be said that while Theophanes and Germanos hint at a lack of fighting on the walls,[70] this may still be something of an argument from silence and/or a judging of the more general impression of a lack of fighting throughout the entire year of the siege. The Arabs surely made early attempts to storm the walls, only to be driven back by a well-organised Roman defence and then settled in for a blockade over the months of poorer weather. If there was no fighting on the walls, this would have been due to the Arabs not wanting there to be any. Maslamah relying solely on blockade, starvation, or diplomacy would not be completely unrealistic due to the strength of Constantinople's defences, but then why did he go to the bother of bringing so many siege engines and artillery? The likelihood is that there were some Arab attempts to force their way in, either through stealth, subterfuge, or storm. They are just not at all prominent in our source material. And complete failures.

While we might think that the sources record something of a dearth of combat on land around Constantinople, there were other Romano-Arab contests taking place further afield that were part of this campaign. The Arab forces which had taken up positions in the major cities and strategic positions along the Asian coast of the Sea of Marmara faced numerous guerrilla attacks. This must have hindered their attempts to resupply the forces outside Constantinople, to rebuild their shattered fleets, or to firmly establish their control of many of those cities. We have already seen the summer raids of Dawid b. Sulayman and Amr b. Qais from Umayyad Syria, but these were joined by further raids led by al-Walid b. Hisham, Abd Allah b. Umar, and possibly Amr b. Qais again. Even if there was no intention for such raids to reinforce Maslamah at Constantinople directly,[71] they will have further hampered the ability of the Romans to bring aid to Leo as they pinned down the Armeniac, Anatolic, and probably Thrakesian themes, who had to defend their lands and so could do little to intervene at the capital, or bolster the attacks on Maslamah's supply lines. We will see later that Romano-Arab conflict was not the only martial aspect of the siege of Constantinople. The extent of the communications blackout from the capital led to a usurpation in Italy, which Leo would have to deal with later.

A second reason why Maslamah himself might have felt the need of reinforcements from Umar is that any hopes he had for a diplomatic solution to the expedition's aims had fallen completely flat. He had been overjoyed at Leo becoming emperor 'supposing that he would thereby find an opportunity to fulfil his promise and deliver the city to him.'[72] Leo further encouraged this notion through correspondence, while using the time to continue preparing the defence of Constantinople. You might expect that once Maslamah had recognised the extent to which Leo had strung him along over the previous year and the siege of Constantinople had begun that diplomatic actions meant to bring about the surrender of the city peacefully would have ended. However, various historiographical traditions – Arab, Armenian, Syriac and even Constantinopolitan – present diplomatic and political interactions continuing even after the blockade had been initiated. A significant portion of these traditions have prominent Arab leaders and commanders entering Constantinople and/or meetings between these leaders and the emperor.

Perhaps the most incredible aspect of these contacts is the Arab tradition – it appears both in the *Kitab al-Uyun* and Tabari[73] – that even when the siege was underway, Leo was still able to string along Maslamah with the idea that he was going to deliver Constantinople to the Arabs. This reputedly culminated in what Tabari describes as 'a trick that would shame even a woman.'[74] As 'Maslamah prosecuted the siege vigorously',[75] either through emissaries or in person, Leo asked the Arab general to relent from his pressure on the walls. Seeing an opportunity to capture the city without a fight, Maslamah agreed and entered negotiations with the emperor. Leo told him that his mass preparations for a long siege was sending the wrong message to the defenders: due to all the supplies the Arabs had piled up in their camp, the Romans viewed it not as a concerted effort to take the city but as an Arab acceptance that they could not win in battle. Leo suggested that a more decisive message would be to destroy grain stores and prepare for an all-out attack; this would demoralise the Romans, who would then capitulate in a few days. Inexplicably, Maslamah accepted this advice, but then doubled down on this stupidity by listening to Leo's further advice in allowing the Romans to have some of his stores before he destroyed the rest![76] Supposedly, such magnanimity would reflect well on Maslamah and make the Arabs seem supremely confident in their ability to take the city by storm.

Having followed Leo's advice, Maslamah then sent Suleiman and al-Battal to the emperor to negotiate what the Arab general thought was the surrender of the Roman capital – here, while accepting that he had broken faith with Maslamah, Leo reveals how completely he has fooled and manipulated him throughout 716 and 717:

> I will not come out of my kingdom… Do you think I will leave all that the emperors have collected in times past up to this day and come out to you? If I do this, I have neither intelligence nor religion… I have left you no provisions or provender, but he had burnt it all at my orders; and you will perish in a short time, and there is no succour for you and no one to seek aid [from], and you have nothing.[77]

So confident was Leo in the reversal of the strategic positions that he promised Maslamah safe passage through Roman territory back to Syria if he abandoned the siege – 'But if he is not willing to do this, then he will meet with real war, very different from that in which he has been engaged.'[78] The emissaries returned to Maslamah, who was shocked, angry, and despairing of the seeming totality of his deception by Leo. He absolved al-Battal of blame, but suspected Suleiman, which could have lingered since the failure to secure Amorion the previous year. When he voiced some aspect of this suspicion to al-Battal, the sub-commander did not back up Suleiman. This suspicion seems to have led

Suleiman to commit suicide through poison, either on the spot or sometime later. Maslamah was so outraged at this that he had Suleiman's body crucified.[79] Command of the Arab fleet reverted to Umar b. Hubayra.

Understandably, this Leonid manipulation and the humiliation it caused him made Maslamah much more wary of diplomatic dealings with the Romans; however, such dealings did continue. When Leo dispatched a patrician seemingly called Tessarakontapechys – 'the son of forty cubits' – to treat with Maslamah, upon listening to those around him, the Arab commander refused to meet with him, sending Umar instead. Tessarakontapechys and Umar had a protracted conversation that eventually led to the patrician offering to ransom Constantinople at a rate of a *denarius* per adult male, so that the Arabs would lift the siege. Umar felt that this was a good deal, but rightly thought that Maslamah would not accept it. In this the admiral was proven correct, with the humiliation and the orders of Sulayman to not retreat before the city was taken seeing Maslamah reply 'No, by God, I will take it by storm, or else Leo shall come out to me on the conditions on which he left me'.[80]

Other significant diplomatic meetings are recorded. A *synaxaria* – collection of biographical notes surrounding the lives of saints and martyrs – from around the late-eighth/early-ninth century,[81] claims that caliph Sulayman was struck from his horse when trying to enter the city. A similar story is recorded in the *De Administrando Imperio* of Constantine VII, where the emphasis is put on the Virgin Mary 'by whose inviolate and holy image Sulayman himself was awed and put to shame, and he fell from his horse'.[82] There are considerable issues with such a story – as we have seen, caliph Sulayman was never present at the siege and was dead by September 717. Suleiman b. Mu'ad was present at the siege and is recorded talking to Leo either before the walls or within the city, although he too may have been dead in early October 717. It could be that such a story was about the 'Arab leader' of the forces at Constantinople, i.e. Maslamah. Other sources relate the idea that he entered the city near the end of the siege. The *Zuqnin Chronicle* has him being allowed into the city by Leo for a tour at the end of the siege. Later Arab traditions follow the *Zuqnin Chronicle*, but have Maslamah being far more antagonistic – a sore loser, particularly with his fooling by Leo, to the point that he breaks a cross in a church and carries it with him upside down. The Armenian tradition also has Maslamah enter Constantinople in a non-diplomatic way, either by being captured or by trying to steal into the city, only to be caught and brought before Leo.[83]

Perhaps such was the level of diplomatic interaction during the siege that later tradition would have it that the first mosque built in Constantinople, near the *praetorium*, was associated with Maslamah.[84] This is not entirely preposterous given how we have already seen Leo's fleet taking prisoners of war and suggestions that various diplomatic visits were paid to the city at this time. However, this association and date are mistakes and it is more likely that this mosque was built after an Arab embassy to the city in 860.[85] There were also traditions linking mosques in Galata to Maslamah, particularly the 'Mosque of the Arabs', but that is erroneously dated to 685–686, which is closer to the 'First Siege' of Constantinople than that of Maslamah.[86] Given their dispositions and time spent in those positions, it is probable that mosques of some kind were built in the Arab-controlled suburbs of Constantinople, such as Hebdomon, Chalcedon and north of Galata, but such a construction inside the walls of either Constantinople or Galata seems unlikely.

A much less surprising aspect of the siege recorded by the *synaxarion* is the suggestion that the Arabs raised a usurper in the suburbs of Constantinople. It would not be surprising to find Maslamah attempting such a political move. He had already had some success in interfering in Roman imperial politics with Leo around Amorion and the persistent usurpations in the empire were surely common knowledge. And even if he was not ultimately successful in placing his new candidate on the throne, the presence of a suburban usurper might have circumvented some of the defensive zeal of the city. It would also not be surprising to find Maslamah and his men reaching out to any remaining partisans of Anastasius II or Theodosius III, either within Constantinople itself or in the Roman army. However, a suburban usurpation receives no corroboration from anywhere else in the source record. This does not completely rule it out but does make it much less likely. It must also be said that any such diplomatic and political manoeuvrings by Maslamah may also hint at the Arab general looking for other avenues to bring about victory as his military options were declining.[87]

Potentially straddling the military and diplomatic actions at the time of the siege of Constantinople and contributing to the argument for reinforcements being sent to Maslamah is the Chinese tradition that the Tang emperor Xuanzong (712–756) was visited by a Roman embassy.

> In the first month of the seventh year of the period K'ai-yuan [719], their lord sent the *ta-shou-ling* [an officer of high rank] of T'u-huo-lo [Khazarstan] to offer lions and ling-yang [antelopes], two of each. A few months after, he further sent *ta-te-seng* ['priests of great virtue'] to our court with tribute.[88]

It would not be surprising to see Leo III or his immediate predecessors reaching out to any and all potential allies in the coming siege of Constantinople, but this embassy to the Far East was almost certainly far more targeted. This was because at the time that the forces of the Umayyad caliphate were preparing to attack the Roman imperial capital, they were also probing Ferghana in Central Asia. In deposing a local king, the Arabs sparked a reaction from Tang China, whose Anxi Protectorate stretched into this region. The Chinese defeated the Arab puppet in Ferghana in 715, only for the Anxi Protectorate itself to be targeted by the Arabs and their Turkic allies, with Kashgar being captured in 717. As they pressed on to the Aksu region, the Arab force was intercepted by a Sino-Turkic army. The resultant Battle of Aksu was a heavy Arab defeat, with the Chinese facilitating repeated Turkic attacks which removed the Arabs from Ferghana. Even though the Chinese historical tradition only mentions tribute being sent to court of Xuanzong, there was surely some encouragement to continue to take the fight to the Arab forces in Central Asia.

And that the Khazars were the intermediary between the Romans and the Chinese highlights another diplomatic contact from Constantinople. It may be no coincidence that 717–718 not only saw Sino-Arab conflict, but an Arab-Khazar confrontation as well. There had been various Khazar raids through the Caucasus throughout the seventh and on into the eighth century, with the Arabs reacting with strikes north of their own, so the Khazar attack on Azerbaijan in 717 did not occur in a vacuum. However, the deployment of significant Arab forces against Constantinople and in Ferghana, along with some Roman financial encouragement, must have helped the Khazar khagan decide to launch his latest raid at this time. Of course, such Umayyad deployments elsewhere in their empire will have been a potential reason for Umar II to *not* send reinforcements to Maslamah, with the caliphate reputedly being so short of manpower that it could muster only 4,000 men to repel the 20,000 Khazars in Azerbaijan.[89]

The biggest reason why Umar II felt it necessary to send significant reinforcements to Maslamah was that the winter of 717/718 was extremely harsh. Arctic blasts of wind brought 100 days of hail, sleet, snow, and freezing temperatures.[90] This hindered the gathering of any provisions in Thrace and prevented the caliph[91] from sending reinforcements and supplies. This meant that 'the Muslim army suffered what no army had suffered previously, to the extent that a soldier was afraid to leave camp by himself. They ate animals, skins, tree roots, leaves – indeed, everything except dirt.'[92] The Syriac tradition suggests that 'everything' included human flesh and the dung of their pack-animals.[93] Such a combination of severe weather and famine spawned disease in the Arab camp, while the frozen ground meant that the bodies of the dead (those that were not eaten) had to be disposed of by being thrown into the sea.

The Romans took advantage of their more comfortable position, launching raids on the Arab forces under cover of fog, snow, and dark. So hard did Leo press the Arabs that it was the Arabs who were the besieged rather than the

Romans.[94] The 'besieged' Arabs also faced constant harassment from the Bulgars,[95] possibly in response to increasingly far-ranging Arab foraging into Bulgar territory. At some point during the siege, the Arab general charged with protecting the western approaches to the Arab position, Sharahil b. Abd was attacked, defeated, and slain by what must have been a sizeable Bulgar army.[96]

The Arab land forces were not the only arm of the expedition to face increasingly poor conditions – the Arab fleet declined in quality as well. On top of damage inflicting by Romans raids and Greek fire, the increasingly poor conditions in the Arab camp saw wood supplies set aside for ship maintenance appropriated for the building of makeshift houses and burning for warmth. This then escalated to the cannibalising of the ships themselves, taking their wood and stripping their pitch protection for sustenance. The deaths caused by the poor conditions will have seen the remaining seaworthy ships depleted of sufficient manpower.

Whatever preparations the Arabs had made for a prolonged siege, they were rendered inadequate by the losses suffered against Leo's *dromons*, the raids of the Bulgars and the harshness of the winter. The need to forage in an already-depleted Thrace made the Arabs more vulnerable to Bulgar attacks, ranging further and further from their defensive positions. The miserable conditions of cold and depleting food supplies rendered the Arab host increasingly impotent against Bulgar raids, Roman sallies, and the walls of Constantinople. Theophanes suggests that, through the hardships they faced, the Arabs came to 'learn by experience that God and the all-holy Virgin, the Mother of God, protect this City and the Christian Empire.'[97] The Arabs could certainly be susceptible to such ideas, given how the launching of the expedition itself had an air of prophetic destiny.

However, for all the seeming direness of their position through the winter of 717/718, there is little hint of Arab capitulation; they proved willing to endure those hardships to secure the victory that was thought to be ahead. It might also be asked where any deserters could conceivably have gone … Bulgar and Roman raiders would have picked off any looking to disappear into Europe, while the Dardanelles, Sea of Marmara and the Bosphorus formed an impregnable barrier (unless they fancied a Byron-esque swim) for those looking to escape to Asia.

Help the Cause and Defect

Arab faith in the expedition and Maslamah's leadership was rewarded when spring came. Their farming endeavours in Thrace proved successful and reinforcements were finally able to arrive at the Sea of Marmara, bringing much needed manpower and supplies. These reinforcements were comprised of three separate forces, two fleets and one army. The larger of the two relief fleets, that of Sufyan, came from Egypt and was comprised of supposedly 400 warships and *katenai* laden with men, supplies and arms. Upon his arrival, Sufyan was informed of the threat posed by Leo's Greek fire-wielding *dromons* and so took his fleet to Kalos Agros, near the mouth of the Gulf of Nicomedia on the Asian side of the Sea of Marmara. The second Arab relief fleet of 360 supply-laden *katenai* arrived from Africa under the command of Yezid. He too steered clear of the city, anchoring at Satyros, Bryas and Kartalimen on the Asian shore of the Sea of Marmara (the latter is some 30 miles from Constantinople). The third wing of Umar's reinforcements was an army marching through the Cilician Gates overland under the command of Mardasan. By the time Sufyan and Yezid had arrived at Constantinople, Mardasan's army had passed Iconium and was approaching Nicaea.

While these forces looked to have tipped the balance in favour of Maslamah, bringing with them much needed manpower and resources, the fleets brought a whole other problem with them – mass desertion. The source of this issue was that in recruiting their naval expeditions, Sufyan and Yezid had made extensive use of Egyptian Christians. This was problematic because, while they had little love for the 'imperial orthodoxy' of Constantinople, the Egyptians were increasingly annoyed at Umayyad rule. In religious terms, the promise of freedom of worship for the Egyptian Christians was no longer being lived up to.[98] Furthermore, being a rich and well-populated province, the burden of war fell heavily upon Egypt. The Arab taxes imposed on conquered peoples – the *risq*, which provided supplies for the military, and the *andrismos*, which was a poll tax to be paid by all males over 14 – were also increasingly burdensome. Sulayman is said to have ordered his Egyptian governor and tax collectors to extract as much material as possible, no matter how much it pained the peoples of Egypt, to build ships, man them, provide resources for resupply, and skilled workers to maintain the ships. The burden was so heavy and unpopular that it was said to be worse than that imposed on Israel by Pharaoh.[99]

With the walls of the great Christian capital before them, these untrained and unwilling Egyptian conscripts decided that they could not partake in an attack on Constantinople. This was not a decision they will have taken lightly. Desertion or defection would have seen them all face death should Constantinople fall and even in victory, they could never go home, and their families may have faced punishment for their treachery. Despite these considerations, during the night when they had been assigned watch duty,[100] the Egyptian crews stole away in many of the smaller craft and *katenai* of Sufyan's fleet, sailing across to Constantinople, where they proclaimed their support for Leo.[101] The loss of so many crewmen, ships, and likely some supplies will have had a detrimental effect on Arab morale and naval capabilities, while bolstering those of the Romans; however, the most important aspect of the Egyptian defection was something else that they brought with them: intelligence.

The defectors told Leo where the various Arab fleets were anchored in the Gulf of Nicomedia and around the Asian coast of the Sea of Marmara, many in small, unprotected ports. Buoyed by both the defection and the knowledge that his *dromons* could inflict significant damage on the Arab fleets, Leo seized this opportunity. He sent out his Greek fire-equipped ships to attack the fleets of Sufyan and Yezid. Emerging from the Golden Horn, the Roman fleet wrought such havoc that they captured significant amounts of Arab supplies as well as destroy significant numbers of Arab ships.[102] Such was the impact of this strike and the enfeeblement of the Arab fleet through defection and destruction, that it could be said that this victory effectively ended the blockade of Constantinople. Roman fishing boats began plying their trade in the waters around the capital again, lines of communication were reopened with the rest of the empire, and reinforcements and supplies could move in and out of the capital once more.

Perhaps the most important military development of the re-establishing of Roman control of the Bosphorus and parts of the Sea of Marmara was that it allowed Leo to send some forces under *basilikoi* (imperial officers) to Bithynia, where they joined up with Opsikon forces. These thematic forces had been harassing Arab positions along the Asian coast of the Hellespont, Sea of Marmara and the Bosphorus. But their reinforcing from the capital allowed them to launch a more audacious attack. As the newly-arrived Arab army of Mardasan was operating between Nicaea and Nicomedia, the reinforced Opsikon forces staged an ambush and Mardasan marched straight into it. As there are two positions of ambush mentioned – Libos and Sophon – it could be that Mardasan marched past a Roman force in hiding. He then found his way blocked by another and when he engaged this force, the Romans sprung the trap, with the bypassed army falling upon the Arab rear. Under this pressure, the Arab army broke into pieces and the remnants were forced to withdraw from western Asia Minor.[103]

This combination of naval and land victory effectively secured the Roman reclamation of the waterways between Europe and Asia, marking the decisive turning point of the siege of Constantinople. So quickly had the relief fleets been destroyed that it appears that they may have brought little relief to Maslamah's depleted army and navy. And the defeat of Mardasan and the reinforcing of the Opsikon made sure that Maslamah's men, already suffering from the deprivations of the winter, were completely cut off from any lines of resupply, with his original fleet in no shape to challenge the Roman navy's control of the straits. Soon, any respite the spring harvest had brought was used up and it is here that

Theophanes speaks of their eating of pack animals, human flesh and bread made from dung.[104] Even allowing for some exaggeration, circumstances in the Arab camp were clearly dire and it comes as no surprise that it was recorded facing the Four Horseman of the Apocalypse once more as Famine and Pestilence rejoined War and Death: combining together they 'killed an infinite number of them.'[105] Theophanes would have it that this Arab tale of woe was compounded by a significant defeat of an Arab force of 22,000, likely the screening force of Sharahil b. Abd, by the Bulgars.[106] Again, the chronology of this defeat is not clear, but it would not be at all surprising to find Arab forces foraging further and further into Bulgar territory and coming to grief as a result.

Nothing to Do but Retreat

The whole expedition was on the verge of collapse: the men were starving and hemmed in by their own defences between Romans and Bulgars; the remnant of the fleet was increasingly unseaworthy, never mind in any state to challenge the imperial navy. Maslamah appears to have stopped sending updates back to the caliph,[107] with Umar II, annoyed by the deafening silence emanating from Constantinople, despatching an emissary to inquire about the situation. In response to this caliphal order for information, Maslamah sent Umar what was considered a 'letter full of lies,'[108] claiming the army was in excellent condition and that the city was about to fall.[109] The emissary reported the truth to Umar with the caliph reputedly weeping at their plight. Umar therefore decided that it was time to cut their losses and sent an emissary to Maslamah with a letter ordering the general to 'Leave that place, lest you and all that are with you should die of hunger!'[110] The caliph also sent supplies with his emissary, but only to facilitate the retreat to Syria. Knowing his general's fighting spirit, Umar also empowered his emissary to bypass Maslamah and take the order directly to the Arab army and fleet should Maslamah make any move to ignore it. Indeed, Maslamah does seem to have made some attempt to hide the order to retreat, but word of Umar's order reached the soldiery, which was overjoyed at the news that they were going home.[111] Maslamah begged for just a few more days to capture the city, only for Umar's emissary to reply 'No, by God, not an hour.'[112]

Even though he still thought to implore Umar for more time, another story from the last days of the siege seems to show that Maslamah recognised that his opportunity to take the Roman imperial capital had passed. Keen to see what he had failed to acquire, the Arab general asked the emperor for an interview within the city walls. Magnanimous in his unfolding victory, Leo allowed Maslamah to enter Constantinople with a personal guard of 30 horsemen. The

Arab general was shown around the imperial capital, marvelling at its sites. He was then 'dismissed and left the city with nothing accomplished'.[113]

And with that, Maslamah followed his orders and struck camp. On the 15 August 718, the great siege of Constantinople was over.[114] It had been a significant failure given the time, effort, and resources put into it. The Arabs had lost large numbers of men and ships through attrition, the harsh winter, the destructive power of the Greek fire-fuelled imperial fleet, and the attacks by Roman and Bulgar forces. And there was still worse to come. While there is no record of Roman strikes against the retreating Arabs – to the point that we might speculate that there was some kind of agreement between Leo and Maslamah – it would seem unlikely that the Arab retreat to the coast, particularly if they did not all take ship at Hebdomon but rather headed back to Sestus, faced some harassment from either the Romans or the Bulgars. Having finally made it to sea, the Arab fleet was pulverised by a fierce storm in the Sea of Marmara, which saw many of its ships wrecked on the islands and promontories of the area. Those ships that made it to the Aegean Sea might have expected that the worst was over. Far from it.

They were struck by a storm of hail – but this was not a hail of the meteorological type. It was not even a hail of missiles from a pursuing imperial fleet. It was instead a 'fiery hail… [which] brought the sea-water to a boil, and as the pitch of their keels dissolved, their ships sank in the deep, crews and all.'[115] We might scoff at what seems like apocalyptic, divine wrath being visited on enemies of Christianity, but the early-eighth century was a period of significant volcanic activity in the Aegean.[116] The remnants of Umar's fleet being battered by waves caused by seismic activity and pummelled by 'flaming hail' being spewed from 'the fiery furnace… between the islands of Thera and Therasia'[117] is by no means beyond the realms of credulity.

Perhaps less believable is the sheer level of destruction reputedly inflicted upon the Arab fleet during the entire expedition and the subsequent withdrawal. Theophanes records that only ten ships of the 2,500 of the original expeditionary force and the relief fleets made it out of the Aegean. A further attack by the Romans, presumably naval forces situated in southern Asia Minor, reduced this Arab remnant to just five ships to limp home to tell their sorry tale of the strength of Constantinople's walls, the barbarity of the Bulgars, the byzantine scheming of Leo and the burning napalm death of the sea being on fire. Of course, we may doubt such catastrophic casualty rates. Had the Arabs lost the virtual entirety of the expeditionary navy and its relief fleets, we would surely expect to hear more about Roman activity in re-establishing their presence in the Aegean and eastern Mediterranean. But even if we doubt the sheer scale of the reported Arab losses, there is no getting away from how the expedition and the withdrawal was a disaster for the Arab navy.

While the Arabs could point to the poor luck of bad weather and volcanic activity ruining their retreating fleet, the collapse of their fleet might have been partially self-inflicted. The Arabs had needed to cannibalise their ships and their maintenance supplies for fuel in the harsh winter; however, the suggestions that their ships had fallen into disrepair within months of their arrival at Constantinople could point to how they were not newly-constructed or were poorly constructed. The lack of specialists that the Arabs faced with the Roman 'brain-drain' and some refusing to serve them could explain either of the latter: the Arabs may still have lacked the expertise to build quality ships themselves and so had to rely on captured Roman vessels of increasing age, which said lack of expertise meant they could not maintain. Even the volcanic activity destroying caulk could be more evidence of shoddy building and maintenance issues.

While it was certainly disastrous, the Umayyad retreat was not an unmitigated disaster. Maslamah himself survived to return to Syria, so either he was immensely fortunate to be on one of the 'five' ships that survived the expedition or there was another avenue of Arab retreat – overland through Anatolia. We have seen that there were Arab forces active in the coastal regions of the Opsikon, securing supply lines to Maslamah's forces, and they could have helped a section of Maslamah's land forces cross to Asia and retreat overland. However, we have also seen that these Arab positions in the Opsikon were vulnerable to raids from Roman forces still present there, a vulnerability only increased by Leo's transferring of reinforcements to Asia after the breaking of the blockade of Constantinople. This was shown in the defeat of Mardasan and his relief army.

Therefore, as it crossed Asia Minor, the remnant of the Arab expedition may have faced harassment from Roman thematic forces; however, it does not seem that Leo and his *strategoi* made any attempt to force anything approaching a full-scale battle. This was perhaps because more of the Arab expedition survived to the end of the siege than might be thought. Certainly, Maslamah did not arrive back in Syria alone. And as we have seen, Umar II sent supplies to help the retreat, including horses and mules. The caliph had also allocated 10 gold coins per man and put out a call to his empire and the families of the men on the expedition to send provisions to help them return home. The problems with the record of the size of the expedition and its reinforcements, coupled now with the exaggeration or silence on the casualties it endured, make it virtually impossible to give any viable figures for the losses Maslamah's army and fleet faced. Later Arab sources would claim that the expedition cost the caliphate 150,000 men and 'while certainly inflated, [this figure] is nevertheless indicative of the enormity of the disaster in medieval eyes'.[118]

Reasons for Defeat

The siege of Constantinople in 717–718 'was the first battle for almost a century in which eastern Roman rulers … at the head of their army had defeated an invader so decisively.'[119] But what were the reasons for this turn around? It may be that, for all their preparation, the Arabs did not have sufficient stores to survive the extended length of the siege. Perhaps Maslamah had not planned for it to last that long or had underestimated the task at hand. It could be that the defences of Constantinople, when in good order and well-manned, were too strong for the military technology of the time. That said, Maslamah could not have legislated for the harshness of the winter and the devastation it would wreak on his men and supplies. Maslamah could also not have done much with the defection of the Egyptian crews of Sufyan and Yezid, but that reliance on so much conscripted manpower was a weakness of the expedition. Another weakness may have been a lack of preparation for dealing with Greek fire, although such a problem may be falling into the possibly ill-founded notion that Greek fire was the decisive weapon in the Roman naval victory, rather than Leo's ability to take advantage of the opportunities presented to him by the weather and defections. Another misstep that could be attributable to the upper echelons of the Umayyad hierarchy as a whole was the failure to shut down the threat the Bulgars and Slavs posed. Maslamah and his commanders on the ground – Suleiman, Umar, Sharahil, al-Bakhtari, al-Battal etc. – may then have exacerbated that problem by failing to restrain their men from raiding Bulgar territory through arrogant carelessness or increasing necessity of supplies. Dealing with the Bulgars/Slavs proved an unwanted diversion of attention and resources.

However, perhaps Maslamah's greatest misstep was putting too much faith in his dealings with Leo. Allowing himself to be lured into viewing him as a personal client who would betray Constantinople to the caliphate might have seen the Arabs miss opportunities to press the siege more successfully. Such a view became increasingly irrational as Leo traded up from *strategos* to emperor, but it seems that Maslamah was an honourable man unwilling to assume anything dishonourable from his 'client'. Or it could be that he could not bring himself to fully accept how seriously he had been outwitted by his supposed puppet emperor. The *Kitab al-Uyan* hints that while a valiant man, Maslamah lacked suitable counsel within himself and amongst his companions.[120] For all his skill and success as a general, could it have been that Maslamah was not the man for this specific job, particularly when there was a diplomatic angle?

For all the potential missteps by Maslamah and the Arab expedition as a whole, we must not overlook the skilled operating of Leo III in the run up to and during the siege. Even if there was initially some collusion with Suleiman/Maslamah, either to secure his position at Amorion or even to jumpstart his imperial accession, Leo used it successfully to delay, distract, and delude the Arab commanders. The Bulgar involvement may also highlight the success of Roman diplomacy. Militarily, the emperor and his admirals made excellent use of the opportunities presented by the weather and Egyptian defection to inflict enough damage and fear on the Arab navy to first slacken and then effectively break the Umayyad blockade of the city. While there is little record of action along the walls, Leo and his commanders must have maintained sufficient discipline amongst the Roman defenders, despite the deprivations they themselves faced, to prevent the Arabs making any headway.

But we cannot just focus on Leo III himself and his regime. He may have provided stout and skilful leadership in a time of ultimate crisis and his troops carried out those orders bravely in defence of their capital, but the contribution of the likes of Justinian II, Anastasius II and Theodosius III cannot be overlooked. All three were far more useful and/or competent than might first be thought due to the circumstances of their reigns. In providing the diplomatic, fiscal, military, naval, defensive and organisational reform and repair basis which Leo built upon, these men helped bring about the Roman victory over Maslamah. Specifically, it could be said that the repulsing of the Arabs was as much a logistical victory as it was a military or naval one, with the reducing of the population, building up of stores, and having some capability of providing food inside the city.[121]

Unsurprisingly, the likes of Theophanes do not give Leo the credit for the successful defence of Constantinople in 717–718, attributing it instead to 'intercession of the all-pure Theotokos [Virgin Mary].'[122] This might seem like an iconodule historian denying a supposed iconoclast emperor his due credit, but it may reflect public belief in the immediate aftermath of the rebuffing of the siege. Indeed, it appears that 'the capital's citizens were not quick to give credit where credit was due.'[123] Leo III is absent from the annual anniversary eulogy given by patriarch Germanos. If this reflects a growing belief in the divine protection of Constantinople and by extension the Roman Empire as a whole at the expense of imperial authority, might this partially explain some of the religious policies embraced by the Isaurian dynasty in the coming years?[124]

The Umayyad failure to capture Constantinople, together with Frankish resistance that culminated in the Battle of Tours/Poitiers in 732, is usually thought to be the high-water mark of the Islamic advance against the empire and into Europe. However, while there should be no underestimating the importance of the Second Arab Siege of Constantinople – it represented 'the climactic episode in the initial bout of warfare between two great monotheistic religions'[125] – we must be careful in presenting this as a truly epochal event in Romano-Arab interactions. There was a noticeable shift in said interactions. The failure at Constantinople was most certainly a great calamity for the Umayyad caliphate, with the devastating losses of manpower and material it suffered contributing to 'the waning of Arab pressure'[126] on Roman Anatolia. But while there was 'some stuttering in the Muslim war machine'[127] and Maslamah's expedition was the last Arab attempt to conquer the Roman Empire 'with a single, convulsive battle,'[128] this does not represent a major sea-change in Arab strategy. If anything, the retreat to the Taurus Mountains, which were to delineate the Romano-Muslim frontier for most of the next four centuries, and the recommencing of annual raids soon after, with the occasional Roman counterstrike, are themselves the *status quo*. The grand expedition against Constantinople in 717–718 was the deviation from the norm. The Muslim Arab world had come to see the Roman Empire 'as a foe to be treated with respect, and as a neighbour who was not about to disappear.'[129]

Some of the Arab sources attempted to play down the defeat before Constantinople in 717–718 – 'the reality... was masked by a blast of propaganda about Umar II as an exemplary Islamic ruler, pious and determined to improve the religious and social ordering of the world he governed.'[130] We have already seen the prophetic nature that the fall of Constantinople had taken on with the name of Sulayman and the year 100 in the Muslim calendar; the survival of the city in 717–718 and the general resilience of the Roman state only exacerbated the apocalyptic connotations. But those same Muslim failures saw the fall of Constantinople be projected further and further into the future, as well as it becoming a central sign, alongside the fall of Jerusalem, of the end times in Islamic eschatology and Christian apocalyptic literature.[131] Umar II's inward social and religious focus after the failure at Constantinople may also mask internal tensions the Umayyad caliphate faced dynastically and provincially. The loss of manpower and resources involved in Maslamah's expedition can only have upped any pre-existing pressure.

This inward focus by the Umayyads presented an opportunity to the Romans. They had shown themselves capable of military, diplomatic, and organisational defiance and with the confidence their successful resistance brought, within a year, there was some attempt to take the fight to the Umayyads. The Asian thematic armies reclaimed the territory evacuated by the retreating Arabs, while the Anatolic and Armeniac armies pressured remaining Arab possessions north of the Taurus, with the caliph ordering the fortification of Cilician Mopsuestia and Armenian Melitene. There may also have been a naval attack on Laodicea in northern Syria, which carried off a large section of its population. The Romans could have made more of Arab weakness post-718, not only in the form of raids similar to that on Laodicea, but also perhaps reclaiming some islands and coastal regions.[132] As it was, Leo was more concerned with asserting control over his empire. Events in and around the capital suggest that even with his victory over Maslamah, Leo's rule was not fully accepted in the empire.

Chapter 7

Internal Enemies: The Rebellions Against Leo III

'An empire toppled by its enemies can rise again. But one that crumbles from within, that's dead. Forever.'

Helmut Zemo, *Captain America: Civil War* (2016)

Dynastic Developments

In the successful resistance of his imperial capital against Maslamah's expedition, it might be thought that something of a crescendo has been reached in the story covered by this book – but as the reader can tell, we are not even half through. That is because as the Arab expedition slunk its way back to Syria in late summer 718, it was still only 18 months into Leo III's reign, a reign that was to last 24 years. Given that Leo was to have such a prolonged imperial tenure, it might also be expected that the great victory over the Arab expedition marked the end of the period of so-called 'military anarchy' that had so crippled the Roman Empire for the previous two decades. However, Leo's accession and victory over Maslamah did not bring an end to internal challenges to the emperor's position.

That Leo recognised the precariousness of his political position, even without the massive Arab army literally knocking at his door throughout much of 717 and 718, can be seen in his dynastic moves around the same time as the siege. We have already met Leo's wife, Maria and have already brought up some of the chronological issues regarding when they might have been married. Indeed, there is little information regarding Maria at all, despite her being the Roman empress and officially crowned *Augusta* on 25 December 718.[1] We do know that she and Leo had four children and it is the two eldest who are the most prominent in the dynastic moves surrounding Leo III early in his reign.

Their first child was a daughter called Anna. Much like her mother, there is little information about most of Anna's life. Her date of birth is unrecorded and can only be inferred from her role in the dynastic arrangements made by her father. A significant part of Leo's rise to power had been his alliance with the Armeniac *strategos*, Artabasdos, and part of that agreement was the promise that Artabasdos would marry Anna – 'a promise [Leo] carried out.'[2] There is no record of when that marriage occurred, but Theophanes has it take place 'after [Leo] had become emperor'[3] and coupled to Artabasdos' elevation to *kouroplates* – 'master of the palace' – a promotion that cannot have happened *before* Leo's elevation to emperor on 25 March 717.

We might ask why there was a delay in the marriage between Anna and Artabasdos had it been contracted at least a couple of years before it took place. The political and military situation in Anatolia and Constantinople would certainly present difficult enough circumstances to prevent it from happening, but it could be that Anna was not yet of marriageable age when the alliance between her father and future husband was initially made. While solid dating material is lacking, the likelihood is that Leo himself was only just over 30 at the time of his accession. This in turn increases the likelihood that Anna was in her teens at that point, as well as the possibility that she was initially not old enough to marry Artabasdos. Whatever its circumstances, the marriage between Anna and Artabasdos would be a fruitful one, producing up to nine children; however, that marriage would also help bring about further rebellion against an Isaurian emperor.

That Isaurian emperor is the other of Leo and Maria's two eldest children – their son, Constantine V. Again, an exact date for his birth is not recorded, but it does seem to have occurred in mid-718, possibly 13 years or more after the birth of Anna. Theophanes refers to Constantine's birth at the beginning of AM6211, which covers the period 1 September 718 – 31 August 719, while Nikephoros merely places it just before the lifting of the siege of Constantinople on 15 August 718 in his text.[4] The latter is usually preferred, but the suggestion that Maria gave birth in July 718 is only a supposition. Even with the lack of clear dating, it would seem that the entirety of Maria's pregnancy with Constantine took place during the siege of Constantinople. The birth of a new heir to the throne can only have provided a boon to the Constantinopolitan defenders privy to the information.

That Leo and Maria would seek to have another child is not surprising – at this point, Leo was relying on Artabasdos to be his heir, reflected in the latter's promotion to *kouroplates*[5] – but the timing, with the 'barbarians' at the gate, raises contrary thoughts of desperation or confidence. The conception of Constantine is likely to have taken place relatively early in the siege and could correspond to either when things looked their bleakest, with the capital surrounded by Maslamah's army and navy, or when there was a significant ray of hope with Leo's initial victory over the Arab naval rear-guard at the mouth of the Golden Horn.

ABD AL-MALIK: gold aniconic dinar, issued in AH80 (699–700) from the Damascus mint. *Courtesy of Noble Numismatics* (http://www.noble.com.au/)

JUSTINIAN II: (second reign, 705–711): gold *solidus*, issued in 705 from the Constantinople mint. Obverse: facing bust of Christ, with cross behind head, curly hair and close beard, wears pallium and colobium, raising hand in benediction, dN IhS ChS REX REGNANTIUM. Reverse: crowned facing bust of Justinian, wearing loros and holding crosses, DN IUSTINIA NUS MULTUS A, PAX. *Courtesy of Classical Numismatic Group, Inc.* (http://www.cngcoins.com)

LIUTPRAND: gold *tremissis* issued during his reign (712–744) from the Pavia mint. Obverse: bust looking right, DN LI TPRAN; P in right field. Reverse: St Michael standing left, SCS MIHHIL, holding long cross and shield. *Courtesy of Classical Numismatic Group, Inc.* (http://www.cngcoins.com)

Al-WALID I: gold aniconic dinar, issued in AH94–95 (713) from the Damascus mint. *Courtesy of Noble Numismatics* (http://www.noble.com.au/)

PHILIPPIKOS BARDANES: gold *solidus*, issued between 711 and 713 from the Constantinople mint. Obverse: facing and crowned bust of Philippikos, DN FILIPICЧS MЧL TЧS [AN], wearing loros, holding cross globe and eagle-tipped sceptre. Reverse: cross on steps, VICTORIA AЧGЧ Z/CONOB. *Courtesy of Classical Numismatic Group, Inc.* (http://www.cngcoins.com)

ANASTASIUS II: gold *solidus*, issued between 713 and 715 from the Constantinople mint. Obverse: facing, crowned and draped bust of Anastasius, ∂ N APTЄMIЧS A NASTASIЧS MЧL, holding cross globe and akakia. Reverse: cross on steps, VICTORIA AЧGЧ ΘΘ/ CONOB. *Courtesy of Classical Numismatic Group, Inc.* (http:// www.cngcoins.com)

THEODOSIUS III: gold *solidus*, issued between 715 and 717 from the Constantinople mint. Obverse: facing crowned bust, ∂ N TհЄO∂O SIЧS MЧL A, wearing loros, and holding akakia and cross globus. Reverse: cross on steps, VICTORIA AЧGЧ H/ CONOB. (© *Otto Nickl*)

SULAYMAN: gold aniconic dinar, issued in AH97 (715–716) from the Damascus mint. *Courtesy of Classical Numismatic Group, Inc.* (http://www.cngcoins.com)

LEO III: gold *solidus*, issued between 717–720 from the Constantinople mint. Obverse: facing crowned and draped bust, ∂ N D LEO N PA MЧL, holding cross globe and akakia. Reverse: cross on steps, VICTOR[IA AVGЧ Δ/CONOB. *Courtesy of Noble Numismatics* (http://www.noble.com.au/)

LEO III and CONSTANTINE V: gold *solidus*, issued between 737–741 from the Constantinople mint. Obverse: facing crowned bust of Leo, ∂ N D LEO N PA MЧL N, wearing chlamys and holding cross globe and akakia. Reverse: facing crowned bust of Constantine, ∂ N CONS TANTINЧ Θ, wearing chlamys and holding cross globe and akakia. *Courtesy of Classical Numismatic Group, Inc.* (http://www.cngcoins.com)

LEO III and CONSTANTINE V: silver *miliaresion*, issued between 720 and 741 from the Constantinople mint. Obverse: cross on steps, IhSUS XRISTЧS NICA. Reverse: LEON/ S CONST/ANTINE E/ C**QEЧ bA/ SILIS. *Courtesy of Noble Numismatics* (http://www.noble.com.au/)

UMAR II: gold aniconic dinar, issued in AH101 (719–720) from Damascus mint. *Courtesy of MANTIS* (http://numismatics.org/collection/1971.49.297)

YAZID II: silver aniconic dirham, issued in AH103 (721–722) from Damascus mint. *Courtesy of Classical Numismatic Group, Inc.* (http://www.cngcoins.com)

TIBERIUS PETASIUS: gold *solidus* issued in 728 or 730–731 from a mint in Blera or Naples. Obverse: facing, crowned bust, ∂ N TIЧERIЧS MЧLTЧS A, wearing chlamys and holding cross globe and akakia. Reverse: cross on steps, VICTOR IVTGTA(?)/CONOB. *Courtesy of Classical Numismatic Group, Inc.* (http://www.cngcoins.com)

HISHAM: gold aniconic dinar, issued in AH119 (737) from the Damascus mint. *Courtesy of MANTIS* (http://numismatics.org/collection/1917.215.3401)

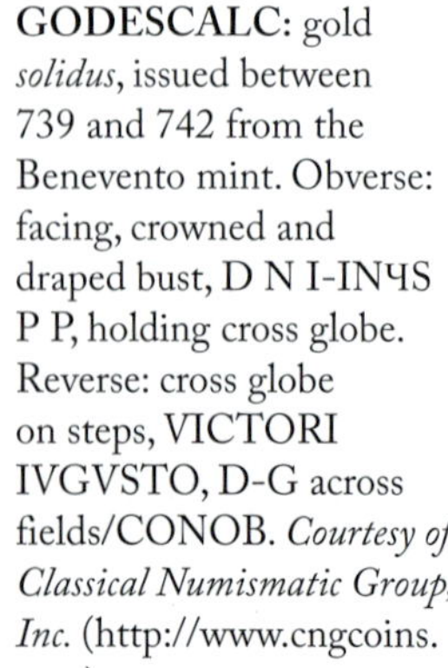

GODESCALC: gold *solidus*, issued between 739 and 742 from the Benevento mint. Obverse: facing, crowned and draped bust, D N I-INЧS P P, holding cross globe. Reverse: cross globe on steps, VICTORI IVGVSTO, D-G across fields/CONOB. *Courtesy of Classical Numismatic Group, Inc.* (http://www.cngcoins.com)

CONSTANTINE V and LEO IV: gold *solidus* issued between 751 and 757 from the Constantinople mint. Obverse: facing crowned busts of Constantine V and Leo IV, CONSTANTINOIS S LEON O NEOS, wearing chlamys, cross above. Reverse: facing bust of Leo III, ∂ LE ON PA MЧL, holding cross potent. *Courtesy of Noble Numismatics* (http://www.noble.com.au/)

ARTABASDOS: gold *solidus*, issued between 742 and 743 from Constantinople mint. Obverse: facing, crowned and draped bust of Artabasdos, ∂ APTAЧA-SDOS MЧLT, holding patriarchal cross. Reverse: facing, crowned and draped bust of Nikephoros, ∂ NIChFORЧS MЧLTЧM, holding patriarchal cross. *Courtesy of Classical Numismatic Group, Inc.* (http://www.cngcoins.com)

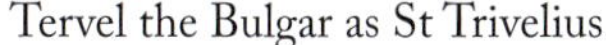

Tervel the Bulgar as St Trivelius.

Pope Constantine, *Nuremburg Chronicle,* 1493.

Pope Gregory II, *Nuremburg Chronicle,* 1493.

Detail of Chludov Psalter, ninth century, depicting an act of iconoclasm.

'Charles Martel divides the realm between Pepin and Carloman', *Grandes Chroniques de France*, Bibliothèque Nationale, Ms. fr. 2615, fol. 72.

Pope Gregory III, eighth century papal medallion. (© *ASKI*)

Patriarch Germanos.

'Argument about icons', *Codex Skylitzes Matritensis*, fol. 50vb.

'The fleet of the Romans setting ablaze the fleet of the enemies', *Codex Skylitzes Matritensis*, fol. 34vb.

'The Arabs attacking Constantinople during the reign of emperor Leo III', Constantine Manasses, *Chronicle*, miniature 47.

Inscription commemorating the successful defence of Nicaea and the restoration of its walls.

The birth of a male child was a great benefit to the Isaurian dynasty. And once he had survived his first few months, a grand state occasion was held on Christmas Day 718 to celebrate the coronation of Maria as *Augusta* and the baptism of Constantine. Maria's crowning took place in the triklinos dining room of the Augusteion, and after she had prayed alone, the new *Augusta* joined the emperor in the baptistery, where Constantine was baptised by patriarch Germanos. While he would go on to be a long-lived and successful Roman emperor, it is Constantine V's supposed involuntary actions at his infant baptism that had the most lasting influence on his reputation. 'The boy because he was so young, gave a terrible, foul-smelling harbinger: he defecated in the holy font.'[6] This is the origin of Constantine's derisive nickname – *Kopronymos*: 'the Dung-named.' This unfortunate incident led Germanos to supposedly declare 'this is a sign that in the future, great evil shall befall the Christians and the church because of him.' This declaration seems unlikely given the presence of the imperial couple and is tinged with the benefit of hindsight regarding the religious policies connected to Leo and Constantine. Despite the soiling of the baptismal font and the patriarchal prophecy of Christian doom, Constantine was shown off to the Senate and leaders of the themes as their new imperial heir. Together with her son, Maria listened to the divine liturgy and then travelled from the church to the Chalke Gate of the palace, distributing largesse to the people.

Constantine's position as the heir apparent would be further secured on Easter Day 720, when he was crowned co-emperor in the Tribunal of the Nineteen Akkubita, a ceremonial banquet hall on the western side of the palace of Constantine I. Again, there is a dating issue, with Nikephoros claiming he was crowned 'on the 25th of March of the 3rd indiction (which was the day of Christ's salutary resurrection);'[7] however, Easter would have been on 31 March in 720.[8] There is another slight difference between Nikephoros and Theophanes on the coronation of Constantine V, with the latter stating that he was crowned by his father Leo, while the former claims that Germanos carried it out. Constantine began to appear on the reverse of Leo's coinage, replacing the cross portent, and he would reign alongside his father until the latter's death in 741, succeeding him (not without challenge) and then ruling in his own right until 775. From a dynastic point of view, the Roman imperial succession appeared to have some security to it.

There had been some other significant dynastic changes by the coronation of Constantine V. In early February 720, after falling ill on a journey from Damascus to Aleppo, Umar II died after a reign of only 28 months. The succession plan that had been put in place by Sulayman came to fruition, with Umar succeeded by another son of Abd al-Malik, Yazid II. His reign was immediately faced by a serious rebellion in Persia under Yazid b. Muhullab.[9] The new caliph reacted quickly, dispatching Maslamah east to put down the revolt and bring Persia back under Umayyad control. The brutality of that subjection would not only come back to haunt the Umayyad dynasty with revenge for the Muhallabs being a rallying cry for the Abbasid revolt, it may also have encouraged more militaristic tendencies in Yazid II's reign, veering away from the reformist polices of Umar II. The *jizya* poll tax on non-Arab Muslim converts was reimposed, with significant opposition in Khurasan and Africa, while there was more fighting against Romans, Khazars and Franks.

The third competitor of the siege of Constantinople – the Bulgar khanate – may also have seen a transition of ruler. We have already seen the issues with the Bulgar succession around this time, specifically with the date of Tervel's death. He may still have been alive by the time of Constantine V's coronation, but not for long, with the latest date for Tervel's reign given as 721, when he was succeeded either by Komesiey or Sevar.

The 'Loyalist' Usurpation of Basil Tiberius in Sicily

The first rebellion faced by Leo was somewhat different to the rebellions that had punctuated the 'Twenty's Years Anarchy'. Upon hearing of the enormity of the Arab army and fleet besieging Constantinople, and becoming increasingly worried by the totality of the communication blackout emanating from the imperial capital as a result, the Sicilian *strategos*, Sergios the *protospatharios*, had a certain Basil, son of Gregory Onomagoulus and a native of Constantinople, crowned as another emperor Tiberius.[10] While Basil Tiberius was to be the 'emperor', that he only 'appointed his own dignitaries with the consent of … Sergius'[11] suggests where the power lay in this Sicilian usurpation. This may not be just another attempt to take the imperial throne away from an unpopular emperor or an opportunistic power grab by an ambitious commander. There is a possibility that there was a 'loyalist' streak to this usurpation – Sergios may have heard rumours of the impending capture of the imperial capital and so was not acting against Leo III, but raising his own emperor to provide some imperial continuity in the face of the loss of Constantinople. Might he have viewed the elevation of Basil Tiberius as being the only way to maintain the existence of the Roman Empire?

Regardless, this was a challenge to Leo's imperial rule. Therefore, once he was able, Leo reacted by turning to a member of his own household, Paul the *chartularius*, 'a faithful friend and experienced in military matters.'[12] Paul was promoted to both patrician[13] and *strategos* of Sicily and dispatched from Constantinople with imperial orders for the thematic forces of Sicily and a *sacra* to be read to the people. Together with a band of followers, including two *spatharii*, Paul stole out of Constantinople in a *dromon* by night, making for Cyzicus. From there, this small expeditionary force travelled across both land and sea, avoiding Arab and Slav forces, to eventually arrive in Sicily. Such was the speed of his arrival that Paul and his crew achieved complete surprise with their arrival in Syracuse. Sergios was so surprised at this imperial delegation's existence, let alone its arrival, that he fled the island, crossing over to territory that the Lombard duke of Benevento held in Calabria. Theophanes states that Sergios fled without a fight because he 'recognised his own guilt,'[14] which can be somewhat ambiguous in terms of motive – recognition, despite his own good intentions, of the official imperial representative or that his powerplay had been foiled – although ultimately either reflects a fear of execution.

Having assumed control of Syracuse, Paul read the imperial *sacra* to a congregation of the people and army, which informed them that Constantinople still held firm, as impregnable as ever, against the Arabs and had recently won great victories over the two relief fleets of Sufyan and Yezid. Their faith in the empire restored, the people and army of Syracuse reaffirmed their allegiance to Leo III and surrendered Basil Tiberius and his officials to Paul. The new *strategos* had Basil and his commander-in-chief (possibly the George mentioned by Nikephoros) beheaded; their heads sent to Leo preserved in vinegar in the care of the two *spatharii*. The other members of Basil's brief regime Paul had either beaten, scourged, or their noses cut off before they were sent into exile.

Given this brutal treatment of those who had prominent roles in the attempted usurpation, it might be expected that its instigator would face the worst of it; however, Sergios managed to get away with it. Seeing the ease with which Paul had defeated his usurpation, Sergios promised to surrender himself to the *chartularius* on the promise of safe conduct and immunity, which was granted, his fate going unrecorded. Had he been able to explain to Paul that he had only elevated Basil because he had been told of the fall of Constantinople and acted only for the benefit of the Roman Empire? Both Theophanes and Nikephoros claimed that the subjugation of Basil Tiberius saw 'the affairs of the West returned to peace and tranquillity;'[15] however, we shall see later that Italy was far from 'pacified',[16] with other rebellions and usurpations against the rule of Leo III.

An Attempted Return: Anastasius II

Not long after the end of the Arab siege of Constantinople,[17] an attempted coup was initiated in the two major cities of the empire – Thessalonica and the imperial capital itself. Which of these two was the initial focus of the rebellion depends on which of the sources is relied upon: Theophanes or Nikephoros. On this occasion, it is Nikephoros who provides more information about the latest usurpation faced by Leo III. As it is unlikely that Nikephoros would suddenly find a different source for this one specific incident than that which he shared with Theophanes, it would seem that Theophanes has 'deliberately condensed and altered the narrative.'[18]

Nikephoros has it that the rebellion of 719 originated in Thessalonica, when the deposed and tonsured emperor Anastasius II 'attempted once again to win the empire.'[19] Nothing had been heard from Anastasius II since late 715 and there is no reason to suspect that he had been an active opponent of the regime of his successor. This has not stopped there being an attempt to connect him with a conspiracy by Maurus and Kouver that is recorded, without date, in the *Miracles of St Demetrius*, and in turn connect this conspiracy to the attempt to reinstall Anastasius at the expense of Leo III;[20] however, this has been successfully opposed,[21] with this 'Kouver' possibly to be identified with the Bulgar tribal leader, Kuber, a son of Kubrat and therefore an uncle of Tervel, who was active around the norther Aegean some 40 years before Anastasius' attempted imperial revival.

Anastasius may have felt that the Arab siege and the usurpation of Basil Tiberius had made the government of Leo III appear weak. It might also be remembered that the lack of chronological clarity in this era could see the rebellion of Anastasius II viewed in a similar manner to the supposed 'loyalism' of the revolt of Sergios and Basil Tiberius – the deposed emperor, hearing word of the siege of Constantinople set out to aid the empire, only to be too late. Anastasius may have sought loyalty not just from men in Constantinople who had previously served him, but specifically from the highest profile supposed supporters of his regime – the men he seemingly appointed as Armeniac and Anatolic *strategoi*: the *kouroplates* Artabasdos and the emperor himself, Leo III. Could Anastasius have been hoping there was some truth in Leo's initial reasoning – support for Anastasius II – for resisting the regime of Theodosius III?

According to Nikephoros, from his Thessalonian monastic exile, Anastasius wrote to the patrician Sisinnios Rhendakios, who was in Bulgarian territory on the order of Leo looking to conclude a treaty between the khanate and empire against the Umayyad caliphate. Anastasius asked Sisinnios for help in regaining the throne and to ask the Bulgar khan to provide the military muscle. Sisinnios agreed to try. The deposed emperor also contacted several prominent individuals within Leo's regime stationed in Constantinople: the *magister officiorum* Niketas Xylinites; Theoktistos the *protoasekretis* (principal imperial secretary); Niketas Anthrax, commander of the walls;[22] and Isoes, *comes Opsikon*. Isoes 'may have resented the success of the Anatolic and Armeniac troops in raising Leo to the throne.'[23] He asked for their help to deliver the capital to him, reminding them of their own friendships, which suggests that the accession of Theodosius III and Leo III had not seen much disruption to the imperial hierarchy. However, these epistolary pleas were immediately revealed to the emperor, who had the recipients arrested and tortured into confessing – Xylinites and Theoktistos were executed, while Isoes and Anthrax had their property confiscated and were exiled.

As the Constantinopolitan portion of the rebellion collapsed, Anastasius had had some success in rousing support from the Bulgars through Sisinnios. He had advanced as far as Herakleia at the head of a Bulgar force, with a rudimentary fleet of *monoxyla* boats from Thessalonica shadowing them, possibly hinting at some Slavic involvement. This has led to the suggestion that the Bulgars Sisinnios had been negotiating with were those settled near Thessalonica, rather than those of the khanate.[24] Indeed, Nikephoros does not mention Tervel or either of his potential successors in connection with Anastasius' rebellion, although Theophanes does name Tervel.

Whomever these Bulgars were, their heart was not completely in supporting Anastasius or it was drained out of them as it became apparent that they had been lied to by Sisinnios and Anastasius about the extent of support for their cause in Constantinople. Word may have reached them about the arrest of Anastasius' allies and a general lack of appetite to remove Leo. And when a letter arrived from the emperor offering them a peaceful retreat in return for the handing over of the rebels, they quickly acquiesced. Anastasius, the bishop of Thessalonica and others were surrendered to imperial forces, while Sisinnios was beheaded by the Bulgars (did he know too much?) before they departed home with no imperial consequences.

The rapidity of the Bulgar capitulation could suggest that they had not forsaken any peace they had with the empire. Could it even be that, rather than supporting Anastasius and Niketas, they had always planned to hand over the deposed emperor and his supporters for execution by Leo? This seems a little farfetched, particularly if these are not Tervel's Bulgars. At best, we might suggest that these Bulgars were hedging their bets – providing Anastasius with support, but with enough plausible deniability should the rebellion fail. With the rebels now in his clutches, Leo made a public spectacle of their punishment. Anastasius and the bishop of Thessalonica were beheaded, their heads paraded around the Hippodrome on pikes as part of a large horse race. The other conspirators not yet punished were beaten, their noses mutilated, their possessions confiscated and then exiled.

Not only does Theophanes give a more truncated version of this attempt to reinstall Anastasius II on the throne, he also gives different emphasis to the roles of certain parties involved in it. Rather than Anastasius being the driving force, Theophanes posits Niketas Xylinites as the first mover in the plot. From Constantinople, Niketas wrote to Anastasius in his Thessalonian monastery urging him to go to Tervel and ask for Bulgar backing in overthrowing Leo III. That Anastasius 'consented' to this gives the impression that Niketas was the man in control. There is no mention here of Sisinnios Rhendakios in negotiations with Tervel; only his execution by the Bulgars is mentioned. Indeed, the other named players in Nikephoros' version – Isoes, Theoktistos and Niketas Anthrax – are also only mentioned by Theophanes when they are executed after the failure of the plot. It is Anastasius himself who escapes his monastic custody and travels to the Bulgar court, where he received not only armed support from Tervel, but also 50 *centenaria* of gold – 5,000lbs – only for the Bulgars to betray him to Leo, who 'duly rewarded'[25] them. While we might rely more on Nikephoros' account, the possibility that Theophanes still retains extra information, such as the amount of cash the Bulgars may have provided to Anastasius cannot be dismissed out of hand – it is not the kind of trivia that Theophanes would have invented.

In Theophanes's account, there is no hint of the Bulgars acquiescing to Leo's plea for peace, with them only giving up the usurper and beheading Sisinnios when 'the City did not accept [Anastasius].'[26] The difference in the possible role of the Bulgars between the accounts of Theophanes and Nikephoros was perhaps due to the more heightened anti-Bulgar bias of the former, with him intentionally playing down any actions that might have benefitted the Roman Empire.[27] Even if it is accepted that the Bulgars involved with Anastasius were those of the khanate *and* that they did actually attempt to overthrow Leo, Romano-Bulgar relations remained largely peaceful throughout most of Leo's reign. His son Constantine V would try to take advantage of the in-fighting that broke out at the end of Tervel's dynastic line. This led to a back-and-forth contest between the empire and khanate for dominance in the Balkans, which would continue virtually unabated until the elimination of the Bulgarian Empire in the early-eleventh century. And even that Roman conquest only lasted until the late-twelfth century, with a revived Bulgarian state playing a significant role in Balkan affairs right up to 1422.

Upon his execution, Anastasius II was permitted burial in the mausoleum of Justinian in the Church of the Holy Apostles, seemingly at the behest of his wife, Irene, who was also later buried there.[28] Why might Leo have allowed this exalted final resting place for someone who had rebelled against him? He might have felt magnanimous in victory or even some personal appreciation to Anastasius himself, but Leo's reasoning was surely much more pragmatic in nature. Treating an imperial predecessor with respect not only reflected well on Leo personally, but also on the imperial position itself. It must also not be forgotten that Leo had based a lot of his initial imperial legitimacy on his support for Anastasius II. A total demolition of Anastasius' reputation could therefore reflect poorly on Leo in more than one way. But perhaps the more important reason for his respectful post-mortem treatment of Anastasius II is that the abortive plot to restore him had demonstrated that there was still support for the deposed emperor in the highest offices of state. So while their relationship ended with rebellion and execution, Leo III may have been careful to show respect to his predecessor for fear of damaging his own reputation or stoking opposition.

The attempt to restore Anastasius II may have been a failure, but that should not underestimate the threat that it had posed to the regime of Leo III. While it collapsed before any military confrontation, the areas from where Anastasius derived support – Bulgars, Slavs(?) and high-level officials in Thessalonica and Constantinople – could have been problematic for the emperor. The revealing of the Anastasian correspondence with Xylinites, Anthrax, Theoktistos and Isoes ultimately brought an end to the conspiracy, as it likely dissipated the Bulgar support for the endeavour. However, Leo was fortunate that Isoes' support for the conspiracy was not reflected within the Opsikons. Their strategic position would have enabled them to block Leo's communications with his Anatolic and Armeniac troops. Opsikon and hierarchic opposition in the city, together with Bulgar pressure outside the walls (where they might not have remained for too long if Anthrax was in command of an outer wall), could have proven a significant challenge to Leo's still fledgling regime. As it was, the betrayal of the letters, the emperor's rapid response, and a lack of demand for Leo's replacing/ Anastasius' restoration retained the Isaurian's throne.

'Moved by Divine Zeal': The Thematic Usurpation of Kosmas

The failure of Anastasius II demonstrates that Leo III, in his successful defence of Constantinople, had made some strides in overturning the years of 'anarchy' that had engulfed the imperial position. It would be several years before he was challenged again. When it did come, details are scant. Even the year it took place is unclear, with Theophanes making an error in placing it in his entry for AM6218 (725/726), but then stating that its crescendo took place on 18 April of the 10th indiction, which was in 727. It seems more likely that the latter date is correct if it is taken as read that the destruction of the Brazen House icon, a reputedly major event in the initiation of Leo III's iconoclasm in late-summer/ autumn 726, was a catalyst for the latest revolt faced by that emperor. But as will be seen later, the dates and very initiation of a Leonid iconoclasm are by no means secure. Furthermore, while Theophanes and Nikephoros posit this latest rebellion as being 'moved by divine zeal'[29] due to opposition to iconoclasm, the same dating and iconoclasm origin issues raises scepticism about the rebellion of 726/727 having a religious basis.

There are some details about this latest rebellion that generate much less scepticism. Geographically, its basis was in the Helladic theme of Greece and the Cyclades islands of the Aegean Sea. The Hellas theme was largely focused on Boeotia and Attica and offshore islands like Euboea. There was little penetration into the Greek hinterlands beyond these areas that the Roman navy could help maintain before the early-ninth century. In its foundation by Justinian II, it is possible that the Hellas theme was territory detached from the Karabisianoi with thousands of Mardaites settled in Helladic territory to provide naval manpower,[30] which could have the forces of the Hellas theme heavily weighted in favour of oarsmen over land forces.[31] This infers that, alongside the Cycladic forces, the revolt faced by Leo III in 726/727 had a naval basis.

In some secondary descriptions of this revolt, a Cyclades 'theme' is mentioned, but this is anachronistic as the Cyclades were not incorporated into a fully-fledged Aegean theme until the mid-ninth century. There is some suggestion of specific administrative reorganisation of the Late Roman province of *Provincia Insularum* (ἐπαρχία νήσων/*eparchia nēsōn*) that encompassed the Aegean islands by the early-eighth century. An *apo eparchon* and general *kommerkiarios* of the *apotheke* of the *Aigaion Pelagos* was recorded during the reign of Philippikos Bardanes (711–713), while a *stratelates* and general *kommerkiarios* of the *apotheke* of the Cycladic Islands may have appeared in 687.[32] The Justinianic connection of the Aegean islands to the *quaestor exercitus* also sees the administration of the Cyclades become part of the controversy surrounding the fate of those various regions commanded by this 'quaestor of the army'. Specific to the naval forces of the Cyclades is the argument over the possible transformation of the *quaestura* into the basis for the Karabisianoi 'theme'.[33] The involvement of Cycladic naval units in a rebellion may have encouraged further reorganisation of the imperial navy by Leo III, with the Cyclades becoming part of the first *thema nautikon* of the Kibyrrhaeots.[34]

There are three individuals named as part of the rebellion of 726/727: Kosmas, Stephen and Agallianos Kontoskeles. While he would be the rebellion's imperial candidate, virtually nothing is known about Kosmas. He need not have been a prominent military commander or even a high-level civilian official. He could simply have been a public servant in Greece of middling standing thrust into imperial contention by the thematic military command as a figurehead. But even this is a supposition with no supporting evidence. We have a similar lack of information on Stephen. There is some suggestion that he was a naval commander in the Cyclades, but this is only due to the recorded involvement of those islands in the rebellion and not due to any record in the sources. Indeed, there is little reason why Kosmas was not the Cycladic representative.

The only other individual named in connection with the rebellion of 726/727 is the man about whom we are told the most, although even that is not all that much: Agallianos Kontoskeles (Agallianos the 'short-leg'). Because he is the only one of the three named rebels to have their official position recorded, it is usually inferred that Agallianos was the leader of the rebellion. However, peculiarly, Agallianos was only a *tourmarches* of the Helladic theme, rather than the *strategos*. This could play into the arguments regarding the establishment of the Hellas theme with our source material not referring to Hellas as a theme throughout most of the eighth century, but rather a στρατηγία/*strategia*; they do, however, refer to a Helladic *strategos* as early as 695.[35] Was Agallianos then a mistitled *strategos*? Was there no appointed Helladic *strategos* at this point, with the record of a Helladic *strategos* in 695 an anachronism? Could Kosmas have been *strategos*? Or was Agallianos the *tourmarches* also rebelling against his *strategos* superior? We have no answers.

And why did this naval conglomeration of Helladic and Cycladic forces rebel against Leo III? We have already suggested that a reaction to the iconoclastic actions of Leo might not be the case, but without that to blame, the causes of the revolt are obscure. Was it more a rebellion against general Leonid policies? The renewed Roman military operations on both land and sea in the aftermath of the defeat of the Umayyad siege of Constantinople would have involved thematic resources being used elsewhere. Hellas and the Cyclades may have already seen much of their manpower seconded for the defence of Constantinople, and then, rather than receive some recompense or relief, these provinces were again tapped for resources for Leo's offensives. Taking the fight to the Arabs may also have undermined east-west trade routes that benefitted the economies of maritime Greece and the Aegean islands. Any failure by Leo to address a subsequent financial or mercantile decline in the Aegean could have stoked armed opposition to his rule. Furthermore, might the Cycladeans in particular have been disgruntled over a lack of sufficient aid to their islands in the aftermath of the volcanic eruption near Thera in 726?[36]

Whatever the reasons, the naval forces of the Helladic theme and the Cyclades joined together under the leadership of Agallianos, Kosmas, and probably Stephen in rebellion against Leo III. Together, they marshalled together a 'great fleet'[37] and sailed into the Sea of Marmara, arriving on 18 April. It is unlikely that they had any intention of trying to besiege the imperial capital, hoping instead to either achieve an incursion through surprise or to establish themselves in the waters around the capital long enough for a rising within Constantinople to topple Leo. We have seen that there was some potential opposition to Leo's rule from amongst his own officials. Or at least there had been some seven years previous. And even then, that had been abortive. The usurpation of Kosmas did not have the imperial experience of Anastasius, the backing of the Bulgars, or the recorded backing of highly placed officials within the city. So when the 'great fleet' of Agallianos, Kosmas and Stephen arrived at Constantinople on 18 April and the gates were not immediately flung open to them in welcome, a confrontation was inevitable.

The rebellion of the Hellenes and Cycladeans ultimately came to grief in the same manner that the Umayyad siege had – the strength of the imperial navy. The remote chance of placing Kosmas on the throne was quickly swept away in a storm of Greek fire before the sea walls of Constantinople. As some of the rebel fleet was set alight, many of its crews either burned or drowned near the Golden Horn. This included Agallianos himself, who seeing the defeat unfolding 'despaired of his salvation and cast himself in the deep.'[38] And because of his heavy armour, rather than swim away to potential safety, he sank without trace. There was a harbour in Constantinople – the Kontoskalion (also known as the Harbour of Julian/Sophia, *Portus Novus* or the 'Harbour of the Galleys' by the Ottomans) – that was supposedly named for Agallianos due to his presence when it was being rebuilt, but this seems unlikely. Kontoskalion and Konstokeles do not necessarily share an etymology, although this legend does show some memory of Agallianos within the city.[39] But ultimately, this erroneous attribution (and further damage to Helladic and Aegean forces) were the only tangible results of this latest failed rebellion against Leo III.

This is because the fiery destruction saw the rest of the 'great fleet' surrender to the forces of Leo, handing over both Kosmas and Stephen. Leo likely had both of these men beheaded at the Kynegion, where the likes of Leontios, Tiberius III and Anastasius II had been executed in the previous two decades. While there is a decreasing support for the notion that this usurpation of Kosmas stemmed from an adverse reaction to Leo's iconoclasm, if that is the truth of its origins, Leo's ability to defeat a rebellion raised in support of the icons strengthened not just his politico-military position, but also his religious stance. Indeed, even the arch-iconodule Theophanes saw Leo's victory over Agallianos as intensifying Leo's iconoclastic zeal.[40]

Ghosts of the Past – The Pseudo-Tiberioi

So far we have seen the regime of Leo III face down four separate usurpations/rebellions – the unnamed Arab candidate during the siege of Constantinople, Basil Tiberius, Anastasius II and Kosmas. He also faced imperial challenges of a slightly different variety. During his reign, two different men claimed to be Tiberios, son of Justinian II. It could be that the first of these 'Pseudo-Tiberioi' appeared during the Arab siege of Constantinople and was therefore the suburban usurper supported by Maslamah. Unfortunately, there is no information about him.

There is more recorded in Roman and Syriac sources on the second Pseudo-Tiberios.[41] His actual identity was claimed as Bešer/Bâshîr from either Pergamum or Cappadocia. He was captured or defected to the Arabs during a raid of Roman territory carried out by Souleiman, son of caliph Hisham, in 737/738. As part of his new life in Umayyad Syria, Bešer came into contact with a Roman inhabitant of Harran called Theophantus (Theopitus according to Bar Hebraeus). Together, they hatched a plot that saw Theophantus go to Souleiman and claim that he knew the whereabouts of Tiberios, son of Justinian II. The caliphal son demanded that he be taken to this Roman imperial, which Theophantus agreed to in return for a sizeable reward. When Souleiman then met Bešer, the latter fervently denied that he was Tiberios, but this only galvanised the Umayyad prince's belief that he had a Heraclian son before him. It was only after extracting sizeable promises of safety and reward that Bešer 'admitted' that he was Tiberios. Souleiman sent this news to his father, Hisham, who gave instructions to treat 'Tiberios' as a Roman emperor, leading him in procession through various major cities in royal robes and surrounded with an 'imperial' guard, starting with Edessa and eventually arriving at the court of Hisham. Theophanes has 'Tiberios' being sent to Jerusalem, a destination not mentioned in the other sources.

The caliph not only presented 'Tiberios' as the Roman emperor within his own territory; he sent an embassy to Constantinople that declared that Tiberios was still alive and allied to the Umayyads. While there was little intimation that Hisham was going to send an expedition to establish 'Tiberios' on the Roman throne, the existence of the son of Justinian II could have presented some issues for Leo III. Tiberios, should he be still alive, would not only be the rightful emperor as the son of Justinian, but also a member of the Heraclian dynasty that had saved the Roman Empire, first from the Persians and Avars and then from the Arabs. Such a lineage could have rallied significant support to his cause. So prominent were the Heraclians in Roman history that they took up a significant role in Muslim eschatological tradition.[42] Part of the 'end times' was thought to involve a massive Roman invasion of Syria under the leadership of a member of the Heraclian dynasty, specifically called Tiberios. This tradition along with that which we have already seen regarding the potential fall of Constantinople around the Muslim year AH100 (718/719) could further back the notion of Maslamah embracing a Pseudo-Tiberios during the siege of the Roman imperial city. However, it is likely that the Tiberian part of this eschatological tradition did not develop until the very late Umayyad dynasty, i.e. after the two occasions of Pseudo-Tiberioi, even if the likes of Nu'aym b. Hammad's *Kitab al-Fitan* accords this prediction to the Prophet Muhammad.

With such a lofty position and/or influence on Arab religious convention, it would be thought that this Pseudo-Tiberios played a significant role in Romano-Umayyad relations post-737; however, that would not be the case. The Umayyads were either wilfully ignorant or had not done their homework on their 'imperial' guest or on Roman history. One could well imagine that the Umayyad ambassadorial pronouncement of the presence of 'Tiberios' at the court of Hisham to the Romans was met with a 'No, he's dead … killed as a child when his monstrous father was done away with'. They may also have sent some information about what 'Tiberios, son of Justinian' should look like – he most likely should have had blond hair for example. Indeed, the Arabs might even have been surprised at the mention of Justinian. This was because their 'Tiberios', at least in the Arab tradition, seemingly claimed to be the son of an emperor Constantine, rather than of Justinian II. This was problematic for the then current co-emperor Constantine V had yet to have any children by 737 (and would never have any called Tiberios). Tiberios, son of Justinian II, would have been a grandson of Constantine IV, while the last Tiberius, son of an imperial 'Constantine' was the youngest son of Constans II (who reigned as Constantine), removed from imperial contention by his eldest brother Constantine IV in 681, a considerable period of time earlier. Clearly, there were holes in Bešer's imperial presentation and while we are not informed how the whole endeavour unravelled, we are told that it did, with Bešer Tiberios executed, possibly by crucifixion in Edessa, before he could provide any real nuisance to the regime of Leo III.

While ultimately nothing came out of either of these Pseudo-Tiberian episodes, the sheer fact that some Romans and Arabs believed in them suggests that there was some latent loyalty to the Heraclian dynasty, which could be problematic for Leo III. Perhaps because of this, and his own personal issues with Justinian II, Leo himself could have been the originator of much of the anti-Justinian propaganda that unjustly blackened that emperor's name. The Isaurian 'may well have felt that [it] was a helpful measure in squelching the aspirations of anyone who might claim the throne as the fallen monarch's heir.'[43]

There was clearly something appealing about the imperial name 'Tiberius' during this period. The usurper Apsimar had taken it as his imperial name in 698, but it was hardly an appellation with a prolific imperial heritage – he was only the third emperor 'Tiberius'. And the first two were much more distantly removed: Tiberius II Constantine reigned 574–582 and the original Tiberius AD 14–37 (the combination of something 'new' and something 'old' could be the point). We have also seen the Sicilian usurper, Basil Onomagoulus, take it as his imperial name, while another Italian usurper in c.730/731 would also use it. There were also the Pseudo-Tiberioi, but they are not choosing the name 'Tiberius', they are choosing to be 'Tiberios, son of Justinian II'. 'Tiberius' had been used by the Heraclian dynasty – both Heraclius and Constans II gave sons the name before Justinian II named his son and heir Tiberios.[44] While it is clear that the Pseudo-Tiberioi were looking to channel this Tiberian imperial heritage in a very specific way, were the likes of Basil Tiberius and Tiberius Petasius appealing to this heritage or looking to gain some support by claiming the name of the last Heraclian? Or was it a little bit of both?

Fix the Problem?

Leo's accession is usually considered the end of the 'Twenty Years of Anarchy,' but such a designation only came about with the fullness of time. Leo's reign might have eventually run to 24 years, but the initial years showed little indication that anarchy was at an end. Given the dire straits that the Roman Empire found itself in, it is not surprising that we see slack army discipline and poor performance, even under skilled emperors like Constans II and Constantine IV, whose armies had routed in battle, protested, and rebelled.[45] And while these events gave opportunities for individual emperors to show strong leadership,[46] the decline of imperial power and resources saw more influence disseminate upon the thematic commanders, who became more interventionist than the guard units around the emperor. This might also reflect the growing influence and stature of the *strategoi* not just in terms of pressuring the emperor, but also a lightning rod for the dissatisfaction of the soldiery, who, along with the clergy, were increasingly viewed as '[representing] provincial opinion.'[47] However, 'by the beginning of the eighth century it became more questionable whether army units might … be able to establish themselves in an emperor-making or permanently 'praetorianist' role.'[48] The Opsikons might have resented the loss of influence and favour, which could have been the basis of such a 'praetorianist' role, that came with the overthrow of Justinian. This in turn may have sparked their roles in overthrowing Bardanes and Anastasius II.

Leo 'recognised that the ability to crush rivals was an essential part of [his] staying power,'[49] both in specific terms of saving his rule directly and also the message that was to be sent out by the manner of his response. A census taken in Sicily and Italy in the aftermath of the subjugation of Basil Tiberius, which had been rapid in its enactment, might have been largely for tax purposes, but could also have incorporated some level of punishment for those who had supported the usurper, with some tax exemptions rescinded and other taxes increased. This was a similar punishment Leo seems to have used towards the papacy. We have also seen the ruthless executions of those revealed to be involved in the plots surrounding Anastasius II and Kosmas, the latter of which also involved decisive naval action.

A significant aspect of his ability to stave off rebellion was that Leo could rely on support from several areas – his Anatolic theme likely continued to offer him as much military backing as it could, while defending the Romano-Arab frontier. He also received important backing from the people of Constantinople at various points – the Arab siege, the plot of Anastasius II, and the Helladic revolt. However, perhaps his most consistent and vital support came from a single individual – his original partner in rebellion, Artabasdos. Against all of the revolts, rebellions, and usurpations, the emperor's Armeniac ally and son-in-law stayed steadfast. There will have been more than a hint of self-preservation in this allegiance. If Leo III were to be toppled, Artabasdos being a prominent member of that regime *and* the Isaurian extended family meant that, unless he was doing the toppling, he and his household would be eliminated.

Whatever its origins, that loyalty saw Artabasdos be the only man that Leo felt he could trust with the potentially dangerous position of *comes Opsikon* in the aftermath of the rebellious actions of Isoes. The success of tying Artabasdos to him through personal and familial connections, and in shoring up loyalty from important sections of the empire may have encouraged Leo III to entrust other thematic commands to members of his extended family. We see Sisinnius, seemingly a nephew of Leo III, serving as Thrakesian *strategos*,[50] while two of Artabasdos' sons (grandsons of Leo) would command the Armeniac and Thracian armies. These latter appointments likely belong to the months after Leo's death, but it is possible that these imperial grandsons had received some command experience under Leo.

That Leo had not completely solved the issues of army loyalty to the throne would be seen after his death, with the revolt of Artabasdos in 741. This demonstrated the 'danger inherent in allowing members of one family to command several theme armies,'[51] even when it was members of the imperial family. Indeed, Leo 'either failed to anticipate difficulties between [Artabasdos] and Constantine or foresaw them but found himself unable to solve them.'[52] However, there was enough progress in certain respects for the accession of Leo III to be the last revolt from the eastern armies to put a commander on the throne until the tenth century. Indeed, Leo's accession was the first and perhaps only time that the Armeniacs successfully intervened in the imperial succession – they would try and fail in the future, including against Constantine V. Their only civil conflict successes would come when supporting the reigning emperor, such as Constantine VI and Michael II. Due to their connection to

Leo III, the Anatolian thematic armies replaced the Opsikons as the main arbiters of imperial power throughout the Isaurian period. Perhaps because of this role, Leo may have targeted the Anatolics for some reduction. It would be Constantine V who would significantly reduce the size and power of the Opsikons, whose threat to imperial authority along with the Anatolics was only gradually replaced by the new *tagmata* guard units.

And while the development of the theme 'system' allowed for dissemination of power to the *strategoi*, it did so to the extent that no single thematic commander, bar perhaps the *comes Opsikon* due more to proximity, could have challenged the emperor successfully alone. Leo's accession required an alliance between the Anatolic and Armeniac themes, while the civil war between Constantine V and Artabasdos would essentially be a contest between two competing thematic alliances – Anatolic/Thrakesian vs Armeniac/Opsikon. While 'the fusion of civil and military powers in the hands of the *strategos* improved his ability to begin and accomplish a military revolt… the theme 'system' [actually] kept the army divided, to the basic benefit of the government in Constantinople.'[53] Indeed, before the civil war between Constantine V and Artabasdos, there had been a marked absence of pitched battle between the main thematic armies. This may reflect how many of the revolts of the period of 'military anarchy' 'owed their planning, execution, and success to military circumstances … Timing and access to the capital, not sheer quantities of troops or resources, were the key elements.'[54]

This would seem to be a change from the previous century when several revolts could trace their outbreak to the emperor's entrusting of 'large numbers of men to certain commanders for specific military expeditions.'[55] The decline of imperial manpower in the wake of the Arab conquests, together with the 'codifying' of the themes, essentially removed this aspect of army size from revolts. It is perhaps also worth noting that a central tenet of the Third Century Crisis – a general looking to use the popularity he gained from military success to seize the throne – played little role in the anarchy of the late-seventh/early-eighth century. There are hints in the period of 695–711 that thematic armies had a willingness to change sides when faced with a challenge, rather than fight for their emperor.[56] Loyalty, it seems, or a lack thereof, was still an issue. The prominence of naval forces in the rebellions of the 'military anarchy' should also not be overlooked – Bardanes, Tiberius III and Theodosius III all used ships to good effect, while the Helladic/Cycladean revolt was solely naval in nature. This prevalence of naval forces in successive revolts probably encouraged Leo III to reorganise the Roman fleet, which in turn 'contributed to the diminished participation of fleets in military unrest during the remainder of the eighth century.'[57]

For all the issues faced by the imperial government from the military, some of which clearly continued throughout the Isaurian dynasty, such 'unrest did not completely paralyze the empire's defences.'[58] Not only were all the revolts and rebellions defeated, but this was achieved on a background of stability on the frontiers. Push back against the Bulgars, Slavs and Arabs might not have wielded spectacular results, but the situation had not gotten any worse. And when coupled with Leo's prolonged reign, the groundwork was laid for a more offensive stance under Constantine V.

And as has been seen above, for the Isaurians to be such in a position, Leo had had to deal with a succession of attempts on his rule. Strangely, none of Leo's successful repulsing of rebellion involved military victory on his part. The only usurper actually defeated in battle – Tiberius Petasius – had, as we shall see below, virtually nothing to do with Leo and only a minor role by imperial forces. Instead, the emperor succeeded through a combination of decisive action, the strength of the imperial navy, good dealings with the Bulgars, general incompetence/weakness of those attempts and most influentially, the legacy of awe and loyalty inspired by his defeat of Maslamah.

These victories allowed Leo time to address internal issues, such as provincial and military organisation, administration and law, but by far the most significant reform he supposedly oversaw was in the realm of religion and it was to have a damaging impact on his reputation.

Chapter 8

Deliberate Destruction of Icons?: Leonid Religious Policies

'Salvation lies not in the faithfulness to forms, but in the liberation from them.'

Boris Pasternak, *Doctor Zhivago*

Outline and Terminology

While the Arab siege of Constantinople was the most important single event in the reign of Leo III, its importance lay in something that that *did not* happen – Constantinople did not fall. Perhaps the most important thing that *did* happen, with repercussions felt not just throughout the Roman world but throughout the Middle Ages and down to modern times, was the 'Byzantine iconoclasm' – the ban and destruction of religious images and even the persecution of their venerators. Purely in the realm of religion, it would greatly change Orthodox Christian worship, strongly shape aspects of the English Reformation and the French Revolution, and even influence policies of the Taliban and Islamic State in the twenty-first century.[1] But so all-encompassing was the iconoclastic movement and the reaction to it that it had wide-ranging cultural, societal, economic, ideological, and even political consequences for the Roman Empire and the world beyond. As much as the politico-military crises of the seventh century, the struggle over the icons of the eighth/ninth century transformed the Roman Empire into its medieval/'Byzantine' form.[2] That said, it is difficult to determine how involved aspects of iconoclasm were in 'the complex pattern of the social, cultural, political, and institutional history of Byzantium,'[3] although the period of iconoclasm did coincide with the period when the Roman Empire changed from being a threatened and disrupted state into a secure kingdom.

While the prevailing understanding has long been that iconoclasm emerged under Leo III sometime between 726 and 730, this assumption, along with several others regarding its destructive impact on Roman religious imagery, artistic development and various sections of society, may be 'incorrect'.[4] And even if it is still decided that Leo played some role in the institution of iconoclasm, it cannot be denied that it was his son Constantine V who was 'the principal mover and thinker of the iconoclasts.'[5] It would be from Constantine's own pen and 'penetrating intellect'[6] that iconoclasm would develop a doctrinal base, one to be presented and disputed at church councils. It must also be said that while iconoclasm may have helped drive social, religious, and political change, it was itself *driven* by already on-going developments in those arenas.[7] And such is the centre stage that it was given, 'even when issues such as the military or fiscal organisation of the empire [were] at stake',[8] that it is perhaps detrimental to a true representation of iconoclasm's actual influence. Indeed, aspects of the Roman world went largely untouched by the narrower ideology of iconoclasm: certain structures, practices, and ways of living continued as they had before.

But before we get into the potential origins of iconoclasm under Leo III, we must look at the terminology used in this dispute. The core word is 'icon', from the Greek εικον, meaning 'image'. In pre-Christian times, it was a term used for portraits of humans before becoming associated with Christian religious art because it was not tainted by association with pagan deities and received some 'authorisation' from the Bible: Genesis 1:26 – 'let us make man according to our image'.[9] Such icons could be any medium painted in tempera or encaustic on wood panels.[10] There were alternative terms for images with non-Christian religious links – ειδολον i.e. idols, while αγαλμα was used to describe images of Greek and Roman gods.[11] The compound word spawned from εικων to describe those who supported the attack on such icons was εικονοκλαστες – iconoclasts – meaning 'breakers of images'. The first recorded usage of the term comes in the 720s, and would gradually become a term for 'heretic', particularly after the Second Council of Nicaea in 787. More modern usage of 'iconoclast' is a little more positive than the always-negative in the surviving ancient texts, where it is used to contrast 'iconophile' or 'iconodule' – 'lover of images'. Perhaps surprisingly, while used to mean the debate around the role of images in the seventh-ninth centuries, applying the term 'iconoclasm' to that period is anachronistic. It is not even strictly a Greek word, deriving instead from the Latin *iconoclasmus*, which did not appear in print until the mid-sixteenth century, when it was used to describe the actions of an early-ninth century bishop of Turin. It was then used in relation to opposition to religious art from Protestants and during the French Revolution of the eighteenth century. Indeed, in the English-speaking world, 'iconoclasm' was not attached to the events of the seventh-ninth centuries until 1953. Instead, the name used by the Romans was εικονομαχία – *iconomachy* – meaning 'image struggle', which is more in keeping with what happened regarding the argument over the role of portraits of Christ, the Virgin Mary and various saints.

Sources of Iconoclasm: Information and Origins

As a religiously-based dispute, iconoclasm inspired fierce responses from both sides of the debate, although the eventual iconodule victory sees their 'history' and reimagining of it become the 'only' story, to the detriment of general iconoclast views and the overall historical picture, as most iconoclast writing was destroyed after 843 with the 'Triumph of Orthodoxy'. This leaves much of what we know about iconoclasm 'the product of … spin with authors rewriting the past to justify their own behaviours and beliefs.'[12] So while there is plenty of information about iconoclasm, much of it is highly problematic. What survives is highly polemical and prone to rhetorical exaggeration, with the likes of Theophanes writing 'with the deliberate intention of blackening the [Isaurian] dynasty's reputation.'[13] Because much of the contemporary material was rewritten or destroyed post-843, the material we do have is somewhat anachronistic, reflecting post-iconoclasm attitudes rather than what people thought during the debates. Iconoclasts, buoyed by imperial support, were not above such rewriting and destroying of iconodule works as well.[14] Virtually all our contemporary sources, from both sides, stem from two very small segments of Roman society: men of urban elite or Christian clergy backgrounds. This narrows the scope of information/attitudes we have and contributes to the wariness of just how all-pervasive and affecting the debates of iconoclasm were across the various levels of Roman society.

Information can also be gleaned from art and archaeology, but while these two areas provide a wide spectrum of material, there are significant issues. There is a slight discrepancy in what the Romans thought most art should be compared to more modern perceptions – 'while technical skill was highly valued, innovation and individuality and artistic expression was not considered desirable.'[15] That is something to be wary of, but the real problems are the limited amount of visual imagery from the period and the limited scope of what does survive. The iconoclastic period reduced the amount of iconographic art from before it, with the destruction of certain types of images.[16] Large mosaics in various prominent churches and cities – Constantinople, Thessalonica, Nicaea – were replaced, which can highlight artistic/dogmatic choices within the iconoclastic movement, such as the use of a plain cross or secular scenes over figurative images.[17] In terms of archaeology, there may be more evidence out there to be connected to both sides of the iconoclasm debate, but 'Byzantine' archaeology itself remains a relatively young subject as a whole, even with some positive strides being made. This combination of alteration, destruction, and a lack of modern archaeological investigation makes it very difficult to bring together an objective and reliable account of iconoclasm. This difficulty, along with its importance and influence, is reflected in the significant amount of secondary literature that has been produced on iconoclasm.

While it became an extremely contentious debate in the eighth century, the roots of iconoclasm had been put down long before. Iconoclasts would claim that icon veneration had no backing in the ancient church; there was even Early Christian opposition to the 'cult of images' or at least to depicting God. And it is easy to see why – the seeming clarity of the commandment against idolatry, general influence from Jewish traditions, and in a pagan world of images,[18] opposition to images would differentiate a new faith. But such dogmatic 'iconophobia' was difficult to stick to in the face of the practical acceptance of figurative art in Mediterranean society and the prominence of images in Roman paganism. Therefore, images were embraced by Christianity as the empire became Christian; this is despite the connection between the Christian icon and who it depicted being distinctly 'pagan' in nature: a cosmic and timeless connection.[19]

Aspects of Christian art continued to have some reservations over their depiction of human figures. The early-fourth century synod of Elvira ruled that 'there must be no pictures in the church, that the walls should have no images of that which is revered and worshipped;'[20] Eusebius of Caesarea referred to the worship of images of Jesus and the apostle Peter and Paul as 'a habit of the Gentiles',[21] while Epiphanius of Salamis went as far as to tear down a church curtain as its depiction of Jesus/a saint 'defiled the church.'[22] Areas of the empire received icon veneration in different ways, including acts of iconoclasm e.g. Palestine,[23] due to influence from different belief systems, such as non-orthodox Christians, Gnostics, Arians, Manichaeans, Monophysites, Zoroastrians, Jews etc..

Even with the disasters of the seventh century encouraging debate over the efficacy of prayer to cults, relics, and images to inspire divine intervention on behalf of the Roman Empire, it is important to look at earlier developments in specific religious belief and practice regarding icons. Ancient Christians rarely invoked God directly with their prayers; instead, they would seek the intercession of a saint or the Virgin Mary to help have their plea heard by Christ. This shows that saints were not only seen as friends of God, but by the mid-fifth century, the holiness of a saint was considered to stay attached to his earthly remains. Therefore, being buried near a saint's tomb (burial *ad sanctos*) was thought to aid divine intercession. This bred not only a cult of saints, but also a cult of their relics, which were thought to retain that holiness even after their removal from the main part of the saint's body. This holiness could also be transferred to objects that had touched the saintly body and its relics. That idea of saintly intercession could be passed to portraits of those saints, which saw these icons become assimilated into the cult of saints.

This was underway by the late-sixth century with *acheiropoietoi* – images 'not made by human hands'. None of these survive down to the modern day, so we are relying on written accounts, all of which detail portraits of Christ on cloth. The earliest recorded was found miraculously dry in a well in 569 in Syrian Kamoulianai, which made its way to Constantinople; another is recorded in Egyptian Memphis in 570 and was reputedly created by Christ pressing his face into the cloth, with the *mandylion* of Edessa from 590 reputedly being made in a similar way. The most famous example of this type of icon 'not made by human hands' would be the Turin Shroud, although it is some 700 years younger than these early examples. Such *acheiropoietoi* images of Christ were cast as protectors of cities: the Edessa image was said to have saved the city from the Persians in the 610s, while the Kamoulianai image was probably paraded around the walls of the capital during the Avar siege of 626.

Such protective icons almost certainly developed out of the Graeco-Roman *palladia*, a cult image of reputedly mythical origin: the most famous example would be the Palladium removed from Troy by Odysseus and Diomedes, which was either an image or statue of the goddess Athena.[24] Such 'pagan' influence would be condemned by Christians when it came to portraits made by human hands. The second-century bishop of Lyon, Irenaeus, thought the displaying of wreaths supporting Christ's face heretical, while the third(?) century *Acts of John* saw the hanging of garlands and candles before an image of the saint as a pagan practice. Giving special attention to images at all may have been seen as distinctly un-Christian in its earliest centuries. And while we do see painted images becoming more prominent from the fourth century onward, there was a lack of 'pagan' veneration, even by the late seventh century. At this point, the images were 'intended to preserve the memory of the person represented, to provide an inspiring model for imitation, to honour the figure portrayed, or to express thanks to a saint who had answered prayer (*ex voto* images)'.[25]

There is a perceptible change in the role of icons in the second half of the seventh century. The boundary between *acheiropoieta* and man-made icons began to fade, with images of Christ, the Virgin Mary and saints taking on a connection to the divine, much as relics and *acheiropoieta* had. Icons become more visible in literary texts, with Anastasius of Sinai invoking them in the 680s, while a decade later Stephen of Bostra was writing positively about honouring icons with candles, curtains, and incense.[26] Usually such religio-political developments stemmed from the top – emperor, imperial court, church hierarchies etc., but in the case of icon worship, its expansion appears more an organic development amongst provincials. It could well be then that some of the background to iconoclasm stemmed from day-to-day religious practice rather than Church orthodoxy.[27]

That is not to say that these ideas did not appear in the imperial capital and were not reflected in imperial policies. Prominent examples of the increasing importance of icons in the late-seventh century come in the actions of Justinian II. The Heraclian dynasty had attached great importance to icon veneration, but it is only with Justinian that we see policies with overt iconic aspects. Part of the Quinisext Council involved the first 'ecumenical' canons regarding images. Representing Christ as a lamb in art was prohibited by canon 82, while canon 73 forbade the use of crosses in floor designs.[28] These canons might reflect some imperial/church worry that people thought Christ appeared as a lamb[29] and demand for more general respect for the Cross, rather than iconodule feelings that would develop over the course of the eighth century. The banning of the depiction of Christ as a lamb raised opposition from Pope Sergius I, who had a personal liking of that depiction and added the *Agnus Dei* – 'the Lamb of God' – invocation to the celebration of Mass.[30] This could be a prelude to papal opposition to iconoclasm. Canon 100 insisted on the distinction between good and bad images, defining the latter as those that invoked the 'shameful pleasures'. There were three other Quinisext canons that dealt with artisanal production, which could be 'an attempt to regulate and control the new powers of sacred images'.[31] Again, it cannot be said with certainty that these canons were meant as part of a nascent iconoclasm debate or were 'trying to stem the tide of a cult that was threatening to undermine their authority,'[32] but they originate from the same religio-political milieu.

Justinian II's other iconic action was to put a full-faced image of Christ on the obverse of his gold coins. It is 'difficult to ascertain [its] meaning,'[33] but it may have encouraged the Umayyad caliph, Abd al-Malik, to move to a purely aniconic Islamic coinage, rather than using Roman coins. While this might seem like a pro- and anti-image numismatic divide, this was not really the case – the Muslims certainly went down an aniconic route, rejecting all imagery; however, it is difficult to attribute any 'iconodule' motives to Justinian II's Christ coinage. While it was a precedent that was ignored for 150 years, this choice to depict Christ on Roman coinage was surely influenced in some part by the growing importance of icons in Roman society.

But even if it is the case that these Justinianic policies lack any true connection to the debates that took place regarding iconoclasm in the eighth/ninth century,[34] they were clearly products of the same period of increased interest in icons. And even if Quinisext did not openly state that icons should be prayed to, it 'intended that images of Christ should be used to support Christological orthodoxy'[35] and that it was acceptable to make icons of Christ because of his human incarnation.[36] So even if these policies were not meant as part of any debate over the 'breaking' or 'loving' of icons, hints at the battle lines that would later be drawn can be seen in them. Together, Quinisext and the Christ coins represent 'the most significant instance of imperial concern for proper use of icons in the pre-iconoclastic era.'[37] And in presenting icons as part of the bedrock of Christological orthodoxy, they made it that 'iconoclasm [became] the climax of a movement that had its roots in the spirituality of the Christian concept of the divinity,'[38] which provided the tools to make the debate over icons even more deeply entrenched when it came. Attempting to find a Christological context for icon support or opposition might be overlooking how unlike other doctrinal disputes the icon struggle was. Christological arguments were completely absent in the forming of iconoclasm – 'it is almost as if the whole issue of Christology had been introduced as it were out of habit, simply because that had become the traditional battle ground for controversy.'[39]

But why was it now in the last quarter of the seventh century that the role of icons began to change? The existential threat posed by the Arab caliphate was a significant part of the religious, political, social, and financial insecurity felt by the Roman Empire that sparked much soul-searching about the efficacy of religious ritual and belief; however, by the first reign of Justinian II (685–695), that threat had been around for half a century. The iconic developments may have arisen due to a lull in the fighting, a lull which provided 'time to think and to write.'[40] The sharp existential anxiety that came with on-going conflict gave way to a more measured investigation of the practical and spiritual situation of the Roman Empire. But more time to think and write did not necessarily mean a better picture of the imperial future emerged. If anything, the limited military successes against the Arabs proved that the empire was incapable of turning back the Islamic tide any time soon. The Taurus Mountains were not the high-water mark of a freak tidal surge; they were the new coastline and that tide would continue to lap into Roman territory for the foreseeable future.

The re-evaluation of icons was not just limited to within the Roman Empire – apocalyptic texts were being produced by Christians living under Arab rule: for example, Anastasius of Sinai's *Questions and Answers* speaks of the late-seventh century facing a spiritual crisis. This extramural influence, as well as the organic, provincial origin of these iconic developments, worried the Church, as this type of uncontrolled change could challenge not only the 'purity of Christian ritual,'[41] but also the Church's own power over orthodox practice and belief. The imperial and Church reaction to this may be seen in attempts by Quinisext to standardise some aspects of practice, although the lack of a clear programme demonstrates a failure to fully identify the problem or the solution to the increasing power of icons. Justinian II's use of Christ on his gold coinage could be taken as not only 'a blatant imperial stamp of approval for the new power of Christian portraiture and, perhaps, an attempt to harness some of that power for the continued security of the empire,'[42] but possibly also a recognition of the initial failure of Church regulation of icons. There was some resistance to the expansion of the intercessional presence of saints in their relics and *acheiropoietoi* to those portraits painted by men. Asking a painted image of a person like they were present was a little too close to idol worship, a clear violation of the commandment regarding graven images.[43] Indeed, that it would take decades to disentangle 'icon' from 'idol' provides insight into the strength and veracity of the opposition to the increasing prominence of icons.

Influences on Leo's Iconoclasm

It is not only influence from extramural Christians that might have affected iconic thought in the Roman Empire. The rise of aniconic Islam may have raised questions amongst Christian politicians about not only the efficacy of iconic intercessional reference, but its very propriety. Might the very use of images have angered God and therefore led to the Roman Empire's century of poor fortunes? While this seems like a logical connection, there is a significant difference between Islamic aniconism and Christian iconoclasm. Islam was in the process of rejecting pictorial representation almost completely, while 'Byzantine' iconoclasm focused on the holy presence in images. But even with this innate difference, we should not ignore the influences the Romano-Christian and Muslim Arab world could have upon one another. It is taken as a given that Abd al-Malik set the Umayyad caliphate on the road to aniconism at least in part due to unwanted influences from the Roman world. Care should also be taken not to view the Roman and Arab worlds as two separate entities. As the frontier was porous and the Arabs inhabited territory that had been Roman for 700 years, the intermixing of cultures, ideas, and practice was inevitable. That iconoclasm might have emerged in areas of the most Romano-Arab interaction in Asia Minor could also be telling – debates over icons, even if Islam and Christianity took differing paths and stressed distinct aspects of those debates, could demonstrate a general discussion over images across the Eastern Mediterranean.

However, just because we might not reject mutual influence regarding icons between the Romano-Christian and Muslim Arab milieu, it does not mean that we accept the stories presented by iconodule Roman sources about the spark of iconoclasm in Leo III reputedly stemming from his familiarity with Islam. We have already seen his residence in Germanikeia,[44] a settlement at the forefront of Romano-Arab fighting in the middle decades of the seventh century. It may have only been mere months after Leo's birth in c.685 that the Romans reclaimed the city, meaning that the young Leo (Konon) grew up in rather Arabised surroundings, including his learning of Arabic and surely some versing in the tenets of Islam. This provides some basis, along with his supposed iconoclasm, for Theophanes to call Leo 'σαρακηνοφρων' – 'Saracen-minded.'[45]

And that 'Saracen mind' may have helped see Leo enter correspondence with the Umayyad caliph in the aftermath of the siege of Constantinople. Said defeat, along with a significant earthquake in Syria the same year, seemingly sparked religious zeal in Umar II. His response included the banning of wine, which as Islam already forbade Muslims from partaking in alcohol was targeting his non-Muslim subjects. Umar is also recorded persecuting Christians, demanding that they apostatise, offering financial incentives for them to do so. He ordered that no Christian could testify against a Muslim in court, with some of those who did not comply being martyred. Umar even went as far as to write a doctrinal letter to Leo himself, trying to persuade him to convert.[46] This AM6210 entry of Theophanes does not elaborate further on the contents of Umar's letter or the extent of the correspondence, but various oriental sources mention it – Syriac, Armenian, Georgian and Arabic, 'which were not passed through the sieve of consistent iconophile bias and censorship.'[47] Several of them have Leo replying to Umar's letter. However, such sources are not always believable; for example, the version of Leo's response to Umar preserved as the Armenian historian, Ghevond, is eleventh-thirteenth century in origin, as it refers to Islamic matters of that time, despite Ghevond himself living in the eighth century.[48] Furthermore, there are some issues with the dating of such correspondence, particularly if the originals are claimed to be authentic and had some immediate iconoclastic influence on Leo. Any such letter from Umar to Leo had to be from before Umar's death in early February 720, making any connection to iconoclasm the earliest Roman mention of the controversy, which raises red flags. Further scrutiny of the various versions and translations of this correspondence suggests that the original text of the Leonid reply was from the pen of an anonymous Melkite monk of the second half of the eighth century, rather than that of the emperor.[49]

However, the existence of such correspondence should not be dismissed out of hand just because these surviving versions did not originate from the pen of Leo himself. There is circumstantial evidence to the effect that Umar II could have sent such a letter to the Roman emperor. The caliph's religious zeal is demonstrated elsewhere in his writing to Transoxianaians, Sindh and Berbers in attempts to get them to accept Islam. There are other records of Umar being in contact with the Romans, such as in the *Kitab al-Aghani* and al-Baladhuri, and while these were not religious in nature, they show epistolary contact. Also, in general, Muslims already had 'a long tradition of epistolary invitation to Islam [dating] … back to the time of the prophet Muhammad,'[50] who is claimed to have written to the emperor Heraclius.

It would not be surprising for Leo to partake in any such religious correspondence. As we shall see below, he was involved in efforts to spread orthodox Christianity to Jews and heretics, and his willingness to indulge in theological disputes is seen in his correspondence with Pope Gregory II. The latter also demonstrates that Leo thought the position of emperor involved some idea of being a priest. The *Georgian Chronicle* gives the text of two letters of Leo to local leaders, with the emperor expressing the idea of holy war against the Arabs, highlighting that not only did he send letters on religious matters, but that he also saw Islam as a target for holy war. Proselytising through letter-writing was also a Christian pastime – there was the legend of correspondence between Jesus and Abgar of Edessa, while 22 of 27 Books of the New Testament stemmed at least partly from epistles written to people or communities.

If we assume that there was a factual basis to this caliphal-imperial correspondence, then why might Theophanes have neglected to mention that Leo responded to Umar's attempt to convert him to Islam? Might it be because Leo III's actual response, rather than embrace aniconism as iconodules might want to claim, 'gloriously refuted the claims of Islam'?[51] References in the Armenian histories of Thomas Ardzruni and Kirakos of Gandzac have Leo's reply being so 'glorious' as to shame Umar into reforming his treatment of Muslims and Christians. Such a learned and persuasive defence of Christianity in the face of a religious caliph is not material that anti-iconoclastic chronicles would want promulgated. Better to leave that part out and rely on 'knowledge' of Leo's reputed iconoclastic actions to fill in the gaps.

The supposed Islamic influence on iconoclasm continued with Yazid II. Theophanes, Nikephoros and the report of John of Jerusalem given at the Second Council of Nicaea in 787 claim Jewish and Arab influences on iconoclasm,[52] with a particular instance stemming from Yazid. In 721/722,[53] the caliph was approached by a Jewish 'magician' from Laodicea or Tiberias, possibly called Tessarakontapechys – 'forty cubits high'. He told Yazid that if he wished to rule for 40 years, the caliph should condemn and destroy the holy icons that were venerated by Christians in Umayyad territory. Yazid accepted this and 'promulgated an all-embracing edict against the holy icons,'[54] possibly appointing Maslamah to oversee its enforcement. The text of the edict is lost, but archaeological evidence supports its implementation, with enough information from various literary and material sources evidence to reconstruct some idea of its focus and results.

Despite the influence that the Roman sources apply to it, this iconoclastic edict of Yazid was extraordinary rather than the norm. There might have been some antipathy for images emerging in the caliphate, but this was not necessarily encouraged by Yazid's edict. At best then, it could be a next step in the development of Islamic aniconism, a step that Islam as a whole did not yet take. Many Muslim sources largely ignored it because it was essentially a failed law, with Yazid's successor, Hisham I, revoking it not long after his accession. Furthermore, the archaeological evidence that supports the existence of a brief wave of Umayyad iconoclasm is confined to Yazid's power base in the southern Levant. This suggests that not only was the edict short-lived, but it was also not widely enforced. 'Perhaps it is not a surprise that medieval Muslims forgot what Yazid had done.'[55] The lack of impact and longevity of this iconoclastic decree has seen it downplayed to the point that its very existence is doubted.[56] Any actual impact and possibly even the aim of Yazid's edict may have come in the political realm, with it being 'a great act of sabre-rattling – a symbolic gesture aimed at cowing Christians at a time of heightened social unrest and apocalyptic angst or as a way of placating religious hardliners at court – rather than a law with serious legal force.'[57]

You might ask what these supposed iconoclastic actions of Yazid II have to do with Leo III? Oriental sources like Michael the Syrian and Gregory Bar Hebraeus claim that it was a direct influence on Leo III's own iconoclastic policies,[58] with Theophanes mentioning Leo's iconoclasm immediately after Yazid's, even if they did not happen in the same year and there is little elaboration on what this influence was. Beyond the mutual influence of the Roman and Arab worlds, there has been some attempt to posit a direct personal influence connecting the iconoclasms of Yazid II and Leo III through the Jewish 'magician', Tessarakontapechys. Leo is recorded as having his own ally in iconoclasm called Besr, a name that could be a shortened version of Tessarakontapechys. And with the name of Yazid's Jewish 'magician' meaning 'forty cubits high', likely a reflection of his physical stature, Theophanes stating that part of the reason Besr came to Leo's attention was due to his physical strength and boorishness suggests that Besr and Tessarakontapechys were both large men.[59] However, there are differences between Besr and Tessarakontapechys. With all the will in the world, their names are different enough to not have to be the same. And there are others known to have each of these names, lessening the chances that this is the same person. Furthermore, there are significant differences in the back stories of these men. While Tessarakontapechys is recorded as a Jewish 'magician' from Laodicea or Tiberias, Besr was a Christian taken captive to Syria, where he converted to Islam, before returning to Roman territory. The likes of the Jewish 'magician' and Besr could even have been invented by iconodule sources to provide a connection between Leo and Yazid that did not exist.[60]

Further eroding of any Islamic influence on Leo is that Islamic aniconism was not the same as iconoclasm. The Qur'an says little about images, although when it does broach the subject it states 'statues are an abomination of the work of Satan.'[61] The actions prevalent in Muslim iconoclasm when it did occur – beheading an image or making a hole in its abdomen to 'kill' the icon – were never part of Roman image breaking. Indeed, Muslim aniconism and Roman iconoclasm were far enough removed both socially, religiously, and politically for Muslim lands to become havens for iconodules during the height of Roman iconoclasm later in the eighth century. It could even be that this Roman iconoclasm was a reaction in the opposite direction – rather than an attempt to remove veneration of the sacred Christian icon, it was an attempt to purify it to differentiate Christian beliefs from those of Islam and Judaism. Instead of being aniconic, Roman iconoclasm may have been looking to suppress aspects of icon veneration that were too easily construed as idolatrous, but without removing icon veneration altogether. There is some notion of this in iconoclastic actions in Palestine.[62] It must also be said that in removing some of the more obviously 'idolatrous' practices Leo III was helping to make Christianity more tolerable to Jews and Muslims who found icon veneration abhorrent.

Jewish antipathy to Christian images is frequently mentioned in Roman material; however, contemporary Jewish literature and archaeological evidence is much less conclusive on any Jewish dislike of images. Indeed, Leo III and iconoclasm are markedly absent from Jewish sources. As with claims of direct Islamic influence, it was perhaps convenient for iconodule Roman sources to portray iconoclasm being influenced by Jews, a charge absent in oriental sources. Indeed, far from being in any way 'Judaising', Leo III may have overseen the forced baptism of Jews.[63]

On top of trying to highlight some non-Christian influences on Leo's 'grievous and illicit'[64] religious error, iconodules like Theophanes were keen to point out the consequences faced by the iconoclastic Yazid. Rather than enjoy a decades-long reign, Yazid II died on 26 January 724 after less than four years on the caliphal throne, reputedly of consumption or a dissolute life. Indeed, so keen was Theophanes to highlight Yazid's demise that he mentions it in consecutive years.[65] And the reason for Yazid's sudden demise, according to Theophanes? Divine intervention by Jesus Christ, the Virgin Mary, and all the saints in response to Yazid's 'satanic constitution.'[66] Of course, if iconodules of the 720s hoped that their icon-breaking Roman emperor would face a similar divine punishment, they were to be greatly disappointed. Upon Yazid II's death in 724, the reign of Leo III still had another 17 years to go.

Leo's origins on the Romano-Umayyad frontier opened him up to other cultural influences. It has been postulated that the other great power of the seventh century and influence on the Roman eastern provinces – Sassanid Persia – saw 'militant, intentional iconoclasm';[67] however, care must be taken in such ascriptions. While there were some aspects of aniconism in Zoroastrianism, 'aniconism is not necessarily accompanied by iconoclasm'[68] and while Sassanid society did not represent the divine in its art, it was not iconoclastic, with figures, divine and royal, depicted on coins and rock-reliefs. The area around Germanikeia was a hotbed of Monophysitism, with many prominent holders to that doctrine, such as Severus and Philoxenus, described as being active iconoclasts. There had been instances of icon breaking in Syria in previous centuries, with Antioch and Edessa seeing some anti-icon upheaval in the sixth and seventh centuries.[69] However, this could also be another instance of the iconodule sources looking for an 'other' to blame for iconoclasm, as it could not possibly be a result of thinking from within orthodox Christianity. Later sources like Michael the Syrian record some late-seventh century Monophysites being 'just as ardent worshippers of image and relics as the Chalcedonians.'[70] This may be reflected in the *Acts* of the Second Council of Nicaea in 787, where Monophysitism was described as 'the many-headed but headless hydra,' so polycephallic that not only is it difficult to fully refute Monophysite leanings for iconoclasts,[71] but in some contexts iconodules find themselves being labelled as part of this 'beast'. If Leo was influenced by the Monophysitism (or Jacobite Miaphysitism) of his surroundings in his early life, he had let it go by the time of his accession, with the oriental sources presenting him as uniformly Chalcedonian.[72] And the version of iconoclasm attributed to Leo had no such Monophysite ideas.

Leo also had numerous Armenians around him too, such as David Hypatos, future bishop Stephen Siwnik and possibly Artabasdos. There is some evidence of seventh-century ascetic Armenians following a doctrine that could be iconoclastic, while also venerating the cross,[73] a combination that would come to reflect Roman iconoclasm. Another prominent Armenian sect of this time were the Paulicians, who reputedly rejected various aspects of Christian worship – baptism by water, eucharist, cross veneration and icons. Much like the Jews, it is difficult to attribute much or any Paulician influence on Leo III as he is recorded ordering the Paulician heresiarch Gegnesius to venerate the cross, with the very idea of a rejection of cross veneration being against Roman iconoclasm (not to mention the rejection of other vital aspects of orthodox Christianity). The later iconoclastic focus on the eucharist as the only true image may have stemmed in part from the Paulician belief in the words of the *Logos* being the only true icons.[74] However, arguments like this, along with lack of Paulician persecution under Leo III and Constantine V and the presence of Paulician soldiers in the Isaurian army, ring hollow as evidence of a Paulician influence over the Isaurian emperors.

While the possible influences on Leo III focus on non-Christian and heretical sources, more general Christian influences should not be forgotten. It is difficult to find clear indications of Leo's thoughts as the historical record has been purged of information claimed as iconoclastic. One source might be the introduction to the Isaurian law code, the *Ekloga*. It may present Leo's sentiments not only on his law-giving mission, but in general. The Leo of the *Ekloga* is 'serenely convinced of divine guidance in his task, who sees no need for an ecclesiastical hierarchy to interpret for him the divine directives.'[75] There is almost some quasi-caesaropapism in such an outline.[76] And such was the biblical simplicity that Leo seemed to follow that it could be that he took a straightforward view of icons as being idolatrous images.

Such straightforward thinking could also affect Leo's treatment of icons should those icons be connected to any who might have thought to 'usurp' any of his prerogatives.[77] This could be seen in the growing role of some icons as a focus of local patriotism as a substitute for the local 'holy man'. The contraction of Roman imperial authority in its own lands[78] saw the influence of these holy men grow, along with the icons that served as their stand-ins. Roman authorities felt the need to break this power. Perhaps this was 'monachomachy' rather than iconomachy;[79] less a war on icons and more a war on monastic holy men, with icons a secondary target. However, the anti-monastic movement was more a policy of Constantine V, making it unlikely to be a driving force behind any iconoclasm under Leo III. It could also be that this anti-monasticism was separate from iconoclasm itself, particularly as there were iconoclastic monks.

In his iconoclasm, might Leo have been attempting to reach out to populations and groups in Asia Minor, specifically the bishops and the thematic armies?[80] Evidence of contact between Leo and the Asian bishops is lacking, and said Asian bishops, even Monophysites, were not necessarily iconoclasts. This idea likely exaggerates the influence of iconoclastic bishops in Asia Minor,[81] while the thematic armies of Leo III were lacking interest in the entire discussion of icons. It was not until the reign of Constantine V that iconodule/iconoclast became more of a dividing line amongst the soldiery.[82] And even then, there would be a lack of unanimity regarding icons amongst the themes, with the example of Artabasdos relying on the Opsikon and Armeniac themes, both heavily iconoclastic, but then also restoring icons. This may add more regional rivalry to iconoclasm, and possibly even an aristocratic element to the dispute.[83]

The arguments regarding influences on Leo and his potential iconoclasm are lacking clarity on what the actual purpose of it was. There are plenty of potential answers, if not exactly consensus, on why iconoclasm happened – 'an undercurrent of hostility towards religious images [had been] present for several centuries,'[84] – while the answer to 'why now' seems slightly more settled. The correct observance of religious practice affecting military and political success had been part of Roman life for centuries, causing significant religious tension and even bouts of persecution. It was no different under Christian emperors.

Defeat was a punishment, and while there had been some suggestions of the Muslim tide receding in the last quarter of the seventh century, the second Muslim wave of conquest shattered this illusion – what grave sin had caused this repeated ruin of imperial territory? Some decided that it was idolatrous veneration of icons. But while opposition to image-worship may have been galvanising in certain parts of the eastern Mediterranean, reverence for and worship of icons continued to spread across much of the Christian world, with images of Christ, Mary, saints, and Biblical scenes decorating churches in the form of mosaics, frescoes, carvings, and illuminated manuscripts. The belief that these were miraculous conduits to those depicted to act as intercessors with God was going to be hard to shake.

A Volcanic Spark?

Having looked at the possible reasons 'why' for iconoclasm, we must now look at 'when' Leo's iconoclasm actually occurred, if at all. If Nikephoros is followed, which is tempting but difficult given his abbreviated style, the iconoclasm of Leo III had a literal volcanic spark. In the Aegean Sea, near the islands of Thera and Therasia, there was an eruption of 'smoky steam', followed by a fire burst that ejected so much pumice that it created a new island and saw pieces float as far as Abydos. Reputedly, the water became so hot that people could not touch it.[85] There seems to have been a long precursor to such seismic and volatile activity, such as the 'fiery hail' and boiling sea that afflicted the Arab fleet in 718.[86] Nikephoros would have it that Leo saw these volcanic eruptions as 'signs of divine wrath'[87] and responded to it by planning to remove holy icons, as he thought that God was telling him to stop their idolatrous adoration. Nikephoros does little to posit a year for these volcanic and iconoclastic eruptions, merely stating that they occurred 'in those days' and 'during the summer season.'[88] He has them take place after the coronation of Constantine V in Easter 720 and before the rebellion of the Hellenes and Cyclades (which he claims was due to iconoclasm), but his style of writing does not give any hint of how long after that coronation or before the rebellion the Theran eruption took place. Such chronological issues will be a consistent problem when looking at almost any part of the outbreak of iconoclasm.

Theophanes records this volcanic eruption in similar terms – 'a vapour from a fiery furnace', with pumice floating throughout the Aegean and a new island being formed[89] – and places it in the summer of 726. He also connects this eruption to Leo's iconoclasm, but does not have it as the specific spark in his chronological order. That is because by his entry of AM6218, Theophanes has already addressed the iconoclasm of Leo III on at least two occasions

– AM6215 (722/723), in connecting it to the iconoclastic edict of Yazid II, where he also mentioned the influence of 'boorish' Besr, and in AM6217 (724/725) where Theophanes has Leo making 'pronouncements' against the holy and venerable icons. Such was the extent of these pronouncements a year before the supposed Nikephoran spark of iconoclasm, that Theophanes has Pope Gregory II withholding the taxes of 'Italy and of Rome' and sending the emperor a doctrinal letter stating that 'it was not proper for the Emperor to issue a command concerning the faith or to make innovations in the ancient doctrines of the church, which had been established by the holy fathers.'[90] Theophanes would have the Theran eruption see Leo, encouraged by Besr, double down on his iconoclastic policies rather than see the eruption as a warning to cease his 'ruthless war on the holy and venerable icons.'[91]

Due to his epitomising, Nikephoros does give the more straightforward account, while Theophanes is a little more muddled; however, it is unlikely that Leo III suddenly jumped into a policy of iconoclasm due to a single volcanic event as the former suggests, and we have already laid out a list of potential influences to make Leo an iconoclast. It could even be that the reason Theophanes has information regarding Leo's iconoclastic ideas from before the Theran eruption is because Leo had been trying to persuade his imperial subjects through peaceful discussion in the years prior to his turning to edicts, a notion that might explain why he tolerated the iconodule Germanos as patriarch for so long.[92] However, this may be giving too much credence to Theophanes' chronology. He was not above making errors in his own records. Regarding the two pre-Theran claims of Leonid iconoclasm, connecting Leo to Yazid's iconoclasm is fraught with problems, with the AM6217 entry containing substantial issues, not necessarily of Theophanes' making, but still damaging to the account. Firstly, and more importantly, the word used by Theophanes for Leo's 'pronouncements' regarding the removal of icons – λόγον – is problematic, with 'a bewildering multiplicity of possible meanings.'[93] This can be seen in the *Oxford Classical Greek Dictionary*, which for λόγος lists…

> 'saying, speaking, speech, mode of speaking; eloquence, discourse; conversation, talk; word, expression; assertion; principle, maxim; proverb; oracle; promise; order; command; proposal; condition, agreement; stipulation, decision; pretext; fable, news, story, report, legend; prose-writing, history, book, essay, oration; affair, incident; thought, reason, reckoning, computation, reflection, deliberation, account, consideration, opinion; cause, end; argument, demonstration; meaning, value; proportion; *New Testament* the Word.'

There is a colossal difference between an authoritative, imperial 'order' to remove icons and the initiating of a discussion regarding them, but both have received support.[94] Is Theophanes claiming that Leo initiated iconoclasm at this point in 724/725? Nikephoros would seem to have it after the summer of 726 (without actually telling us), while the *Vita Stephani iunioris*,[95] the most detailed hagiographic account of iconoclasm, places the outbreak of iconoclasm in the tenth year of Leo's reign – 726 in inclusive counting. It is also important to note that if there was an imperial 'order', no text has survived.

There are also factual issues highlighted in Theophanes' AM6217 entry. He conflates popes Gregory II (715–731) and Gregory III (731–741) into a single pope of that name with a reign of 725–734. And the *Liber Pontificalis* indicates that the taxation issue between the papacy and the empire was already happening *before* any 'order/discussion' on icons was initiated by Leo III in 724/725. Indeed, it does not state that iconoclasm was partly a result of the economic falling out between Gregory II and Leo III – instead, imperial authorities reputedly responded to Gregory's withholding of tax revenue by trying to remove the pope and even kill him.[96] There is also significant discussion about the existence of Gregory's doctrinal letter to Leo. It may even be in reference to two late-eighth/early-ninth century letters of dubious authenticity. And even if they are genuine or record some actual contemporary papal contact with Constantinople, their content gives allusions to the Lombard capture of Ravenna, which was not until 732 or definitively in 751, undermining the chronological position of this Gregorian 'doctrinal' letter.[97] This gives little concrete in chronological terms, only to further prove that we face considerable trouble in determining when, or even if, Leo's iconoclasm was initiated.

Instances of Icon Breaking: The Chalke Gate and Walls of Nicaea

On this already shaking historiographical ground, we move on to what is considered the first open act of Leonid iconoclasm: the removal/destruction of the icon of the Chalke Gate. This image – depicting the Lord above an entrance to the imperial palace – would seem to be of considerable prominence; however, even in iconodule writings, it was not accorded 'any outstanding significance.'[98] This could demonstrate that at least the Chalke Gate icon and maybe icons in general were not as widely revered as iconodules would later suggest; at least not until its removal. There are several versions of the story of this initiative iconoclastic act, each with their own additional/alternative aspects. Theophanes has the 'Lord's image' that hung above the Bronze/Chalke Gate taken down by men of Leo in the immediate aftermath of the Theran eruption.[99] Already roused in opposition to the 'new-fangled doctrines'[100] of the emperor regarding icons, the populace of Constantinople attacked and killed some of these men. Leo responded with 'mutilation, lashes, exile and fines', creating the first iconodule martyrs. Theophanes also suggests that in his iconoclastic anger, Leo targeted many of noble birth and high learning, destroying many of the schools and education systems that had been around since the Christianising of the empire.

Such a pronouncement of a Leonid destruction of Roman education at this point is specific to Theophanes. The iconoclastic age was not a great one for art, but some traditions continued, and some influences were absorbed from abroad, giving the era its own distinct flavour. There was a parallel decline in some expertise, but this was not necessarily due to iconoclasm itself, as many of the richer cities of the empire were already showing decline by the late-sixth century, followed by the upheavals of the seventh. This decline was long claimed to be in marked contrast to the artistic boom that encapsulated the 'Carolingian Renaissance' in the Frankish Empire, but this is incorrect due to iconodule sources presenting the 'Byzantine Renaissance' as beginning much later than it did. The green shoots of Roman recovery were Isaurian in date and origin. That said, the iconoclastic period did see a significant change in the basic education programme. While philosophy, rhetoric, mathematics and their many constituents remained part of Roman education by the late-eighth century, the core changed from classical elements like Homer to biblical texts.

A more detailed story of the Chalke Gate incident comes in the first letter of Gregory II to Leo III, although it does not appear to be a contemporary text, either a later interpolation or a complete fabrication.[101] It records Leo sending a *spatharocandidatus* called Julian (some manuscripts call him Jovinus) to the Chalke Gate to destroy the image of the Saviour, which had been the site of many miracles. When he arrived there, Julian was met by a group of zealous women, who begged him not to carry out his task. The *spatharocandidatus* did not listen, climbing a ladder and starting to hack away at the icon with an axe. Upon seeing this, the women pulled down the ladder and beat Julian to death. Gregory bemoans how Leo sent his soldiers to punish and kill many of these women. 'The specific details of this account … appear at first sight to be due to an eye-witness,'[102] but it is instead problematic. Not only does it entail exaggeration, the text misidentifies the location and therefore the actual icon targeted – it speaks of the Chalkoprateia, the name of a quarter of Constantinople and a church. This could be a mistake based on the similar names, but other comments suggest that the identification of the Chalkoprateia was intended and understood, detailing the account from a Constantinopolitan origin, who would not have made such a mistake. Such is the problem that even those who argue in favour of the authenticity of these Gregorian letters find the whole

'Chalkoprateia' incident to be so problematic that they posit the whole section as a later interpolation into an authentic contemporary source.

The *Vita Stephani iunioris* has Leo III order the Chalke icon be taken down and burned. It repeats the pious women pulling down the ladder and killing the *spatharius* charged with the deed, but adds that they made for the patriarchal palace where they threw stones at the patriarch. The *Vita* also provides an extra piece of information regarding the nature of the Chalke icon. There has been argument over what exactly the icon above the Chalke Gate was made from. It could have been a stone statue, more easily connected to pagan practice and therefore explains why Germanos did not strenuously attack Leo's actions in 726/727. In such a notion, the dispute between the emperor and patriarch only came later when iconoclasm was escalated in 730 with paintings being targets. However, that Leo would target the Chalke icon for destruction through burning increases the likelihood that it was a wooden painted panel rather than a stone statue.

Other hagiographic sources provide slightly different forms of this Chalke incident, specifically what are considered the 'Marian' and 'Theodosian' versions. The 'Marian' version stems from an anonymous *Passio*, also called 'The Acts of the Ten Martyrs', which belongs to the second half of the ninth century and relies heavily on Theophanes and the *Vita Stephani iunioris*, following the latter in terms of date. It also places Besr at the head of the group of soldiers undertaking the destruction. A group, led by a patrician woman of imperial lineage called Mary, but also containing ten others – Gregory the *protospatharius*, Julian, Marcian, John, James, Alexius, Demetrius, Leontius, Photius and Peter – attacked and killed a *spatharius*. The incensed Leo sent 500 soldiers against the people, killing many. The group were thrown in prison for eight months, where they were punished daily. After that, they were brought before the emperor, who tried to make them renounce their support for the icons. When they refused, Leo had their faces branded with hot irons, before they were beheaded at the Kynegion, their bodies thrown into the *ta Pelagiou*, the burial place for criminals on 9 August. Their bodies would later be moved to the Church of St Demetrius at the Aninas monastery. The 'Theodosian' version first appeared in the *Menologium* of Basil II of c.1000 and replaces Mary with Theodosia the nun. Theodosia was executed with a ram's horn, a peculiar method. Showing some naivety, the *Menologium* has Theodosia live during the reign of Constantine V, despite having been martyred under Leo III. This is not completely incorrect as Constantine was co-ruler with his father from 720.

Another aside from the Chalke incident is the suggestion that Leo replaced the Christ icon with a plain cross, using an epigram of Theodore the Studite. This epigram could refer to Leo V and his son Symbatios-Constantine,[103] although it would not be surprising for Isaurian emperors to mount a cross above the Chalke Gate due to the prominence they gave to the cross in their iconoclastic policies. It was also claimed that the Chalke Gate image was not destroyed, making its way to the papal collection in the Lateran. While this has been refuted as a myth,[104] it shows that regardless of whether it happened or not, the incident at the Chalke Gate and the icon itself had taken on significant importance for iconodule opposition to Isaurian icon policies.

The most significant issue raised by the sources on the Chalke Gate incident is of date – when exactly did this incident happen? This might seem somewhat insignificant, but it has ramifications for the outbreak of iconoclasm and the veracity of some of the source material. Based on Theophanes' placing of the incident between the Theran eruption and the Helladic/Cycladean revolt, the earlier date is 726/727. The other sources that also have this date – Anastasius, Cedrenus, *Historia Miscella* – got their information from Theophanes and so are not providing independent corroboration. The letter of Gregory II to the emperor claims that the Chalke icon's destruction occurred ten years into Leo's reign, which began on 25 March 717. Gregory records that this letter was in reply to a previous imperial missive of the 9th indiction, i.e. 725–726; he also mentions Germanos as still being patriarch, a reign that did not end until 730. The section of Gregory's letter that deals with the Chalke Gate incident is considered 'particularly dubious,'[105] and does not provide much backing. Even with that though, 726–727 is the most accepted date for any such Chalke Gate incident.

The other proposed date for this event is 730, with the *Vita Stephani iunioris* claiming that the Chalke icon was destroyed immediately after the resignation of Germanos and the accession of Anastasius as patriarch on 22 January 730, with it being Anastasius who the women threw the stones at and who encouraged Leo to have said women executed as punishment. The late-ninth century 'Acts of the Ten Martyrs' dates the Chalke icon incident to 19 January 730. This does not completely line up with the *Vita Stephani iunioris*, as it has Anastasius as patriarch, a position he did not take up until 22 January. Some support for 730 could come from other sources: it could be logical for it to occur just after the *silentium* of 17 January 730, especially if there had yet to be an imperial edict against the icons, an idea supported by the interview between Leo and Germanos in 728/729. Here, the patriarch states 'We have heard it said that there will be a destruction of the holy and venerable icons, but not in your reign.'[106] Germanos would not have said this had there been an iconoclastic 'order' in 724/725 and the Chalke Gate icon had been destroyed in 726/727. Indeed, very little icon breaking is recorded before 730. Some iconodule sources may be presenting

Germanos in an uncompromising light, moving the entire Chalke Gate incident to 3–4 years later to connect it directly to his resignation as patriarch.

There is a third 'chronological' option that had been put forward ... rather than 726/727 or 730, could it be that the destruction of the Chalke Gate icon did not happen at all, possibly because no such image actually existed at that point?[107] On the backdrop of some doubts surrounding many aspects of the Leonid iconoclasm, doubting the existence of the Chalke Gate incident does not seem all that far-fetched. If the very idea of the Chalke Gate incident being moved to a later date cannot be completely rejected, then neither can the idea that the entire incident never took place at all ... Unfortunately, none of these arguments are decisive, leaving the date of the Chalke Gate incident up in the air.

While there is much focus on the incident at the Chalke Gate, there was another similar incident at Nicaea in 727. Supposedly at the head of 100,000 men, two Arab generals, Ameros and Mauias (Amr and Mu'awiyah), struck across Anatolia and put Nicaea under siege. While the city was supposedly unprepared, it resisted the Arab attack. Amidst this siege, Theophanes relays the story of Constantine, a *strator* of Artabasdos, throwing a stone at an image of the Virgin Mary. This caused it to fall to the ground, where Constantine stamped on it. Such an action may reflect an underway iconoclasm or a more specific belief that that icon *palladia* had failed to protect so many Roman cities from Arab attack. The iconodule Theophanes has Constantine suitably punished for his act of sacrilegious iconoclasm. First, the *strator* was visited by a vision of Mary, who warns 'See, what a brave thing you have done to me! Verily, upon your head have you done it.' And the next day, in the face of another Arab assault, Constantine raced to the walls – Theophanes shows his slavish copying of a less iconodule source by calling this dreadful iconoclast a 'brave soldier' – where he had his head smashed by a large stone launched from an Arab siege engine: 'a just reward for his impiety.'[108]

Nikephoros gives a shorter version of the siege, mentioning nothing of Constantine's icon breaking,[109] which raises concerns over the veracity of Theophanes' account. Indeed, some of the awkwardness of the original Theophanic Greek could stem from Theophanes inserting an image story to add an iconodule slant.[110] As well as the Constantine incident, he also claims that Nicaea was saved not by the soldiers defending it, but by 'acceptable prayers' and the images of the Nicene Fathers in the Church of the Holy Fathers. However, while the existence of such images is backed up in other sources,[111] Theophanes fails to present the salvation of Nicaea as a victory for icons. The entire Nicaea incident, other than the death of Constantine, does nothing to present iconoclasm as being rejected by divine authority. Not only was the city not punished for Constantine's or indeed Leo's iconoclasm, it was *saved* from Arab sack in the aftermath of the destruction of an icon of the Virgin.

The somewhat throwaway Theophanic line that 'after a long siege and a partial destruction of the walls, they did not overpower the town'[112] has archaeological and epigraphic backing. The walls of Nicaea, now in the Turkish city of Iznik, were rebuilt in the late-720s, with an inscription, still extant, which gives credit to the rebuilding to the emperors and Artabasdos, without any pro- or anti-icon stance. This inscription not only gives credence to the siege of Nicaea itself, which is not attested in Arab sources (likely due to its failure), and the destruction of part of the city walls, it highlights the involvement of Artabasdos. This would explain the presence of his *strator*; however, it does not highlight any truth to Constantine's supposed iconoclasm. Theophanes might sneeringly claim that Leo presented this victory as affirmation of his iconoclastic policies, which there is no other evidence for, but in reality he is somewhat bereft of explanation for the military victory of an iconoclastic emperor. This would be a problem: iconodules were going to be faced with several decades of trying to understand how a 'heretic' dynasty was winning so many victories for the Roman Empire.

There was some attempt to connect the Helladic/Cycladic revolt directly to the iconoclastic policies of Leo III. But not only is there dispute about how iconoclastic Leo's policies were, this revolt was likely defeated by April 726, which was *before* the removal of the Chalke Gate icon, which was late summer/autumn 726 at the very earliest. Indeed, it was extremely early for *any* iconoclastic measures. This has led to other suggestions of economic and more general lack of authority reasons for the revolt. The resistance faced by Agallianos, Kosmas and their allies from the citizenry of Constantinople, supposedly a hotbed of iconodule support, would also suggest that iconoclasm was not a part of the rebellion. Similar iconodule leanings would be attributed to the usurpation of Artabasdos in how he restored the icons on his capture of Constantinople in 743, but this does not appear to be the case.[113]

Emperor vs Patriarch

After these reputed incidents of iconoclasm at the Chalke Gate and Nicaea, both Nikephoros and Theophanes switch their attention to the growing dispute between Leo III and his patriarch Germanos. Before he came to stand up to any iconoclastic policies of Leo, Germanos had already played a prominent role in Roman imperial politics. His father is recorded as a patrician called Justinian who was executed for his role in the assassination of Constans II in 668 and the subsequent usurpation of Mezizios. This saw Constantine IV have the already young man, Germanos, castrated and sent into the church.[114] By 712, he was the metropolitan of Cyzicus and was then promoted to being patriarch of Constantinople in August 715. From this position, he partook in the successive negotiations that saw Theodosius III replace Anastasius II in 715, and then Leo III replace Theodosius III in 717. The patriarch and emperor likely had a reasonably close relationship, with Germanos presiding over the baptism and accession of Constantine V, while Leo will surely have tapped into Germanos' patriarchal prominence to help galvanise the imperial city during the Arab siege.

However, when it came to religious doctrine and hierarchies, the pair were on divergent paths. The patriarch, along with the pope, saw the emperor's role as 'to watch and guard over the Church, not to change its doctrine;'[115] however, Leo felt that it was his legal right to make his own religious views law for his subjects, reputedly even stating to Gregory II that 'I am emperor and priest.'[116] This was not a claim of state supremacy over the church, but rather 'a re-establishment of the traditional view of the emperor within the Christian schema',[117] a view crafted after the conversion of Constantine by the likes of Eusebius of Caesarea to make the imperial position more palatable to Christians, using the outline of Hellenistic kingship – the emperor was not a god amongst men, but a man with 'a divine commission to bring peace and justice to the world.'[118] Such a view looked to present Leo III not as a heretic innovator but as a traditionalist restorer of imperial Christianity. This would also fit in with the idea of imperial iconoclasts looking to remove objects or individuals – icons, monks – that had taken focus of authority from the emperor. Removing images of God, Christ, the Virgin, and saints would have left the emperor as the most prevalent individual in the empire, and it is no surprise that imperial depictions increase during iconoclasm. Any such 'turning back of the clock' with regards to imperial authority and the roles of icons, monks, saints etc. did mean that Leo 'found fault with all the emperors, chief prelates, and Christian folk who had preceded him, [not just] on the ground that they had been idolaters because of their reverence for the august, holy icons,'[119] but also because they had contributed to the undermining of imperial authority.

Germanos had already been involved in formal outward debate over the images during the 720s, shown in a series of his letters.[120] The first of these letters concerned Constantine, bishop of Nakoleia, a Phrygian city 300km south-east of Constantinople, who was an iconoclastic ally of Leo III.[121] Germanos wrote to Constantine's superior, John, bishop of Synada, treating it as a case of local discipline rather than a church-wide issue. Any quiet dealing with the issue by John failed, leading to the patriarch writing directly to Constantine, expressing his annoyance over his refusal to honour images by performing *proskynesis* (bowing/prostration) before them. Constantine argued that such an honour was due only to God, but the patriarch said that the honour given to the icons was different to the honour given to God. This argument became central to the iconoclasm dispute. Iconodules like Germanos came to recognise that there was some issue with icon veneration, at least in technical terms if not in practice (recognising a practical issue would be admitting that a long-standing aspect of Christian worship involving icons was a church error). A clear distinction had to be made between idolatry and icon veneration, with the latter needing to be shown not to be outright worship; an honour 'directed not to the material of which the images were made but to the person represented.'[122] This required new phraseology in the form of σχετική προσκύνησις (*schetike proskynesis*), translated as something akin to 'relative veneration' or 'qualified veneration'.[123] Germanos thought that he had convinced Constantine of this distinction, with the bishop agreeing to follow tradition and not to scandalise or confuse the populace. Instead, Constantine retained his 'anti-image position'. It is not exactly clear if Constantine did anything else other than fail to bow before the images, but the two letters showed that in the 720s at least one church man had a problem with the honour being bestowed on the sacred portraits. There is little or no evidence that this was a widespread problem – yet.

The third letter of Germanos was sent to Thomas, bishop of Klaudiopolis, who came under the direct jurisdiction of the Constantinpolitan patriarchate. This letter was read out at the Second Council of Nicaea in 787, defending the veneration shown to icons. It has a much different tone than those to John and Constantine and so has been claimed to come from late in or even after Germanos' patriarchate, when the iconoclasm dispute had grown. The patriarch recalled his meetings with Thomas, who complained about an icon failing to provide its miraculous ointment, possibly displaying dismay at the powerlessness of icons in general. Much like with Constantine, Germanos thought that his arguments over notions such as σχετική προσκύνησις had swayed Thomas back into a more 'orthodox' stance; however, the bishop of Klaudiopolis had been hardened in his doubts over the veracity of icon veneration as he had the icons in his church removed. Germanos complained that in these actions, Thomas was opening the church to Jewish and Muslim slander, was going against tradition and scripture, and was denying his congregation the saintly models of behaviour. The patriarch reminded Thomas, somewhat peculiarly, that Leo III had erected an image of the apostles, prophets, and the cross in front of the palace as a demonstration of imperial faith. This suggestion that Leo installed images of anything other than the cross flies in the face of the usual depiction of him as the arch iconoclast and is something we will return to later. As both of these Asian provincial bishops had been reprimanded by the patriarch for their stances on icons, it could be that Constantine and Thomas had contact with Leo III; however, evidence of such contact between emperor and Asian bishops, while an attractive explanation, is lacking.

And while we are looking for potential iconoclastic allies of Leo III, we must also look for prominent opponents beyond Germanos. Two successive papal Gregorys were opposed to iconoclasm, while in Damascus, John Chrysorrhoas ('flowing with gold') wrote extensively against iconoclasm – *Treatises Against Those Who Deprecate the Holy Images* – and specifically against Leo's attacking of the honour due to the saints. Indeed, the works of John of Damascus (730s/740s) provide much of the theological basis for images and icons – a divine presence in sanctified matter – that would be tested by iconoclasts at the Council of Hieria in 754 and ultimately become the iconodule 'orthodoxy' and 'the basis for a medieval view of the image as fully equal with Scripture.'[124] Hagiographic sources suggest that, despite being in Umayyad territory, Leo III attempted to silence John Chrysorrhoas – a ninth-century Arabic life and a tenth-century Greek *Vita* of John have Leo's secretaries planting a forged letter that presented John as inviting Roman attack on Damascus. For this treachery, John lost a hand only for the Virgin Mary to restore it – 'the entire story is a fiction designed to glorify the saintly servant of the Caliphs at the expense of the iconoclastic emperor.'[125] Instead, being in Arab territory insulated John of Damascus almost completely from imperial reprisal. Similarly, the increasingly detached status of Italy from the Roman Empire provided the pope with some separation. However, their distance to Constantinople also reduced the support and protection they could offer to the likes of Germanos.

But before any thought to the patriarch needing protection arose, having turned his attention to Germanos, Leo attempted to convince the patriarch to support iconoclasm. It might be thought that Leo was wasting his time in attempting to sway Germanos away from iconodule 'orthodoxy'; however, Germanos had not always been the great champion of orthodoxy – when bishop of Cyzicus, he had acquiesced to Philippikos Bardanes' attempts to revive Monothelitism and rescind of the Sixth Ecumenical Council. 'The spirit of accommodation he showed at this juncture may have been a factor in his transfer to the see of Constantinople, but once elevated to the highest ecclesiastical dignity, he seems to have acquired a firmness of conviction that he had lacked before.'[126] In response to this imperial outreach, Germanos recalled a prophecy known within the church: 'we have heard there will be a condemnation of the holy and revered icons, but not during your reign.' Leo then forced the patriarch to reveal whose reign would see a great iconoclasm – 'During the reign of Konon.' When the emperor then revealed that his baptismal name was Konon, Germanos retorted 'Heaven forbid, my lord, that this evil should come to pass through your rule. For he who does it is the forerunner of the Antichrist and the overthrower of the incarnate and divine dispensation.'[127] The emperor was angered by this patriarchal snub and escalated the pressure on Germanos 'just as Herod once had on John the Baptist.' The patriarch stayed firm, reminding Leo of the promises he had made when he assumed the throne, 'that he would in no way disturb God's church from its apostolic laws.'[128] This failed to shame Leo away from his iconoclastic path, with the emperor threatening to depose Germanos if he felt the patriarch was acting against his imperial wishes.

In this contest with the patriarch, Leo found a well-placed ally in one Anastasius, a pupil and *synkellos* of Germanos.[129] The patriarch was aware of Anastasius' leanings and reminded his *synkellos* of the consequences of betrayal. When that did nothing to sway Anastasius, Germanos warned him as he went in to meet with the emperor 'Don't hurry, for you will enter the gate through which chariots come.'[130] If Germanos meant it as a prediction, it was one that took fifteen years to come to fruition, when Anastasius was beaten, whipped, blinded, and paraded naked through the streets of Constantinople on a donkey, passing through the gate of chariots when entering the Hippodrome – Anastasius' crime had been supporting the rebel Artabasdos against Constantine V in 744.[131]

Having seized the initiative, Leo called a *silentium*, a meeting of leading secular and church officials (mistaken in some sources for a synod), targeting icons for 7 January 730.[132] The patriarch was present, and Leo tried one last time to persuade him to back iconoclasm. Germanos' refusal to comply marked the end of his patriarchate. There is a slight deviation between Theophanes and Nikephoros about Germanos' reply. While the former has Germanos state that 'I cannot make innovations in the faith without an ecumenical conference,'[133] the latter has him say that 'without an ecumenical synod I cannot make a written declaration of faith.'[134] This is either incorrect/poor recording by Nikephoros or by the shared source of Theophanes and Nikephoros, with Theophanes correcting the statement – Germanos could not change faith or doctrine without a church council, but his declaration of faith was personal and could say basically whatever he wanted.

The two do agree that Germanos gave up the patriarchate in the face of this imperial opposition;[135] however, the *Liber Pontificalis* has Germanos 'expelled from his see through the emperor's wickedness.'[136] It is difficult to judge which of these sources is correct – Theophanes and Nikephoros being closer geographically and their source rivalling the possible contemporaneousness of the *Liber Pontificalis*. In an earlier pronouncement, Theophanes mentioned that Germanos was 'exiled'[137] in the thirteenth year of Leo's reign, which might hint more at the end of Germanos' patriarchate being Leo's doing. It was also suggested that Germanos was eventually hanged on the order of Leo,[138] which could also hint at an imperial order being behind the end of Germanos' patriarchate. In more modern sources and retellings, it is more usual to talk about Germanos being dismissed.[139] However it came about, Germanos' patriarchate ended after just over fourteen years in the role. He is said to have gone into seclusion at his ancestral home, possibly at Platanaion, to live out his days, but even this is not completely clear. He may have been exiled there or confined to the Chora monastery and then exiled to his home; or retired to his home and then later exiled to Chora where he was possibly executed.[140] Any ramping up of his punishments could indicate that even after losing his patriarchate, Germanos did not remove himself from iconoclasm arguments, possibly in the form of his letter to Thomas of Klaudiopolis.

With Germanos removed, Leo appointed a supportive patriarch in the form of Anastasius. Unsurprisingly, the new patriarch accepted Leo's iconoclasm, seeing it become not only imperial but church policy. At least in the east, for equally unsurprisingly, the papal Gregorys both rejected Anastasius' elevation and his statement of faith, condemning Leo for his attacks on icons. Leo was furious with this papal rejection and 'intensified the assault on the holy icons. Many clerics, monks and pious laymen faced danger on behalf of the true faith and won the crown of martyrdom.'[141]

With such pronouncements and the emperor having the backing of his new patriarch, it would be expected that the last eleven years of Leo III's reign would see a significant escalation of iconoclastic actions. However, there is still a significant lack of clarity over the exact nature and timing of any actions or how forcefully any iconoclasm was carried out. The claim of an iconoclastic edict in 726/727 does not seem to fit with Germanos, the arch anti-iconoclast, remaining in post for another four years. Some of this confusion may be due to iconodule rewrites trying to distance Germanos from having worked with Leo III. We are also poorly informed about what went on at the *silentium* in early 730. Did this council reaffirm or expand a previous decree or was this the first iteration of an anti-icon edict, hence Germanos' outright refusal to cooperate and then his removal as patriarch? There is some evidence of the removal of icons after 730, possibly with iconoclasts having relics distanced from altars so as not to taint the eucharist;[142] however, there is increasing doubt over there being widespread destruction of images, murals, altar covers, and relics and persecution of priests, monks and laymen who defended those icons post-730. These claims have been seen as 'deliberately magnified'[143] and even complete iconodule fabrications,[144] with any systematic iconoclasm during the reign of Leo III to possibly be considered out of the question. Indeed, it is 'by no means certain that the iconophiles suffered serious persecution till mid-way through the reign of Leo III's son, Constantine V,'[145] who appears a much more fervent and active iconoclast than his father. Even the most prominent iconodule sources, who we would expect to hear more from about any considerable imperially-mandated attack on the icons, give little-to-no information about iconoclasm post-730. For example, while some of the annual entries in the *Chronographia* of Theophanes had focused almost solely on iconoclasm up to AM6221, during the last eleven years of Leo III's reign, there is nothing said about iconoclasm until Theophanes' goes on something of a rant about Leo and his 'evil doctrine'[146] upon the emperor's death in 741. This raises questions of whether a Leonid iconoclasm was underway to any real degree. Or is this an argument from silence?

One of the basic arguments for iconoclasm became 'the favourable military and political records of the iconoclastic Emperors Leo III and Constantine V, their long reigns and success.'[147] Other later iconoclastic emperors such as Michael II and Theophilos were not so militarily successful, and therefore not so successful in implementing their religious policy. And at the head of these military victories of Leo and Constantine was the cross, the championing of which the emperors could say anchored them in tradition and Christian faith.[148] Such a military focus could contribute to any imperial iconoclasm in a practical sense. Rather than focus on making/venerating such images, perhaps those energies and resources should have been expended on something more 'useful' – such utilitarianism might be a more modern idea, but could a military-minded Leo III have had similar thoughts? Rather than seeing no utility in veneration of any kind, the practical Roman of this period might have wanted to not waste time on veneration that was clearly not 'working'.

A significant attack on icons and their supporters is suggested by the recording of refuges for iconodules by *Vita Stephani iunioris*. These refuges were all maritime – Black Sea coast, southern Italy and Cyprus – and were all regions of the empire where Roman control was less than complete. It also mentions the 'Propontis', without specifying which one: the Cimmerian Bosphoros and the straits between Cyprus and Anatolia are described as 'Propontic'; however, the more usual 'Propontis' is the Sea of Marmara, so the *Vita* might be suggesting that the environs of the imperial capital contained an iconodule refuge. If true, it was surely sporadic, for iconoclasm was at its most stringent in and around the capital. It could even be that iconoclasm was used to re-impose imperial control on the provinces, which in some ways makes it 'a Constantinopolitan phenomenon, which invaded the provinces.'[149] The sheer fact that arguments can be made to present 'Byzantine iconoclasm' as either sprouting from the imperial capital and spreading into the provinces *or* an eastern provincial idea that gradually made its way to the capital demonstrates the difficulty in presenting a clear picture of iconoclasm. While these areas of iconodule refuge suggest a vociferous and successful imposition of iconoclasm, the source record might be presenting a slightly skewed grand picture. This is because the iconodule sources focus on the provinces where imperial control was strongest and therefore where iconoclasm was more forcefully imposed. Because of this, could it be that the iconodules themselves give a more 'successful' picture of iconoclasm than was the case? These places of iconodule refuge had also been frequent sites of imperial exile, which may add a further political dimension for these regions to take up against iconoclasm.

Even this idea of certain regions or groups being fervent defenders or detractors of iconoclasm must be treated carefully. Not all monks were stringent iconodules, with several prominent monastic communities won over to iconoclasm due to a concerted effort by the authorities. This suggests that they tried to talk people round before resorting to force and persecution. And the army, which under Constantine V was seen as an iconoclast bastion, also contained pockets of iconodule support. So, while there were more general divides between iconodule west and iconoclast east, between a general populace following imperial policy and upper classes holding to tradition, these are by no means clear delineations of who supported or opposed iconoclasm.

Reaction in the West

Imperio-papal relations had been very up and down during the seventh century. The Monothelite controversy had seen Constans II depose and exile a pope. Constantine IV had succeeded in coming to an accommodation with the papacy, which largely held even with Justinian II's initial heavy-handedness over Quinisext. It is usually seen that Leo's iconoclasm was the spark for the latest downturn in east-west relations, but Rome and Constantinople were already at loggerheads over taxation and waning imperial authority over Italy. Iconoclasm merely added to those disagreements, rather than spark them. That is not to say that iconoclasm did not have some impact on imperio-papal relations. While it might be that papal opinion on icons was not staunchly held before the outbreak, when it came, the papacy took a hard-line iconodule stance. Gregory II held a synod in the late-720s that condemned iconoclasm and, according to Theophanes, had Leo III excommunicated; however, no western source records such an action. As we have seen, equally doubted are the pair of letters reputedly sent to Leo by Gregory II, telling the emperor that he had no right to interfere in matters of church doctrine. Upon his accession, Gregory III in 731 appealed to Leo to moderate his iconoclasm, which may show some papal recognition that icon veneration had veered too closely to idolatry. When Leo's response was to arrest the papal representative, Gregory called a synod that condemned iconoclasm outright and withheld papal recognition of Anastasius. There was some iconoclast support in Italy – Otranto had an iconoclast bishop and even in the past, the papacy had shown some support for iconoclastic measures. When a late-sixth century bishop of Marseilles had ordered all icons be removed and destroyed, he was praised by Pope Gregory I, although the pope condemned the actual destruction, seeing icons as educational.[150]

The lack of separation between the ancient state and religion meant that any imperial policy against icons had political ramifications, particularly in Italy with the growing position of the pope. Leo III tried various ways to depose the successive Gregorian popes for their iconodule stance – he appointed a favourable exarch with orders to remove the pope; he encouraged opposition from the Lombards and Roman dukes and then even launched an expedition of his own to Italy. None of this worked. Part of this political dimension saw the transferring of Illyricum, Sicily and southern Italy from papal jurisdiction to that of Constantinople, but there is considerable dispute about when this action happened, and even which emperor was behind it.[151] It is usually linked to the outbreak of iconoclasm and therefore to the reign of Leo III in around 732–733;[152] however, it has also been claimed to be an action detached from iconoclasm and rather part of 'the general Isaurian scheme for tidying the administration of the empire.'[153]

Even though various areas of the peninsula welcomed iconodule refugees, significant portions of Italian iconodule support may have been political in nature i.e. opposing all policies of Leo III, rather than any fervent opposition to iconoclasm itself. This would help them project their independence from the imperial government. It was claimed that the initial iconoclastic 'pronouncement' sparked rebellion in Ravenna, although there are similar issues with this being sparked by iconoclasm or other economic and political issues. This will be looked at in more detail in a later chapter, but this shows the lack of political unity between Constantinople and its Italian holdings. Care must be taken in not viewing 'Italy' as one monocephalic entity, political or religious. Even though the seventh-century Catholic conversion of the Lombards had unified the peninsula religiously, the numerous political allegiances – popes, Lombard kings, Roman emperors, exarchs and various dukes – left the peninsula frequently fragmented. Disputes amongst the various political entities could see differing religious policies. For example, while the *Liber Pontificalis* might see more image descriptions as the eighth century progresses, the Ravennate writer Agnellus says nothing about iconoclasm directly. This silence does not reveal anything about Ravenna's beliefs about icons, but rather more about the long-running dispute between the Ravennate bishopric and the papacy.[154] Again, iconoclasm was merely a tool in Italian politics, rather a central issue.

In terms of its independence, we may see an escalation in what the papacy aimed for: from a mere retention of the Heraclian accommodations with the empire, to an exchanging of suzerain for one more militarily capable, more religiously amenable to papal primacy and more supportive of icons, and then even a harkening back to the Constantinian age for an 'historical', if not necessarily factual, basis for its claim to independence. The lattermost may be seen in what would become the so-called *Donation of Constantine*. This was a document issued by Constantine I in the early-fourth century that supposedly transferred authority over Rome and the western provinces of the Roman Empire to the papacy. This would be used as a basis of papal independence during the medieval disputes between the pope and various Holy Roman emperors; however, even during those struggles it was claimed to be a forgery and eventually by the fifteenth century, even the papal bureaucracy admitted that philologically the document could not belong to the fourth century. The language of the text has suggested an origin in the eighth century, likely demonstrating the growing independent feelings prevalent in papal Rome. However, it is by no means sure that papal independence was a definitive policy during the reign of Leo III – even with significant disagreements, Gregory II had not lost his allegiance to the Roman Empire, helping deal with an imperial usurper in c.730/731. The break did not come until the 750s under Constantine V.[155]

Was Leo III an Iconoclast?

With all this deep discussion about what iconoclasm was, when it was, where it came from, its effects etc., there is one extremely important question that was left largely unasked: was Leo III actually an iconoclast? On the surface, this seems like as strange an imperio-religious question as 'was Diocletian a persecutor of Christians?' or questioning if Constantine ever actually embraced Christianity in any form. The answer appears clear – what became the 'Byzantine iconoclasm' formerly began with Leo III …

> 'a period of massive destruction of religious imagery across the Byzantine world … hugely divisive, tearing apart Byzantine society … a period of artistic stagnation … its fiercest opponents were monks and possibly women … [and begun] by removing an icon of Christ from above the main ceremonial entrance to the palace, the Chalke Gate in either 726 or 730, perhaps as a reaction to have a volcanic eruption on the Aegean island of Thera.'[156]

However, it could be that 'every one of these assumptions is incorrect,'[157] to the extent that Leo III had almost nothing to do with iconoclasm. Such a notion would render much of the discussion over the meaning of 'λογον', Germanos' letters, and much of what the likes of Theophanes had to say about Leo's religious policies as largely moot or even completely wrong.

Certainly, Leo was not an open iconoclast upon his accession, perhaps seen in his absence from the anniversary eulogy for the defeat of the Arab attack on Constantinople, with the Virgin Mary and perhaps the icon devoted to her given the credit.[158] There is the story of Maslamah's horse rearing when approaching the image of the Virgin at the Bosphoran Gate, which was claimed as a victory of the icons during the Arab siege, but this is a later interpolation. He was still not openly iconoclastic by 720 when he had a seal with the legend 'Leo and Constantine' and depicting himself wearing a crossed diadem while the other side had the Virgin holding an infant Jesus. And while the coins he minted with Constantine V on the reverse could be somewhat iconoclastic due to the replacing of the cross portent, this was almost certainly a purely dynastic measure as the cross continued to appear on Leonid silver coinage. Indeed, iconoclastic focus on the cross saw it rise in prominence, not diminish.[159]

Indeed, there was no great activity against icons in the first nine years of his reign, before sources such as Theophanes claim that there was a significant attack initiated between 726–730. And then there is nothing else in the annual account of the *Chronographia* during the eleven years after that. Leo did undertake other religious activity, focusing on Jews and Montanists, activities which may be indicative of his willingness to demand and even force 'religious orthodoxy'; a demand that could have led to iconoclastic action. But even with that potential, 'it is by no means certain that the iconophiles suffered serious persecution till mid-way through the reign of Leo III's son, Constantine V.'[160]

The depiction of Leo as an iconoclast, whilst prevalent in virtually all source material, primary and secondary, relies largely on three documents, all of which are problematic. The *Liber Pontificalis*, which is largely contemporaneous with eighth-century events and independent of the eastern iconodule tradition, deals with imperio-papal relations, but focused more on taxation and land ownership issues. There are three brief mentions of Leo's supposed actions against icons, 'but all have been shown to be later insertions intended to enhance the anti-iconoclast credentials of the popes.'[161] If this is the case, then the *Liber Pontificalis* says nothing contemporary about Leo's dealings with the icons. The *Vita Stephani iunioris*, which was written in 807/809 and called Leo 'the new Doek', referencing Doeg the Edomite who slew a priest for Saul,[162] was a propaganda piece to promote monks and denigrate the Isaurian dynasty. It may even be that 'truth' was not the aim in its telling of the Chalke Gate incident; rather it should be seen as 'a moral tale'[163] and therefore not necessarily based in fact or bearing any semblance of reality. The same can be said of Theophanes' *Chronographia*, with both it and the *Vita* being 'constructions of opposition,'[164] quite possibly using the same core source. This further depletes their veracity as sources for Leo's actions, to the degree that there may be no material written during Leo's reign that attests to any significant iconoclastic acts perpetrated by him. There may not even be anything written before the early ninth century. Such reinvention is not necessarily conscious misrepresentation, with the Isaurian dynasty becoming tied up with iconoclasm, even if not all of its members were iconoclasts. Could it be as straightforward as 'Leo III initiated the Isaurian dynasty so he must have initiated iconoclasm too'?

It may be that we have little clear indication of Leo III's beliefs regarding icons; indeed, if the *Liber Pontificalis*, *Vita Stephani iunioris* and Theophanes are removed from contention as providers of valuable information, we are left with *very* little. There are other sources that could be used to infer aspects of Leo's iconoclasm, such as the poems of Theodore the Studite, the letters of pope Gregory II to Leo, and some other hagiographic texts, but these suffer from various problems of anachronism and veracity. We have seen that the tone and inferences of the *Ekloga* could present some notion of biblical simplicity in Leo's beliefs, while the only other source of information that might have contemporary information are the letters of Germanos to John, Constantine, and Thomas. This might be expected to provide a heavily slanted view of the 'iconoclastic heretic' Leo, but instead we find something surprising. In his letter to Thomas of Klaudiopolis, Germanos not only claims that Leo was a 'Christ-loving, pious emperor' but that he had also had an image of the apostles, prophets, and the cross created in front of the imperial palace. While there may have been some personal and even political reason behind such a claim of invoking an orthodox imperial faith, the Leo in Germanos' letter to Thomas looks like an imperial iconodule… if this was true, then Leo has been done a major historiographic disservice because by 'the 9th century he was the villain of a legend about the beginning of the image struggle.'[165] It may well be that the earliest years of iconomachy were in no way an imperial movement.[166] It must be said though that Germanos' letters also accuse Leo of growing impiety, while John considered the emperor impious and worthy of anathemas.

We have also looked at the potential geographic, cultural, and personal influences that Leo could have felt, whether it be the Monophysitism of Islam of his Syrian homeland, various Anatolian bishops,[167] an active but 'unduly magnified'[168] iconoclast feeling in Phrygia, the environs of Constantinople, or individuals like Besr, Umar II, and Yazid II. And while this seems like a lot of influences, they all come with significant caveats over how there is little-to-no evidence of those influences playing out in Leo's beliefs and actions.

Cutting through the historiographical bias and various potential influences that the emperor could have been under reveals a simpler championing of the commandment against idolatry and a more general look to restore Roman Christianity to its traditional roots, as seen in the *Ekloga*. Iconoclasm was too complex to be solely based on the religious, cultural, and political interests of Leo III. And while the more sophisticated arguments over iconoclasm come later through the philosophising of Constantine V, his supporters, and indeed his opponents, there was already a philosophical and religious basis for it from paganism, Christianity, and other belief systems in contact with the Roman world. Perhaps the only idea to be extrapolated from the time of Leo III that would become part of iconoclasm is the increasing focus and importance of the cross.

Another significant issue with trying to decipher Leo's beliefs and those of others regarding iconoclasm is that the two sides of the debate may not have been as far apart philosophically as the polemic literature would have it[169] – both retained the (pagan) belief in a connection between the icon/image and who/what it depicted, but differed on the nature of that connection. However, this philosophical proximity was overshadowed by its practical applications, with iconoclasts coming to view icon veneration as little better than idolatry or 'veiled animism.'[170] Conversely, iconodules appealed to unwritten traditions, which included various church practices, and to the claim that images had a long history in the church, although many of the examples given were later interpolations, with the earliest authentic examples being fourth century in date.

Even after going into such largely superficial depth on aspects of iconoclasm, there are significant questions to be answered, dependent on which view of Leo's iconoclasm you take. For example, if Leo had nothing to do with iconoclasm, why did Germanos' patriarchate come to an end in early 730 if not for his opposition to iconoclasm? Conversely, if Leo III was such a vociferous iconoclast and felt so vehemently that his imperial predecessors and the church had strayed from accepted practice and doctrine with regard to icons, surely we would expect that he would look to enforce this 'anti-idolatry' doctrine with an ecumenical council?

Outside Iconoclasm: Leo and other Religions

The religious policies of Leo III are dominated by iconoclasm; however, he did deal with various other religions and heresies. Reputedly, one of Leo's major policies towards these other faiths was forced baptism. For his entry for 720/721, Theophanes claims that the emperor targeted both Jews and Montanists.[171] Such a measure against Jews also appears in oriental sources like *Chronicle to 1234*,

Elias of Nisibis, Michael the Syrian and Agapios,[172] with there being enough difference to suggest that this tradition was separate from that of Theophanes, adding a little more credence. That said, there are discussions to be had over the historicity of such forced baptism,[173] particularly when Theophanes manages, even when he admits that they 'were baptised against their will', to judge the Jews negatively as having 'defiled the faith' by washing off their baptism and consuming the eucharist on a full stomach. It should also not be overlooked that the Jews could also be something of an obstacle for the Umayyads as well, with a certain Severus of Marde claiming to be the Messiah in 720/721 in Syria. He himself was a Christian, but he garnered support from local Jewish populations.[174]

Montanism, a Phyrgian sect from as early as the second century, followed the basic tenets of Christianity, with a focus on the teachings of St John, particularly his Gospel and Revelation. They did, however, hold several heterodox beliefs concerning the Trinity, denial of the power of a priest to forgive post-baptismal sins, and acceptance of themselves as vessels for the Holy Spirit or even God to add new divine revelations and prophecies to Christian belief. Such heresy so close to the core of the Roman Empire may have encouraged Leo to target them. Within the *Ekloga*, 'Montanists shall be punished with the sword;'[175] the inference being that they accept forced baptism or face execution. A band of Montanists found a third option – after listening to some of their new divine revelations, on an appointed day, they gathered within one of their churches and immolated themselves.[176] So drastic an action may be doubted; however, almost two centuries earlier, when Justinian I had confiscated Montanist property, they 'shut themselves up in their own churches and at once set these buildings on fire, perishing with them.'[177] While there are doubts over Leo's actions against the Montanists, if he did take such action, he may have helped establish another heresy in the regions of Phyrgia and Lycaonia in the form of the Athinganoi, who appear in Theophanes' record of Michael I's reign (811–813).[178] However, the name 'Athinganoi' was used for a sect in Phrygia at the turn of the seventh century and, demonstrating the lack of clarity on their origins and beliefs, they have been suggested as Manichees, gnostics, Judaising heretics, proto-Romani or even Indo-Greeks.[179]

This also leads us to perhaps the most active heresy during the reign of Leo III: the Paulicians.[180] This Armenian sect reputedly rejected baptism by water, eucharist, cross veneration and icons. It was also an adoptionist, nontrinitarian church, which believed that Jesus did not become the Son of God until his baptism.[181] Some of their teachings were condemned by a synod at Antioch in 268, before the group that became known as the Paulicians appeared in the mid-sixth century Caucasian region, possibly being condemned along with Nestorianism at the Council of Dvin (554–555). This heresy enjoyed a growth spurt sometime during the mid-seventh century. This new wave of Paulicians may have started out as followers of Mani, only for attempts to make their beliefs more acceptable to Christian ears effectively changed them into a Christian sect with great reverence for St Paul. This acquaintance with Manichaeanism has been challenged, with the dualism of both sects seeing them mistaken for one another,[182] along with the general trend of calling various heretics by the same names and knowing very little about their actual beliefs. The very notions of the Paulicians being adoptionist or dualist are uncertain, with later missionaries not finding any dualistic beliefs amongst Balkan Paulicians. They may not have been any more dualist than orthodox Christians, with Satan as the opponent of God.[183]

Paulicians were heretical enough for their growth to draw imperial attention. Their leader, Constantine-Silvanus, was killed in c.681 during a persecution by Constantine IV, although this did little to deaden Paulician zeal. By 690, the leadership of Symeon-Titus, who had been an imperial official sent to deal with these heretics only to become one of them, had seen the Paulicians cause enough alarm for the local bishop to complain to Justinian II. The emperor responded viciously, launching a persecution that killed Symeon-Titus and most of his followers. This attack quietened the Paulicians for half a century.[184] The sect only survived due to the escape of a certain Paul, who revived the Paulicians with his sons Gegnesios and Theodore. But they did not escape imperial attention for long. Possibly knowing of them from his time as Anatolic *strategos* and his attention drawn to them due to disruption caused by a falling out between Gegnesios and Theodore after Paul's death in 715, Leo III had dealings with the Paulicians. The emperor had Gegnesios brought to Constantinople to defend his faith before the patriarch.[185] In the subsequent interview, the patriarch found little wrong in Gegnesios' beliefs, either by being deceived by the Paulicians' arguments or because Gegnesios professed orthodox beliefs to save his skin. The bias and anachronism of our sources make it difficult to ascertain which is the case.[186] However he managed it, Gegnesios felt it would not work again, so the sect fled imperial territory, settling in Umayyad Syria. This self-imposed exile lasted the remaining years of Leo III's reign. Internal strife and heavy Arab taxation would eventually see many Paulicians return to Roman territory, so many that imperial authorities of Constantine V saw them as an Arab-sponsored 'fifth column'. The Paulicians then spread their wings, by choice and imperial intervention, with communities in rural Anatolia, as well as in major cities such as Pisidian Antioch and Constantinople.

The timing of this expansion of the Paulicians – mid-eighth century – sees some attempts to connect them to the iconoclasts. They did hold some similar beliefs – they were opponents of monks, possibly repudiated the use of images, and did not give any special role to the Virgin Mary. These were clear policies of Constantine V, but there is less clarity about whether Leo III followed similar ideas. However, there were significant doctrinal differences. Iconoclasts did not follow dualism (if the Paulicians did), nor did they reject the Old Testament; neither did they follow any Marcionite or Manichaean beliefs. The Paulicians also forbade the use of the cross, substituting the outstretched arms of Christ; they also substituted the body and blood of Christ for his words. The iconoclasts championed the cross and the eucharist as the true symbols of Christianity and did not seek the destruction of ecclesiastical organisation that the Paulicians wanted – they considered the clergy to be an obstacle to the truth promised in the Bible, particularly the non-Biblical ban on laymen reading the Scripture alone. The Paulicians considered only themselves to be 'Christian'. Such a deep doctrinal divide made any alliance between the state and the Paulicians impossible.

Despite this divide, it is unclear just how far either emperor tolerated Paulicians. Constantine V is beyond the scope of this work,[187] but while Leo III seemed willing to leave the Paulicians alone once Gegnesios passed the patriarchal orthodoxy test, there is a legal argument to the contrary. The same law of the *Ekloga* – 17.52 – that demanded Montanists face the sword demanded the same punishment for Manichaeans, and if the Paulicians were identified by eighth-century authorities as Manichaeans, then it would apply to them too. Indeed, the combination of 'Manichaeans and Montanists' in this law might have it that Leo III merely meant that 'heretics' were to be put to the sword. But even if there was some imperial opposition, it did not vanquish the Paulician heresy, which would continue to increase in size and power to the point that they founded their own independent statelet that proved a thorn in the imperial side throughout the ninth century.

In general, Leo's actions against various heresies seem indicative of his aim to restore 'religious orthodoxy' amongst his subjects. It may also link to Leo's restoration of imperial authority in the face of limited decentralisation with it 'likely that the identification of these communities with heretical beliefs reflected at the same time traditional opposition to the central government and its demands as much as it reflected an ideological difference.'[188]

Even with this look at the religious policies of Leo III, we are left with an unclear picture of his aims and actions. When we dig a little below the surface of the source material, we find a diverse picture of Leo. For all the accusations of wickedness, impiety, cultural terrorism, and megalomania levelled at Leo (and Constantine) by iconodule sources,[189] there are positive views. Leo had a high reputation amongst certain Syro-Palestinian Christians – the *Passio of Sixty Martyrs of Jerusalem* refers to him as 'of holy memory', 'God-crowned emperor of the Romans' and 'a most God-beloved and pious emperor', and this is despite its Syriac author being orthodox, although not necessarily anti-iconoclastic. This demonstrates the lack of iconodule unity throughout the empire and beyond. And the same can be said for the iconoclasts too: 'the entire official discourse after the "Triumph of Orthodoxy" falsely suggests a strict binary division between iconodules and iconoclasts.'[190] Evidence does not help distinguish 'iconoclast' and 'iconodule' regions of the empire; iconoclasts and iconodules lived side by side in the empire: 'the differences of their attitudes was founded on social and economic factors rather than geographical, and on their fidelity to traditions rooted in differing cultures.'[191] It may even be that a sizeable proportion of the population of the empire was largely indifferent to iconoclasm, and yet the literature produced during and after iconoclasm sparked the growth of an ever-changing cultural milieu that influenced and was influenced by socio-political developments – 'the result was the creation of a cultural heritage and identity that survived until the final days of Byzantium.'[192]

And this is even before we go into the political and military views of Leo held by some religious groups. To the Melkites of Syria and Palestine, Leo stood out for having proven that the Muslim Arabs were not invincible. The Armenian chronicles have Leo seen as a Moses figure 'who strikes the waves of the sea with a cross, prays, and conjure the elements, stirring up a storm which destroys the Arab fleet.'[193] This fits in with the iconoclastic view of Leo as 'pious towards God and capable in war'[194] who saved the Roman Empire through such strong military leadership and efficient administration.[195] This was a view that had to be removed by iconodules – there was to be no praise for the emperor's actions during the Arab siege of Constantinople; instead, it was those who carried the True Cross and image of the Virgin asking for divine intercession whilst parading around the walls who were responsible for the deliverance of the capital. In such iconophile sources, Leo is either not mentioned, mentioned only in passing, or denigrated.

If Leo did have something to do with iconoclasm, it was not because he was an infidel or anti-religion, but because he was a man of sincere and simple belief, who was keen to purge the Roman faith of perceived errors.[196] These were the pagan aspects of image worship and adoration of relics. In addressing these issues, he not only saw 'ecclesiastical authority intertwined even further with imperial power,'[197] but also laid the foundations of a social, cultural, religious, and political dispute that was to last over a century and to influence 'Byzantine' society until its final demise over 700 years later.[198] For all the discussions and arguments about aspects of iconoclasm, if there was any hint that Leo and then Constantine tried to use iconoclasm as a unifying force in the empire, it was a significant failure.

Chapter 9

Law and Order: The Administration of Leo III

'In the criminal justice system, the people are represented by two separate yet equally important groups. The police who investigate crime and the district attorneys who prosecute the offenders. These are their stories.'

Law and Order

Ekloge ton nomon – 'Selection of the Laws'

While iconoclasm was tremendously important to the moulding of the medieval 'Byzantine' Roman Empire, such is its overwhelming position in the historical narrative that his reputed role in it has overshadowed the other significant achievements of Leo III's reign. We have already looked at one such achievement in the successful defence of Constantinople (without which there would likely have been no era-shaping iconoclasm), but there are also various other military, financial, legal and administrative reforms that Leo undertook during his 24-year reign that were to re-shape the Roman Empire.

The most important modifications undertaken by Leo III came in the realm of legislation, with legal reform being a significant part of his plan for dynastic security. Upon his accession to the throne, the main law code of the Roman Empire remained that of Justinian I – the various sections of the *Corpus Juris Civilis*;[1] – however, not only was that corpus so enormous as to hinder access, by 717, it was nearly 200 years old, an intervening period that had changed the state it had provided the legal structures for. Furthermore, the increasing predominance of Greek in the Roman Empire provided added difficulty of access as the Justinianic corpus was in Latin.

While new legislation had declined post-Justinian and there was considerable disruption during the seventh century, the late antique legal infrastructure had survived largely intact. The resultant Isaurian law code – the *Ekloga* – mentions still-existent judges, notaries, magistrates, and courts at various levels, rather than having to re-establish such infrastructure. This was the result of not only the long-standing integration of Roman law into society, but also efforts to make Justinianic law more accessible through commentaries, translations, and epitomes in Greek. It is these works that the compilers of the *Ekloga* used rather than the original Justinianic texts, although the *Ekloga* prologue itself complains about the fragmentation of Roman law that such epitomes represent. So rather than 'operating within a legal vacuum, [or] reanimating the corpse of law,'[2] Leo and the Isaurians were reinvigorating legal discourse and infrastructures and adapting existing ideas to meet the requirements of the eighth century. And while 'no law can ever be simply read as an accurate description of the society that produced it… [the *Ekloga* and associated laws] offer a precious window onto a little understood age,'[3] or at least one untinged by iconoclasm and iconodule rewrites.

As will be seen with virtually all the legal texts connected to the Isaurian dynasty, there is trouble with the dating of the *Ekloga*. Its title section declares that it was issued by Leo III and Constantine V in March of the 9th indiction in *Anno Mundi* 6248. This may seem like a clear-cut date, but it is not without issues. Due to its length, the reign of Leo III encompassed two '9th indictions'; one in 726 and another in 741. There has been some argument that 726 is meant due to the lack of mention of iconoclasm in the *Ekloga*; however, this could instead be evidence of a lack of iconoclastic action under Leo. It should also be stated that equating AM6248 to 740/741 is not entirely certain due to different dating system versions of *Anno Mundi*; for example, that of Theophanes equates AM6248 to the year 755/756. However, the most prominent dating for the promulgation of the *Ekloga* is March 741, very late in the reign of Leo III.[4]

The name '*Ekloga*' means 'selection' 'and that is broadly what it is'[5] – a concise, utilitarian, selection of Roman law, specifically from the Justinianic corpus. That is not to say that the *Ekloga* was entirely derivative. There was significant editorial input, some deviation from Justinianic law, and significant simplifications and omissions – just one part of the *Corpus Juris Civilis*, the *Digesta*, contained 150,000 lines of Latin, while the *Ekloga* as a whole was made up of under 1,000 lines of Greek. There were also new Isaurian laws within the *Ekloga*.[6] Ultimately, the work done to compile the Isaurian law code 'probably ranges considerably from significant reworking to almost verbatim copying.'[7] But who carried out that work? While we have no names of those charged with the editorial job, the commission was made up of 'our most glorious patricians, the most glorious *quaestor*, and the most glorious consuls and *antigrapheis*.'[8] By this point, the *quaestor* was 'the pre-eminent legal officer in the empire, an amalgam of imperial spokesman, and spin doctor, high court judge, and legal draftsman.'[9] The *antigrapheis* were the *quaestor*'s deputies, who served as the head of the secretarial bureau, preparing legislation, court cases and answering legal questions.

But what did this commission come up with? The resulting 'selection' contained 18 titles, focused mainly on civil and some criminal law, tackling subjects ranging from marriage, betrothal, dowries, testaments, intestacies, wardship, enfranchising of slaves, witnesses, sale liabilities, purchases, rent etc. In the simplest terms, the *Ekloga* aimed to resolve practical problems, a vital concern in an empire which had faced so many issues undermining the rule of law. This meant that for the most part the *Ekloga* was a restatement of Roman private law. The only sizeable section of new legislation came in the realm of marriage and sexual morality. There were to be very limited grounds for divorce and significant punishments for acts of sexual immorality, much of which reflected the religiously-based ethics of the Isaurian additions.

These ethics are also seen in how the *Ekloga* and Isaurian legal texts in general contain a significant amount on crime and punishment. The section on criminal law – XVII – is the longest in the *Ekloga* and incorporates penalties for various crimes such as treason, murder, and theft. While based on Roman law, there was some innovation within this section, which also harkened back to the ancient past. This was seen most prominently in the rise of corporal punishment, with mutilation used over execution, exile, and fines.

Mutilation as a legal punishment had a long history before its appearance in the *Ekloga*. It was extensively prescribed in the law code of the Babylonian king Hammurabi in c.1754 BC.[10] *Rhinokopia*, the removal of the nose, was a punishment for abuse of power, adultery, and conspiracy in thirteenth- and twelfth-century BC Egypt, while ancient India had developed advanced nasal reconstructive surgery, suggesting nose removal was a frequent occurrence. Various forms of amputation are also seen as punishments in early Peruvian cultures.[11] While not unheard of, punitive mutilation was not prominent in the Roman world before Late Antiquity.[12] While there is no definitive correlation, maiming as a punishment coincided with the Christianisation of the empire, perhaps using the Biblical justification provided by Matthew 5:29–30 – 'Cut your hand or your foot if it scandalizes you,' and 'better being lame or crippled rather than able-bodied and damned.'

Somewhat counterintuitively, such punitive mutilation was a downgrade in severity of punishment as it was 'a merciful substitute for the death penalty.'[13] There had been a general lessening of the severity of legal punishments since the reign of Justinian I,[14] continuing through the seventh century until it became codified by the *Ekloga* and other Isaurian legal texts. The *Ekloga* deals mostly with crimes against the state, such as counterfeiting and forgery, which were punishable by losing a hand; however, it also stipulates *rhinokopia* as punishment for adultery.[15] In connection with such punishments, the *Ekloga* claimed that criminals of all backgrounds, rich or poor, would be treated the same, but this was not the case in practice. The doling out of punishment, including mutilation, depended very much on the wealth of the accused, with a rich person allowed to pay a fine for their crime, while a poor person was forced to pay with a part of their body.

This turn towards mutilation as a punishment in criminal law was perhaps a reflection of how it had already become a prominent practice within imperial politics. Such physical mutilation had been used to remove an individual from the Roman imperial succession for perhaps over 300 years,[16] and this only increased with the Christianising of the imperial position. Being a divinely-cast ruler required the emperor to be physically 'perfect'. This was not a new concept – his family had sought to hide Claudius away from public view due to his physical maladies, although that did not stop him being elevated to the imperial title and ruling for thirteen years.[17] It was under the Heraclian dynasty that such political mutilation became more widely used. Even if the mutilation of John Athalarichos, illegitimate son of Heraclius, in 637 on a charge of conspiracy was meant more as a punitive punishment rather than a political removal, it opened the door to clearer instances of mutilation as a political tool. Within four years, three of Heraclius' sons by his second wife (and niece) Martina – Heraklonas, David Tiberios and Marinus – had their noses mutilated as part of their removal from positions of power. Martina herself had her nose and tongue cut out for her perceived interference in imperial politics.[18]

This opened something of a political disfigurement floodgate – Constantine IV had his two brothers mutilated, Leontios had Justinian II mutilated, who in turn had Tiberius III mutilated (and executed) upon his return to power, which, of course, demonstrates that such mutilation did not always prevent someone from being emperor. This is also not to say that mutilation was always carried out against those removed from power – while Philippikos Bardanes was blinded upon his deposition, neither Anastasius II nor Theodosius III faced any physical deprivation upon their initial removal from office. Indeed, at a time when mutilation was becoming an everyday punishment under the Isaurian dynasty, the removal of bodily appendages was becoming less prevalent in politics. Its failure to remove Justinian II from imperial contention may have led to the preference moving on to blinding. Indeed, throughout the eighth century, dozens of emperors, imperial candidates, patriarchs, generals, and plotters were blinded.[19] It would continue as the dynastic preventative throughout the remainder of Roman imperial history.

The Roman Empire was not the only state of the period to embrace punitive mutilation. The Frankish kingdom of the sixth century saw hand, nose, and ear removal as a punishment, while perhaps the most well-known use of mutilation as a punishment is in Islamic law. It called for amputation as a punishment for crimes said to violate Allah's *hudud* – 'boundaries' – in the Qur'an, namely what we might consider 'highway robbery' and types of theft. It must be said that Muslim jurisprudence had such a high evidentiary standard that any such punitive mutilation was exceeding rare.[20]

The *Ekloga* commission also recognised the need to reform the judiciary that was to enforce these selected laws. In making law more accessible to all and stamp out corruption, legal officers were salaried and forbidden from accepting gifts, another reform that appealed to the Bible by hoping to avoid 'the selling of righteous for silver'.[21] This demonstrates recognition that Roman law was not universally understood by those Romans covered by it and that it did not necessarily work for them either, particularly outside Constantinople. This may even be an example of the 'metropolitan elite' recognising it lived in a bubble detached from the general life of the state they governed, legislated for and ultimately depended on for revenue and manpower. The *Ekloga* replaced the Justinianic *Institutes* as the manual for teaching law until the mid-ninth century, and even when the *Ekloga* was supplanted, its chapters were reused and its text revised. This demonstrates its significance not just in its 150 years of direct use 'to meet the demands of the living realities of the period,'[22] but also how it influenced the judicial collections of the Orthodox Church, ancient Slavic law and the Arabs.

Given the significance and influence of the *Ekloga*, it could be tempting to see Leo III as a great legislator; however, this is not strictly the case. The *Ekloga* was largely a restating of pre-existing Roman law and even the new sections on marriage, morality, and mutilation were all influenced by long-standing Biblical teachings and/or trends in the Mediterranean world. That said, Leo clearly understood the importance of an established, comprehensible, and fairly-enforced law code to the future of the Roman Empire and his dynasty.

Religion, Imperial Propaganda and Isaurian Law

The influence of the *Ekloga* was not only in the realm of dynastic security and legislative reform; it also presents a significant reshaping of the imperial law, order, and justice with the Old Testament. It was presented as a restoration of the covenant between God and his chosen people, except in this case the chosen people were Christian Romans, with Leo and Constantine the successors of Moses and Solomon. Part of the perceived necessity of this realisation of a Christian kingdom based on Old Testament rhetoric and model was how 'Islam forced Christians to examine, defend, or alter their religious practice and private morality in response to the evident displeasure of heaven.'[23]

The traditional imperial response would have been to play into the idea of universal Roman Christian power; however, that was no longer a safe bet. The 75 years after the Islamic explosion proved that the loss of the eastern provinces was not ephemeral, while the 20 years of political instability following the first deposition of Justinian II in 695 suggested that the empire's power was not only not universal, but dangerously close to disappearing altogether. Indeed, when Leo III usurped the throne in 717, it was perhaps expected that the empire would not survive the year. Under Isaurian leadership, the threat of annihilation abated but 'the imperial dream was jettisoned',[24] born out of Leo III's and Constantine V's realistic appraisal of the political and military situation, 'adopting policies suited to their reduced powers and relinquishing utopian ideals of world domination.'[25] To even think about going on the offensive and reclaiming lost lands, the empire needed to be reforged into something different, doing away with systems broken by conquests and migrations and codifying and building upon the improvised systems that had proven useful in staving off total defeat.

Because of this, imperial rhetoric changed from the 'universal empire of Christian New Rome', encapsulated in civil and canon law, to a greater rhetorical and legal reliance on the Old Testament, which provided an analogue of God's chosen being surrounded by earthly powers intent on their destruction. With the Isaurians, this redirection also involved the identifying and rectifying of the reasons for their troubles, such as improper religious observance and private immorality in the form of sexual misconduct. This redirection was codified in the *Ekloga* and other Isaurian legal texts, which were also looking to organise the resources of the truncated imperial state.

Such was the extent of this redirection that the *Ekloga* embraced how the Quinisext canons presented the Roman Empire as Christian rather than Roman. Indeed, the term 'Roman' is frequently absent from the *Ekloga*, with 'Christian' used instead: it was a law code for and about Christians, with no reference to Jews or pagans and only the briefest mention of heretics. It represented the final embracing of the religiosity of the imperial position, presented with the claim of divine appointment and the authority of a bishop;[26] 'a sacralisation of the Roman *politeia* (state) itself.'[27]

The religious influence can be seen beyond such pronouncements of Christian influence, morality, and being 'chosen'. Specific laws in the *Ekloga* were very much Christian in origin. There were some rulings on personal morality, marriage, sexual conduct and correct religious practice.[28] The prominence of crime and punishment in Isaurian legal texts was part of 'an eschatological plan to heal the souls of the sinful sick, in order to restore health to the empire.'[29] And while Christian clemency was encouraged, even the idea that 'deemed judicial mutilation a merciful substitute for the death penalty'[30] relied on Biblical backing from Matthew 5:30.

> the law was conceived as a heaven-sent implement of correction, which would advance Christian morality by protecting the weak, deterring those with any propensity to evil and punishing the wicked, both for the sake of stern justice in upholding God's commandments, and for the purgation of sin.[31]

This harkening back to Biblical teachings in Isaurian legal reforms may also have influenced the development of iconoclastic policies. A core component of Leo's iconoclasm, if it existed at all, was the Biblical opposition to idolatry.[32] This did not mean a removal of all icons, but a promotion of imperially approved imagery,[33] specifically the cross and the eucharist, which were foundational aspects of the Christian church. And yet, iconoclasm was initially not introduced with assent from church authorities, with the emperor claiming that his imperial position gave him the right to legislate in both civil and religious matters. In this light, together with the concurrent creation of the *Donation of Constantine*, iconoclasm could be seen as the latest round in the long struggle over the limits of imperial and church jurisdiction. And such harkening back to the past were part of Leo's attempt to win that struggle, repositioning the emperor as 'the sole and undisputed leader of society, with the Church subordinate to his authority and regulatory care.'[34] Such a position was reflected in the *Ekloga* and given some credence by the emperor's power to appoint and depose patriarchs. An aspect of iconoclasm in line with imperial authority may also have been to gain some control over monks, many of whom had flourished under the stable conditions of Isaurian rule. However, as with iconoclasm in general, care must be taken with their reputed monastic policies for they are open to distortion. The policy, if it can even be attributed to Leo III, looked to place monks and monasteries under the control of bishops and restrict them to charity, piety, and exemplary living, rather than claiming any authority through connection to images.[35]

Roman law was no longer completely sufficient, but still able to form the basis for three major divergent states. The 'renaissances' under the Carolingians and Abbasids are well-documented; however, the 'Byzantine' revival was usually placed a century later under the Macedonian dynasty 'due to the distorting miasma of iconophile rhetoric.'[36] Contrarily, the historical and hagiographic sources of the late-eighth century, which did so much to denigrate the iconoclastic Isaurians, are actually proof of the 'renaissance' nurtured under said Isaurians but dismissed by iconophiles. In the west, the Latin miniscule invented in the second half of the eighth century is usually taken as a symbol of the need for a more accessible script as interest in reading and writing spread as part of the 'Carolingian Renaissance'; however, it is overlooked that there was a concurrent development of the Greek miniscule, surely for similar reasons – increasing administration bureaucracy showing re-centralisation, legal texts for judges etc., all of which are hallmarks of strong central government.

The Isaurian Legal Corpus

The *Ekloga* is not the only legal text attributed to the Isaurian era and possibly to be linked to Leo himself. There is the *Decision Concerning Soldiers who are Son-in-laws*. It has issues with dating and its imperial attribution, but there are hints that it was to be directly attached to the *Ekloga* itself. Its mention of there being more than one emperor at the time of its promulgation narrows its date to the period between the publication of the *Ekloga* and the death of Leo III in June 741 and after the elevation of Leo IV to co-emperor in 751. It could even be that this 'decision' was meant to be part of a 19th title of the *Ekloga* or was a case raised following the publication of the *Ekloga* but before the death of Leo. Its content highlights how the Roman thematic army was supported by households in return for certain privileges, such as tax breaks, claims to soldierly property and income. This was an important contribution to the empire's ability to field an army of any size to defend against the Arabs. In general terms, this 'decision' may show how the *Ekloga* was not meant to be a rigid edifice from the very outset.

Also dealing with aspects of the military is the *Nomos Stratiotikos* – the *Soldier's Law*. Some manuscripts had it as a title added to the *Ekloga*, rather than a separate legal text that the name *nomos* suggests. Therefore, it could be connected directly to titles 17 and 18 of the *Ekloga* or it could be part of the *Appendix Eklogae*. The first section of the *Soldier's Law* is lifted from the late-sixth century *Strategikon*, with the rest derived from the Justinianic corpus; the second covers martial penalties (all harsh) for the likes of flight and disobedience, and the third looks at statuses that might affect a soldier's continued service, such as suicide attempts or adultery. It does appear likely that this law was promulgated under Constantine V, with it fitting in with his military reforms, but it likely still reflects the ideas of Leo III.[37]

In spite of its name, the *Appendix Eklogae* is not a coherent 14 title appendix to the *Ekloga*; indeed, no surviving manuscript contains all 14 titles. There is evidence of editing and significant copy-and-pasting, specifically from the Justinianic corpus. The titles deal with a wide range of content – marriage, adultery, inheritance, boundaries, witnesses, penalties for heretics, pagans etc.

As they do not cover the same ground as the *Ekloga*, they were meant as a supplement. This is further shown by the lack of an imperial name on any section of the *Appendix*. Despite this lack of attribution, the likelihood is that it was Constantine V who saw the promulgation of these appendices, although again possibly reflecting the aims and practices of his father.

The *Rhodian Sea Law*, another composite text, regulates maritime commerce. It is divided into three parts, although it takes the form of a *nomos*. It largely follows established Roman maritime law,[38] only embellishing and expanding on it with specific scenarios and circumstances. This was intended to be read by judges who applied the rules and faced some of the scenarios. The opening section is a legendary account of its supposed origins that was added later. The second part contains 19 chapters of short pronouncements about division of profits, regulation of behaviour on ship, and legal matters of deposits and loans, which largely follow Justinianic precedents. This section can be so concise as to cloud the actual meaning. The third part contains 47 chapters, with many subjects covered, although liability regarding general damage, contract infringements, and jettison are the most prominent.

Based on some linguistic overlap and similarity of style with the *Ekloga*, it has been placed at least in the period AD 600–800, although its familiarity with the punishments of the *Ekloga* and it not repeating much from it suggests that it was meant to bolster the *Ekloga*.[39] While Isaurian in origin, it was likely promulgated well after Leo's death. The need for such a revamping of maritime law reflects the rise of piracy in the seventh century, which required legal clarifications and outlines of insurance. The *Rhodian Sea Law* was to have long-standing influence down to the twelfth century. This also highlights that Roman sea commerce did not substantially change after the seventh century, which means it never really improved following the decline induced by the Arab conquests and/or the rules of *Rhodian Sea Law* were sufficient for any such recovery.

Another extended law – 85 chapters long – with a wide disparity of suggested dates is the *Nomos Georgikos* – the *Farmer's Law*.[40] The importance of farming and therefore its legislation should not be overlooked, although it can be exaggerated too. This is because it was long thought that the development of the themes saw the new armies made up of small landowners, who farmed the land in peacetime and defended it in war.[41] However, while many recruits will have been from rural backgrounds, the still existent professional element of the Roman army will have seen such recruits forget their past lives. They might have been housed in and supplied from rural settings and even given land grants upon their retirement, but the growth of a 'farmer soldier' army during the seventh century appears incorrect.[42] However, the number of small landowners did increase throughout the seventh century. This was caused by a boom in the population density of the empire as armies and peoples evacuated the lands conquered by the Arabs, Bulgars, and Slavs. This saw to the fragmentation of Roman landholding and the creation of more small independent farms.[43] Such were their numbers that small landowners became targeted by those in power, either land-hungry aristocrats looking to take their land or an emperor looking to garner support against the nobility. Maintaining this new independent farmer class would also maintain tax and recruiting resources for the empire.

While there was still some public land, the *Farmer's Law* highlights a world of private land with various tenders: landowners, tenants, hired labours, slaves. Its greatest focus is on aspects of property, such as tenancy, theft, construction, damage etc. or compensation for negligent/deliberate acts. This presents a variegated, stratified, complex society, with an active legal system right down to village level, which gives it 'a degree of universality,'[44] explaining its significant reuse over an extended period.

What that period was is difficult to ascertain, with anything from Justinian I to the late-ninth century being suggested, although most ideas cluster around AD 600–800. Justinian II seems to have followed the socio-political route offered by the growth of the small independent farmer class, with it having some influence on his deposition in 695. This has led to attempts to attribute the *Farmer's Law* to his reign, due to it containing numerous laws aiding the farming class. An inscription at the beginning of the work calls the *Farmer's Law* 'an extract from the book of Justinian.' This would seem to connect the *Nomos Georgikos* to Justinian I,[45] but sections of it contradict agrarian policies of the *Corpus Juris Civilis*. Indeed, the *Farmer's Law* does not reflect the agricultural picture of the Justinianic era, focusing on small landowners rather than serfs and tenant farmers.[46] But then Justinian II is not known to have had written any significant pieces of legislation.[47]

The lack of clear dating could suggest that the *Farmer's Law* appeared in various forms over an extended period, initially being a private collection of Justinianic laws and local customs that was given official sanction by later Heraclian or Isaurian emperors. It records four different types of mutilation as punishment for crimes against the individual:

1. Blinding, for a third offence of theft (chs. 42, 68, 69)
2. Branding, for destruction of property (ch. 58)
3. Cutting out the tongue, for swearing falsely (ch.28)
4. Cutting off a hand(s), for more grievous destruction of property (chs. 44, 59, 65, 66, 80)[48]

This provides evidence of a similar style to the *Ekloga* and other legal texts like the *Rhodian Sea Law* and the *Soldier's Law*, and it seems to purposely not repeat parts of the *Ekloga*, which place at least some of its editing after Leo's reign. However, even if it does not belong to Leo III, his aim to establish firm Isaurian central control may be reflected in aspects of the *Farmer's Law*. As it also employs Biblical language, this may show the impact of Leo's aims and methods even if he did not promulgate the *Farmer's Law*.

There is one section of the Isaurian legal corpus that is not derived from Roman law – the *Mosaic Law*. The reason for this is that 'just as the emperor was legitimised through his closeness to and imitation of God, so Isaurian legislation was justified by its closeness to and imitation of the law of Moses.'[49] And due to this prominence of religion in Leo's regime, it is not surprising that the *Mosaic Law* was used in some *Ekloga* manuscripts as an 'ideological frontispiece.'[50] As different versions use the Pentateuch or the Septaugint, the Isaurian *Mosaic Law* covers a varied array of subject matter, although property disputes and sexual immorality were the most prominent. This was not a slavish following of the original text, with some necessary changes/omissions made, as aspects of Roman/church life were not reflected in Mosaic laws.

As with other Isaurian legal texts, the similar terminology between the *Mosaic Law* and the *Ekloga* marks a connection between the two, although there is little clarity on date other than how the *Novels* of Irene present some complaints about use of Mosaic law as a bedrock for Roman law, showing that the *Mosaic Law* predates the reign of Irene (797–802). The reign of Constantine V is most likely, but again it reflects the foundations laid by Leo III. While part of the Isaurian corpus, the *Novels* of Irene are definitively not connected to Leo, but are evidence of how the Isaurians had re-established some 'normality' to Roman law.

Leo and the Isaurians also made changes to the judicial hierarchies that were to impose the new law codes. The *anthypatoi*, successors of proconsular civil governors, were attached to the new thematic hierarchies, so we see '*anthypatoi* of the themes' or an '*anthypatos* of the Anatolikoi'. Could it even be that every thematic military commander was given an *anthypatos*, to whom the *praitores* could appeal? We also see village-level courts under *oikodespotai* recorded in the *Nomos Georgikos*, but as this position was noted in the seventh century, it could be that these courts had developed at the same time, with Leo and the Isaurians responsible for their formalising rather than their invention.[51] This would fit in with much of the general reforming action of Leo and his dynasty – not necessarily innovative, but of vital importance in permanently establishing the practices that had developed during the seventh century.

Collecting Gold, Silver and Bronze

The legislative system of the empire was far from the only area that Leo III attempted to reform. The 25 years before Leo's accession had seen significant numismatic developments both within and without the Roman Empire. While the gold *solidus*, minted only in Constantinople, had remained the core currency of the Roman state and a significant part of imperial propaganda, under Justinian II, its obverse sported a depiction of Christ, with the imperial bust relegated to the reverse.[52] Justinian was indicating his subservience to Christ, while also linking himself to the divine by 'literally forming two sides of the same coin.'[53] The Christ coin would have long-term consequences for Roman art and numismatics as its design would influence the depiction of Christ that would be used for centuries to come; however, in the short-term, its internal impact was minimal as Justinian's immediate successors did not take on the Christ coin design. Its short-term impact may have come in foreign affairs. In so clearly uniting imperial rule with Christianity, Justinian may have stirred up the Umayyads, providing a possible avenue for the outbreak of war in 692 (although this has been doubted[54]), and encouraging them to make significant (and overdue) numismatic innovation of their own.

The centrality of the *solidus* was not just limited to the Roman financial system. Along with Roman copper coins and the Persian silver drachm, the *solidus* had been the centrepiece of the economy of the Muslim world as well. In its first 50 years of existence, the Arab caliphate had yet to divest itself of the pre-existing tax systems inherited from the lands it had conquered.[55] When they were not using or directly copying Roman coins,[56] the Umayyads only employed minimal levels of innovation in attempts to make those Roman coins their own. It was not until the reign of Abd al-Malik (685–705) that Islamic coinage came into its own. Through a period of experimentation 'with new symbols and designs – not all of the imagery is fully understood today,'[57] by 699 Abd al-Malik, taking a cue from Kharijite rebels, found Islam's defining numismatic, artistic, and dogmatic style in aniconism. There would be no pictorial representations on Islamic coins; instead, the *shahadah*, the profession of the Muslim faith, was to be the central inscription.[58] Not only were these new Muslim coins newly minted by Umayyad authorities and divested of the Roman pictorial milieu, the resultant dinar was slightly thinner and therefore contained less gold than the *solidus*. There was similar aniconic innovation with the Umayyad silver coinage, using the Persian drachm as a basis for the new dirham. This marked the complete separation of Muslim numismatics from its Roman and Persian counterparts by the end of the seventh century.

But it was more than even that. Given the size of the Umayyad caliphate, the dinar and the dirham broke the centuries-long Roman monopoly on Mediterranean coinage. The extent of this influence can be seen in the numismatic reforms of Leo III. When he came to introduce a new Roman silver coinage in 720, instead of taking his cues from previous Roman silver issues such as the *antoninianus* or *siliqua*, he used the dirham as a template.[59] This reformed Leonid silver coin was the *miliaresion*. Technically, this was something of a re-introduction as there had been a *miliaresion/miliarense* issued intermittently since the fourth century,[60] but this Leonid iteration was thinner and wider than previous versions. This new *miliaresion* sported no imperial portrait on either side. It was not completely aniconic as the obverse hosted a cross-portent. Surrounding that cross, rather than a traditional Latin numismatic pronouncement such as *VICTORIA AVGVSTI*, there was a Christian inscription in Greek that read *Iesus Christus Nika* – 'Jesus Christ Victorious'. The reverse, like the dirham, was purely inscriptional, displaying 'Leo and Constantine, by [grace of] God, emperor'; however, rather than *Augustus*, this was the first coin to use the Greek word *basileus*. This combination of cross, Jesus, and *basileus* demonstrates the close link between divine and imperial authority that Leo and the Isaurian dynasty were promoting.

There has been some suggestion that this new *miliaresion* was more ceremonial than functional in nature,[61] but then it was valued at 1⁄12 of a *nomisma/solidus*, while its incorporation of a triple dot border, again like that of the dirham, might highlight that it was expected to have a wide enough circulation to face clipping. There may have been some other fractional silver coins briefly used under the Isaurians, but for the most part, by being a significant fraction of the *nomisma/solidus*, the *miliaresion* sparked a decline in such fractional issues; however, it did serve 'as an important intermediary between the bronze fiduciary coinage and the gold.'[62] And whatever it was actually meant for, its inscriptional outline remained standard for Roman silver coinage throughout the Isaurian dynasty and beyond.

It was not just silver coinage that saw reform under the Isaurians. While the base purity and weight of the *nomisma/solidus* was not changed, the propagandist depictions on it did. Leo's initial issues – 717–720 – followed the more traditional approach of an imperial portrait on the obverse surrounded by his imperial title, and a cross portent on the reverse surrounded by the *VICTORIA-AVϚЧ* legend. However, this changed with the elevation of Constantine V to co-emperor in 720. Leo had a new *nomisma/solidus* minted to mark the occasion, which had the same obverse style – his imperial portrait and legend, but on the reverse, there was a virtually identical portrait of Constantine, with his own imperial legend. The only major difference was that Leo sported a beard in comparison to the cleanly shaven Constantine. Junior emperors had appeared on the coinage of their fathers before, but usually on the same side as the senior emperor. Constantine being portrayed on his own whilst being the junior emperor was the innovation here. This also marked a trend of numismatic portraiture becoming less distinctive, being replaced with a more standardised image, with all Isaurians looking the same; indeed, Constantine is said to appear 'as a miniature Leo.'[63]

This focus on the emperors demonstrates that for Leo and the Isaurians 'the centrality of the dynasty trumped even religious symbolism.'[64] Constantine V and his successors would double down on this through the portrayal of deceased ancestors on their coinage; for example, post-751, the *nomismata/solidi* of Constantine V would depict himself and his newly elevated son, Leo IV, side by side on the obverse, with Leo III on the reverse. Such a portrayal was unprecedented and presents an Isaurian imperative to celebrate dynastic success, continuity, and longevity.[65] Indeed, Leo's dual-headed coin would be used throughout the eighth century and on into the first half of the ninth century by iconoclast and iconodule emperors. It would even see some use post-843. Perhaps the most crowded example of this trend would be the coins from the reign of Constantine VI, which saw him and his mother Irene portrayed on the obverse, with Leo III, Constantine V and Leo IV standing abreast on the reverse.

While there was also, along with limited numbers of silver fractions, a Leonid *tremissis*, which was worth a third of a *nomisma/solidus* and sported a similar dual-headed style, Isaurian numismatic policy focused on rationalising denominations, gradually removing fractional issues aside from one per metal. This numismatic triumvirate was represented by the *nomisma/solidus*, the new *miliaresion* and the bronze *follis*. The latter had declined in size throughout the seventh century, defying reform by Constantine IV in 669.[66] These wide discrepancies in weight of Roman bronze coinage, even within a single class, was 'due to lack of care in mint supervision and workmanship.'[67] However, even in the throes of 'military anarchy', the Roman government showed some ability to 'enforce its fiduciary value [which] made such fluctuations less damaging to the continuing role of the bronze in the system.'[68] Again highlighting that not all fractional issues were removed immediately, there were some *decanummium* from early in Leo's reign, which were overstruck *folles* and half-*folles*. For the decade after Constantine's elevation, Leonid copper coins followed the dual-head formula, although in the 730s, they reverted to the side-by-side busts on the obverse and a mark of value on the reverse.

When looking at the Leonid coinage formulas used on all three metals, there were some aspects conspicuous by their absence. There is no date on any Leonid coins. Mintmarks were also done away with after appearing on the initial run of Leonid *nomismata/solidi*. This was presumably because Constantinople was the only eastern mint in operation, making its identification unnecessary. That said, western mints continued to issue – Sicily, Naples, Rome, and Ravenna, although their coins were debased during Leo's reign, possibly a result of the emperor's confiscation of papal revenues.

Numismatic policy and propaganda can also be seen on imperial seals, the development of which under Leo and the Isaurians largely followed the same path as their coinage. Seals can provide more clarity of chronology than coins for many have the indiction date listed on them. Initially, from 717–720, Leo retained the pre-existing form of imperial seal – depicting the Virgin Mary holding the infant Christ – which had been favoured since the reign of Constantine IV. There was also a seal that depicted the imperial bust on the obverse and an inscription listing the position of an imperial customs official. From the elevation of Constantine V, he too appears on Leonid seals. There is a type like the *nomisma/solidus*, with Leo on the obverse and a beardless Constantine on the reverse. There is also an imperial customs official version that has Leo and Constantine holding the same cross globe between them on the obverse and an inscription naming the office on the reverse. Somewhat mirroring the *miliaresion*, there was another seal that has a cross on the obverse, with an inscription that continues on the reverse – 'In the name of the Father, and of the Son and of the Holy Spirit, Leo and Constantine, faithful emperors of the Romans'. This was the first imperial seal not to depict the emperor, while the extended inscription was the first to use Greek language, although it was still inscribed in Latin letters. The dual headed seal and the cross/inscription types were copied through the next century, while Leo III continued to appear on the seals of his successors up to at least the Council of Nicaea in 787, if not later.

In combination with numismatic reform, Leo also saw to the overhaul of the financial administration of his empire. This is seen in the changes to hierarchies of supply and taxation. The *genikoi kommerkiarioi*, who were fiscal crisis managers mostly responsible for the supply of the army, gradually disappeared during the course of the 720s.[69] The regulation of trade and taxation was taken on by the lower-ranking *kommerkiarioi*, by whom the *kommerkion* customs levy would be collected by the end of the eighth century. The *basilika kommerkiarioi* were appointed to oversee the fiscal running of the thematic provinces, while the *dioiketai*, acting under the authority of the *logothete* of the *genikon*, acted as tax collectors in the themes. The thematic connection of these officials hints at 'their immediate and overriding purpose [in this permanent organisation]: the supply of the army.'[70] Indeed, much of Leo's financial reform matched the military infrastructure. And as this military system was based on the thematic provinces, the new financial system reflected its increasing regionalism and militarism. There were also some general reforms of how tax was paid. The system of prepaying taxes which had weighed heavily upon wealthier proprietors was abolished, while more tax revenues were paid in cash rather than pre-agreed kind.[71]

Part of Leo's financial reforms may be seen in his dealings with regions of Italy. Theophanes claimed that Leo raised the poll tax in Sicily and Calabria by 33 per cent out of greed and in response to the papacy's rejection of iconoclasm. However, this supposed tax hike was merely a recalculation of the tax rate following the coinage reforms. This means that regions like Sicily and Calabria had been underpaying their taxes due to the disturbances of the seventh century and the attendant debasing of the coinage, which was markedly more widespread in Italy. This so-called tax increase was making these regions pay what they were supposed to.[72]

Expanding Themes

While the Roman Empire was a state of intricate and well-developed governmental and judicial mechanisms and hierarchies, it remained a military empire facing considerable military danger. This meant that for all his other reforms, the most important Leo had to undertake was to do with the thematic provinces and their armies. It was only with the turn of the eighth century that the Romans came to recognise the permanence of the new situation caused by the Arab conquests and how imperial forces were overmatched by those of the caliphate. This led to a change in tactics and strategies: large-scale campaigns of reconquest were abandoned for lower-level harassment and containment through the building of fortresses and depopulation of the frontier zone. It also saw the acceptance of the new thematic army that had gradually evolved over the previous half century.[73] Such a gradual evolution included significant aspects of unevenness and lack of planning. In that, Leo III had inherited a state 'marked by ad hoc additions and modulations to the late antique system.'[74]

Having proven himself a capable military leader in the Caucasus, Anatolia and at Constantinople, Leo had some breathing room to permanently organise the improvised themes. His experience at the head of thematic armies meant that Leo will have appreciated their benefits and drawbacks, with administrative and military usefulness conflicting with the competition and separatist tendencies they could foster. He therefore faced the balancing act of limiting the power of individual *strategoi* without compromising the theme system. Unfortunately, eighth-century source material provides very little information on Leo's provincial organisation. To discern almost any Isaurian thematic expansion, we are relying on comparisons and inferences from late-seventh and early-ninth century lists, such as the 687 *iussio* of Justinian II and the Arab geographer Ibn Khordadhbeh.[75]

Therefore, it might be speculated that Leo III enshrined the thematic *strategos* in common Roman practice, but there is little evidentiary backing for it.

As a product of thematic revolt himself, Leo III may have thought to reduce the sizes of the thematic armies to minimise the chances of a repeat. It was previously thought that the Thrakesian theme was not one of the original themes to appear in the second half of the seventh century. It was even suggested that its initial appearance in military action when the Thrakesian *tourmarches*, Christopher, was sent to Cherson in 711, does not prove the existence of a Thrakesian theme; only that there were Thrakesian *turmae*, possibly a subcommand of the Anatolic *strategos*. An actual Thrakesian *strategos* is not mentioned until 741, when its holder Sisinnius sided with Constantine V against Artabasdos. This led to suggestions that it was Leo III who elevated the Thrakesian *turmae* to a fully-fledged theme. This is rendered moot by the identification of the *Thracianus exercitus* in the Justinianic *iussio* of 687 as the Thrakesian thematic army; however, it does not rule out Leo altering the Thrakesian theme during his reign. He could have redistributed some thematic land, particularly that of the Anatolikon. Some of its western territory may have been given to the Thrakesion, while some of its southern coast went to the Kibyrrhaeots. Of course, this was not a general reduction policy as he would surely have targeted the interfering Opsikon if he had. But then why did he target the Anatolics, the theme that he had based his own power on? His knowledge and experience may have awakened Leo to an imbalance in thematic resources. The emperor could also have been wary of someone following in his footsteps in using the Anatolic army to obtain the imperial throne.

If there was any such Leonid display of thematic reduction to ease the threat of revolt, it did not work all that well. There were various rebellions during his reign and there would be more after it. This may be because if Leo sought to restrict rebellious acts by reducing the size of the forces under the command of a single *strategos*, he had misunderstood the origins of the thematic rebellions of 695–711. Rather than the size of any single thematic army, these were based more on opportunism offered by proximity to the capital, the concentration of more than one army in the same place, or individual, political circumstances, such as fear of punishment after a military failure.

If it did occur between the Thrakesian and Anatolic themes, this was not the only example of land transfer between imperial jurisdictions. The territories of Illyricum, Sicily, and southern Italy were transferred from papal jurisdiction to that of Constantinople, which is usually linked to papal opposition to iconoclasm, much as Leo supposedly did with the poll tax in Sicily and Calabria. Of course, this argument would be fatally undermined if Leo III had nothing to do with iconoclasm. This transfer was merely to do with 'the general Isaurian scheme for tidying the administration of the empire.'[76] That this assertion would focus on the Isaurians rather than specifically Leo III may reflect the dispute over the dating of this transfer. It has been posited in 732–733 or in the early 750s, which would make it either the action of Leo III or Constantine V.[77] Such land transfers and reorganising of the themes and provinces were likely accompanied by censuses and land registries, all helping to maximise the efficiency of tax collecting. Leo may even have ordered the continuing updating of the citizenship register, having all newly-born male children recorded. Unsurprisingly, Theophanes thought this a hideous idea, harkening back to the Egyptian Pharaoh's treatment of the Jews, with all the supposed evil intentions.[78]

All at Sea?

There is a specific section of the Roman themes and their military forces that Leo III is usually attributed a significant say in reforming – the navy and its supporting provinces.[79] However, there is very little clarity on the named naval squadrons of the late-seventh/early-eighth century and whether they had anything approaching thematic organisation. What might have been the main (or even the entire) Roman naval force, the Karabisiani, was gradually replaced by the Kibyrrhaeots and other regional squadrons. The last mention of the Karabisian *strategos* came in 710/711, although it continued in existence for some years after that. Two different reasonings have been given for the eventual abolition of the Karabisiani: repeated poor performance or involvement in rebellion. Two dates are also proposed, which in themselves provide hints at what led to the elimination of the Karabisiani.

One view is that the abolition came in around 719/720 in the aftermath of the Arab siege of Constantinople, with the reason being a combination of poor performance and rebellion.[80] There are issues with this suggestion. What rebellion had there been recently? Aside from a minor one in Sicily, which might have had nothing to do with the Karabisiani, the most recent rebellion that might have involved Roman naval forces was that of Theodosius III against Anastasius II. Of course, they had been involved in other previous rebellions against the sitting emperor and Leo may well have just taken some time to ensure that the Arab fleet was not coming back to the Aegean and to take stock of the Karabisian track record and its unwieldy size. If he was looking at the most recent record of the imperial navy, poor performance would not necessarily have been an issue, particularly during the siege of Constantinople where the navy played a significant role.

The other date suggested for the proposed disbanding of the Karabisiani is c.727, much more specifically tied to the revolt of Kosmas and Agallianos

Kontoskeles, which involved Stephen, who was possibly the commander of the Karabisian naval district of the Cyclades.[81] There was also a revolt in Venice in 726, which could have made Leo III feel that large sections of the navy were not to be trusted. Such timing would seem logical, but it also lacks evidentiary backing. Could it be that the lack of a record of the abolition of the Karabisiani is because there was no such abolition? Rather than any conscious decision to get rid of it through poor performance, rebellious action, or any other idea, it might just be that the Karabisiani was subdivided out of existence. Both dates attributed to the demise of the Karabisiani are during the reign of Leo III, meaning that if nothing else, the consensus is that he was responsible for the end of the Karabisiani.

A possible connection to the end of Karabisiani could be seen in the promotion of the Kibyrrhaeots to thematic status, if not necessarily yet as an official *thema nautikon*. The earliest mention of the Kibyrrhaeot *strategos* does not come until 732, when the current office holder, Manes, saw his fleet destroyed in a storm en route to Italy.[82] This does not give the Kibyrrhaeot theme a Leonid origin as no official elevation of it to thematic status is recorded, and the 'men of Cibyrrha' appear in the late-690s.[83] The Kibyrrhaeot 'theme' likely developed out of a *droungos* subdivision along the south coast of Asia Minor, bolstered by Mardaite recruits, to protect the entrance of the Aegean, before then receiving the more usual (although not universal) thematic hierarchy of *droungoi* and *tourmai*. Due to the source record, it is uncertain exactly how much or even if any of the structuring of the Kibyrrhaeot theme was done under Leo. Much of said development may have already taken place, possibly in connection with the settling of the Mardaites in the region under Justinian II.

The same Justinianic/Mardaite basis was likely involved in the naval forces of the Helladic theme, which was a creation of Justinian II. However, the role of Helladic naval forces in the revolt of Kosmas could have influenced Leo in any dealings he had with not only those forces specifically, but with naval commands in general. Might Leo have decided to detach naval forces from land themes like Hellados and other provincial forces, a further step in the creation of specific *thema nautikon*?

The easiest areas to see possible naval thematic organisation are the various islands and islands groups that the empire still controlled. The *archontate* of Sardinia was something of a lesser theme, with some of the organisation but a smaller size and budget. As an island, the forces raised to defend Sardinia were largely naval in nature. While it may have originated upon the final collapse of the African exarchate in 698, continued development of the infrastructure of Sardinia will have taken place in the decades after that, including under Leo III and the Isaurians. Another island theme possibly developed under the

Isaurians was that of Crete. The first recorded mention of a Cretan *strategos* comes in 767. As we have seen, the first mention of a specific thematic *strategos* does not necessarily date the theme itself as late as that. It could be that Crete was a theme by the 730s;[84] however, this recording of a Cretan *strategos* in 767 might itself by a misidentification by the *Vita Stephani iunoris* (which also uses the title *archisatrap*), with Crete actually being governed by an archon until the early-ninth century.[85] This does not necessarily remove the idea that Crete was organised along thematic lines at this point; indeed, it could be that eighth-century Crete was organised similarly to the Sardinian *archontate*.

There were other possible naval reforms that took place in this period, but are of uncertain date. A separate Aegean theme is not attested until 843, but Leo could have initiated some reform of this region following the revolt of Kosmas. Might he have been involved in a more definitive division of the *Aigaion Pelagos* into separate squadrons focused on island groups in the northern Aegean and the Cyclades? Such island groups were operating not only before the Helladic/Cycladean revolt but also before Leo's reign. Part of the Leonid reorganisation saw the renewing and expansion of the Roman naval presence in southern Italy. Bases such as Vibona on Sicily, Reggio in Calabria and others were rebuilt, while the regional fleet was restored after the fiscal reforms of the 730s, and the Adriatic squadron at Venice was renewed/expanded. The imperial squadron stationed in the Golden Horn and in the waters around Constantinople, which had performed so well during the Arab siege, also had a recent history of not completely supporting the reigning emperor. This combination likely saw Leo act to give it more organisation and loyalty to the Isaurian dynasty.

With all these possible changes, rather than have an overall command, the Leonid/Isaurian navy was more of a conglomeration of squadrons with most attached to what would become naval themes and some others attached to land themes like the Hellados. And while the iconodule sources may not want to admit it, these reforms by Leo III and his successors, building on previous developments, not only reduced unrest amongst the fleet but also spurred some significant naval success for the Roman Empire as the eighth century progressed. Even with the losses entailed in the various civil wars, the Arab siege and the revolt of Kosmas, Leo's reforms allowed for the rebuilding of a navy capable of sending a significant force – reputedly 360 warships – against Umayyad Damietta in 738/739.[86] The naval revival initiated by Leo's reforms continued into the reign of Constantine V, punctuated by a significant victory in the Cypriot harbour of Keramaia in 746. The Alexandrian fleet of the Umayyads sailed north either to attack Roman Cyprus or respond to a Roman fleet doing the same. The result was a decisive victory for the Kibyrrhaeot *strategos*, with Theophanes claiming the unlikelihood of just 3 of 1,000 Arab ships surviving the battle; Anastasius Bibliothecarius more believably states that 30 ships were lost. But even the lesser victory may have broken Umayyad naval power in the Mediterranean.[87] The resultant Roman strangling of Muslim maritime trade, attacks on North African squadrons, and the ousting of the Umayyad dynasty saw the Isaurian navy dominate the seas.[88] The Muslims of the Mediterranean came to fear a devastating Roman seaborne invasion, prompting a new wave of Islamic apocalyptic writing and categorising of coastal guard duty as service in the *jihad*.[89] The tide might have started to turn again by the last years of the eighth century, but Leo III had facilitated a resurgence in Roman naval fortunes.

Locals, Officials and Hierarchies

The Isaurian emperors posed as patrons and defenders of the soldiery, largely as part of an attempt to make the soldiers more loyal to the emperor rather than to their locality, which was a possible problem with the themes. The eighth-century Roman Empire had seen a decline in importance of most of its major cities, with a concurrent rise in the network of villages. This is seen in the prominence of new sub-provincial magistrates in the *Ekloga* and *Nomos Georgikos*, such as the *akroatai*. Other pre-existing provincial governorships like the *anthypatoi* and *praitores* (proconsular and ordinary governors respectively) were retained, which presents some success in maintaining previous chains of command and court justice systems.

The themes may also reflect this local development, with rural land being given to soldiers on their retirement. It is likely that previous emperors and Leo III himself initiated some reforms in the face of this – the rural sections of the *Ekloga* and the *Nomos Georgikos* may provide the best evidence of this; however, it was not until the 750s under Constantine V that it was addressed more directly with the founding of a separate department of the *dromos* under its own *logothete*, which tackled aspects of the postal service, foreign affairs, espionage.[90] This development, along with the post-Leo legal texts, show that the moves to bring legislative reform and administrative coherence to the ad hoc changes made during the seventh century did not stop after his death in 741.

In the process of formalising various officials at various levels, the specialisation of public office and the separation of judicial and fiscal matters,[91] Leo and the Isaurians created a need for 'competent and able persons [in] positions of military and political authority.'[92] To fulfil this need required an increase in capable officials that was beyond the empire's ability to produce. Or at least the emperor felt he could not find enough capable officials he could trust. This led to the rotating of individuals from post to post when the emperor felt the need to have a specifically capable *and* loyal individual in place.[93] Did this demonstrate a good use of skilled manpower? Or a lack of said skilled manpower? Was there also a hint of the emperors not wanting certain skilled individuals gaining a foothold in certain areas of the military/political hierarchies, particularly in the theme system? Keeping offices amongst a tight group would help the emperors keep more of a handle on power as they would appoint men they trusted. This led to 'even greater competition between post-holders and an intensification of the exploitation of offices promoted increasing dependence on the personal favour of the ruler.'[94]

Leo himself will have been wary of the thematic circumstances that enabled his own accession – a power vacuum at the centre of the empire exploited by an alliance amongst *strategoi*; however, he was unsuccessful in dealing with it as seen in the usurpation of Artabasdos against Constantine V, which was essentially a civil war between the alliances of the Armeniac and Opsikon themes (Artabasdos) and the Anatolic and Thrakesian themes (Constantine). After his victory, Constantine would expand the military reorganisation of his father to minimise rebellion, maximise imperial control, and improve military efficiency. He broke up the Opsikon into three separate themes – the Optimatoi, the Bucellarian and a much smaller Opsikon. Constantine also reformed the guard units in the capital into new *tagmata* regiments, which were to provide him with a core group of professional and loyal troops made up exclusively of heavy cavalry.[95] This context of reasserting imperial control and internal discipline should be used to view Isaurian laws regarding the army, such as *Ekloga* 18.1 which 'introduces an entirely new regulation on the division of booty in which the soldiers are specifically singled out for rewards as opposed to their officers … [reflecting] the centrality of soldiers to both society at large and to the emperors.'[96]

There is some claim that Leo III stripped the circus factions of their power, consoling them with a ceremonial position, although it may be that the deme factions never had any real political power to lose. This would mean that any such addition of a ceremonial role saw Leo *increase* the importance of the factions, rather than decrease it.[97] And it was Constantine V who was able to take advantage of this increased importance, using the Hippodrome 'in his campaign against the monks, whipping up popular rage against them by skilfully planted and presented agents provocateurs.'[98]

Another negative misattribution to Leo III comes in the realm of education. Part of the iconodule attack on Leo III by Theophanes was to claim that he targeted the schools and education system to the point that he destroyed an institution that traced its lineage back to Constantine I;[99] however, with this claim we find a counter in the pages of Nikephoros, who much more plausibly attributes the decline of the Roman education system to the neglect caused by 'the frequent assumptions of imperial power and the prevalence of usurpation'[100] in the preceding two decades before Leo's accession.

Isaurian Building and Architecture

As with numismatics and law, Isaurian architecture was used to present a re-founding of the Roman Empire as a Christian kingdom. '[The] creation of a single, coherent image of imperial centrality, dynastic success, and Christian kingship [was] symbolised in the Cross'[101] and in other messages already used elsewhere, such as the repaired walls of Nicaea which had 'Jesus Christ Victorious' on them. This demonstrated how the city had resisted the Arabs and so was able to celebrate its divinely-inspired defiance. This symbolism is seen on other Leonid buildings as well, whether it be the mosaic of the Cross and Scripture excerpts in the apse of Hagia Eirene or image of the prophets and apostles outside the imperial palace. A further dynastic symbol was the building of a porphyry palace chamber, although while it may be attractive to think of this as an example of the promotion of *porphyrogenitus* – 'born in the purple' succession – it was another century before that term was firmly attributed. That is not to say that the idea of precedence being given to children born after their father had become emperor, and was therefore divinely anointed, had not arisen – it had been referred to in the late-fifth century, while Constantine V himself could point to his own being a *porphyrogenitus*.[102]

Leo also had to initiate a major rebuilding effort in the last months of his reign for on 26 October 740,[103] Constantinople and the surrounding area was struck by a massive earthquake. It was large enough that 'in some places the sea withdrew from its own boundaries,'[104] with the area also suffering a year of aftershocks, which saw many move out of the city to makeshift huts beyond the walls.[105] As one can imagine, there were significant casualties and many buildings and structures were destroyed. Along with numerous churches and monasteries, including part of Hagia Eirene,[106] Theophanes mentions the collapse of several imperial statues – that of Constantine I on the Gate of Attalos, which was a gate in the Constantinian Walls on the Mese and possibly the original Golden Gate, that of Arcadius on the Xerolophos column, and that of Theodosius I on the Golden Gate. Parts of the land walls, other towns and villages in Thrace, Nicomedia, Nicaea and others are also mentioned as suffering significant damage. Reputedly, only one church survived in Nicaea.[107]

While most of the repair work will have taken place under Constantine V, Theophanes records Leo III initiating a state-led rebuilding programme for the walls, to be paid for by a new tax of a *miliaresion* per *nomisma/solidus*.[108]

Theophanes seems to suggest that this wall-upkeep tax became permanent (if it was not already), with it being 'customary to give the officials two *keratia*.'[109] Repairs to the Constantinopolitan land walls are well-documented and we have already seen that the walls of Nicaea received repairs under Leo III. The combination of the earthquake and its aftershocks and the attempts to retrieve the military security of the empire likely saw Leo and then Constantine undertake the restoration of other walls and structures around Roman territory.

The Isaurians inherited a hodge-podge system still struggling to deal with the new political and military realities of the eighth century. And yet Leo and his successors succeeded in transforming it into something capable of defending itself, ruling itself and even prospering in the burgeoning medieval world. In organisational terms, it is not clear if Leo founded any themes himself, naval or land. Some dates given for the first appearance of a theme or thematic official might make it appear that they were Leonid foundations, but they could be from before his accession. But then, the same logic should be extended to the reign of his son, Constantine, with some of the themes first mentioned under him, such as a separate Thracian theme or a Cretan theme in 742 and 767 respectively, possibly belonging to Leo. Whatever Leo III did with the themes, it continued their crystallising into permanence, if not necessarily a 'system' *per se*. The Isaurian dynasty and its successors would continue to add new themes through reclamation, reorganisation, and subdivision, to encompass a list of several dozen themes over the succeeding 300 years, a duration that demonstrates the usefulness of thematic organisation in military, political, logistical, governmental, financial, and judicial terms.

A significant aspect of the regularising of the theme 'system' was the in-built ideas of soldiers protecting their own lands, as well as the empire. Leo and the Isaurians also built upon these 'nationalistic feelings'[110] by injecting religious iconography in the form of the cross and promoting the notion that their military successes was due to divine favour.[111] The civilian and military unity provided by such 'Byzantine nationalism' was much needed in the face of the Arab, Slav, and Bulgar threats, but was also another example of the (temporary) abandonment of 'Roman universalism' and 'global empire'.

Caution should be maintained when it comes to how the political, religious, and military reorganisation that may be plausibly but not definitively attributed to Leo and Constantine engendered loyalty from the themes and general security within the empire. It may have been the victories that Leo had won over the Arabs and rebels that did more to generate loyalty to him. The continuation of the political, legal, social, administrative, and ideological reforms Leo initiated was contingent on his ability to bring peace, security, and success to the empire. And while the initial months of his reign had brought significant successes against the Arabs and subsequent years saw the defeat of rebels, the respite these victories brought could not be relied upon to endure. Leo and his forces were going to have to win further victories if that respite was to continue.

Chapter 10

From Constantinople to Akroinon: Romano-Arab Conflict 718–741

'Be merry! We meet again, at the turn of the tide. A great storm is coming, but the tide has turned.'

Gandalf the White, *Lord of the Rings: The Two Towers*

The Raids Return

We have already seen the naval turnaround that took place through the reign of Leo III, with the Romans breaking Umayyad control of the Mediterranean, imposing some control of their own, and even sparking some existential worry in the caliphate. But how had things been going in the land war? There was a lull in Romano-Umayyad conflict after the significant Arab losses suffered at Constantinople and during a serious earthquake in Syria in 717/718. The Arabs were also hindered by some political upheaval, with the death of Umar II less than eighteen months after the end of siege. He was succeeded by his cousin Yazid b. Abd al-Malik, who was faced not only with establishing his regime but also an immediate revolt from a Yazid b. al-Muhallab. Son of a prominent general of the late-seventh century, this rebel Yazid had fallen foul of a court faction, been dismissed as governor of Khurasan and then imprisoned in 704. He managed to escape and was granted asylum in Palestine and when Sulayman became caliph in 715, Yazid was restored to favour, serving as governor of Iraq and Khurasan. While he was militarily successful, subduing Tabaristan, a feat that had eluded the Arabs for over half a century, he allowed his thirst for revenge to colour his political and tribal dealings. This meant that when Sulayman died, Umar II had Yazid imprisoned again. When he heard that Umar was ill, Yazid escaped his prison for fear of further punishment from Yazid II, who was a member of the opposing faction. He fled to Basra and raised the flag of revolt, even declaring holy war against the Umayyads in 720. He received support from Kufa, various tribes, and non-Arab populations, but the caliph was able to call upon veteran commanders in Maslamah and al-Abbas and send them against the rebels with experienced Syrian armies. And all it took to break the rebel spirit was for Maslamah to make an aggressive move across the Euphrates. The al-Muhallabid army irretrievably fractured without a fight, with Yazid and a small number of supporters left to launch an attack of forlorn hope against the Syrians. It ended as you might imagine – Yazid and his rebels were slaughtered.[1]

Even with these political, military, and geological distractions, the respite for Roman Anatolia did not last as long as might be thought. Within a year of the defeat of the al-Muhallabids, al-Abbas had sacked Thebasa in Lycaonia and carried off 20,000 people from Paphlagonia and Umar b. Hubayra had defeated Armeniac forces in Sophene, taking 700 prisoners. Such raids quickly became annual once more. Twin raids by Marwan b. Muhammad and Uthman b. Hayyan al-Murri in 722 struck into Cilicia, possibly capturing Dalisandus, while al-Abbas led a less successful winter campaign. Uthman, along with Abd al-Rahman b. Salim captured Sibora in Armenia and a fortress at Cappadocian Caesarea in 723. Before there could be another raid, Yazid II died of consumption and was succeeded by his half-brother Hisham b. Abd al-Malik. While again faced with the disruption of establishing a new regime and conflict elsewhere in the caliphate, whether it be confronting a Sogdian army in 722/723, a Turkic coalition in 724 (and beyond) or, as will be seen below, fighting with the Khazars,[2] the annual raids did not skip a year under Hisham. If anything, they increased in scope.

Under Yazid II, Umayyad raids were restricted to areas on or near the Romano-Umayyad frontier, possibly explaining why Theophanes does not mention these raids at all. This could call into question the reliability of the Arab sources or could suggest that these raids did so little damage that they escaped notice by Roman sources. We could posit that it is Theophanes who is unreliable here, although he would surely not miss out on an occasion to paint the reign of Leo III in a negative light. It could be that the initial raids launched under Yazid II were limited to the frontier zone because they had to reduce the frontier defences that Leo and his *strategoi* had been able to rebuild. Umar II had been keen to withdraw from frontier regions across the caliphate in the wake of the losses suffered at Constantinople. And while he was persuaded not to go through with the more drastic withdrawal he had proposed – all of Spain, Transoxiana and anything beyond the Taurus – all bases in Anatolia, western Armenia, and Cilicia (apart from Mopsuestia) had been evacuated, allowing Roman forces to re-establish themselves there.

The raids of Yazid II therefore laid a foundation for the increase in scope that Hisham was able to achieve within months of his accession. In 724, Marwan and Sa'id b. Abd al-Malik drove through the frontier zone, capturing the Cilician fortress at Kamakhon and raiding Iconium. Mu'awiyah b. Hisham followed up the next year by driving through the Anatolic theme as far as Dorylaeum, which was in the Opsikon theme. And despite an eruption of plague in Syria,[3] several raids were sent across Anatolia in 726, while Maslamah succeeded in capturing Cappadocian Caesarea and Mu'awiyah sacked the fort of Ateous in Phrygia/Galatia.[4] The combination of these raids and the capture of major settlements could seem like part of an Umayyad strategy to conquer parts of Anatolia; however, if viewed in more traditional terms, the increasing range and larger targets of the Muslim raiding columns may be a result of the success of previous raids. 'As more and more towns were devastated, those left containing any worthwhile quantities of booty became harder to find,'[5] forcing raiders to go further and further west, becoming increasingly distant from their own bases.[6] It does not appear that the Arabs attempted to keep many of the fortresses and cities they captured during these raids.

It might seem that the Romans failed to react to these raids, accepting their inevitability as if they had no manpower to confront them; however, this would be to do them a disservice. Rather than lying prostrate before the Umayyad hordes, refusing to confront them was part of an intentional hard-point defensive strategy by Leo and his generals. The frontier zone of the Taurus and most of Anatolia was dotted with fortified positions – this is seen in the sheer number of different sites named as targets for Arab raids.[7] In these positions, supplies, materials, and manpower could be congregated and protected by thematic garrisons. As they wanted to get at these resources and carry them back to Syria, the Arabs would have to spend time capturing these fortresses and fortified settlements. And as there would be Roman forces within these hard-points, this would take time, limiting the damage these raiders could do every year and opening them to potentially disastrous counterattacks by thematic armies.

The Romans had used such a hard point defensive strategy on their eastern frontier before during the fourth century against the Persians, and while unpopular – considered 'un-Roman' to hide behind walls – it had been successful and its abandoning in favour of more traditional Roman military campaigning had led to disaster. Granted, such a strategy involved an acceptance of some material loss and the constant uprooting of populations and resources to these defensive positions, but burned fields and lost resources were more recoverable than lost manpower. Furthermore, it opened the Arab columns up to trouble should Roman forces strike back – for example, the Anatolian raids led by Kathir b. Rabiah and Sa'id b. Abd al-Malik in 723–724 are recorded as not only meeting with little success but also suffering heavy casualties.[8] And as the raiders were forced to move deeper and deeper into Roman territory, the threat of significant reverse increased. Ultimately, the strategies employed by the Romans and Umayyads saw the conflict descend into 'a grinding and monotonous pattern in which each side attempted to wear the other down.'[9]

The Siege of Nicaea 727

The first major flashpoint between Constantinople and Damascus post-718 came because of these opposing strategies and their inherent dangers. Not long after the defeat of the usurpation of Kosmas in late spring 727,[10] a large Arab army drove through Anatolia. It consisted of two corps – a fast-moving vanguard under Abdallah al-Battal and a main force under Mu'awiyah. There is some disagreement in the sources over who Mu'awiyah's co-commander was, for while the Muslim sources are uniform in naming Abdallah, Theophanes and Nikephoros name a certain Amer/Ameros, possibly to be identified with Ghamr b. Yazid.[11] Normally, it would be usual to accept the unambiguous Arab record, but the history of the personage of al-Battal raises some questions. Despite not having an overly distinguished career – he served at Constantinople, Nicaea and later Akroinon, where he died – we have seen that al-Battal became the basis for a legendary Turkish warrior called Battal Gazi. The building up of his character to literally legendary heights raises doubts over his actual achievements.

There is a third option – this 'Amer' was not a mistaken 'Ghamr', but the personal or patronymic name of Abdallah al-Battal, making him either Amr b. Abdallah al-Battal or Abdallah b. Amr al-Battal. The name 'Abdallah' could be something of an honorific too – it meant 'servant of Allah' and was often a name given to new converts to Islam, marking either al-Battal or possibly his father as a *mawla*.[12] There is room to doubt Theophanes' account of this episode due to the size of forces he attributes to the command of 'Amer' and Mu'awiyah – a vanguard of 15,000 and a main force of 85,000, to make a nice, round total of 100,000: surely far too big. That said, both Amer/al-Battal and Mu'awiyah must have had significant enough forces under their command to penetrate as far as Bithynia and target major cities.

This two-pronged attack achieved some success, with al-Battal sacking the Paphlagonian city of Gangra. He then used his fast-moving raiders to strike towards the capital of the Opsikon theme, Nicaea, catching its garrison unawares. He was then joined there by the main army of Mu'awiyah, whose capture of Ateous may have been part of this campaign, recalled as Tabya by Arab sources. The capture of Gangra and the advance to Nicaea was one of the greater Umayyad successes against the Romans of this post-718 period, only bested by Maslamah's capture of Caesarea the previous year.[13] But even these early successes in 727 were tempered by the heavy casualties suffered at Tabya/Ateous.

Despite finding the Nicaean garrison unready, al-Battal and Mu'awiyah were unable to capture the city by storm, but rather than withdraw, they settled in for a siege once the Romans refused to meet them in battle. The Nicaean garrison may have been commanded by Artabasdos due to his position as *comes Opsikon*, although his role as *kouroplates* might have kept him in Constantinople. Whether the *comes/kouroplates* was present or not, Nicaea resisted resolutely. Even with the partial destruction of its walls by Arab siege engines, the city remained untaken for forty days. At this point, Michael the Syrian claims that the Nicaeans, thinking further resistance was futile, took ship and sailed away across Lake Ascania, leaving the Arabs to capture and destroy this city. This is clearly a mistake as Nicaea remained in Roman hands until the early-fourteenth century, with only a brief Seljuk interlude between 1081 and 1097. If there was to be a kernel of truth in this 'retreat' recorded by Michael, perhaps a Nicaean squadron departed with word of the siege, rather than an abandonment of the city. Any word being sent to imperial authorities over the vulnerability of the Arabs fully deployed below the walls of Nicaea could have encouraged their decision to withdraw without capturing the city, gathering the prisoners and booty they had accumulated and heading back to Syria.

The resistance of Nicaea against this Arab attack was commemorated by an inscription on the repaired walls, which is still extant today. Just west of the Istanbul Gate in modern Iznik near Tower 71 and carved in raised letters reads…

> At the place where, with divine help, the insolence of the enemy was put to shame, there our Christ-loving emperors Leo and Constantine restored with zeal the city of Nicaea, having erected in demonstration of their deed a trophy of victory by setting up a *kentenarion* tower, which Artabasdos, the glorious *patrikios* and *kouropalates*, completed by his toil.[14]

This inscription surely marks the stretch of the Nicaean walls, not only that around Tower 71 but between Towers 70 and 72, that had been battered down by the forces of Mu'awiyah and Amer/al-Battal. This section was reconstructed during the eighth century with reused marble blocks and columns from surrounding buildings. And if such a large section of the walls had been reduced, it may infer some aspects of the siege. It could reflect just how exaggerated the size of Mu'awiyah's army was, as surely an army of 100,000 men would not have failed to storm such a large gap. It may also reflect the extent of the Nicaean garrison, which would be unsurprising with it being the thematic capital and with the *comes Opsikon/kouroplates* possibly present. More generally, it might reflect the success of any hard-point strategy employed by Leo and the fighting ability still present in the Roman army.

Leo III trumpeted the successful defence of such a large, important, and religiously significant city as a great achievement for the empire and him personally. Feeling the need to present it being nothing to do with the 'iconoclast'

Leo, Theophanes gave the kudos to the iconodule prayers of the Nicaeans, the city's own ecumenical past, and the intercession of the Blessed Virgin and the holy icons of the Church Fathers present in the city. Indeed, Theophanes upped the iconodule rhetoric with the story of Constantine the *strator* destroying the icon of the Virgin Mary and receiving 'a just reward for his impiety.'[15]

A Useful Distraction – the Second Arab-Khazar War

While it did not mark the end of Arab raids of Roman Anatolia, the siege of Nicaea marked the last high point of this period for the Umayyads. As their attention was drawn to other frontiers, they would never again strike so deeply into Roman territory. The one frontier to take the attention of the Umayyads that saw some Roman involvement was that of the Caucasus. Here, the Umayyads faced two sources of trouble – the lesser came from the Transcaucasian Christian kingdoms of Iberia, Lazica, and Abasgia; the graver threat came from further north with the Khazars. Arab-Khazar conflict was not a new development. The First Arab-Khazar war had been fought as early as the 640s, with the Arabs possibly looking to cut trade routes to Constantinople, warning the Khazars about aiding the recently conquered Caucasians or even out and out conquest to aid in an attack on the Roman Empire from the steppe. The first major Arab strike through the Derbent pass into Khazaria saw Abd al-Rahman reach Balanjar unhindered, with his cavalry vanguard approaching the Volga in c.643. The succeeding decade saw al-Rahman launch various small-scale raids from Derbent into Khazaria.[16] This culminated in a rash attempt to capture Balanjar itself in 652, which saw Abd al-Rahman and 4,000 Arabs killed by a large Khazar force.

There would be limited Arab-Khazar conflict for the next 70 years, with plundering raids of Transcaucasia launched by the Khazars and their subjects in the early 660s and 680s, taking advantage of periods of Muslim civil war to perhaps achieve some short-lived Khazar suzerainty over Albania.[17] This was challenged and largely overthrown by the Umayyads before the seventh century was out, although an attempt to recapture Derbent failed in 692/693. Several more attempts by the most prominent Umayyad generals, Muhammad b. Marwan and Maslamah, to retake Derbent ended in failure in 707, 708 and 709, before the latter succeeded in 713/714. The Khazar response was to raid into Albania (709/715) and Azerbaijan (717), only to be defeated by an Arab force under Hasan b. al-Nu'man.

This Azerbaijan raid could have had a more direct effect on Roman affairs as it came at a time when the caliphate had gone all out to conquer Constantinople. Hasan could only scrape together 4,000 men to confront up to 20,000 Khazar raiders. Indeed, the timing of this Khazar attack was so providential for the Romans that it raises the possibility that Leo III, or his predecessors, had reached out to the khagan. The ability of the Khazars to threaten Arab-held territory in Transcaucasia through the Caucasian passes made them an attractive ally for the Roman Empire. And although Justinian II's marriage alliance with the Khazars in the last years of the seventh century might have been made for more personal motives, good relations between Constantinople and Khazaria were to continue to be useful for the Isaurians going forward.

Conflict with the Khazars could have influenced why the initial restarting of Umayyad raids of Roman territory did not stray too far from the Syrian border. In early 722, a Khazar force of up to 30,000 men forced its way past Derbent, raided Umayyad Armenia and then inflicted a heavy defeat on the local governor, Ma'laq b. Saffar al-Bahrani at the Battle of Marj al-Hijara – the Battle of the Rocky Meadow. In response, Yazid II sent a large army north under al-Jarrah b. Abdallah al-Hakami to drive out the Khazars. Upon collecting troops from vassal princes, al-Jarrah's force likely matched that of the Khazars. And as Derbent was still in Arab hands, al-Jarrah advanced into Khazaria unhindered, where he defeated a Khazar force on the al-Ran river and then forged on to Balanjar. They found the city's defences in poor shape, with the Khazar garrison having to literally circle the wagons around their citadel. It proved futile with al-Jarrah capturing and systematically sacking Balanjar, killing or enslaving most of its inhabitants.

Upon his return south, al-Jarrah asked the caliph for reinforcements, suggesting that he felt that the northern threat had not been quashed.[18] He was not wrong as the Khazar host returned south of the Caucasus in early 724. Al-Jarrah was victorious in a subsequent days-long battle, but it was not a decisive rout. For the rest of the year and on into 725, Arab commanders looked to solidify Umayyad control of Transcaucasia and the routes into it. Al-Jarrah subdued Iberia by taking Tiflis, before then becoming the first Arab commander to traverse the Darial Pass, securing it for the caliphate. This removed a route of Khazar attack, whilst also providing the Arabs with a second route of invasion into Khazaria.

The command was then given to Maslamah, highlighting that caliph Hisham was putting more focus on the area by charging his best general with the job. Initially, Maslamah busied himself with dealing with the Romans and building up his forces, while his sub-commander al-Harith b. Amr al-Ta'i consolidated Umayyad control of Transcaucasia. This was necessary as the Khazars returned in force in 726, raiding Albania and Azerbaijan, as well as laying siege to Vardanakert, an attempt that involved the use of mangonels, which demonstrates that the Khazars were more militarily sophisticated than usually thought.[19] But even then, al-Harith proved their match, defeating them on the banks of the Araxes river.

The escalation in the Arab-Khazar conflict continued, as not only did Maslamah take personal command of the front in 727, so did the khagan and his son. The Umayyad general reclaimed the Darial Pass, lost since 724, before launching raids into Khazaria in 727 and 728. This second invasion almost ended in disaster, for while the Arabs defeated the Khazar army in an extended month-long battle in August/September 728, they were ambushed during their return south. In a headlong flight through the Darial Pass, the Arab army had to abandon their baggage train.[20] This reverse not only saw Maslamah replaced by al-Jarrah but also the loss of Albania and Derbent by 729. Al-Jarrah was also faced with defending Azerbaijan from another Khazar raid. Adding to the tit-for-tat nature of this conflict, al-Jarrah followed up in 729/730 with another advance through Tiflis and the Darial Pass. It is improbably claimed by Arab sources that al-Jarrah reached the Volga, although he was far enough away from the Caucasus to be outmanoeuvred and bypassed by a Khazar army that again invaded Albania and Azerbaijan.

Al-Jarrah raced back south, eventually catching up with the Khazars besieging the regional capital at Ardabil. In the resultant three-day Battle of Ardabil of 7–9 December 730, the Arab army came apart under the combination of Khazar attacks and exhaustion. Al-Jarrah himself and up to 20,000 Arab soldiers were killed, with another 40,000 (improbably) taken prisoner after the sack of Ardabil.[21] Such was the destruction of al-Jarrah's army that the Khazars were able to divide their forces (which brings suspicion upon the numbers attributed to the prisoners they had taken as they could not have looked after them), sending raiding columns far and wide across Transcaucasia and Azerbaijan, sacking Ganza and other settlements. One column reached Mosul before being repulsed. This was a significant shock for the caliphate and surely a welcome boon for the Romans, for as the Arabs had to throw more forces into dealing with the Khazars, there were fewer forces available to threaten Anatolia.[22]

Hisham responded by dispatching Sa'id b. Amr to retrieve the situation on the ground, whilst charging Maslamah with preparing a sizeable army to strike back. Despite the limited troops at his immediate disposal, Sa'id took advantage of the splitting up of the Khazar army to recover some settlements and prisoners. There is some hint of exaggeration in the reporting of this Sa'id counter-offensive, with him reputedly beating several armies of much bigger size and even killing the khagan's son in single combat. It may well be that Sa'id simply won a single engagement at Bajarwan, which encouraged the Khazars to return home, happy with their work.[23] Maslamah then arrived with a Syrian army, with which he re-established Umayyad control of Albania and then drove through the Derbent Pass once more. As with other events of this conflict, this raid of Khazaria is chronologically confusing, possibly conflated with other raids, but Maslamah may have driven deeply into Turkic territory, capturing several major settlements, including Balanjar again. However, when he was confronted by the full Khazar army under the personal command of the khagan, Maslamah wisely retreated to Derbent. The base was still in the hands of the Khazars and while al-Harith had been posted there with a force to keep the route open to the Arabs, the Khazar khagan was able to catch up. The subsequent battle was in the balance until an elite unit stole through the Khazar lines and attacked the khagan in his own tent. This swung the battle in favour of the Arabs, who then starved out the Khazar garrison of Derbent and established a military colony of 24,000 men there.

Even with this success, Maslamah was replaced in early 732,[24] with Hisham giving the job to Marwan b. Muhammad. His first Khazar campaign also falls into the chronologically dubious category, looking reminiscent of the previous raids of Maslamah. Perhaps more believable is the report of Marwan's forces probing the lands just north of Derbent, securing its approaches before withdrawing there for the winter. A reason for Marwan being less ambitious north of the Caucasus was his dealings with the Transcaucasian kingdoms. He is seen granting the Armenians some autonomy in return for manpower for the caliphal armies, a concession that highlights Umayyad manpower problems.[25]

While we may posit an on-going relationship between the Roman Empire and Khazar khaganate since Justinian II's exile, it is around this time that we hear direct reference to contact between the two states. In 731/732,[26] what must have been an extended period of high-level negotiations resulted in an alliance between Leo III and Khagan Bihar, cemented by the marriage of Constantine to Bihar's daughter. She is listed as being named Tzitzak, possibly a Hellenised version of the Proto-Turkic word for 'flower', but Constantine VII used *tzitzakia* to refer to an imperial garment influenced by the Khazar presence in the imperial court.[27] It could be that *tzitzak* was a descriptor of the Khazar princess' dress.[28] Upon her marriage to Constantine, 'Tzitzak' was obliged to convert to Christianity and take the name Irene. She became known for her piety and her opposition to iconoclasm.[29] It could also be that Irene was extremely young when she married Constantine, who was himself only 14, for their first child – the future Leo IV – was not born until 25 January 750. And given that Constantine V was married to Maria by the following year, it is possible that Irene died in childbirth. What this Romano-Khazar alliance entailed can only be guessed at. It could have involved trade agreements, allowing the Khazars access to the Black Sea and the Romans access to the north routes to the Far East, avoiding Umayyad territory. Militarily, the Khazars may have undertaken to continue their raids into Transcaucasia, while the Romans may have promised to send more aid to the Khazars to continue such actions, and to their other allies in the region – Abasgians, Apsilians, Alans and any factions amongst the Armenians, Iberians and Albanians still fighting against Arab dominance.

But if the Khazars did promise to continue their raids, it was one they did not keep. The campaigning seasons following Marwan's limited expedition of 732 saw little action on both sides. Marwan had been replaced as the Umayyad governor of Armenia and Azerbaijan in early 733 by Sa'id b. Amr, who undertook no campaigns of any substance. This could reflect the need to consolidate the achievements of the previous years both in Transcaucasia and Derbent, but it could also reflect increasing manpower issues. There was a similar Arab lull in fighting on the north-eastern frontier of the caliphate after some costly reverses suffered against the Turkic Turgesh, again hinting at Umayyad manpower resources being overstretched.[30] This is not to say that there was a lack of appetite for the fight amongst the Umayyads. Even after his replacement, Marwan pleaded with Hisham to take the fight to the Khazars by sending him and an army of up to 120,000 to see to their subjection. And in 735, when Sa'id asked to be relieved due to his failing eyesight, Hisham fulfilled half of this plea – Marwan was restored to the Caucasian command; however, it appears that the caliph would not or could not provide the overwhelming manpower. Thus, Marwan's second tenure initially proved as lacking in major engagement as Sa'id's had. Such was the lack of Arab-Khazar conflict post-732 that sources like Agapios and Michael the Syrian posit an official peace. Muslim sources ignore this possibility or suggest that Marwan was intentionally lulling the Khazars into a false sense of security.[31]

While there was no immediate attack on Khazar territory, Marwan was hardly inactive in Transcaucasia. He repaired and expanded Umayyad infrastructure, establishing a new base at Kasak near Tiflis; he subdued Armenian opposition to the Umayyad vassal prince, secured control of the Darial Pass by lifting fortresses from the Alans, restored an Alan prince to his territory as an Umayyad subject and defeated another and, as will be seen below, launched a devastating campaign across the western Caucasus. And in the background, Marwan was planning the biggest strike yet against the Khazars. His pleas had reputedly been answered by 737, with a force of 120,000 Syrians, Jazirans, jihadi volunteers, Caucasian allies and armed camp followers at his disposal, although this seems like a significant exaggeration; however, the strategies Marwan employed would require significant manpower resources, so he must have had an army of substantial size.

Under a pretence of peace negotiations, Marwan launched a two-pronged attack on eastern Khazaria. The Derbent governor, Asid b. Zafir al-Sulami led

30,000 men from the garrison and Caucasian allies up the coast of the Caspian Sea beyond the ruins of Balanjar. Marwan marched through the Darial Pass with a larger force and struck north-east towards Samandar, where he was to meet up with Asid. The strength of these Arab armies and a Khazar strategy of non-engagement saw Marwan and Asid meet no resistance, meaning they had to rethink their strategy once they converged at Samandar. Keen to bring the Khazars to battle, Marwan set out for the Volga, aiming for the nomadic camp 'capital' at Itil. The khagan withdrew further north, but the area was defended by a large army. Marwan gave chase along the Volga, shadowed by the Khazar army on the opposite bank. Growing frustrated and a little concerned, Marwan launched a daring strike across the river, which caught the Khazars off-guard in swampy land, where up to 10,000 were killed and another 7,000 taken prisoner. Muslim sources would have it that the khagan sued for peace in the aftermath and agreed to accept Islam.

But for what looks like a spectacular crescendo to the Second Arab-Khazar War, Marwan's campaign had been something of a damp squib. The swampy contest along the Volga was the only battle of note in the entire campaign. For all the distance covered, Marwan did not accomplish much. The show of force might have been the catalyst for the end of Khazar raids south of the Caucasus, but there was little beyond that, particularly if the expedition had aimed at breaking Khazar power.[32] Perhaps the only material achievement of this campaign was the large number of captives that Marwan reputedly took – up to 50,000 in total, including some Khazars who converted to Islam, but could not continue to live amongst their Turkic brethren, demonstrating that the story of the conversion of the khagan is untrue.[33]

Whilst not achieving much given the scale of the undertaking, Marwan's campaign was the last major contest between the Khazars and Arabs for two decades. There may have been some Arab raiding beyond Derbent up until 741, possibly intent on securing the approaches to the Caucasian pass and seizing plunder to help pay for the upkeep of the Derbent garrison. This lack of result does not mean that Marwan's 737 campaign was folly from the start. Indeed, it has been proposed that Marwan was close to conquering at least southern Khazaria. Had the attack across the Volga killed the khagan rather than just his leading general, a peace treaty may have involved significantly more concessions and established an Umayyad presence north of Derbent.[34] As this did not materialise, and even though they did not make any permanent in-roads into Umayyad territory, the Khazar role in stemming the Arab tide, alongside the Romans, Bulgars, and the Franks should not be overlooked. Specifically for Leo III, the Umayyad material and time spent against the Khazars was material and time not spent against the Roman Empire. And even when some headway was made in the form of the garrisoning of Derbent, it required valuable Syrian troops who would have otherwise been focused on dealing with the Romans.

Dealings with the Caucasian Kingdoms

Leonid interactions with the Caucasus were not limited to his dealings with the Khazars and their strikes into Arab Transcaucasia. His personal experience amongst the Alans, Apsilians, and Abasgians may have led to some connections in the region and even some impetus above imperial concerns to achieve a positive result there. Leo was encouraged to intervene by a letter sent by a namesake – Leon I, prince of Abasgia, asking for aid against the Umayyads. The chronology is not clear, but this plea for help likely came on the back of Transcaucasian campaigning of Marwan in 735–737. The Arab commander had ousted Stephan of Iberia, forcing his sons, Mirian and Archil, to flee to Lazica and then Abasgia. These Christian dynasts called upon Leo III for help, who responded by looking to bring some hierarchical order to the region. The emperor gave his official stamp of approval to Leon's hereditary rule of Abasgia and suggested that he accept Archil, the *de jure* ruler of Iberia after the death of Mirian, as his suzerain to best present a united front against the Arabs. Further highlighting the vassalisation of Abasgia, Leo III bestowed the title of archon upon Leon, which may have involved the dynast receiving some Roman aid (and possibly pay some Roman taxation). This alliance between Archil and Leon I was strengthened by Leon's marriage with Gurandukht, a daughter of Mirian. Indeed, such marriages played a significant role in the solidifying of this Transcaucasian alliance, with Mirian alone having seven daughters who were married off for political gain by Archil.

The Abasgia-Iberia alliance did not look like it would last long as the Umayyads struck deep into the western Caucasus with up to 60,000 men. Marwan captured several Alan fortresses (suggesting their involvement in the alliance), and then moved against Abasgia, where they ravaged the countryside and captured its major settlements, all except the fortress of Anacopia. Archil had retreated there to take advantage of its natural and man-made defences. Leon I does not seem to have been present, as he was then in negotiations with the Alans at Sobhi. The defenders at Anacopia reputedly numbered only 2,000 Abasgians and 1,000 Iberians, but this is likely missing out some other retreating allies such as Lazicans and Alans. Even if there were a few thousand more defenders at Anacopia, they still paled in comparison to the size of Marwan's army. If the Arab general had 60,000 upon his initial strike against Iberia, he will have taken casualties and established garrisons in Iberia, Lazica and Abasgia. Therefore, the Umayyad army that appeared at Anacopia might have been greatly reduced in size, but was still several times larger than that of Archil and his allies – possibly 20,000 at a minimum.

The defenders needed a miracle and, as the story goes, they got one. Answering the prayer of Archil, the Arab column was wracked with an outbreak of disease, likely brought on by the combination of the climate, exhaustion, and close quarters of their camp. This epidemic may have killed thousands of Marwan's men and demoralised the rest to the point that a sally by the Abasgi-Iberian garrison ejected the Umayyads from western Abasgia. It is unlikely that Marwan suffered the extent of casualties that some sources claim – 38,000 of the 40,000 that assailed Anacopia! – but he did withdraw from Abasgia as a whole. And while he led a second invasion in 739–740, he only extracted some tribute. It is not certain that outright conquest was the aim of Marwan's first Transcaucasia campaign, for in 737 he would launch his great attack on Khazaria, so it could be that the attacks on Iberia, Abasgia, and the Alans were to secure his flank and rear. If that is the case, Marwan had made a strategic error as his heavy-handed presence drove the Transcaucasian kingdoms into alliance with one another and the Roman Empire.

By 738, Marwan and his lieutenants were having to campaign against these regional alliances and recalcitrant tributaries throughout the Caucasus. Over the course of the next four years, the Arabs had repeated success in their dealings with the Alans, Iberians, Albanians, and Armenians; however, the sheer fact that these 'successes' could be called 'repeated' may considerably undermine their actual extent. As an example, Marwan's forces attacked the same Alan princeling several times. These Arab incursions were not severe enough to prevent Caucasians from acting contrary to the agreements they had come to with the caliphate. They may have been little more than raids, designed to add plunder and enforce tribute that Marwan needed to keep his troops happy. He could also not afford to inflict heavy casualties on what were his additional sources of manpower, so even these raids might have been little more than demonstrations, with so little actual fighting 'that most of the sources have not even deigned to notice.'[35]

We might even propose that for the Caucasian principalities to continually challenge Marwan through non-payment of tribute obligations, they may have had outside encouragement, either from the Khazars or the Romans. It does not appear that Leo III provided military aid to the Abasgi-Iberian alliance and other Caucasian princelings, but some material aid cannot be ruled out. The renaissance of Roman naval strength under Leo would have provided a useful avenue of support to the Christian peoples of the eastern shores of the Black Sea. The Abasgi-Iberian alliance might not have lasted long beyond the reign of Leo III, but it had helped lay the foundations of the restoration of Iberia by saving its ruling dynasty and preserved Abasgia as a nominally independent state, an independence it would use a generation later to liberate and absorb Lazica, founding the kingdom of Abkhazia. The two kingdoms enabled by this short-lived alliance would later unify in the early-eleventh century to become the Kingdom of Georgia.

We should not go too far in denigrating the Arabs for their dealings with the Khazars and the Caucasus. By 741, the region was largely stabilised through Arab control of several important bases, such as Derbent and the Darial Pass, while the Khazar raiding had stopped. The problem was that this result had required a significant investment of manpower, material, and money, resources that may have been better deployed elsewhere. This was not just because it might have improved Umayyad outcomes on other frontiers, but also because the Caucasus region lacked the resources to make controlling it profitable. And not only was it unable to provide a surplus to the caliphate, it sucked more manpower, material, and money away from the centre.

Their campaigns in Transcaucasia and against the Khazars were not the only major areas of conflict that took Umayyad attention away from Roman Anatolia. We have already mentioned the eastern campaigns against the Sogdians and the Turkic Turgesh, where the Arabs suffered significant reverses throughout the mid-eighth century. In the Indian subcontinent, the Arab advance was halted by the Chalukya, before they were then ejected from northern India by the Pratiharas. Far to the west, the Arabs had spent the first quarter of the eighth century conquering the Iberian Peninsula and probing into Gaul. This expansion had been facilitated by the conversion of the Berbers and while Frankish leaders such as Charles Martel and Odo of Aquitaine halted the Umayyad advance in Gaul, perhaps the most important episode in making sure they never returned was the major Berber revolt of 740–743. This almost cost the Umayyads their territory west of Libya, and while they succeeded in regaining control of Tunisia, eastern Algeria and Spain, what are now Morocco and western Algeria were lost to the caliphate. The Syrian manpower needed to curb this revolt played a significant role in the dissipating the Umayyad threat to the Roman Empire and undermining the Umayyad caliphate itself.

The Road to Akroinon

Umayyad incursions into Anatolia did not cease upon the failure at Nicaea and the intensifying of war with the Khazars. In 728, Mu'awiyah captured the fortresses of Semalouos and al-Mawa in the Armeniac theme; the next year saw Sa'id reach Cappadocian Caesarea and Mu'awiyah lead a raid of less success.[36] Through the late-720s, the Umayyad navy was also taking to the seas once more, suggesting that Arab sea power 'had somewhat recovered since the debacle at Constantinople, though their extent is unknown and no brilliant exploits are recorded.'[37] The year 730 focused on Cappadocia, with Mu'awiyah striking from Malatya to take the fortress at Charsianon[38] and burn the unidentified Farandiyya, although there is no campaign recorded for the summer of 731. This may show the strain on caliphal resources, with Mu'awiyah possibly restricted to frontier duty due to the need of his soldiers in Caucasia following the Khazar sack of Ardabil late in 730. A raid later in the year by al-Battal met with failure.

Keen to avenge this reverse, Mu'awiyah and al-Battal struck more deeply into Anatolia in 732/733, reaching Akroinon. Seeing the Arabs driving as far west as Akroinon as an opportunity to inflict another defeat, a Roman army under a certain Constantine tried to intercept this Umayyad column; however, al-Battal succeeded in defeating Constantine, taking the Roman commander prisoner. There is some suggestion in Syrian sources of another Arab reverse after Mu'awiyah withdrew, but this could be a misinterpretation of al-Battal's defeat the previous year and/or his confrontation with Constantine. It could also be influenced by the less successful raid by Souleiman b. Hisham towards Cappadocian Caesarea in the same year.

The siege of Nicaea, while a tremendous success for Leo and his defensive strategy, was not a significant defeat for the Umayyad forces. Raids in the years immediately following the retreat struck at major cities and thematic fortresses; however, there were signs of trouble in the lull of summer 731 and some reverses, which show a combination of stretched Umayyad resources and renewing Roman fortunes. And successes were only to become less frequent through the early/mid-730s, even as the annual raids expanded their range. In late 733, Mu'awiyah reached Paphlagonia, taking prisoners and possibly sacking a town, before raiding again the following summer, seemingly achieving little. The Umayyad raids of Anatolia were not helped by the outbreak of plague in Syria in 732/733.[39] In 735, we see the Umayyad raiding parties again striking further and further from the border. Mu'awiyah's column reached Sibora in Pontus, while another column reached Sardis in the Thrakesian theme. As mentioned earlier, this is not evidence of the strength of the Umayyad raids, but perhaps of the strengthening of the Roman hardpoint defence, with Mu'awiyah's men having to raid further to find towns, cities and fortresses they could capture, opening them to counterattack. These raids of 735, while wide-ranging are not recorded as capturing any settlements, even if Theophanes comments that Mu'awiyah 'devastated Asia.'[40] Following up on the attack on Sibora the same year, Souleiman led a multi-pronged raid of Armenia and while it is not clear if this is to be considered parts of Roman-controlled Armenia or the parts of Armenia rankling under Umayyad control, it appears to have achieved little.[41]

Raiding of similar scope and lack of achievement seems to have taken place in 737, a failure coupled to a naval defeat in the eastern Mediterranean, where the reformed Roman fleet made their return.

Both Mu'awiyah and Souleiman launched further raids of Roman territory in 738, with the latter taking 'many captives in Asia', amongst whom would appear to be the Bešer, the Pseudo-Tiberioi;[42] however, the more consequential event of this campaigning season came within Mu'awiyah's column. It had reached Baluniya, possibly a fortress in Cappadocia, but on the return journey, Mu'awiyah 'fell from his horse and died'[43] whilst out hunting. The loss of the caliphal son who had been given the leading role in the Romano-Arab conflict would seemingly have had a negative effect on the already flagging Umayyad action against Roman territory; however, if anything, it had the opposite effect. While not reflective of Mu'awiyah, the two years after his death saw an uptick in Umayyad success against the Romans as his brothers, Souleiman and Maslama b. Hisham led attacks. In 738, Souleiman captured the fortress of Sideroun, taking many prisoners, including the son of a prominent patrician,[44] with Maslama keeping the pressure on the next year by seizing southern Cappadocia and then marching north to besiege and capture Ancyra in the Opsikon theme.[45]

These successes of the last years of the 730s would explain why in 740 Hisham authorised a seemingly enormous and multi-pronged invasion of Roman territory under the command of three of his sons – Muhammad, Maslama and Souleiman. Muhammad and Maslama were charged with raiding campaigns, with the added incentive of distracting any Roman counterattack, while Souleiman led an army of up to 90,000 into the heart of the Anatolic theme. Not only was such a total unlikely for a caliphate facing manpower issues, whatever size it was, it was not concentrated under Souleiman's direct command. Instead, it was divided into three. The vanguard of 10,000 light troops under Ghamr b. Yazid was sent deep into enemy territory to reconnoitre and/or pin down Thrakesian forces. This column was followed by a cavalry force of 20,000 under Malik b. Shu'ayb and al-Battal, who struck out across the Anatolic theme, eventually reaching Akroinon. Souleiman would then march through the Taurus with his main force of 60,000, raid across southern Cappadocia, and secure its reincorporation as caliphal territory by capturing the fortress of Tyana.

Each of these columns met with mixed results. Souleiman inflicted considerable damage on southern Cappadocia 'destroying a large number of men, women and beasts of burden,'[46] before withdrawing unharmed; however, he had failed in his main objective as Tyana remained in Roman hands. This would suggest that Souleiman did not have an army of 60,000 under his direct command as Tyana would surely not have been able to resist. Ghamr is attributed with inflicting similar devastation on the Thrakesian theme, before also retreating unharmed;

however, he would seem to have failed not only in capturing any settlements but also in any reconnaissance he was charged with. This most westerly column of the Arab attack of 740 failed to report the presence of a substantial, imperially-led Roman army in the field. He could even be accused of not backing up the Arab cavalry force at Akroinon when it was approached by this Roman army. There is room to divert some blame away from Ghamr for what was about to happen – he may well have found the Roman army, reported its movements to Malik and al-Battal and even offered his assistance only to be rejected. The source record does not provide sufficient information to come to any conclusion.

The result was a disaster for the cavalry column at Akroinon and the entire expedition, which had already achieved very little with respect to the layout of men and material entailed. Again, there is little depth in the record of the subsequent Battle of Akroinon. It is recorded[47] that a Roman army marched to intercept Malik and al-Battal and that it was commanded by Leo III and Constantine V, but there is no mention of what this army was made up of. We could surmise that the main Thrakesian and Anatolic armies were charged with keeping track of Ghamr and Souleiman respectively, while it appears a little out of the way for the Armeniac army. This could have seen the army of Leo and Constantine constituted from the Thracian and Opsikon armies, with some Thrakesian and Anatolic garrison forces collected en route. It would also be expected that Leo would not have risked such a battle in person if he did not at least have numerical parity, if not a strong superiority, over Malik and al-Battal's 20,000 (if that number is to be believed). As Malik and al-Battal commanded a cavalry force, for them to be drawn into a decisive contest would require that they were either taken by surprise by Leo's arrival, were consummately out-generalled, fell into a trap laid by the Romans, or were so over-confident as to suffer a combination of all three.

However the Battle of Akroinon came to be and then played out, Malik and al-Battal reputedly suffered 66 per cent casualties, with 13,200 of their 20,000 lost, including the two commanders themselves.[48] Of the 6,800 that survived, they managed to make it to Synnada and then on to re-join the column of Souleiman after suffering much hardship and lack of supplies.[49] Sources such as Agapios and Pseudo-Dionysius posit even higher Arab casualties for the campaign as a whole – anything from 20,000 to 45,000. Even if these are exaggerations, the Umayyads were in no position to sustain even the low end of 13,200 casualties, particularly to the Syrian forces that were the core of Umayyad power. Indeed, the Umayyad position became even more stretched before the year was out. Many of those men who had just returned to Syria from their less than successful campaign in Anatolia had to be dispatched to Africa to help deal with the Berber revolt, which had won the 'Battle of the

Nobles' near Tangiers. And this expedition led by Kulthum b. Iyad, governor of Damascus, was to be another disaster for the Umayyads, with heavy losses at Bagdoura in late 741.[50]

It was long held that the Battle of Akroinon had a significant impact on the history of the Mediterranean: a significant victory for the Romans, providing them with a first major land victory over the Arabs in decades, while being equally catastrophic for the Umayyad caliphate, initiating its final decline into the Third Fitna and eventual overthrow by the Abbasids in 750. However, the effects of this singular battle have been exaggerated. The manpower losses it involved for the caliphate were ill-timed, but taken in isolation, they do not represent a significant loss for the Umayyads, particularly if the bloated sizes attributed to Souleiman's army as a whole and the casualties it incurred are to be considered exaggerations. While not coincidental with the collapse of Umayyad leadership,[51] Akroinon's impact on the caliphate comes as only a part of a drawn-out progression of manpower losses and overstretching of resources on various frontiers involving the Romans, Khazars, Turgesh, Indians, Berbers and Franks.[52]

And even with those problems, the forces under Souleiman were able to launch another attack on Roman territory the following summer. Geographical specifics beyond 'a fortress in Anatolia' are lacking, but at the very least it shows that this Umayyad army charged with raiding Roman territory had not been debilitated by the combination of Akroinon and the transfers to Africa. Although Hisham and Souleiman may have soon wished they had been unable to launch such an attack as the latter proved incapable of capturing the targeted fortress due to an outbreak of plague in his camp. And given the various occurrences of plague recorded under Hisham, the Umayyad army in Syria must have felt the impact of this throughout the period. But it was not just plague that ravaged Souleiman's army – it was also devastated by famine, possibly due to a lack of supplies either brought with them or gathered from raids. This saw most of the Umayyad horses die, with the Romans taking advantage of this combination of Arab debilitations to launch a stinging counterattack. Souleiman made it back to Umayyad territory, but Agapios claims that a number of Muslim troops surrendered to the Romans and converted to Christianity due to the wretchedness of their existence.[53] This again could all be exaggeration, but could still give an insight into the deterioration in conditions within the Syrian forces of the caliphate.

Some of the Arab and Syriac sources claim that Souleiman's campaign of 741 was a success, although they may be conflating that plague-ridden disaster with the more successful campaigns of 742 and 743, when Umayyad forces took advantage of the civil war between Constantine V and Artabasdos to raid widely across Roman Anatolia. This again shows that the losses of Ardabil, Akroinon, and Bagdoura had not incapacitated the caliphate's military, although the sources for these raids of 742 and 743 do not present any significant achievement, beyond the taking of prisoners.

While the downturn in caliphal fortunes was a state-wide problem exacerbated by defeats like Akroinon rather than caused by it, that defeat of Malik and al-Battal marked something of a sea change in Roman strategy and fortunes in Anatolia. Akroinon 'is presented in the sources as an encouraging sign,'[54] with the previous decade of successful hardpoint defence building enough confidence for Leo and Constantine to take to the field and defeat a sizeable Arab raiding column. That growing Roman confidence was also demonstrated at sea. In 740, some kind of 'incident' of Roman instigation occurred on the Syrian coast, which required the calling up of reserve troops in Damascus. This was almost certainly a Roman naval raid on the area of what is now Lebanon, an ominous sign of renewed Roman sea power.[55]

And in the last months of Leo III's life, or even just after his death on 18 June 741, the more aggressive Roman stance was laid bare by an attack on the Umayyad base at Melitene. An army of 20,000, likely a combination of thematic forces, launched a surprise attack, catching the Melitene garrison unawares and perhaps away from its station. This would not be surprising given the years without a Roman threat to this area. While it may be a made-up story, the suggestion that Muslim women within the city had to disguise themselves as men to pretend that the walls were defended highlights the lack of Arab manpower in the area. This was also seen in how the relief force sent to Melitene was led by caliph Hisham himself, the only time that he led troops in person during his reign. And even though the city remained in Umayyad hands, the Romans pillaged the surrounding area extensively without risking their own numbers, marking a shift in the strategies employed in Anatolia from Roman resistance to Umayyad raids to mutual raiding.

Umayyad disgruntlement with this change of emphasis may be seen in an incident dated to 741. Hisham sent an order to Souleiman to execute all Roman prisoners held by the Umayyads in various cities. It was later reported that Hisham's murderous anger was piqued by a false report that Leo III had ordered a similar massacre of Muslim prisoners taken by the Romans.[56] As there is no reporting of this in Roman sources, even those keen to depict Leo as a bloodthirsty tyrant, it is more likely that the downturn in Umayyad fortunes on various frontiers had gotten the better of Hisham. The combination of Akroinon and the Roman strike at Melitene may have been the final straw, seeing caliphal ire being targeted on Christians within his power. There could also have been some Christian/pro-Roman disgruntlement within parts of the caliphate, possibly hinted at in the pages of Theophanes in the years prior, with caliphal camels being destroyed and a prominent Christian, Theodore, son of Mansour, being banished to the desert.[57]

Overall, the Romano-Umayyad contest during Leo III's reign must be seen as up-and-down for both sides. In the grand scheme of things, it reminds the historian of the Romano-Persian conflicts of old – significant resources expended with little to show for it as there was no appreciable change in the frontier. As the state on the offensive, this must see the period labelled as one of ultimate but not on-going failure for the Umayyad caliphate. It was bookended by the colossal defeat at Constantinople and the less disastrous but still damaging loss at Akroinon and punctuated by the successful Roman defence of Nicaea and the Roman reclamation of the seas; however, looking past these more major episodes, the period of 717–741 was one of largely unbroken raiding success for the Umayyads. Their columns raided far and wide across Constantinople's Asian territories and the number of prisoners and resources those raiders hauled back to Syria from Anatolia must at times have been eye-watering; however, Leo and his *strategoi* gradually organised a strategic withdrawal and hardpoint defence that first stemmed and then began to reverse the tide.

While the deeper the Umayyad raids went into Roman territory would seem to reflect their repeated success, they could highlight the growing capabilities of the Roman army and the population in reacting to these raids. As settlements and resource centres along the Romano-Umayyad frontier and then in central Anatolia become more adept at removing themselves to hardpoint defences and then defending them from an assault or siege, the raiders had to go deeper and deeper into Roman territory to find plunder – or in strategic terms, they had to go further and further from the safety of their own territory, opening them to counterattack by increasingly confident and even numerically superior Roman forces.

These successes laid the groundwork for a more aggressive strategy, seen at Akroinon and then Melitene, as well as at sea. This aggression was forestalled somewhat by Leo III's death and the civil war that followed, but the Umayyads proved incapable of taking full advantage of this, even though both Constantine V and Artabasdos offered Hisham's successor, al-Walid II, an alliance. And when the civil war ended in late 743, Umayyad leadership of the Arab caliphate was facing serious jeopardy. Indeed, Isaurian control of the Roman Empire was to outlast the Umayyad caliphate by over half a century. You would have been given long odds on that being the case when Leo III ascended the throne with Maslamah's immense expedition on his doorstep in 717. The collapse of Umayyad leadership and its replacing by the Abbasids altered the balance of power within the caliphate, particularly with the eastern origins of the new

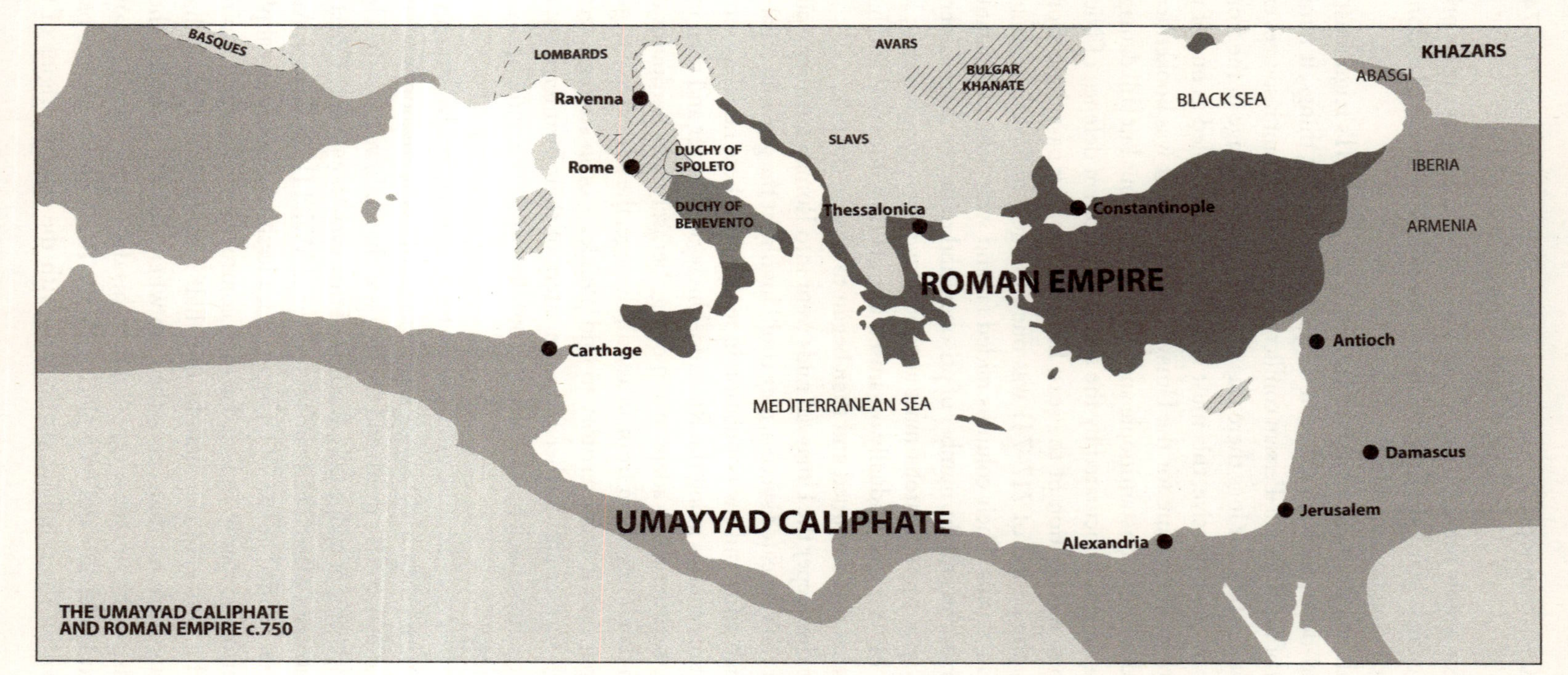

THE UMAYYAD CALIPHATE AND ROMAN EMPIRE c.750

rulers and their foundation of Baghdad. This redirected Arab attention away from the Roman frontier somewhat, allowing Constantine V to resume a more aggressive stance in Anatolia 'and from the 750s the changed character of the conflict between empire and caliphate gradually produced a more balanced, if still not even, contest'[58] for the remainder of the eighth century.

While it would become a major theatre of war under Constantine V, relations with the Bulgars under Leo III appear to have been peaceful. This is something of an argument from silence, as the sources say almost nothing of the Romano-Bulgar relations during the reign of Leo after the failure of the plot to restore Anastasius II. To say that the agreement reached between Theodosius III and Tervel and renewed by Leo held for over 35 years would be an optimistic reading of the situation. There is little to prove or disprove such an assertion. There are similarly few written source records about the other imperial opponent in Eastern Europe during the reign of Leo III, the Slavs. The meagre record does still show Slavic progress in 'colonising' areas of Greece, escaping Bulgar overlordship and thwarting any Roman attempts to stop them. During his pilgrimage to Jerusalem in 724, the Bavarian bishop Willibald is recorded stopping off in Monemvasia in the Peloponnese, which is described as being 'in the land of Slavinia.'[59] Other areas of Greece, such as Dyrrhacium and Athens, were heavily Slavicised by the late-eighth century to the point that empress Irene sent an expedition to the Peloponnese through Thessalonica and central Greece in an attempt to recover the region.[60] Some of this Slavic encroachment was likely the result of population transfer carried out by Leo in order to keep land in circulation and to supply recruits for the army. This was a policy that had not only been used by some of his immediate predecessors like Justinian II, but had been a repeated Roman policy basically since the foundation of Rome itself.

Chapter 11

Italian Afterthought: Papacy, Lombards and Franks

'You cannot be the leader of the free world and sit on the sidelines and tweet and think you're going to get the job done.'

Kevin McCarthy

Background

The area of the Roman Empire that saw the most intricate and on-going military and political action during the reign of Leo III was where the empire had the least power in lands – the Italian peninsula. We have a group of sources that illuminates the activities of the various sides striving for survival or supremacy: the *Historia Langobardorum* of Paul the Deacon, the *Liber Pontificalis* and the *Liber Pontificalis Ecclesiae Ravennatis* of Agnellus; these three each present a different view of the conflict – Lombard, papal, Ravennate. Indeed, the side of this multi-faceted conflict that we hear the least from is the Roman Empire itself, with Italy relegated to an imperial sideshow. This also highlights the diminishing imperial presence in its former heartland, a persistent reality to be revisited frequently during this chapter.

By the time of Leo's appearance in the early-eighth century, the Lombards had overcome a serious ducal revolt, an unstable king, and divided rule to establish a strong central monarchy through men like Rothari (636–652) and Grimuald I (662–671). This had allowed the Lombards to expand their territory – the central kingdom covered the entirety of the Po Valley, Tuscany and Liguria, while the independent Lombard duchies of Spoleto and Benevento had taken virtually all of central and southern Italy – and to resist Roman imperial attempts to push them back. On the flip side, the rivalry between the Lombard kings and dukes, along with geographical issues, prevented them from conquering the rest of the peninsula.

The territory still in Roman hands was largely that which could be supported by the Roman navy, so the hinterlands of and duchies centred on major cities like Ravenna, Rome, Naples, and Venice, as well as the heel and toe of the Italian boot. This focus on naval strength is also seen in continued imperial control of Sicily, Sardinia, and Corsica. On the surface, this suggests that even though the Lombards controlled most of the peninsula, the empire still had a secure position from which to resist further attempts at conquest and to take advantage of Lombard divisions in reclaiming some territory. However, scratching beneath the surface reveals that what remained of Roman Italy was not the monocephalic edifice it was supposed to be, which was the Ravennate exarch carrying out the orders and policies of the emperor. The decline in power of the exarchate in the wake of Lombard expansion could have been mollified by the establishing of the Sicilian theme in the late-seventh century. The Sicilian *strategos* was perhaps the most powerful individual in the Italian theatre, besides the Lombard king himself, and could have rallied the disparate regions of Roman Italy into a successful resistance. However, the threat of Umayyad Africa took up much of the *strategos*' attention, to the point that he appears far less in the succeeding story of Italy during the reign of Leo III than would be expected.

Roman resistance was also greatly undermined by one of the reasons for its survival – its disparate geography. The same coastal fringes and mountainous defences that hindered the Lombards also hindered communication and coordination between the various regions of Roman Italy. It could even be that the navy maintained a Roman presence in Italy beyond the capabilities of the forces available to the exarch. This left regional leaders – exarchs, *strategoi*, *archontes*, *duces* – having to fend for themselves, which could mean acting directly against imperial interests. Indeed, so fragmented was the Roman position in Italy that the term 'Roman' itself becomes problematic as the *dux* of Rome became a player in his own right, with aims and policies that could be at odds with the central authority of the Roman Empire. As we progress through this chapter, the Roman Empire will be represented more by the demonym 'imperial', while the *dux* and people of Rome will be known as the 'Romans.'

This multiplication of Roman officials acting for themselves only takes in the political/military realm – there was also the religious and civil realms. The latter is less important in the grand scheme, but it should not be forgotten that the fragmentation of Roman Italy saw even the most local civilian magistrate potentially thrust into a leadership position against any number of hostile opponents. The former, however, is far more important. Leaders within the Christian church were taking on not just their religious duties but also branching out into other realms. While there are local priests and bishops who will play their part, there are two of particular importance: the bishop of Ravenna and the pope in Rome. Both positions took on increasingly prominent political roles: the Ravennate bishop overtook the exarch as a leader of that city and its territory, and the pope emerged as not just the dominant character in Rome over the *dux*, but also as the entity that many of the players in Italy turned to for spiritual and political leadership.

The messiness of this fragmentation of Roman authority and the blending of politico-religious influence may be seen in the earliest years of Leo's imperial service under Justinian II. During his first reign (685–695), Justinian had had a significant falling out with the papacy over the Quinisext council, only to repair relations when he returned to power in 705. Part of this restoration of relations was to help deal with some of the pope's problems, and one such problem was the rivalry between the papacy and the archbishopric of Ravenna. Based on both cities having been an imperial capital and Ravenna being the capital of the exarchate, this rivalry had had another dimension added to it in 666, when Constans II granted autocephaly to the Ravennate archbishopric, removing it from papal jurisdiction. In his aim to repair imperio-papal relations, strained by Monothelitism, Constantine IV revoked this grant, necessitating the Ravennate archbishop having to swear obedience to the pope upon his election.

There had been about thirty years of uneasy peace by the election of archbishop Felix in 709, who refused to swear such obedience and declared Ravenna's removal from papal jurisdiction. Pope Constantine could not accept such a challenge to his authority. And to highlight that this dispute was not limited to the religious realm, just four years previously the Ravennate exarch, Theophylact, had marched on Rome soon after the election of Pope John VI. The reason for this attack is not given, but it shows the messiness of Roman Italy, while the claim that the pope was defended by 'the army of all Italy',[1] certainly hyperbolic, could offer insight into the direction of travel for loyalty on the Italian peninsula.

Whether doing a favour to the pope or feeling that Felix's actions constituted an attack on his imperial authority, Justinian interjected in this Rome-Ravenna feud.[2] And again showing the extra dimensions to this dispute, Felix received backing from various civilian and military leaders within Ravenna. The imperial intervention saw a delegation under Theodore, Sicilian *strategos*, arrest and deport the leaders, including Felix, to Constantinople through deceit. And when the city did not immediately capitulate after that, it was subjected to a sack by an imperial army. Agnellus would have it that this intervention not only failed to cow Ravenna, but emboldened the rebellious city to launch a military revolt or even a usurpation, proclaiming a certain George, son of Johannicus as emperor. Details of the actions of these rebels are so scant as to raise the possibility that this revolt did not occur. The 'ignominious death'[3] of Theophylact's replacement as exarch, John III Rizocopus, in Ravenna in late-710 could be connected to on-going issues in the city, but the *Liber Pontificalis* presents Rizocopus' death as punishment for his execution of several papal officials in Rome. This purge lacks explanation in the sources, but of the possible reasons – imperial warning, imperio-papal reaction to corruption, political opposition, exarchate rebellion – only the lattermost could be linked to any on-going trouble in Ravenna.[4] Rizocopus may then have died fighting alongside or against the rebels of George; either is very tenuous. There is a lack of mention of murder or fighting in connection with his death and the use of the term '*turpissima* may hint that it was the result of some foul disease.'[5]

Due to the rebellion of Ravenna and growing imperial distractions in Constantinople, the demise of Rizocopus led to an exarchate 'interregnum' for over a year. And by the time a new exarch was appointed in 713, Justinian II had been overthrown and executed. This end of the Heraclian dynasty was supposedly met with celebration in Ravenna,[6] but as we have seen, the Monothelitism of Philippikos Bardanes caused trouble with the confirmation of Peter as *dux Romae*, leading to riotous violence on the *Via Sacra*. Soon after, with word of Bardanes' deposition came a new exarch, Scholasticus, who also brought Anastasius II's proclamation of orthodoxy. And when he arrived in Ravenna, Scholasticus confirmed Peter as *dux Romae* on the promise that he not cause trouble, suggesting that it had not been Peter's faith or conduct that had so angered the people of Rome, but his association with the regime of Bardanes. Another rehabilitated individual was the blinded Felix, who was restored to the Ravennate bishopric and accepted papal jurisdiction.[7]

The Italian Revolt: No Taxation Without Imperial Protection?

By the time historiographical focus on Italy resumed, the papacy had changed hands, with Constantine succeeded by Gregory II, who has been labelled a 'half revolutionary, half loyal subject' due to the transitional nature of his tenure.[8] Gregory II is most famous for leading the opposition to Leo III's iconoclasm, which we have already dealt with and will not revisit unless it affects the political development of Italy in the period 717–741. Perhaps a more important succession for Italy had taken place a couple of years earlier. In June 712, Ansprand had been succeeded as King of the Lombards by his son, Liutprand. His would be perhaps the most successful of all Lombard reigns, with him essentially becoming 'arbiter of Italy.'[9]

From the outset, Gregory II had to deal with Liutprand, even if the Lombard king was not yet ready to expand his influence over Roman Italy, distracted in the north by Bavarians. The pope was indirectly involved in these dealings, for early in his reign, Theodo, duke of Bavaria, visited Rome to ask Gregory for help in setting up a church hierarchy in his realm. Not only was this an opportunity to spread church influence, but having the Bavarians as allies could be a constraining influence on the Lombards. Theodo had already been involved in Liutprand's accession and when the duke died in 717/718, Lombardo-Bavarian tensions increased again. Perhaps thinking that this distraction might make him more amenable, Gregory's first dealings with Liutprand centred on the pope asking the king to confirm the restoration of the Cottian Alps, originally donated by Aripert II in 706. Liutprand, eager to secure good relations with the pope, confirmed this restoration;[10] however, this want of good relations with Gregory changed by 718.

And Liutprand was not the only Lombard threat that Gregory was immediately faced with. The independent Lombard duchies – Spoleto and Benevento – were causing problems. In 716, Romuald II of Benevento attacked and captured the *castrum* of Cumae in the duchy of Naples. Gregory encouraged Romuald to return it with threats of divine wrath and the promise of gifts, but was rejected. According to the *Liber Pontificalis*, the pope took the lead in organising a riposte by John, *dux* of Naples, although it is more likely that John moved to reclaim Cumae because it was in his territory. The Neapolitan army stole into the Cumae *castrum* at night, killing 300 Lombards and taking 500 prisoners. Gregory still paid the promised bounty to Romuald and considered the *castrum* to now be part of the papal patrimony – this was papal appropriation of imperial territory.[11]

The Spoletan duke, Faroald II, was also active against Roman territory, capturing the *castrum* at Narni in the Roman duchy.[12] Given its position, there must have been negotiations between Gregory and Faroald for the return of Narni and the *Liber Pontificalis* may not mention them because they were unsuccessful.[13] Emboldened by this success, Faraold then turned his attention to the exarchate, capturing Classe, the port of Ravenna. Not for the last time, there is some trouble with our sources over this Spoletan attack: Paul the Deacon has Faraold carry out this attack, only to return Classe on Liutprand's orders, who then besieged Ravenna and took Classe himself.[14] The *Liber Pontificalis* has Liutprand lead the attack on Ravenna that involved the capture of Classe from the start, taking many captives and 'untold wealth.'[15] It might be that the Lombard king forced Faroald's return of Classe out of fear of either growing Spoletan power or the imperial wrath of Leo now that the siege of Constantinople was over. It could even be that Liutprand forced Faraold to hand Classe directly over to him. There is also a chronological issue with this fall of Classe being listed so early in the biography of Gregory II. If it is to be considered close in time to the capture of Narni and before some of the events that follow it in the *Liber Pontificalis*, then this is not the definitive fall of the Ravennate port to the Lombards. In that case, Liutprand must have returned it to the exarchate. If this is a record of the definitive loss of Classe, it is significantly out of order.

It was around the time of the Narni episode that the usurpation of Basil Tiberius took place in Sicily. This did not affect mainland Italy itself directly, but it did see Paul the *chartularius* appointed as Sicilian *strategos* by Leo III, representing imperial intervention in Italy. And this appears to be the first of several interventions in other contexts beyond this political move. There is, of course, the religious intervention that would be iconoclasm, but perhaps the more important initial imperial intervention for impero-papal relations came in the realm of taxation. Such issues pre-dated the reign of Leo III, with the Heraclian emperors giving Italy some tax relief throughout the seventh century. As an example, in the first year of his reign, Justinian II reduced the fiscal burden on papal estates in Sicily and Calabria, along with abolishing 'various other charges which the Roman church had been unable to pay every year.'[16]

The initial point of contention between Leo and the Italians might have been that the latter felt that these Heraclian tax reliefs were not enough in the face of Lombard pressure and declining imperial protection. It may even be that Leo III removed these tax reliefs or introduced new taxes with the aim of having Italy pay for itself. The increased tax burden saw a substantial proportion of resources making its way out of papal/Italian lands into imperial coffers. And as imperial power waned, many imperial citizens in Italy, including the pope, would be forgiven for wondering what their taxes were paying for. Once the likes of the duchy of Rome were having to facilitate their own protection with cash from the papacy, many might wonder why they were paying imperial taxes at all. On such a background then, Gregory II likely became a voice for those who were upset by 'taxation without protection'. And given the action taken by Leo III and his representatives in Italy, the pope likely led the way in refusing to pay some or all of the taxes demanded of him by Constantinople. And refusal to pay imperial tax was effectively political rebellion and imperial officials would be empowered to deal with the perpetrators, even if one of them was the bishop of Rome.

The first move against Gregory II could be linked to this issue of taxation, although it is not expressly stated as such. The *Liber Pontificalis* does not explicitly connect this and the subsequent moves against Gregory to iconoclasm; at least not chronologically, as it has iconoclasm become an issue in *LP* 91.17, *after* its recording of the plots and moves against Gregory in *LP* 91.14–16. It even explicitly states that the reason for imperial targeting of the pope was 'that he was preventing the imposition of tax in the province [and the stripping of] the churches of their wealth;'[17] a pronouncement that highlights that Roman Italy was targeted by the Leonid tax policies, rather than just church lands.

The first plot was centred on *dux* Basil, Jordanes the *chartularius* and a subdeacon called John Lurion. The *Liber Pontificalis* connects the new *dux Romae*, Marinus, an imperial *spatharius* sent to take up this role by Leo, to this plot, having him give it his consent, but not open support.[18] The aim of this plot was reputedly to kill the pope, but they could find no opportunity to carry out this attack. The lack of overt imperial order leaves it open to suggestion that this was a plot by local officials looking to gain imperial favour rather than an imperial mission. 'What is, however, most significant and interesting is the powerlessness of the duke of Rome and the continued willingness of the Romans to protect the pope.'[19]

If Leo, through Marinus, was indirectly involved in this attempted removal of the pope in the early 720s, the initial failure of Basil, Jordanes and John Lurion only encouraged him to take more action. In 723, Scholasticus was replaced as exarch by Paul. This is commonly held to be the same Paul appointed Sicilian *strategos* by Leo in 718. Both this identification and holding of the two offices simultaneously lack corroboration in the source material.[20] Any such dual-office holding is likely to demonstrate the continuing weakness of the position of exarch, with Paul's position as *strategos* providing him with military resources that the exarch did not have. Although in this situation, it is likely that accruing more positions weakened Paul's position rather than strengthened it, as it added to the tasks he faced – Lombard king, Lombard dukes, papacy, Ravenna, Roman duchies, Arabs – without any significant increasing of resources.

The plotters in Rome took heart from this appointment and possibly received some consent from the new *strategos*/exarch. However, their plan to reprise the plot against Gregory was betrayed and the Romans 'all rose up'[21] to stop them. Both Jordanes and John Lurion were killed, while *dux* Basil was forcibly tonsured and lived the rest of his life in monastic captivity. While it is unclear where Basil was supposed to be *dux* of, the fact that he could be undone so easily by the Romans again shows the weakness of imperial officials in the face of the growing support for the pope in the duchy of Rome.

The definitive failure of Basil's plot against Gregory led to Leo instigating a more overt attempt, using an unnamed *spatharius*, who was sent to remove Gregory from the papacy and possibly to take over as *dux Romae* from Marinus, who had proven his ineffectiveness. The *strategos*/exarch provided the *spatharius* with men from the exarchate, although the *Liber Pontificalis* hints at Paul having trouble finding men who would help 'carry out this crime.'[22] When they came to enter the city of Rome, these men were confronted at the Milvian Bridge by a force made up of the men of the Roman duchy, Spoleto and other local Lombard duchies.[23] Paul the Deacon took this to mean that the Lombard dukes of Tuscany, loyal to Liutprand, saved the pope, which is not beyond the realms of possibility; however, it is more likely that it was the duke of Benevento. An alliance between the papacy, Spoleto and Benevento was to be a central part of Italian politics going forward for the remainder of Leo III's reign. It would not be surprising to see it in action here at the Milvian Bridge.[24] Wherever the

Lombard contingent came from, their combining with the Roman duchy and Spoleto drove off the exarchate army sent by Paul, adding the *strategos*/exarch to the list of imperial officials who could not impose the imperial writ on the city of Rome.

It is here in the narrative of the *Liber Pontificalis* that Leo's edict of iconoclasm arrives in Italy, with Gregory II 'arm[ing] himself against the emperor as against an enemy, denouncing his heresy and writing that Christians everywhere must guard against the impiety that had arisen.'[25] Even if it is accepted that iconoclasm did play a significant role in the pan-Italian opposition to Leo III, it was not the spark for the latest downturn in east-west relations. The political and economic disagreements were already happening, meaning that iconoclasm merely added to those disagreements, even if it came to dominate that downturn in some sources.[26] The wave of rebellion that is recorded in response to the iconoclastic edict was perhaps merely the spread of pre-existent anti-imperial/pro-papal sentiment. The dukes of Rome, Spoleto, Benevento and possibly others had already proven willing to fight to protect the pope before the *Liber Pontificalis* mentions iconoclasm. The *duces* of Pentapolis[27] and Venetia – mentioned as rebelling against iconoclasm[28] – may also have risen against the violent plot to remove the pope from an imperial government that they themselves were already disgruntled with over 'taxation without protection.'

The rising of Pentapolis and Venetia escalated the opposition against the mission of the unnamed *spatharius* into an almost pan-Roman Italy revolt against the *strategos*/exarch, isolating him in Ravenna and enforcing a papal anathema upon him. Several imperial duchies may have removed their *duces* and elected their own replacements. They even proposed proclaiming their own emperor, 'openly declaring an end to Byzantine rule.'[29] Such an act was opposed by Gregory, who urged his followers 'not to renounce their love and loyalty to the Roman Empire.'[30] The pope even professed the hope that Leo would be won back to orthodoxy. This profession seems out of step with the papacy's growing independence, but Gregory was demonstrating his grasp of the geo-political reality of Italy in the 720s. The disruption of an Italian emperor would be worse than the current predicament. The fracturing of imperial territory and the growth of independence 'movements' in Ravenna and Venice made the entire peninsula vulnerable to piecemeal Lombard conquest, which would creep closer to a reality should there be a usurpation in Italy dividing the already meagre imperial forces even further. An emperor in Ravenna, which would likely be the usurpation capital, could also be bad for the papacy given their past hostilities. Gregory therefore found it expedient to profess his continued loyalty to the empire, if not the policies of the current emperor.

The ability of the pope to curtail an Italian movement towards imperial usurpation demonstrates the increase in his influence; however, his power was by no means supreme, with even the environs of Rome not free from factional fighting. This was seen in a possible pro-imperial reaction to the revolt against the actions of the *strategos*/exarch. A certain Exhilaratus and his son Hadrian seized control of Campania in the name of the emperor. The *Liber Pontificalis* calls Exhilaratus a *dux* but does not record which duchy he led. We have the names of both the Roman and Neapolitan *duces* at this point in the mid-720s – Peter and Theodore I – so it could be that this is an incorrect ducal attribution. These 'loyalists' may have had a personal grudge against Gregory, who had excommunicated Hadrian for marrying a deaconess. This personal grudge could have been invented to divert attention from Gregory not being in complete control of the duchy of Rome.

Exhilaratus and Hadrian hoped to keep the route from Naples to Rome open as the former was still loyal to the emperor. This was foiled by forces of the Roman duchy overrunning Exhilaratus' position, killing him and Hadrian. Peter, *dux Romae*, was then blinded due to his allegiance to Leo and possibly some connivance with Exhilaratus and the Neapolitan *dux* to hand Rome over to imperial forces.[31] This episode highlights the dichotomy of the pope's and Rome's position – on the one hand, the fates of Peter, Exhilaratus and Hadrian suggest that imperial influence in Rome was effectively over, but on the other, the pope was as yet not secure in Rome itself, with the Neapolitan *dux* and even groups within the Roman duchy, including the *dux Romae*, still loyal to Leo III.

There was another Roman official who was not safe in his capital. With virtually all Roman Italy in revolt against him, Paul the *strategos*/exarch was faced with growing disgruntlement in Ravenna itself. The city and its environs were split into pro- and anti-imperial feeling over Paul's actions towards the pope and taxation, possibly added to by iconoclasm. This dispute broke out into violence, although to what extent is not clear – was it merely rioting in the streets? Or was it a full-blown revolt of anti-imperials with the *strategos*/exarch having to rally what loyalists he could to defend his position in battle? Whichever it was, it resulted in the death of Paul.[32]

The First *Doges* of Venetia?

The demise of Paul the *strategos*/exarch in Ravenna in c.726/727 leads us to another area of Roman Italy neglected so far – the duchy of Venetia. While more detached from the main Italian theatre than other duchies and having five Lombard duchies – Friuli, Ceneda, Treviso, Vicenza, and Mantua – in close proximity, Venetia remained involved in events further south. It had joined the rebellion against Paul and will appear again later. It was also this period of Leo III's reign that later Venetian chroniclers would claim as seeing the founding of the Republic of Venice. And the specific connection to the demise of Paul in Ravenna is that there was a claim that the *strategos*/exarch was the basis for the man claimed as the first Venetian *doge*, Paolo Lucio Anafesto. Such a proposed association relies on the rejection of the more reliable account of Paul surviving a decade beyond the 'recorded' death of Paolo Lucio Anafesto in 717. His successor as *doge* was reputedly Marcello Tegaliano, although if he existed at all (Marcellus is not mentioned until 840, while he does not 'gain' a surname until the late-fourteenth century), he was likely the *magister militum* appointed to run Venetia for the empire. The Paul who formed the basis of Paolo Lucio Anafesto may have been a Lombard duke of Treviso, with Marcello Tegaliano being based on his Roman opponent.[33] Both Paolo Lucio and Marcellus are recorded repelling attacks from the Umayyads, which is unlikely given the distance from Umayyad territory to Venetia. Any kernel of truth likely stems from the historiographical connections to Paul the *strategos*/exarch, who dealt with Umayyad raids in Sicily.[34]

The first historical *doge* is the man who succeeded 'Marcello' – Ursus, possibly one of those *duces* elected during the pan-Roman Italy revolt. He is recorded in later Italian sources as 'Orso Ipato', which reflects not only his Latin name but also the honorific title of ὕπατος/*hypatos* (essentially an honorary consulship) he received from the Roman Empire. During his time as *dux/doge*, Ursus is credited with improving the military and naval organisation of the Venetian duchy. This was within his purview as ducal commander, but the claim that he built up the 'Venetian' navy to the point that it could send eighty ships in response to an upcoming papal plea for help would seem to outstrip the resources available to the mid-eighth century duchy. Rather than doubt such a build-up, there may be an alternative explanation. The timing of this expansion fits in with the naval reforms of Leo III and the restoration of Roman naval power in the eastern Mediterranean. An effective northern Adriatic squadron could easily have been part of the reforms carried out by Leo and placed under the command of the Venetian *dux* at a time when he still professed loyalty to the Roman Empire.

If Ursus is taken as the first *doge*, his rule did not provide the definitive establishment of the position as it did not initially survive the end of his reign. By 737, the Venetian duchy had become embroiled in inter-factional strife and rather than intervene to calm the situation, Ursus sided with his hometown. This led to his lynching either by opponents or more neutral underlings who felt he should not have taken sides. Instead of a new *dux/doge*, he was replaced by a *magister militum per Venetiae*, seemingly imposed by the exarch, suggesting that imperial control tightened somewhat or had not slackened during this initial period of dogeship. This *magister* was replaced annually for the next five years, until in 742, when Ursus' son, Theodatus Hypatus became *dux/doge* through popular vote, marking a more definitive foundation of the lines of *doges.*

Opportunity and Usurpation Makes Strange Bedfellows

While it had nothing to do with the foundation of the Venetian dogeship, the death of Paul the *strategos/*exarch and the on-going dissension within the Romano-imperial ranks in Italy marked a significant opportunity for the Lombards. And a king such as Liutprand was not going to let such an opportunity slip by. Looking to break the land link through the mountains between Rome and Ravenna, Lombard royal forces rolled into Aemilia, capturing the *castra* of Ferronianum, Monteveglio and Verabulum and the towns of Buxum and Persiceto, as well as the town of Osimo in the Pentapolis.[35] If there was a religious dimension to this rebellion, Liutprand may have presented himself as an orthodox liberator as well as a papal ally.[36] Gregory needed to be calm in the face of such 'zeal', for any embracing of a Liutprand 'mission' could quickly have seen the Lombard subjugation of all Italy.[37]

If Gregory's preaching in favour of the Roman Empire was based on some inkling that Liutprand and his 'Catholic zeal' could not be trusted, he was soon proven correct. In the 11th indiction, which equates to 727/728, the Lombard king 'treacherously seized'[38] the *castellum* of Sutri on the border between Lombard and Roman territory. Liutprand held it for about five months before handing it back, but Gregory had to pay an enormous bounty to secure Sutri's return.[39] And even then, while the *castellum* was given back, the surrounding area was retained by the king. The Sutri *castellum* was also not returned to its original owner, either the Roman duchy or the Roman Empire itself. Instead, it was 'donated' by Gregory to the papal patrimony and therefore is the second papal claiming of what had been imperial public land and possibly the first outside the Roman duchy. This could see the so-called 'Donation of Sutri' as the informal beginning of the Papal States.[40]

Liutprand's advances in the 720s were not limited to the Italian mainland. As early as 713, if not before, Corsica had become a target for Arab naval raids. While it was still nominally an imperial possession, the island received little or no help from imperial forces. This provided Liutprand with an opportunity to present himself as a 'protector of the church' to 'defend' the island, subjecting it to Lombard governance in c.725. Sardinia will have been under similar Arab pressure and possible efforts by Liutprand to provide 'protection through subjugation'; however, the Sardinians were better placed to resist the Arabs and

Lombards with their own imperial/ex-African exarchate/archonate forces, even if they continued to drift out of imperial control.

In the face of Roman revolt and Lombard advances, Leo III moved to reassert some imperial influence in Italy. In 727, he dispatched a eunuch patrician called Eutychios to become exarch, although such were the dire straits that had befallen the exarchate that Eutychios went to Naples rather than Ravenna. The new exarch had been sent with similar orders to Paul, Marinus and the unnamed *spatharius* – remove the pope and Roman ducal officials and enforce imperial control of Rome and its duchy. As with the previous attempts, word of the aims got out and any chance of a quiet enforcement evaporated. Eutychios sent a messenger to Rome reiterating the imperial orders should the pope and the Romans continue in their economic/political/religious disobedience. This was met with such outrage in Rome that the people wanted to kill the messenger only for Gregory to intervene; Eutychios was, however, anathematised and the people of Rome pledged their allegiance to the pope.[41]

With his early attempts at forcing obedience in tatters, the new exarch looked around for potential allies in bringing order to the peninsula. His focus fell upon the Lombards, offering gifts for them to relinquish their friendships with the pope. This will have been aimed particularly at the dukes of Spoleto and Benevento, Transamund II and Romuald II respectively, who were driven into an alliance with Gregory II out of fear of Liutprand. Military backing from these two dukes made it difficult for imperial forces in Italy to impose any control on the papacy. All three Lombard leaders openly refused Eutychios' offer, with Transamund and Romuald keen to form a united front against the expansionist Liutprand; however, while the Lombard king professed to not tolerate any 'vexation' of the papacy, behind closed doors Eutychios' bribery and the papal-ducal alliance overrode Liutprand's 'Catholic zeal'.

The result was the division of Italy into two alliances – the pope and the dukes of Spoleto and Benevento on one side and the exarchate and the Lombard king on the other. While the former offered mutual defensive support, the latter saw Eutychios offering aid against Spoleto and Benevento in return for Liutprand's help in restoring imperial control over the Roman duchy.[42] Given the Lombard king's track record in trustworthiness, the exarch had made something of a deal with the devil. The subjugation of Spoleto and Benevento would be a significant blow to the balance of power in Italy. And the Lombard-exarchate alliance was quick to impose its will. An invasion of Spoleto by Liutprand and probably Eutychios saw them overrun the duchy and 'receiv[ing] oaths and hostages from both dukes.'[43]

This Lombardo-exarchate army marched on to Rome, arriving on the Campus Neronis on the right side of the Tiber beyond the site of Castel S. Angelo.[44]

It is difficult to ascertain what happened at the subsequent meeting between pope, king and exarch (Eutychios' presence is not certain). The *Liber Pontificalis* has Gregory persuading Liutprand to withdraw by appealing to his orthodox piety;[45] however, there were political dealings at work here. The thaw in relations between exarch and pope recorded by the *Liber Pontificalis* for the following year suggests that the withdrawal of Liutprand from Rome came as part of an agreement between pope, exarch and king. Any such agreement likely saw the dissolving of the exarchate-royal alliance, as well as an exarch agreement not to act against the pope or to look to impose any heavy taxation or iconoclastic edicts. In return, Gregory had to abandon his alliance with the dukes.

It cannot have escaped the attention of Gregory and Eutychios that this agreement had only been reached through the power and largesse of the Lombard king – essentially 'arbiter of Italy.'[46] His ability to rapidly subdue Spoleto and Benevento and then march a sizeable army to the Tiber, on top of his continued gnawing away at imperial territory in Aemilia and Pentapolis, surely saw the exarch and pope recognise that Liutprand was their most dangerous foe. This fuelled a rapprochement between the two, even if it meant recognising the pope as an imperial ally rather than an imperial subject.

The Usurpation of Tiberius Petasius

Despite the continued slackening of its power in central Italy, Gregory continued to preach loyalty to the Roman Empire, if not to the greedy icon-breaker ruling it; again, he saw the usefulness of the unifying force of the empire. And further political developments in 728 allowed the pope to demonstrate his loyalty to the empire and reconciliation with the exarch with action rather than just words as a new threat emerged before Eutychios had departed Rome. From Monterano, a little over thirty miles north-west of Rome itself in territory that was technically still imperial but likely took its cues from the *dux Romae* (and therefore the pope), news arrived of a usurpation.[47] The proclaimed emperor was a certain Petasius, of whom very little is known. The chances are that he was a military officer, but we might not even know this man's actual name as 'Petasius' may be an epithet from the Greek πετασος (*petasos*) meaning 'sun hat', possibly reflecting a fashion choice. This would see him associated with much more (in)famous emperors who became known by a nickname inspired by their garb – Caligula and Caracalla.

With support from Monterano, Blera, Luna and the surrounding area, Petasius took the imperial name 'Tiberius'. There is no suggestion that this was the same 'Tiberius' who had rebelled in Sicily in 717/718, but it does highlight the popularity of the name 'Tiberius' for such usurpers – there would be four men of imperial aspiration to take that name during Leo III's reign. As already seen, two of them claimed to be the dead son of Justinian II. It seems a little coincidental for Basil Onomagoulos and Petasius to both choose that name for it not to be in some way looking to appeal to any latent Heraclian support in opposition to the Isaurians, even if neither are recorded claiming to be Tiberios, son of Justinian.

As the chief imperial commander in Italy, it was Eutychios' job to deal with this usurper, but he received encouragement and military support from Gregory, who once more refused to accept a usurper. The pope dispatched Roman ducal forces (noting that they and the *dux Romae* now seem like his to command) with whatever exarchate forces Eutychios had brought with him to deal with this threat. This papal-exarchate army marched against Tiberius Petasius at the Monterano *castrum* and quickly overwhelmed him.

Given the lack of forces available to the exarch and the papacy, Petasius had even more meagre forces at his disposal; however, there is one small numismatic hint that could suggest that if Gregory and Eutychios had not acted so quickly and decisively Petasius could have caused significantly more trouble. It comes in the form of a *solidus* minted with the name TIЧERIЧS MЧLTЧS, assigned to Petasius' usurpation. Of course, Petasius needed to mint coins to pay his loyal troops, bribe others and proclaim his rule. And this issue looks like an attempt to copy an imperial issue of Constantinople, down to the CONOB mintmark, from before Leo's numismatic changes in 720. However, the intrigue comes from the suggestion that the style of the coin, rather than be from Monterano, Blera, or Luna, was closest to those of Benevento or Naples. If this coin was from either of these, it poses a question over who was supporting Petasius. It being from Benevento would fit best with the politics of the time as the papal-ducal alliance had just been extinguished. Romuald II may have been looking to divide the papal-exarchate faction by backing an imperial usurper. Had it been minted in Naples, that would signal a significant political shift in the Neapolitan duchy which had so far been staunch in its loyalty to the empire.

Whatever backers he might have had, Petasius was quickly subdued and executed, his head dispatched to Constantinople. While Eutychios was successful in defeating Petasius, the presence of an imperial usurper on imperial territory so close to Rome demonstrates the real dearth of authority of both the exarch and the pope. That said, Gregory again presented his loyalty to the empire and reinforced his message of not supporting usurpation of the imperial title in Italy. Leo III, despite his distance, distractions, and deviation from religious orthodoxy, was still the only emperor he would recognise.

New Pope, Same Problems – Invasions and Taxation

Papal involvement in the subduing of Tiberius Petasius was the last political action of Gregory II recorded by the *Liber Pontificalis*. He died and was buried on 11 February 731, to be succeeded a month later by Gregory III. Unfortunately, the new pope's biography in the *Liber Pontificalis* is spare on political events in Italy, particularly after 733. This sees numerous important events involving Leo III directly and the imperial position in Italy lacking record. And when it does address some matters, they are chronologically disordered and likely later additions to the text.

The agreement forged between Gregory II and Eutychios on the Campus Neronis held during the new papacy, with the exarch moving to Ravenna; however, such continued conciliation took place on the backdrop of increased enmity from Constantinople. Or at least that is what Theophanes claims. In his iconoclastic madness and possibly in response to Gregory III's pronouncements on iconoclasm from a Roman synod in late 731 'which resolutely upheld the iconodule position,'[48] Theophanes has Leo organise an expedition under the command of Manes, the Kibyrrhaeot *strategos*, to deal with 'the secession of Rome and Italy.'[49] However, en route to Italy, this fleet was smashed by a storm in the Adriatic Sea, which Theophanes took as divine punishment for Leo's incessant icon-breaking and attacking of various iconodules. Rather than learn from this, Theophanes then has 'God's enemy' impose a capitation tax on Sicily and Calabria and order that the revenues of the papal patrimonies – 3.5 talents or over 25,000 *solidi* – in those regions be paid into the state treasury instead, 'a crippling financial blow to the papacy.'[50] Theophanes also has Leo order the registration of all male births in Roman Italy, which he presents in religious terms by referring to the historical registration of Jews by 'Pharaoh' and how not even the Muslim Arabs were doing such a thing in the caliphate.[51]

The possibility of Leo not being an iconoclast raises questions about his motives for these actions. Even without iconoclasm, the pope could still be a target for this imperial expedition due to a refusal to pay tax – although this would have Gregory III as just one of several targets, with Manes charged with a more general enforcing of imperial loyalty in Roman Italy, which had seen various forms of disobedience in recent years. Geography could provide some hints at Manes' target. If the pope was the main target, the fleet would have probably sailed to Sicily, Calabria or Naples. The decimation of the imperial expedition in the Adriatic highlights that its primary target was surely on the eastern side of the Italian peninsula – the exarchate or Lombards. Manes may have been ordered to punish Ravenna for the death of Paul. Such an action could also involve protecting the area from the Lombards.[52]

The increasing of the tax burden in Sicily and Calabria, the confiscation of revenues from papal patrimonies and the registration of male babies seem punitive, even sinister in the lattermost, but they could all be part of a provincial reorganisation by an emperor who had accepted the reality of the situation.[53] Events in Italy during his reign to that point had highlighted the weakness of the imperial position even in imperial lands. Addressing the revenues of Sicily and Calabria, i.e. the lands of the Sicilian theme, could be the basis of a consolidation of territory and resources that were still securely imperial. A focus on the Sicilian theme may also reflect that it was part of southern Italy, the more Hellenised and richer part of the peninsula. Might this capitation tax have been part of a burgeoning thematic framework across the empire, bringing the Sicilian theme into line with other themes? In such a view of provincial reorganisation, Theophanes' registration of male babies could be a (wilful) misinterpretation of a census and/or survey of imperial resources in Italy. Leo was instituting 'a new ordering of affairs by reorganising the territories where his power was still effective.'[54] And consolidating rule and finances would not only allow for the preservation of an imperial presence on the peninsula, but it could also lay the groundwork for the reclamation of territory should the opportunity arise.

Potential evidence against this initiative being purely punitive against the papacy comes in its seeming lack of scope. Lands of much less secure loyalty than the Sicilian theme would surely have been targeted for confiscations, even if the emperor felt he did not command the authority to enforce them. For example, the duchy of Rome – surely the least loyal of 'imperial' lands – was not targeted. Neither was the exarchate, which works against this being a general reorganisation of imperial Italy but could be a recognition of irrevocable exarchate weakness and even its impending doom. Eutychios was almost powerless in the face of Liutprand. Perhaps the only region lacking mention that possibly should be in a proposed reorganisation is the Neapolitan duchy, which had been loyal to the emperor (if the possible link to Petasius is dismissed). There has been some suggestion that Leo sent an imperial secretary called Alfanus to Theodore, the Neapolitan *dux*, with orders to enforce similar confiscation of papal patrimonial revenues. Due to his being well-disposed towards the pope and possibly annoyed by the tax hike in his own territory, Theodore refused to comply with this imperial order. This story does not appear in any primary source and may be an invention to make Naples look more pro-papal than it was.[55]

Lombard Strikes at Ravenna and Rome

If Leo had ignored any reorganisation of the exarchate due to an acceptance of its terminal decline, he was about to get further evidence to that point.

Initially, Liutprand looked to avoid confrontation with the papacy, adhering to the agreement struck on the Campus Neronis. But this did not stop him from acting against the other Lombard duchies. Internal disruption upon the death of Romuald II in 732 provided the king with an opportunity to intervene in Benevento. Romuald was succeeded by his son Gisulf, whose minority saw a certain Audelais usurp the duchy. As Gisulf's great-uncle and 'overlord' of the Lombard dukes, Liutprand marched south to overthrow the usurper in 733, putting his own nephew on the ducal throne, unhelpfully also called Gregory. That Gisulf was not re-appointed suggests that he was still too young or that Liutprand was taking the opportunity to bind the Beneventan duchy closer to his crown.

However, it was to be the actions of others that was to bring the Lombard king into conflict with the imperials once more. In around 735, Agatho, *dux* of Perugia, attempted to reclaim Bologna from the Lombards, who had captured the city in the years since Liutprand's attack on Aemilia in c.727. Finding the city defended by the forces of Walcari, Rotcari and Peredeo, duke of Vicenza, the Perugians were routed with 'great slaughter.'[56] In this failure, Agatho had stirred up a hornet's nest in breaking the imperio-Lombard peace. Liutprand's nephew and recently appointed co-ruler Hildeprand[57] and Peredeo combined their forces and struck into the exarchate. Eutychios' forces proved unable to prevent the Lombards driving to and then capturing Ravenna. The seemingly fatal undermining of the exarchate was seen as a disaster – a destruction of the balance of power – by Gregory III, and he and Eutychios moved quickly to bring together an army that could oust Hildeprand and Peredeo. The subsequent diplomatic effort brought together forces from the exarchate, the Roman and Venetian duchies, and the patriarch of Grado. There were likely contingents from other Roman regions in Italy – Naples, Sicily, Apulia etc. Whatever its size and composition, this 'pan-Roman' force proved large enough to reclaim Ravenna, capturing Hildeprand and killing Peredeo. Such an expedition may well have proven Liutprand's wariness over confronting the papacy correct: if they had something to unite against, Roman forces in Italy were still capable of defeating the Lombards.[58]

After the Bologna and Ravenna incidents, the focus of Romano-Lombard hostilities switched to Transamund II, duke of Spoleto. In 737/738, he moved against the *castrum* of Gallese, which was not only in the duchy of Rome but also commanded the overland route between Rome and Ravenna. The source material is not clear if Transamund had captured Gallese or was moving against it – either way, Gregory entered negotiations and bought off the Spoletan duke 'by giving much money.'[59] The pope may also have highlighted to Transamund that his move against Gallese was against the royal prerogative of Liutprand and therefore an act of rebellion.[60] It would also appear that the pope took control of Gallese after the incident, annexing more imperial territory.

There are some chronological issues with Transamund's move against Gallese. In the text of the *Liber Pontificalis*, it is situated *after* Liutprand's second march on Rome, which was partially encouraged by the then-fugitive Transamund, ousted from Spoleto by Liutprand (for the first time) by 16 June 739.[61] There is some problematic interpolation here as the section in question not only does not fit chronologically, it also contains a grammatical issue where it is 'stitched' into the text. It seems much more likely that the Gallese incident helped cause Liutprand's second march on Rome, rather than be somewhat caused by it.

That Transamund's move against Gallese could ultimately spark a series of events that led to a Lombard march on Rome was because of what Gregory warned the Spoletan duke about – his action against Gallese was independent of Liutprand's authority. The Lombard king was already prickly about this due to the mess that Hildeprand's attack on Ravenna turned into. In unravelling the chronological mess of the *Liber Pontificalis* at this point, we may also find something that the negotiations over Gallese produced that sparked Liutprand into action – in his subsequent plea to the Franks, Gregory III hints at a renewed alliance with Spoleto and Benevento, an alliance that was supposed to not exist after Liutprand's previous march on Rome. The interpolated section of the *Liber Pontificalis* also raises issues here, as it has any renewal of the papal-ducal alliance coming *after* Liutprand's second march on Rome, which would be a rather brazen move for the pope and the dukes to undertake with Liutprand already on the warpath.

Transamund's independent action, a restoration of the papal-ducal alliance and the concurrent Beneventan election of the separatist Godescalc[62] as duke combined to spark Liutprand's large-scale invasion of central Italy in 739. The Lombard king may have felt it necessary to reaffirm his military power in Italy after the Lombard defeat at Ravenna, even if he personally had not been involved. The pope and various dukes, Lombard and Roman, needed a reminder of who was the boss. This might also give us a reason why Gregory, Transamund, and Godescalc felt now was the time to test the Lombard king – Roman forces alone had bloodied his nose. Combine that with the forces of Spoleto and Benevento and they might succeed in breaking that power. Liutprand's attention was also elsewhere at this point as he had sent and possibly even led Lombard forces across the Alps to help the Frankish leader Charles Martel eject the Umayyads from Provence in 738.[63]

While this might have felt like an opportune time to strike back against the Lombard king, the pope and his ducal allies quickly found that this was not the case. By mid-739, Liutprand had attacked and captured Spoleto, establishing another nephew, Hilderic, as its duke; however, Transamund had escaped and taken refuge in Rome. Therefore, Liutprand descended upon the duchy of Rome once more. His exact motives are unclear – was he merely after Transamund, as the *Liber Pontificalis* suggests?[64] Was he looking to force Gregory into abandoning his ducal alliance as well? Or was he even taking the next step in unifying all of Italy under his control?

The Lombard king established himself on the Campus Neronis once more, putting pressure on the city of Rome[65] and sending raids into Campania, perhaps to prevent imperial aid arriving from Naples. In concert with the *dux Romae*, Stephen (a lead *bullae* seal found at Blera seems to refer to this man), and all the forces at his command, Gregory refused to hand over Transamund (might we presume that the deposed duke had sought sanctuary in a Roman church?). Liutprand responded by tightening the blockade of Rome and occupying strategic strongholds in the Roman duchy – Aemilia, Orte, Bomarzo and Blera. And yet, even with these successes, Liutprand's blockade of Rome was lifted in August 739, without Transamund in the king's custody or the papal-ducal alliance being decisively broken. Even if we are liberal with the dates and say that Liutprand left Spoleto immediately upon Hilderic's elevation on 16 June, force-marched the 100km to Rome in a couple of days and then left the city again in the last days of August, this Lombard blockade lasted 10 weeks at very most.

So why did it last so little time? It was still prime campaigning season, so this withdrawal will not have been through climatic necessity, bar any unrecorded freak weather. Given his age and previous ill-health, Liutprand may have worried about his own condition. As evidenced by previous papal dealings with Lombard conquerors, Gregory III could have bought off Liutprand, although any deal did not involve the return of the four captured cities, or if it did so the Lombard king immediately reneged. The chronology in the sources is messy enough to suggest, not necessarily all that convincingly, that Liutprand departed from Rome to assist Charles Martel in Provence, rather than attacking the city *after* aiding the Franks against the Umayyads.[66] Liutprand may have felt that his subjugation of Spoleto, capture of the four cities and demonstration against the walls of Rome had made his point. But if this was the case, he was soon to find out that the 'signatories' of the papal-ducal alliance had not understood or cared about what that point was. The example of the pan-Roman alliance to recover Ravenna from Hildeprand will also have been fresh in Liutprand's mind. A prolonged blockade of Rome could have seen him confronted by a combined army of thematic, exarchate, papal and ducal forces; however, there appears to have been no intention or ability of Gregory to bring such a force together again. This is seen in who the pope sent a call for help to – the Frankish ruler, Charles Martel.

This initial papal latter[67] to Charles only received an ambassador to Rome and no aid, but might we speculate that the Frankish ambassador mediated between Gregory and Liutprand, leading to lifting of the blockade? While this seems an attractive notion, it comes up against geographical and political obstacles. The short length of the blockade puts time constraints on the ability of the papal plea and the Frankish response to have gotten there and back in time to influence the blockade – if Charles was still in Provence (he faced a rebellion there in 739), it would have taken a minimum of two weeks for embassies to travel in both directions. The political considerations focus on whether Charles would really side with the pope against Liutprand at this point. The Frank could have thought Gregory had brought the trouble upon himself with his ducal alliance and may still have had need of Lombard aid against Umayyad Spain.[68]

However, while little came of this papal plea, the call for aid to Charles Martel is still a momentous occasion. It marks a shift in papal horizons, looking west for succour rather than east to Constantinople. And the pope could hardly be blamed for such a move. In the face of an expansionist and capable Lombard king, imperial forces in Italy had proven increasingly fractured and impotent, with the Sicilian *strategos* focused on the Muslim threat from Africa, the exarchate in terminal decline, and the emperor either distracted with his own military problems or an active enemy of the pope and the exarch.

This is not to say that Romano-papal forces were completely ineffective in the face of Liutprand. And this, along with the possibility of the Lombard king being distracted with the Muslims in Provence, Bavarians, or Slavs to the north, the exarchate remnant, internal issues, or his own health, may be demonstrated by what occurred after his withdrawal from Rome. Immediately after Liutprand had returned home, Gregory and his allies were planning a counterattack. These plans came to fruition either in December 739 or December 740 – the manuscript of the *Liber Pontificalis* is missing an indiction year – with Transamund, Stephen and Godescalc launching a two-pronged invasion of the Spoletan duchy. The contingent using the *Via Valetia* obtained the surrender of Marsi, Forcona, Valva, and Penne. The second contingent followed the *Via Salaria*, going through Sabina, accepting the surrender of Rieti and then moving against Spoleto itself. Hilderic was defeated and killed, allowing Transamund to become Spoletan duke again.[69]

Twin *Volte Faces*

The restored papal-ducal alliance did not long survive this success. Despite having relied on papal aid to maintain his freedom and regain his duchy, Transamund proved an untrustworthy ally. He refused to facilitate the recovery of Aemilia, Orte, Bomarzo and Blera, which he had surely undertaken to do as part of the agreement that led to his restoration. He may not have wanted to antagonise Liutprand by being involved in an attack on settlements held by royal Lombard forces, but the deposition and execution of Hilderic had already done that – the Lombard king would soon be back in Spoleto for another reckoning. Recognising the poor position he was now in – unable to trust the Spoletan duke, shackled to the exarchate corpse, (mutually) abandoned by thematic Sicily and once more in the crosshairs of the Lombard king, Gregory III resorted to epistolary diplomacy. It could be during this crisis of 739–740 that Gregory sent his second letter to Charles Martel, seeking his aid.[70] Some medieval annalists see the pope proposing that the Roman duchy and the papacy secede from the Roman Empire and accept Charles as their suzerain. Any such plea was more an acceptance of the fait accompli that was the retraction of Constantinople's power on the Italian peninsula. And it would be foolish for the papacy not to seek protection as it remained militarily impotent in the face of a rampant Lombard king; however, at this time, nothing came of this renewed plea.[71]

But while Gregory might have been militarily impotent in the face of Lombard anger, ducal duplicity, and exarchate uselessness, he did find that, through further epistolary diplomacy, he was not religiously impotent. In a letter dated 15 October 740, Gregory reminded the bishops of Lombard Tuscany that their oaths of ordination included the demand to help the church when it faced danger and an exhortation to aid papal envoys going to meet Liutprand to demand the restoration of the four cities. If the Lombard bishops would not help the Holy See, the ill Gregory would make the journey himself – this was 'a subtle but effective reminder that Rome was not without means of stirring up trouble.'[72] This crisis lingered on into 741, a year which saw the death of three of the major players. First and the most important for this book, but by far the least consequential for Italy, was that of Leo III on 18 June. This was followed on 22 October by the demise of Charles Martel and then on 28 November, Gregory III shuffled off this mortal coil.

The successors of all three of these men – Constantine V, Pepin, and Zacharias – would have significant impact on Italy over the remainder of the eighth century, but it is the papal successor on whom focus must fall. This was because one player who was still very much alive was Liutprand, who, along with Hildeprand, had again turned his attention to the exarchate. The latter had raided the lands around Ravenna, before both joined together to attack the duchy of the Pentapolis. It might be expected that the new pope would continue the policies of Gregory III and try to revive the alliances that had seen success against Liutprand's forces. However, Zacharias performed a volte face in papal dealings with the Lombards. While the *Liber Pontificalis* claims that

Liutprand gave way to the pope's admonishments and promised to return the four cities, what actually happened is that Liutprand agreed to return the cities if the pope abandoned the alliance with Spoleto and Benevento. Indeed, when Liutprand moved against Transamund again in 742, the forces of the Roman duchy fought alongside the Lombard king, not the Spoletan duke. Liutprand was then free to march on to Benevento and facilitate the ejection and death of Godescalc. By 743, both Spoleto and Benevento were ruled by nephews of Liutprand and the pope was his ally.[73] The fall out from this papal volte face was not yet complete – Transamund would try again in Spoleto after Liutprand's death in 744, but that is not only well beyond the reign of Leo III but also the policies that emerged during his time on the throne.

The imperial presence in central Italy had been fading before 717 and continued to do so throughout Leo III's reign. There were several important signpost events in that decline, whether it be the papacy taking control of imperial territory through the 'middleman' of Lombard opportunism, papal forces attacking the seemingly pro-imperial faction of Exhilaratus, and imperial intervention taking the form of either land confiscations or military endeavours aimed at recalcitrant exarchs rather than Lombards or 'separatist' popes. Leo might send officials with orders, but in central Italy, there was a combination of unwillingness and inability to carry them out. This may explain the attempts to reorganise what remained 'imperial', such as removing papal revenues in Sicily and Calabria and reordering taxes – Leo recognised that decline of the imperial situation and was looking to make the best of it. The rise of a strong Venetian fleet, capable of helping eject the Lombards from Ravenna in 735, may reflect that Leo's reorganisation of imperial lands in Italy and its environs was not limited to Sicily and Calabria.

But there is no getting away from the fact that significant sections of central Italy had fallen out of imperial control during Leo's reign. This is seen most clearly at the negotiations between Zacharias and Liutprand over the four cities and papal-ducal alliance in 742 – the last time such a negotiation had taken place in c.730, the exarch had been directly involved; now, with Zacharias becoming the first pope to undertake a political mission in person outside 'Roman'/imperial territory, he was acting as the representative of the papacy and the duchy of Rome – there was no involvement of the Roman Empire at all.[74]

However, while imperial influence had been ejected from west-central Italy and what remained of the exarchate had only a decade left, the days of imperial Roman Italy were not numbered by the death of Leo III in 741; far from it. Imperial influence might have continued to wane over Sardinia and the Neapolitan and Venetian duchies, but it remained strong in Sicily and the toe, sole, and heel of Italy – Calabria, Lucania and Apulia. It would even at times expand to encompass the entire Italian 'shoe' over the next 250 years. Sicily would not be lost to the Aghlabids of Tunisia/Libya until 902, while peninsular imperial possessions would be reorganised into the catepanate of Italy in the mid-tenth century and only be definitively lost to the Normans in 1071. Given the messiness of its restoration in the mid-sixth century and the persistent threat from Lombards and Arabs, it was quite the feat for 'Byzantine' Italy to have survived for over 500 years. It is difficult to credit Leo III with much influence on that survival: his attention was elsewhere and his ability to act directly or through his officials had been significantly curtailed; however, while they rely on some supposition, the reorganisation possibly involved in the patrimonial confiscations, tax 'increases', and his naval reforms affecting the Adriatic and possibly Sicilian and Italian coastal waters may have helped galvanise those regions – the Sicilian theme, Lucania and Apulia were to remain Roman imperial possessions for a century or more after the fall of the Isaurian dynasty.

Chapter 12

Leonid End and Isaurian Epilogue: Trouble with the In-Laws

'In-laws can be outlaws that disrupt your peace and happiness.'
Anonymous

Epilogue

On 18 June 741, Leo III succumbed to dropsy, dying 'a physical death, to match his spiritual death.'[1] While the year of his birth is unknown, it is likely that he was in his mid/late-50s by the time he died. Upon his subsequent burial in the Church of the Holy Apostles, the succession seemed secure – Constantine V was now 23 years old and had been associated with the imperial office for over two decades, even joining his father on the campaign that culminated at Akroinon. Leo had also contracted a marriage for Constantine in the form of the daughter of the Khazar khagan, although it has yet to produce any offspring at the time of Leo's demise – the future Leo IV would not be born until 750.

That is not to say that Constantine was the only child of Leo and Maria. There were at least two younger daughters, Kosmo and Irene, about whom very little is known beyond them being buried in a sarcophagus of Proconnesian marble in the Church of the Apostles. Perhaps they died young. However, the second most important child of the emperor, we have already met: Anna. Not only was she the eldest, but she was also married to Leo's most important political and military ally, the *kouroplates* and *comes Opsikon*, Artabasdos. This marriage had been extremely fruitful, with nine children born, two of whom were old enough – Nikephoros and Niketas – to be in positions of power by the time of their grandfather Leo III's death. And circumstances were soon to prove that Artabasdos had an eye for the imperial throne.

Early in his sole reign, Constantine V crossed to Asia and marched through Opsikon territory, ostensibly aiming to launch a raid against the Umayyads to 'crown' his accession; however, upon reaching Krasos, he found Artabasdos at Dorylaion with the Opsikon army: 'they eyed each other suspiciously.'[2] When Constantine then 'asked' his brother-in-law to send Niketas and Nikephoros, to the imperial court, claiming that he wished to see his nephews, Artabasdos recognised it for what it was – a demand for hostages, with him being treated as an enemy of the emperor. The *comes Opsikon* used this thinly-veiled threat to gain the support of the Opsikon army (who may have been happy to regain their influence as king-makers). Artabasdos then attacked the emperor at Krasos, putting his army to flight on 27 June 741. Constantine's flight took him to Amorion, capital of his father's Anatolic theme. The Anatolic *strategos*, Lankinus, threw his lot in with Constantine, allowing the emperor time to reach out to others, securing the support of his cousin, Sisinnius, the Thrakesian *strategos*.[3] Artabasdos had not only the Opsikon army, but also the attached Thracian forces once he took control of Constantinople, and the Armeniac army, which was commanded by his son, Niketas.

This again thrust the constituent parts of the Roman army into the role of 'the ultimate arbiter'[4] in a struggle for the imperial throne. The loyalty of Lankinus and Sisinnius allowed Constantine to bide his time and eventually retake the field and in the process prove himself to be a skilled general. He defeated the Opsikon forces of Artabasdos at Sardis in May 742/743.[5] Three months later, Constantine intercepted and defeated the Armeniac army of Niketas at Modrine. A surprise attack in November reclaimed Constantinople, ending the usurpation with the capture and blinding of Artabasdos and his sons.[6]

Conclusions

While the Isaurian dynasty survived the various rebellions during Leo III's reign and the civil war upon his death, the latter instance 'exposed the deep fissures within the Byzantine army,'[7] giving the clearest evidence that Leo had failed to fix the fundamental problems of loyalty and discipline within the Roman military. The civil war between Artabasdos and Constantine could also suggest a personal conflict between the initial heir apparent and the man who replaced him in that role, a conflict that Leo either failed to recognise or failed to resolve.

Such a contest could be something of an issue with Leo's prolonged reign: 'If Leo had died earlier, when Constantine was still a child, Artabasdos almost certainly would have gained the throne for himself or would have become an all-powerful regent for an heir of minor age.'[8] And Artabasdos had likely enjoyed such a position of heir apparent for fifteen years or more. He will have found it difficult to just lose such a position, while Constantine will have been wary of a man who had wielded such power, even if (or especially because?) he was his brother-in-law. Constantine certainly demonstrated his lack of faith in members of his own family in positions of power for Sisinnius was also deposed and blinded despite supporting the emperor. Perhaps Constantine was recognising 'the danger inherent in allowing members of one family to command several theme armies,'[9] even if it was members of his own imperial family.

Despite these continued problems in fixing ill-discipline and fractures within the Roman army, Leo III did succeed in securing strong support from one very important military edifice – the city of Constantinople itself. Through his repelling of Maslamah and his rule more generally, the city and enough of its hierarchies supported Leo in the face of the rebellions of Anastasius II and Kosmas.[10] Indeed, this Isaurian support carried over into the reign of Constantine V, with Artabasdos only able to claim the city through the rumour of Constantine's death.

Indeed, focusing on Leo's ultimate failure to halt military unrest or foresee conflict over his succession plan overlooks the fact that he was also the empire's saviour. Resisting the existential threat that was the titanic Arab siege of Constantinople was an epochal moment in Roman and even European history, leading some to see Leo as 'the Miltiades of medieval Hellenism.'[11] In inflicting the first great defeat on the Umayyad army and establishing a hardpoint defence strategy in Anatolia, Leo had shown that the Roman Empire was 'a foe to be treated with respect, and as a neighbour who was not about to disappear.'[12] This military and leadership ability also allowed him to survive all the rebellions that arose during his reign, unlike every other emperor for the previous half century.

Leo also proved himself 'an accomplished politician and diplomat'[13] by establishing peace and alliances with various other neighbours – Bulgars, Khazars, Alans, Abasgians. This gave him the prolonged reign necessary to demonstrate that he was also 'a gifted administrator and a wise legislator who understood the problems of his time.[14] His introduction of various military, provincial, numismatic, tax, and legal reforms provided the empire with solidity. This helped bring prosperity back to the provinces through effective and just administration and rejuvenated economic activity, which in turn allowed him and then his son to go on the offensive and continue the restoration of the Roman Empire.[15]

Leo the Isaurian (and Constantine V) was much more successful than the sources would dare admit, with this unwillingness stemming from his reputed initiation of iconoclasm. As Edward Gibbon put it, Leo III is 'known to posterity by the invectives of his enemies'; his noteworthy achievements in military, finance and law are completely overshadowed by his reputed role in iconoclasm, which in turn has seen him fall into relative obscurity, despite his importance to the future of the empire. Whether Leo had a significant impact on that growing religious, social, and political maelstrom or not, the iconodule sources thought that he did, tarnishing his reputation as a result. 'Such evils as befell the Christians during the reign of the impious Leo'[16] – he caused the rebellion in Italy, popular revolts, earthquakes, famines, invasions, plagues; all because of his 'wicked beliefs' (which he may not have had). Leo was so terrible as emperor that his reign only lasted twenty-four years and established a dynasty that was to last into the ninth century.

To conclude, returning to the title of this work, and the question mark attached to it: there is no question that Leo was an 'imperial saviour' – the Roman Empire was unlikely to have survived in any appreciable form had Constantinople fallen in 717/718. And Leo continued in saviour mode throughout his reign, with his various reforms giving solidity, substance, and longevity to the renewed life that he (and his soldiers) had given the Roman state on the walls and seas around Constantinople. Indeed, this might be the only part of the title that is definitively correct. Over the course of the previous pages, we have seen that our main subject was *not* the third emperor to be called 'Leo', rather he was either 'Konon' or 'Leo IV'. He also seems to have not been from Isauria and any Isaurian blood in his family is merely speculative. The only geographic origin we have for him is Germanikeia, in Syria.

The question mark over his status as an 'icon breaker' is not only unexpected, but also much less easy to prove or disprove. Of course, if the traditional view of Leo as the imperial initiator of iconoclasm is upheld, then the question mark can be removed. Even if we follow the track that Leo III was not the instigator of iconoclasm, rather it was his son Constantine V, that later initiation did not occur in a vacuum. Issues with the status of icons had been around for decades or more, and if Leo did not accelerate the discussion, he certainly did not quash it. At the very least, by securing the empire, he paved the way for a deeper discussion on icons and possibly part of the negative reaction to iconoclasm in the west with his policies in Italy.

Perhaps with that summation of partly definitive, partly unclear, and partly incorrect segments of the title, significant alterations to the title are, in order –

Konon/Leo IV the Syrian: Imperial Saviour! Christian Icon Breaker?

Appendix

A Brief History of Greek Fire

'Almost to the point of no return
Everything will burn, baby burn'

'Burn, Baby, Burn'
Ash (written by Tim Wheeler)

While it became most widely associated with the Roman Empire of the seventh/eighth century and beyond, using fire in concert with a projectile weapon on board a ship was an idea from much earlier in history. Thucydides records the use of fireships as early as the climactic Battle of the Great Harbour in 413 BC during the disastrous Athenian expedition to Sicily, while the Tyrians attempted to undermine Alexander the Great's siege of their city in 332 BC by sending a fireship against the causeway his Macedonians were constructing. The Romans and their Rhodian allies made use of fire and fireships against the Seleucid fleet of Antiochus III at the battles of Samian Panormus and Myonessus in 190 BC, while the Carthaginians burned almost the entire Roman fleet of Censorinus outside Carthage in 149 BC. Cassius Longinus made significant use of fireships against Julius Caesar's navy at Messana and Vibo in 48 BC. The Vandals also wrought havoc amongst the expedition of Basiliscus at Cape Mercurium by directing fireships into the Roman navy in AD 468. However, the exact meaning of 'fireships' can be confused, with the sources sometimes not being clear if they mean a ship or ships set on fire to be directed an enemy position or fleet or a ship laden with men throwing or launching missiles which are on fire.[1]

Actual incendiary weapons were not limited to ship-born devices, having been used on battlefields for centuries prior to the invention of Greek fire. The likes of sulphur, petroleum and bitumen had all been used as early as the ninth century BC by the Assyrians.[2] Perhaps most interesting is the contraption Thucydides records the Boeotians using at Delium in 424 BC during the Peloponnesian War. It was a primitive flame-thrower, which used a bellows focused through a long pipe to blow flames at the city walls.[3]

There are numerous other specific mentions of chemicals being used to produce fire – II Maccabees, Livy, Pliny the Elder, Pausanias, St Augustine[4]

– with perhaps the best description coming from the early-third century AD writer Julius Africanus on 'πῦρ αὐτόματον' – 'automatic fire.'

> 'This is the recipe: take equal amounts of sulphur, rock salt, ashes, thunder stone, and pyrite and pound fine in a black mortar at midday sun. Also in equal amounts of each ingredient mix together black mulberry resin and Zakynthian asphalt, the latter in a liquid form and free-flowing, resulting in a product that is sooty coloured. Then add to the asphalt the tiniest amount of quicklime. But because the sun is at its zenith, one must pound it carefully and protect the face, for it will ignite suddenly. When it catches fire, one should seal it in some sort of copper receptacle; in this way you will have it available in a box, without exposing it to the sun. If you should wish to ignite enemy armaments, you will smear it on in the evening, either on the armaments or some other object, but in secret; when the sun comes up, everything will be burnt up.'[5]

These examples highlight that the core principles of Greek fire – chemical-based flame and projecting liquids/fire through tubes under pressure – were known many centuries before a certain Kallinikos of Heliopolis (now Baalbek in Lebanon) arrived in the imperial capital in c.672 with knowledge of a 'napalm-like substance that burned in water and could be projected great distances from the bows of ships.'[6] It is unlikely that the connection of these two technologies had not occurred at some point in previous centuries. Theophanes recorded the Roman navy having fire-carrying and siphon-equipped ships at least a year before the seeming appearance of Kallinikos in Roman territory in c.672 (although that could be to do with Theophanes' style and sources).[7] It could also be that there was no one single inventor of what became known as Greek fire, with it instead being 'invented by chemists in Constantinople who had inherited the discoveries of the Alexandrian chemical school.'[8] It could be that Kallinikos brought ideas that refined the mixture used to produce the fire or upgraded the delivery system to make it so that Greek fire could be more widely implemented at Constantinople and in the imperial navy.

After its use in defending Constantinople from the Arabs on perhaps two occasions in the late-seventh/early-eighth centuries, Greek fire became an invaluable weapon for the Roman Empire. It would be used to expand Roman territory, fight civil wars, and against other opponents throughout the succeeding centuries.[9] The Romans were still using Greek fire by the time Anna Komnena was writing her *Alexiad* in the mid-twelfth century, as she records its deployment against the Pisans and Normans.[10] However, the defence of Constantinople against the Fourth Crusade in 1203–1204 does not seem to have involved the use of Greek fire, which might suggest that the decline of the empire in both territorial and trading terms saw it lose access to the necessary ingredients. Or perhaps the secret of how it was made was simply lost over time.[11]

It might be questioned as to how the Roman Empire could have lost the secrets behind such an important military application. The answer seems to be that the Romans were so keen to keep those secrets that not many people were entrusted with them and of those people, they would only be entrusted with a specific part of the operation – the formula, the devices and techniques used in its creation, the design of the siphon, the training of the *siphonarioi* who used it in battle, and the apparatus for mounting the siphon on specialised ships. The mechanical and chemical production of Greek fire was therefore highly specialised, compartmentalised and centralised.[12] Such a veil of secrecy could not prevent some of the substance and equipment falling into the hands of enemies through military defeat as both the Bulgars and Arabs are recorded capturing siphons and some of the mixture. However, it seems that the formula and the apparatus required enough knowledge and knowhow that they could not reverse engineer the formula or the delivery system.[13] The secrecy behind Greek fire encouraged the unlikely story recorded by George Kedrenos that Kallinikos' descendants, a family called *Lampros*, 'brilliant,' kept the secret of the fire's manufacture down to the eleventh century.[14] Constantine VII even provides the example of a Roman official who was bribed to hand over the secrets of Greek fire to imperial enemies, only to be struck down by 'flame from heaven' as he was about to enter a church.[15]

Due to this secrecy, modern attempts to ascertain the chemical make-up of Greek fire are dependent on limited references in military manuals and historical sources who might have seen it in action or had partial information about the workings of the substance or the apparatus. An example of this is the partial 'recipe' that Anna Komnena provides in her description of the Roman defence of Dyrrhachium against the Normans in 1108.

> 'This fire is made by the following arts. From the pine and certain such evergreen trees inflammable resin is collected. This is rubbed with sulphur and put into tubes of reed, and is blown by men using it with violent and continuous breath. Then in this manner it meets the fire on the tip and catches light and falls like a fiery whirlwind on the faces of the enemies.'[16]

This is by no means enough to recreate Greek fire and the systems used for deploying it. Characteristics have to be 'siphoned' from various literary sources in order to present a fuller picture, and perhaps also eliminating some other assumptions. For example, because the discharge of Greek fire was accompanied

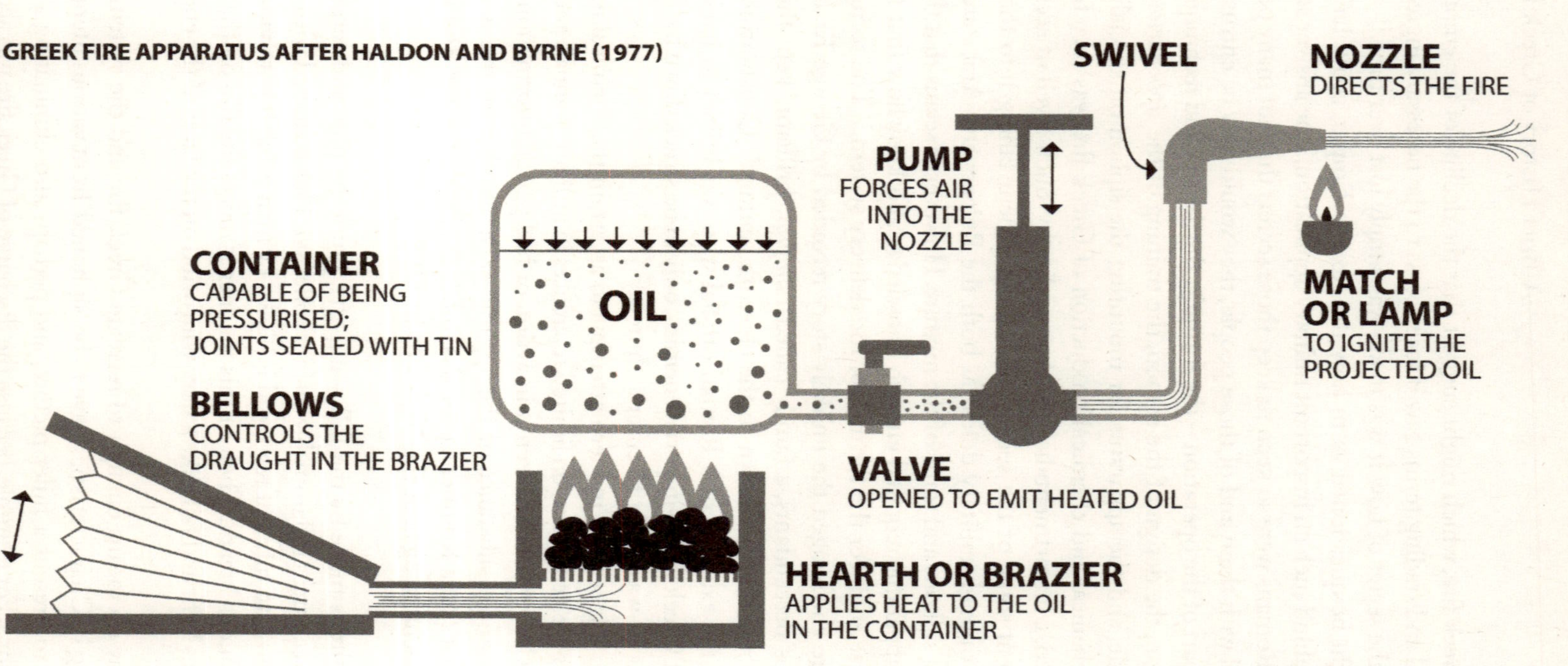
GREEK FIRE APPARATUS AFTER HALDON AND BYRNE (1977)
SWIVEL
NOZZLE
DIRECTS THE FIRE
PUMP
FORCES AIR INTO THE NOZZLE
CONTAINER
CAPABLE OF BEING PRESSURISED; JOINTS SEALED WITH TIN
OIL
MATCH OR LAMP
TO IGNITE THE PROJECTED OIL
BELLOWS
CONTROLS THE DRAUGHT IN THE BRAZIER
VALVE
OPENED TO EMIT HEATED OIL
HEARTH OR BRAZIER
APPLIES HEAT TO THE OIL IN THE CONTAINER

by 'thunder [and] … much smoke,[17] it was long held that saltpetre was used in its composition, making it something of an early form of gunpowder.[18] This would seem to go against the other records of Greek fire being a liquid substance, one that was capable of floating and burning on water. Reports that it could only be extinguished with strong vinegar or urine, along with depriving it of oxygen through a solid substance such as sand, would seem to demonstrate a specific type of chemical reaction occurring similar to other flammable liquids.

The most distinctive form of deployment of Greek fire is it being ejected from a tube called a σίφων, *siphōn*, like a primitive flame-thrower, mounted on the front of ships or on defensive walls.[19] To add to the psychological effect, these projectors could be made to look like animals or monsters, giving the Roman ship it was mounted on the appearance of a fire-breathing dragon.[20] Previous methods of discharging similarly flammable liquids in pots or hand-held grenades were also still used.[21] The distance this *siphon* could spray the flame was also used as 'evidence' of an explosive being used;[22] however, even the suggestion that saltpetre was involved at the ignition stage of the Greek fire process goes against the evidence. Saltpetre was not used in European or Middle Eastern warfare or even mentioned by Muslim or Christian sources until the thirteenth century. Other proposals suggest that the destruction wrought by Greek fire came from an explosive reaction with water, whether it be quicklime or calcium phosphide.[23] Modern experiments have failed to recreate the explosive, flame damage recorded for Greek fire. Furthermore, there are plenty of examples of Greek fire being deployed without contacting water – Leo VI has it being fired directly onto the decks of ships or thrown in grenades, neither of which would see water required as the source of ignition.[24]

It seems likely then that even if there were other ingredients added in – as thickeners to make it sticky, for longer duration or greater intensity[25] – the core ingredient of Greek fire was a liquid hydrocarbon, whether it be fractions of crude oil, natural gas condensates, petroleum distillates or fractional distillates of coal tar or peat, all of which were lumped together under the name *naphtha* in the ancient and medieval worlds. The Romans did have access to such crude oil derivatives around the Black Sea and the Middle East.[26]

Using the source descriptions of Greek fire in action and Roman technological abilities at the time, along with a mixture of crude oil and wood resins, Haldon and Byrne (1977) designed an apparatus consisting of an airtight tank in which the mixture would be pressurised by a bronze pump and heated by a brazier (also adding to the pressure), before then being transferred through a valved pipe to a swivel-mounted nozzle to spray the mixture through a naked flame to produce the flame-thrower effect. When tested, it was found that even modern welding could not contain the twice-pressurised mixture, with potentially explosive results, a problem not mentioned by the sources. This was solved by moving the bronze pump to after the heated mixture came out of the tank through the valve. This allowed for a flame of over 1000°C to be sprayed 15m.[27] This proved that an effective Greek fire flame-thrower could be made with materials and techniques available to the Romans of the seventh century, even if it is not provable that the apparatus of Haldon and Byrne (1977) actually resembled the ancient equivalent.

While the deployment of Greek fire at the 717–718 Arab Siege of Constantinople was extremely useful for the Roman defenders, it was not the all-conquering weapon that it would seem to be. The *siphōn* seemingly did not have a substantial range and relied upon favourable conditions in order for it to do its work. Choppy seas and contrary winds could nullify its deployment, or worse still, see it turned back on Roman ships (some of which were, of course, carrying the extremely flammable mixture). And if it did work as planned, even 'sticky fire' did not sink a ship quickly, particularly in comparison to more conventional weapons such as the ship-borne ram or heavy artillery. There were also ways for the enemy to protect itself against this threat. The most straightforward was to stay out of its effective range, which was much shorter than that of archers or artillery. Muslim navies also made use of the chemical properties of the flammable liquid, covering their hulls and decks with materials soaked in vinegar, which would not burn and could even counteract the Greek fire. These drawbacks and countermeasures do not mean that Greek fire was completely neutralised as a threat. An unaware or under-prepared enemy could still be completely overwhelmed by the physical and psychological impact of the 'fire-breathing' Roman ships. This can be seen in its devastating success against the rebel fleet of Thomas the Slav in 822 and that of Igor I of Kiev in 941.

Notes

Introduction

1. Brubaker and Haldon (2001), xxiii.
2. Brubaker and Haldon (2001), 166.
3. Howard-Johnston (2010), 306–307; Treadgold in Bumazhnov *et al.* (2011), 595; Afinogenov (2002), 11–22; Forrest in Jankowiak and Montinaro (2015), 418.
4. *Suda* T901; a seal of 'Trajan the Consul' could be the same man (*PmbZ* no.8511; *PLRE* IIIb.1335), although this is somewhat tenuous; Treadgold in Bumazhnov *et al.* (2011) extrapolates a potential career outline for Trajan the Patrician; Mango (1990), 16–17; Afinogenov (2002).
5. Forrest in Jankowiak and Montinaro (2015), 444; Howard-Johnston (2010), 306–307; Treadgold in Bumazhnov *et al.* (2011), 595; Aginogenov (2002), 11–22.
6. Speck (1988) 429–430 vs Mango (1990) 1–4.
7. Brubaker and Haldon (2001) 168.
8. Head (1972), 16.
9. Mango (1978) 9–17; Mango and Scott (1997), lv.
10. Treadgold in Bumazhnov *et al.* (2011), 589; Forrest in Jankowiak and Montinaro (2015), 418.
11. Orosz (1948), 3–12; Head (1972), 15–17; Forrest in Jankowiak and Montinaro (2015), 418 n.4.
12. Head (1972), 18.
13. Bar Hebraeus I.110.
14. Head (1972), 16; Theophanes's sources: Brooks (1906), 578–587; Conterno in Jankowiak and Montinaro (2015), 383–400; Debié in Jankowiak and Montinaro (2015), 365–382; Forrest in Jankowiak and Montinaro (2015), 417–444; Howard-Johnston (2010), 295–299; Hoyland in Jankowiak and Montinaro (2015), 355–364; Proudfoot (1974), 400–427.
15. Mango and Scott (1997), lxxxviii; Forrest in Jankowiak and Montinaro (2015), 418.
16. Mango (1990), 12; Breckenridge (1959), 4.
17. Howard-Johnston (2010), 305.
18. Howard-Johnston (2010), 305.
19. McKitterick (2016) 243.
20. Deliyannis (1996).
21. Hoyland (1997), 425; Woods (2011), n.10.
22. Brock (1979); Conrad (1990); Brooks (1906); Debié in Jankowiak and Montinaro (2015).
23. Brubaker and Haldon (2001) 188–189.
24. Conrad (1998), 63; Koscielniak (2004), 10–11.
25. Brubaker and Haldon (2001) 194.
26. Noth and Conrad (1994); Donner (1998).
27. Brubaker and Haldon (2001) 199.
28. Breckenridge (1959), 4.
29. Schneider and Karnapp (1938) no.29.
30. Grierson (1968); (1973) on coins from the era.
31. Zacos and Veglery (1972) on seals.

32. Treadgold (1990), 203; cf. Ostrogorsky (1968), 129–146, 152–156.
33. Treadgold (1990), 225.

Chapter 1: From Heraclian Stability to Military Anarchy – The Roman Empire of 685

1. Jankowiak (2013a).
2. And even that is still young in comparison to many cities in the Near East that the Romans lost control of during the seventh century, such as the site of Damascus, which might have seen human habitation since 9000 BC.
3. Georgacus (1947)
4. Pliny, *NH* IV.18/11; Dionysius of Byzantium, *Anaplous of the Bosporos* 24.
5. Cassius Dio, LXXIV.14.4.
6. Themistius, *Or.* XI.151a.
7. Crow, Bardill and Bayliss (2008).
8. Claims that both late antique Constantinople and Chang'an in China might have reached 1,000,000 inhabitants seems somewhat unlikely; Morris (2010); Modelski (2003); Chandler (1987).
9. *CTh* XV.1.51; *CIL* III.739; Socrates, *HE* VII.1.3; Bardill (2004), 122.
10. Suggestions that this outer wall was a slightly later addition have been doubted – Meyer-Plath and Schneider (1943), 4; Bardill (2004), 123; Philippides and Hanak (2011), 299–302.
11. Mango in *Necipoğlu (2001) 22–25; Bardill (2004) 123 n.21.*
12. Over its 170-year history, 19 men served as exarch of Ravenna, with over 20 years of total vacancies; of that 19, possibly 6 were killed in battle by rebels or when rebelling.
13. While the 'gradual transformation' across decades (or more) is the largely accepted idea for the 'theme system', there were some prominent proponents – Teall (1971), 47–48; Oikonomides (1975), 1–8 – of Heraclius being the sole originator of the 'themes'.
14. Haldon (1990), 215 n.27; Louth in Shepard (2008), 239–240, 266.
15. Kaegi (1967), 39–54.
16. Treadgold (1995), 23–24.
17. Kaegi (1981), 180.
18. Kaegi (1981), 176, 180.
19. Theophanes, *Chron.* AM6265.
20. Treadgold (1995), 64.
21. Treagold (1995), 145–147.
22. Treadgold (1995), 74, table 3.
23. By 773, what had been the Opsikon theme had been divided into several smaller units – the Bucellarian, Optimatoi and smaller Opsikon themes, and the guard regiments of the *tagmata*: the *scholae*, *excubitores*, *arithmos*, *numeri/teicheon* and the *optimates.*
24. An army in Thrace of perhaps 6,000 could also be part of the area initially covered by the *Opsikon.*
25. Theophanes, *Chron.* AM6113.
26. Haldon (1975), 77–78, 96–108 on the success of the *Obsequium* against the Persians possibly forming some of the foundations of the theme system.
27. An actual Thrakesian *strategos* is not mentioned until 741, when its holder, Sisinnius, sided with Constantine V against Artabasdos.
28. Haldon (1990), 216; (1999), 87.
29. Lilie (1977), 7–47; Haldon (1997), 212–214.
30. Head (1972), 81; Kaegi (1967), 39; Charanis (1963), 74–75.
31. Zacos and Veglery (1972), n.2918, 2919; Prigent and Nichanian (2003), 98–99.
32. Oikonomides (1972), 351.
33. Brown in Shepard (2008), 457–459.

34. Pryor and Jeffreys (2006), 35; Cosentino (2008), 602; Ahrweiler (1966), 22–23; Justinian II's *iussio* of 687 mentions the 'Cabarisiani', which would seem to refer to the Karabisiani, but there is some doubt (Diehl (1905), 285; Antoniadis-Bibicou (1966), 63–68)
35. Treadgold (1997), 315; Pryor and Jeffreys (2006), 25 vs Ahrweiler (1966), 23–25.
36. Rhodes, Keos and Samos are also suggested as the base of the Karabisiani *strategos*.
37. Ahrweiler (1966), 24–25.
38. Theophanes, *Chron.* AM6190; Nikephoros, *Brev.* 41, with Nikephoros mentioning a contingent of Kibyrrhaeots from Korykos.
39. Ahrweiler (1966), 50–51.
40. It could be that Mardaite manpower was considered so successful with the Kibyrrhaeots that similar resettlements were employed in other coastal and island themes, such as Hellas, Peloponnese, Epirote Nicopolis and Cephalonia.
41. A Macedonian theme centred on western Thrace and capitaled at Adrianople was formed in the last years of the eighth century, as were Peloponnesian and Cephallonian/Ionian themes; further themes centred on Dyrrhachium and Thessalonica appeared in the early-ninth century; the mid/late-ninth century saw an Epirote theme centred on Nicopolis and then a Dalmatian theme in 870 (Ostrogorsky (1963), 5–6).
42. Kaegi (1981).
43. Theophanes, *Chron.* AM6126.
44. Kaegi (1981), 201.
45. Kaegi (1981), 201.
46. Haldon (2016), 165); Winkelmann (1987).
47. Haldon (2016), 153.
48. Haldon (2016), 152; *Ecloga* 18.1.
49. Nikephoros, *Brev.* 39. There is some suggestion that Justinian II continued the forceful methods of his predecessors at a time when there was little or no unrest may have actually in part *caused* the unrest that he faced (Kaegi (1981), 186; cf. Nikephoros, *Brev.* 37–38; Theophanes, *Chron.* AM6187).
50. Ostrogorsky (1959), 45–47; (1968), 132–137; Charanis (1963); Kaegi (1967), 40–43.
51. Jenkins (1966), 53 considered that the Farmer's Law was 'almost universally attributed' to Justinian II; *contra* Dolger (1944–1945), II.21–48; Lemerle (1958) 49–55; Karayannopulos (1958), 357–373; Ostrogorsky (1968), 90–91, Toševa-Nikolovska (2008), 209 while Medvedev (1984) considers it to be a composition of the sixth century. Ashburner (1912), 68–71 records and refutes the attempts of von Lingenthal to attribute the Farmer's Law to Leo III and Constantine V.
52. Vernadskij (1925), 172; Setton (1953), 233–234.
53. Head (1972), 87; Ashburner (1910); (1912).
54. De Ste Croix (1981), Appendix III provides a long list of imperial settlements of non-Romans on Roman territory.
55. Jenkins (1966), 52 on Justinian transferring 100,000 Slavs, almost certainly a large exaggeration.
56. Charanis (1960–1961), 140–143; Ostrogorsky (1968), 130ff.
57. Lemerle (1954), 265–308; (1958), 63–65 on Slavic infiltration of Roman territory prompting agricultural changes.
58. Stein (1928); Ostrogorsky (1931), 229–240; Ostrogorsky (1968), 137; Setton (1953), 225–259.
59. Ostrogorsky (1931), 237–240.
60. Nikephoros, *Brev.* 37, 39–40; Theophanes, *Chron.* AM6186–6187.
61. Head (1972), 5.
62. The title of *pontifex maximus* was discarded at some indeterminate point – Cameron (2007), 341–384 suggests that Gratian, usually thought to have given it up, kept the title and that Theodosius I may also have used it. There is no evidence that the pope was officially styled as *pontifex maximus* until the Renaissance.

63. Optatus, *Against the Donatists* III.3.
64. Bury (1889), II.317.
65. Ekonomou (2009), 217; *LP* 83.3; cf. Paul the Deacon, *HL* VI.53.
66. *LP* 84.1.
67. *LP* 85.3; Mann (1925), 46; Head (1972), 62; cf. Noye (2015), 346–361, 366–367); Calabria was a useful source of grain, wine, wool, manpower, copper, silver and gold (Noye (2015), 346–348, 354–358 on sources for Calabria).
68. Petrus Siculus, *Historia Manichaeorum* 1281–1282; cf. Garsoian (1967), 117–118; Runciman (1947), 35–38.
69. Hefele (1896), V.222–223; Humphreys (2015), 39–80 on Quinisext.
70. Head (1972), 65; Mansi, *Concilia* XI. 921–1006; Hefele (1896), V.221–242; Fliche and Martin (1930), 194–197; https://www.newadvent.org/fathers/3814.htm.
71. *LP* 86.6–7; Ekonomou (2009), 222–223 on the canons the pope may not have liked.
72. Sergius himself liked that depiction, adding the *Agnus Dei* invocation – 'Lamb of God, you take away the sins of the world, have mercy on us' – to the celebration of Mass at the breaking of the Host.
73. *LP* 86.7.
74. *LP* 86.8.
75. Haldon (2016), 127.
76. Haldon (2016), 91.
77. In the interim, Quinisext had been largely ignored in imperial-papal relations, but that does not mean that there was any real improvement – Tiberius III had looked to cow the pope using his new exarch, while imperial forces had been impotent in the face of an invasion of papal territory by the Beneventan duke.
78. *LP* 88.5; Haldon (2016), 50.
79. Pope Sisinnius was so stricken with gout upon his election (*LP* 89.1) that he appears to have been some kind of stop-gap.
80. Ekonomou (2007), 271.
81. Agnellus, *Lib. Pont. Ecc. Rav.* 366–371 makes claims of Justinian targeting Ravenna due to its involvement in his first deposition. *LP* 90.2 provides some corroboration for the attack on Ravenna, but it seems more a political attack than a revenge mission, with the latter likely part of the 'black legend' of Justinian II that Agnellus had a role in circulating, possibly due to the imperial attack on Ravenna and maybe on members of Agnellus' family. It must be said that the lack of record from Theophanes and Nikephoros about a possible rebellion by and then sack of the exarchate capital in Italy raises some concerns over the dating of this whole affair.
82. *LP* 90.4.
83. Richards (1979), 212; Sansterre (1984), 10–11; Ekonomou (2007), 271.
84. Taddei (2013), 55.
85. *LP* 90.3; Bede, *Anglo Saonis Chronicon* 201; Paul the Deacon, *HL* 225; Constantine would be the last pope to visit Constantinople until 1967.
86. *LP* 90.6.
87. Hefele (1896), V.242; Bede, *De Sex. Aetatibus* 316; *LP* 88.5.
88. *LP* 91.1.

Chapter 2: The Enemies of the Empire

1. Madelung (1997).
2. Madelung (1997), 140, 80–81.
3. Tabari XVIII.173; Madelung (1997), 311–355.
4. On the Second Fitna, Dixon (1971), 34–35, 73–75, 104–110; Hawting (2000), 48–49; Kennedy (2016), 76–80.

5. Mukhtar received mixed depictions in the sources, either as a sincere Alid, a ruthless opportunist or, according to Theophanes, *Chron.* AM6174, a false prophet.
6. Tabari XXI.783–789 on the revolt of al-Ashdaq; Dixon (1971), 126–129 on Umayyad attempts to stir up anti-Zubayrid feeling in Basra.
7. Tabari XXI.807.
8. Tabari XI.829, 852–853.
9. Kaegi (1992), 185; 244–245, 247; Kennedy (2004), 87; Jankowiak (2013), 273.
10. Haldon (2016), 47; Charanis (1961a); Greenwood in Sheperd (2008), 333–364.
11. The earliest mention of 'Avar' comes in the fifth-century *History* of Priscus of Panium, but it could be that the 'Avars' he records (fr.40) and the people established along the Danube a century later are not one and the same (Sinor (1946–1947), 35).
12. Jordanes, *Getica* V.34–35; Tacitus, *Germ.* 46; Pliny, *NH* IV.96–97; Ptolemy, *Geog.* III.5.21; Procopius, *BG* VII.14.30 gives the Sclaveni and the Antae a common ancestor in the Sporoi, a name meaning 'seeds' in Greek; the ninth-century *Bavarian Geographer* connects the Slavs and Suebi, not only listing the 'Suevi' as a Slavic tribes but also suggesting that 'Suevi are not born, they are sown' (cf. Metzner (2011), 321, 347); Curta (1998), (2001), 39–43.
13. Curta (2001), 309; Geary (2003), 145.
14. Schenker (1996), 3–5 on certain vocabulary – sea, amber – missing from proto-Slavic possibly reducing any connection between the Slavs and Baltic peoples.
15. Kortlandt (1990), 4; Sussex and Cubberley (2011), 22.
16. Heather (2009), 390, 391; Heather (2009), 389–390, Map 17.
17. Curta (2001), 7, 11–13; Heather (2009), 391–392.
18. Curta (2001), chs. 3, 6.
19. Pohl in Little and Rosenwein (1998), 20.
20. Curta (2001), 46, 60.
21. Curta (2001), 117–119, 347.
22. Mauricius, *Strat.* IX.3.
23. Mauricius, *Strat.* XI.4.
24. Procopius, *BG* V.27.1–3, VII.14.25; Mauricius, *Strat.* XI.4; Theophylact Simocatta, *Hist.* VII.4.
25. Geary (2003), 145; Procopius, *BG* VII.14.22 goes as far as to say that the Slavs practiced democracy, which may hint at their decentralised leadership.
26. Jordanes, *Getica* 48.247.
27. Procopius, *BG* VII.40.5–6.
28. Procopius, *BG* VII.29.1–3, 38, 40; Procopius, *Secret History* 18.20 suggests that the raids had become annual; Curta (2001), 75–89.
29. Whitby (1988), 156ff.
30. Haldon (2016), 47.
31. Vasiliev (1943), 8.
32. Golden (1992), 103–104 on 'Bulgar' not being used earlier than the fourth century.
33. Maenchen-Helfen (1973), 384; Golden (1992), 104; (2011), 143; (2012) n.37; Chen (2012), 92–97; Simeonov (2008), 108–113.
34. Nikephoros, *Brev.* 24 and Theophanes, *Chron.* AM6171 connects the Danube Bulgars to the Unogundurs; Golden (1992), 104; (2011), 143. They shared land with various peoples – Kutrigurs, Utigurs – who the Romans regarded as 'Hunnic' (cf. Procopius, *BG* VII.2.2–5; Agathias I.3.4–5; Menander VIII.4.13, 5.23, 18.18), although this could be an all-purpose name for steppe barbarians in the same way that 'Scythian' had been for much of antiquity.
35. Keramopulos (1953), 334–336; Detschev (1927), 199–216; Maenchen Helfen (1973), 384.
36. *Chronology of 354, liber generationis II*, 77; Movses Khorenatsi 55–56; Paul the Deacon, *HL* I.16–17; II.26; Dimitrov (1987).
37. John of Antioch fr. 214.7, 303; Malchus fr.22; Zacharias, *HE* III.27; Ennodius, *Pan.* 19 on Theoderic the Amal reputedly killing the Bulgar leader in single combat; Paul the Deacon, *HR* XV.15.

38. Golden (1992), 104.
39. Jordanes, *Get.* V.37 on the 'Bulgari'; Ps-Zacharias Rhetor, *HE* XII.7 on the 'Burgars.'
40. Golden (1992), 100.
41. Kubrat may have spent time in Constantinople as a political hostage at a time of the Romano-Bulgar alliance in the 620s, although it has been suggested that this is misconception due to poor handling of the source material (Mingazov (2012)).
42. The lack of clarity or even the actual multi-ethnicity of this 'proto-state' may be reflected in the various titles and ethnicities Kubrat is referred to as: 'king of the Onogundur Huns, 'lord of the Onuğundur,' 'ruler of the Onuğundur–Bulğars,' 'chief of the Huns,' 'Onogur,' 'Oğuro-Bulğar,' 'Bulgar Hunnic/Hunnic Bulgar,' and various others; Golden (1992), 244, 245, 252; Kim (2013), 16, 101, 138; Hupchick (2017), 8.
43. Golden (1992), 103, 236–237; (2011), 144 on pressure coming from the Turks, specifically an inter-familial feud between the Khazar Ashina and Bulgar Dulo clans.
44. Theophanes, *Chron.* AM6171.
45. Golden (1992), 245, 253–258.
46. Theophanes, *Chron.* AM6171; Curta (2006), 106.
47. Kuber is likely one of the 'uncles at Thessalonica' recorded on the inscription of the Madara Rider (Petkov (2008), 5).
48. Theophanes, *Chron.* AM6171; Paul the Deacon, *HL* V.29.
49. Turtledove (1982), 56 n.125, with the Latin '*angulus*', the Slavic *o(n)gl* – 'angle, corner' or the Turkic *agyl* – 'yard'; Fiedler in Curta and Kovalev (2008), 152.
50. Theophanes, *Chron.* AM6171.
51. Theophanes, *Chron.* AM6171.
52. Theophanes, *Chron.* AM6171.
53. Theophanes, *Chron.* AM6171.
54. Theophanes, *Chron.* AM6171.
55. Theophanes, *Chron.* AM6180.
56. Theophanes, *Chron.* AM6180.
57. Theophanes, *Chron.* AM6180; Head (1972), 8 on these 'Kuber' Bulgars receiving assistance from local Slav tribes instead of the Bulgar khanate. There is some suggestion that this ambush did not happen, with Theophanes possibly duplicating a later Bulgar ambush of Justinian. Nikephoros does not mention any ambush of the Roman army marching back to Constantinople from Thessalonica.
58. Theophanes, *Chron.* AM6196; Nikephoros, *Brev.* 42.
59. Theophanes, *Chron.* AM6196; Nikephoros, *Brev.* 42.
60. Nikephoros, *Brev.* 42; Tervel may also have been given some territory in northern Thrace, specifically a region called Zagora; however, while this region did come into the possession of the Bulgars in the early-eighth century, it would seem to been part of the treaty of 716 between Theodosius III and Tervel.
61. Theophanes, *Chron.* AM6200; Nikephoros, *Brev.* 43.
62. Nikephoros, *Brev.* 45.
63. Nikephoros, *Brev.* 43.
64. Theophanes, *Chron.* AM6200.
65. Theophanes, *Chron.* AM6200; Nikephoros, *Brev.* 43.
66. Dunlop (1954), 34–40; Shirota (2005), 235, 248; Golden (2007a), 15–17; Brooks (2018), 5.
67. Golden (2006), 86; (2007a), 40–41; (2007b), 78; Brook (2018), 4.
68. Head (1972), 103; ibn-Sa'id al-Maghribi I.874 fol.71; cf. Dunlop (1954), 11.
69. Golden (2007b), 133–134, 155–156; Dunlop (1954), 97, 112; Noonan (2001), 77.
70. Golden (2007b), 138; (2006), 79–80, 88; Olsson (2013), 495, 507; Noonan (2007), 211, 217; Koestler (1977), 18.
71. Noonan (2007), 211–214; Golden (2011), 64.

72. Nikephoros, *Brev.* 46; Theophanes, *Chron.* AM6203.
73. Constantine VII, *de adm. imp.* 69–73.
74. Nikephoros, *Brev.* 12 speaks of Turks, while Theophanes, *Chron.* AM 6117 calls them Khazars; Moses Dasxuranci, *Hist.* II.12; Eutychios, *Hist.* 104.
75. Some Khazars are seen serving alongside Roman forces in battles against the Arabs in the 640s.
76. Golden in Reyerson, Stavrou and Tracy (2006), 11–13; Zuckerman in Golden, *Ben*-Shammai, *and* Róna-Tas (2007), 417.
77. *Parastaseis Syntomoi Chronokai* col.678; Dunlop (1954), 171; Artamonov (1962), 196.
78. Theophanes, *Chron.* AM6196; Nikephoros, *Brev.* 42.
79. *Parastaseis Syntomi Chronikai* cols. 678–679; cf. Dunlop (1954), 173.
80. Nikephoros, *Brev.* 45; Theophanes, *Chron.* AM6203.
81. Noonan (1992) 180–181.
82. Lombard sources record that the Langobards were originally called the Winnili and got their new name from a 'silly story' involving Frea and Odin and their 'long beards' (*Origo Gentis Langobardorum* 1; cf. Paul the Deacon, *HL* I.8). Odin himself was known as *Langbarðr,* so the name could reflect their adoption of him as their chief deity. Other suggested etymologies involve the Old High German roots, *barta*, meaning 'axe,' and *börde/börd*, meaning 'river plain' (Priester (2004), 17; Fröhlich (1976), 19; Bruckner (1895), 30–33).
83. Tacitus, *Ger.* 40; Velleius II.106.
84. Suetonius, *Claudius* 1; Dio *LV*.1; Tacitus, *Ann.* II.5–26; IV.44; Velleius II.104.
85. Wegewitz (1964), 19; (1972), 1–29; Priester (2004), 18.
86. Dio, LXXI.3.
87. *Codex Gothanus* 2; Jordanes, *Getica* 116; *Ravennatis Anonymi Cosmographia* I.11; Paul the Deacon, *HL* I.16; Priester (2004), 14; Burns (1984), 37–38; Wolfram (1988), 86–89
88. Procopius, *BG* VIII.26.10–13.
89. Paul the Deacon, *HL* I.27, II.6.
90. Paul the Deacon, *HL* II.6.
91. Paul the Deacon, *HL* II.26–27.
92. Paul the Deacon, *HL* II.28. 31.

Chapter 3: The Origins and Early Career of Leo III

1. Theophanes, *Chron.* AM6221; cf. George Monachus 735.13; Zonaras XIV.28.2.
2. Theophanes, *Chron.* AM6209.
3. Theophanes, *Chron.* AM6232.
4. Gero (1973) 7.
5. Head (1971) 105ff.
6. Nikephoros, *Brev.* 40.
7. John of Antioch fr.306, although somewhat aptly, it would appear that Theophanes, *Chron.* AM5972 mistakes this Isaurian usurper for a Syrian; Malalas XV.13.
8. *Parastaseis syntomoi chronikai* 20.1.
9. Schenk (1896), 296–297.
10. Vasiliev (1964), 234.
11. Theophanes, *Chron.* AM6209.
12. Theophanes, *Chron.* AM6237.
13. Vasiliev (1964), 235.
14. Kim (2017), 35; Brooks (1899), 22.
15. Kim (2017), 35.
16. Theophanes, *Chron.* AM6218.
17. Theophanes, *Chron.* AM6237.
18. Ekonomou (2009), 214.

19. *Kitab al Uyun* in Brooks (1899) 21.
20. *LP* 85.1.
21. Schenk (1896); Vasiliev (1964), 234; Gero (1973), 1–12.
22. *Kitab al Uyun* text from Brooks (1899), 21–22.
23. Brooks (1899), 21 n.7.
24. Brooks (1899), 21.
25. Oberhelman (1981); Calofonos (1985); Mavroudi (2002).
26. Theophanes, *Chron.* AM6209.
27. Brooks (1899), 21 n.11.
28. Theophanes, *Chron.* AM6209.
29. Bury (1889) II.375, 381.
30. Gero (1973), 30–31 vs Mango and Scott (1997), 547 n.3.
31. Haldon (2016), 239.
32. *Chronicle of Zuqnin* AG1028.
33. Crawford (2021), ch.5; Kaegi (1981), 189.
34. Petkov (2008), 5.
35. Crawford (2021) and Head (1972) on Justinian II.
36. *Kitab al Uyun* in Brooks (1899), 22.
37. Theophanes, *Chron.* 6197.
38. *Kitab al Uyun* in Brooks (1899), 22.
39. Theophanes, *Chron.* AM6209.
40. Theophanes, *Chron.* AM6209.
41. Head (1972), 155.
42. Head (1972), x.
43. Michael the Syrian II. 478, who says Justinian executed 'many of the great ones' and sent others into exile; cf. Bar Hebraeus I.105; *Chr. 846* 175; Mas'udi, *Le Livre de l'avertissement* 225; Levcenko (1947), 182.
44. Nikephoros, *Brev.* 42–43; Theophanes, *Chron.* AM6198.
45. Theophanes, *Chron.* AM6198.
46. Nikephoros, *Brev.* 42; Theophanes, *Chron.* AM6198; Bede, *De Sex Aetatius* 317.
47. Head (1972), 118.
48. Theophanes, *Chron.* AM6209.
49. Theophanes, *Chron.* AM6189; Howard-Johnston (2011), 207; Bury (1889), II.374–375 suggests that Justinian II targeted Abasgia for reconquest because it had been Justinian I who had conquered the region.
50. Theophanes, *Chron.* AM6209.
51. Theophanes, *Chron.* AM6209; the detail of this section is further evidence that Theophanes or George Synkellos had access to a source that the likes of Nikephoros did not and one quite close to Leo III, if not reliant on notes from the man himself; Bury (1889), II.375, 381.
52. Theophanes, *Chron.* AM6209.
53. Theophanes, *Chron.* AM6209.
54. Theophanes, *Chron.* AM6209.
55. Theophanes, *Chron.* AM6209.
56. Head (1972), 130.
57. Theophanes, *Chron.* AM6209.
58. Theophanes, *Chron.* AM6209.
59. Mango and Scott (1997), 547 on this 'Itaxes' not being a personal name but a Greek rendering of the Persian-Armenian title 'vitaxa', meaning viceroy; cf. Toumanoff (1963) 155ff.
60. Theophanes, *Chron.* AM6209.
61. Theophanes, *Chron.* AM6209.

62. Theophanes, *Chron.* AM6209.
63. Theophanes, *Chron.* AM6209.
64. Theophanes, *Chron.* AM6209.
65. Theophanes, *Chron.* AM6209.

Chapter 4: 'Only' Six Years Anarchy? Imperial Crisis at the Dawn of the Eighth Century

1. On the reigns of Leontios and Tiberius III, see Crawford (2021) chs. 9–11.
2. Haldon (2016), 50.
3. Head (1972), 155.
4. Dunlop (1954), 174 demonstrated that it was an official Khazar title rather than a personal name, but it being a political position rather than say a diplomatic one is unclear.
5. Head (1972), 144.
6. Charanis (1959); (1963) 15; Brubaker and Haldon (2011) 587
7. Kaldellis (2019) 185.
8. Theophanes, *Chron.* AM6203; cf. Michael the Syrian II.479 *Chr. 1234* 233.
9. Possibly the same Kallistratos monk, Paul, who had 'predicted' and encouraged the usurpation of Leontios in 695 (Theophanes, *Chron.* AM6187; Mango and Scott (1997), 529 n.16).
10. Theophanes, *Chron.* AM6203.
11. Theophanes, *Chron.* AM6203.
12. Theophanes, *Chron.* AM6203; Nikephoros, *Brev.* 45.
13. Theophanes, *Chron.* AM6203.
14. Theophanes, *Chron.* AM6204. Nikephoros makes no mention of Armenian activity under Bardanes.
15. Breckenridge (1959), 16.
16. Michael the Syrian II.479.
17. Theophanes, *Chron.* AM6203.
18. Theophanes, *Chron.* AM6204–6205; Curta (2006), 81–84; Brandes (1989), 63, 77.
19. Theophanes, *Chron.* AM6198.
20. Crawford (2021), 275–277.
21. Agathon the Deacon in Mansi XII.19E = *ACO* 2nd ser. ii/2 (1992), 900.
22. Theophanes, *Chron.* AM6204; Nikephoros, *Brev.* 47.
23. Theophanes, *Chron.* AM6203.
24. Nikephoros, *Brev.* 48.
25. Nikephoros, *Brev.* 48.
26. Theophanes, *Chron.* AM6203.
27. Theophanes, *Chron.* AM6203; Theophanes suggests that the monk went blind.
28. Theophanes, *Chron.* AM6204.
29. cf. Kaegi (1981) 191.
30. Haldon (2016), 51.
31. The *LP*, either through mistake or textual corruption, records a *botarea* 'image' rather than a chest.
32. *LP* 90.8; Bury (1896), 570–571.
33. *LP* 90.10.
34. *LP* 90.10.
35. *LP* 90.10.
36. *LP* 90.10.
37. Kaegi (1981), 191 counsels against such a characterisation of Bardanes being 'an emperor of the old aristocracy.'
38. Kaegi (1981), 204.
39. *Chron. Altin. et Grad.* 108 suggests 20 January 714.

40. Theophanes, *Chron.* AM6207.
41. Sumner (1976) 290; *contra* Mango and Scott (1997) 536 n.1.
42. Haldon (2016), 52.
43. *LP* 90.11.
44. *LP* 90.11.
45. Kaegi (1981), 191.
46. Theophanes, *Chron.* AM6206.
47. Theophanes, *Chron.* AM6206.
48. Theophanes, *Chron.* AM6206; Nikephoros, *Brev.* 49; *Parastaesis syntomoi chronikai* 20.3 records Tiberius III undertaking the repair of the sea walls.
49. Nikephoros, *Brev.* 50.
50. Theophanes, *Chron.* AM6207.
51. Theophanes, *Chron.* AM6207.
52. Nikephoros, *Brev.* 2.
53. Theophanes, *Chron.* AM6245.
54. Sumner (1976), 292 *contra* Mango and Scott (1997) 537, n.6; Kedrenus I.787–788 on Bishop Theodosius' tomb working miracles.
55. Theophanes, *Chron.* AM6207.
56. Haldon (2016), 185.
57. Nikephoros, *Brev.* 51; Theophanes, *Chron.* AM6207.
58. Theophanes, *Chron.* AM6207.
59. *Chron. Altin. et Grad.* 108f.
60. Michael the Syrian II.479.
61. Howard-Johnston (2011), 243.
62. *LP* 91.5.
63. Theophanes, *Chron.* AM6305.
64. Theophanes, *Chron.* AM6305, although this may be an anachronistic mistake from Theophanes in his use of his source for the siege of Constantinople.
65. Theophanes, *Chron.* AM6305.
66. Bury (1912), 338 n.5; Besevliev (1980), 249ff.
67. Theophanes, *Chron.* AM6208.
68. Nikephoros, *Brev.* 52.
69. Theophanes, *Chron.* AM6208.
70. Theophanes, *Chron.* AM6208; Nikephoros, *Brev.* 52.
71. *Vita Stephani iunioris* 1084.
72. *Chronicle of Zuqnin*, s.a. 716–717
73. Nikephoros, *Brev.* 52.
74. Haldon (2016), 53.
75. Haldon (2016), 53.

Chapter 5: A Game of Cat and Mouse in Anatolia

1. Theophanes, *Chron.* AM6209.
2. Kulakovskij (1912–1915), III.324; Canard (1971), 353–357.
3. Bury (1889), II.395.
4. Bar Hebraeus I.110.
5. Head (1972), 18.
6. Nikephoros, *Brev.* 49.
7. Konstantopoulos, Athens, 231; cf. Zacos/Veglery 899.
8. *Epist. Ad Theophilum, PG* 95: 357C; George Monachus 737.
9. *Kitab al-Uyun* (Brooks (1899), 22).
10. Theophanes, *Chron.* AM6207.

11. Theophanes, *Chron.* AM6192, 6195–6196; Tabari XXIII.1185; Crawford (2021), 240–243.
12. Nikephoros, *Brev.* 52.
13. Nikephoros, *Brev.* 52.
14. Michael the Syrian II.484 mistakes him with caliph Sulayman.
15. Agapios, *Kitab* 241.
16. Nikephoros, *Brev.* 52.
17. Tabari XXIV, 1314.
18. *Chr. 1234*, 152.
19. Tabari XXIV, 1314.
20. Kaegi (1981), 192.
21. *Kitab al-Uyun* (Brooks (1899), 22.
22. Theophanes, *Chron.* AM6208.
23. Kaegi (1977), 19–22.
24. Tabari XXIV.1316.
25. *Chr. 1234*, 153.
26. *Chr. 1234*, 155.
27. *Chr. 1234*, 157.
28. *Kitab al-Uyun* (Brooks (1899), 22.
29. Theophanes, *Chron.* AM6208.
30. Theophanes, *Chron.* AM6208.
31. Theophanes, *Chron.* AM6208.
32. Theophanes, *Chron.* AM6208.
33. Theophanes, *Chron.* AM6208.
34. *Chr. 819*, 10, AG 1027; *Chr. 846*, 177; Michael the Syrian II.483.
35. Theophanes, *Chron.* AM6208.
36. Nikephoros, *Brev.* 53.
37. *Chr.1234*, 154.
38. *Chr. 1234*, 154.
39. *Kitab al-Uyun* (Brooks (1899), 24).
40. Theophanes, *Chron.* AM6209.
41. Theophanes, *Chron.* AM6208.
42. *Kitab al-Uyun* (Brooks (1899), 24).
43. Theophanes, *Chron.* AM6208.
44. *Chr. 1234*, 154.
45. Kaegi (1981), 194.
46. Perhaps even rarer is how the abdication of Theodosius III shows troops from the Asian themes pressuring Constantinople without crossing the Bosphorus (Kaegi (1981), 206).
47. *Chr.1234*, 154.
48. *Kitab al-Uyun* (Brooks (1899), 24).

Chapter 6: Imperial Baptism of Fire: The Great Siege of Constantinople 717–718

1. Theophanes, *Chron.* AM6169.
2. Theophanes, *Chron.* AM6162–6164.
3. Theophanes, *Chron.* AM6165.
4. Theophanes, *Chron.* AM6165; Michael the Syrian II.455; Olster (1995), 23–28 on a poem by Theodosius Grammaticus possibly reflecting Constantinople's resisting of multiple Arab raids and Constantine's naval victories over Yazid.
5. Jankowiak in Zuckerman (2013), 242–243.
6. Jankowiak in Zuckerman (2013), 240–241, 239; cf. *ACO*, ser. sec II.612–614; Fischer (1884), 289.
7. Howard-Johnston (2010), 492–493 n.13.

8. Jankowiak in Zuckerman (2013), 273.
9. Howard-Johnston (2010), 492–494; Jankowiak in Zuckerman (2013).
10. Jankowiak in Zuckerman (2013), 316.
11. Howard-Johnston (2010), 303–304.
12. Sebeos 50.
13. O'Sullivan (2004); Cosentino (2008).
14. Sebeos 50.
15. Sebeos 51.
16. Cf. Jankowiak in Zuckerman (2013), 309.
17. See Appendix.
18. Christides in Bumazhnov *et al.* (2011), 511–513.
19. Howard-Johnston (2011), 509.
20. *Chronicle of Zuqnin* AG1028.
21. *Chr. 1234*, 152.
22. Treadgold (1997), 346.
23. Kennedy (2001), 19–21.
24. Kennedy (2001), 47.
25. *Chr. 1234*, 152.
26. *Chr. 1234*, 152.
27. *Chr. 1234*, 152.
28. Tabari XIV.1315; the amount demanded of each cavalryman was two *mudd*, which was a dry measure for grain in Syria and Egypt.
29. Tabari XIV.1315.
30. Tabari XIV.1315.
31. Tabari XIV.1315.
32. Sahih Bukhari IV.52.175.
33. Remondon (1953), nos. 9, 11, 28, 31.
34. Braudel (1976), I.86–90.
35. Christides in Bumazhnov *et al.* (2011), 513.
36. Christides in Bumazhnov *et al.* (2011), 519.
37. Nikephoros, *Brev.* 49.
38. Mango (2005) 89.
39. Mango in Mango and Dagron (1995), 17.
40. Koder Mango and Dagron (1995), 49–56.
41. Michael the Syrian II.484; cf. *Kitab al-Uyun* (Brooks (1899) 27); cf. Magdalino in Mango and Dagron (1995) 35–47.
42. Shepherd (2020), 25.
43. Theophanes, *Chron.* AM6209.
44. *Syn. CP* 904. 18.
45. Olsen (2020), 426–427 n.9, raises the idea but doubts it.
46. Nikephoros, *Brev.* 54.5.
47. Mango and Scott (1997), 548 n.16.
48. Theophanes, *Chron.* AM6209.
49. *Chr.1234* 159.
50. *Chr.1234* 158.
51. Theophanes, *Chron.* AM6209.
52. Tabari XXIV.1317.
53. *Chr.1234* 158.
54. *Kitab al-Uyun* (Brooks (1899), 23.
55. *Chr.1234* 158; cf. Tabari XXIV.1317.

56. *Chr.1234* 159.
57. Theophanes, *Chron*. AM6209.
58. At this point in his text (*Chron*. AM6209), Theophanes is clearly copying from another source as he would never call Leo III, the man who by the early-ninth century when Theophanes was writing, was considered the originator of iconoclasm, 'the pious emperor' who gained God's help against the Arabs…
59. Theophanes, *Chron*. AM6209; cf. Nikephoros, *Brev*. 54.
60. Howard-Johnston (2011), 510.
61. Theophanes, *Chron*. AM6209; cf. Nikephoros, *Brev*. 54.3–18.
62. There are numerous dates given for Sulayman's death: 20 September (Elias of Nisibis 77.26–27); 22 September (mentioned by Tabari XIV.1336); 1 October (Tabari XIV.1336 citing Hisham Abu Mikhnaf and Ahmad b. Thabit); 8 October (Theophanes, *Chron*. AM6209); *Chr. 819* 11 and *Chr. 846* 177 merely mention September, while Michael the Syrian II.485 and *Chr. 1234* 238.21–25 do not mention a day or month (cf. Mango and Scott (1997) 547).
63. Dols (1974), 379.
64. Tabari XIV.1341.
65. Bosworth (1972).
66. Tabari XIV.1341.
67. Tabari XIV.1341.
68. Shaban (1971) 130.
69. Ibn Asakir, *Tarikh Dimashq* (Tritton, MacKenzie and Derrett (1959), 350–352 on a manuscript, *Or*. 9052 f.18r, in the British Museum).
70. Grumel (1958).
71. Tabari XXIV.1317 on the Slavs tricking reinforcements sent by Sulayman under Mas'adah or Amr b. Qais.
72. *Chr.1234* 157.
73. There are some chronological issues with these sources, with the *Kitab al-Uyun* having Leo not present in Constantinople at the outset of the siege, while Tabari XIV.1316 has the following diplomatic contact take place just before the siege began.
74. Tabari XXIV.1316.
75. *Kitab al-Uyun* (Brooks (1899), 23).
76. Tabari XXIV.1316.
77. *Kitab al-Uyun* (Brooks (1899), 25).
78. *Kitab al-Uyun* (Brooks (1899), 26).
79. *Kitab al-Uyun* (Brooks (1899), 26).
80. *Kitab al-Uyun* (Brooks (1899), 27).
81. The relevant *synaxarion* appears in various forms in the *Vindo. Hist. gr.*, *Synaxarium Ecclesiae Constantinopolitae* and the *Menologion of Basil II*; cf. Olsen (2020).
82. Constantine VII, *de adm. imp.* 102.
83. Lewond, *History* 112–113; Stephanos of Taron (Greenwood (2017), 192).
84. Constantine VII, *de adm. imp.* 101–102.
85. Hasluck (1929), II.720.
86. Hasluck (1929), II.717–735; El-Cheikh (2004) 64.
87. Olsen (2020) 439.
88. *Chiu-t'ang-shu* 198; there are similar records of this embassy in the *Hsin-t'ang-shu* 221 and Ma Tuan-lin, *Wen-hsien-t'ung-k'ao* 330, but both of these are more recent than the mid-tenth century *Chiu-t'ang-shu*, and likely derive their information from it; cf. Hirth (1885), 35–96.
89. Dunlop (1954), 60–61; Artamonov (1962), 205.
90. Theophanes, *Chron*. AM6209; Nikephoros, *Brev*. 54.

91. *Kitab al-Uyun* (Brooks (1899), 28) had Sulayman as the caliph who could not resupply Maslamah in the winter of 717/718, but he was dead before then. It will have been Umar II who would have tried and failed to resupply the expedition at this point.
92. Tabari XXIV.1316; cf. *Kitab al-Uyun* (Brooks (1899) 29); Theophanes, *Chron.* AM6209; Nikephoros, *Brev.* 54.
93. Michael the Syrian II.485
94. *Kitab al-Uyun* (Brooks (1899) 29).
95. Michael the Syrian II.485.
96. Tabari XXIV.1317; cf. *Chr.1234* 160.
97. Theophanes, *Chron.* AM6209.
98. Severus b. al-Muqatta III.16.
99. John of Nikiu CXX.32.
100. Michael the Syrian II.485.
101. Theophanes, *Chron.* AM6209; Nikephoros, *Brev.* 54.
102. Theophanes, *Chron.* AM6209; Nikephoros, *Brev.* 54.
103. Theophanes, *Chron.* AM6209.
104. Theophanes, *Chron.* AM6209.
105. Theophanes, *Chron.* AM6209.
106. Theophanes, *Chron.* AM6209; cf. Tabari XXIV.1317; *Chr.1234* 160.
107. *Chron. 1234* 162.
108. *Chron. 1234* 162.
109. *Chron. 1234* 162; cf. *Kitab al-Uyun* (Brooks (1899), 29.
110. *Chronicle of Zuqnin* AG1028.
111. *Chron. 1234* 162.
112. *Kitab al-Uyun* (Brooks (1899), 29).
113. *Chronicle of Zuqnin* AG1028.
114. Nikephoros, *Brev.* 56; *Chronicle of Zuqnin* 13; Michael the Syrian II.486; *Chr. 1234* 239.1–3.
115. Theophanes, *Chron.* AM6210; cf. Germanos, *Hom.* (Grumel (1958), 197).
116. Nikephoros, *Brev.* 56; Theophanes, *Chron.* AM6210.
117. Theophanes, *Chron.* AM6218.
118. Haldon (1990), 83.
119. Haldon (2016), 1.
120. *Kitab al-Uyun* (Brooks (1899), 24).
121. Christides in Bumazhnov *et al.* (2011), 519.
122. Theophanes, *Chron.* AM6209.
123. Turner (1990), 420.
124. Turner (1990), 420–421; Grumel (1958), on Germanos, *Hom.*
125. Howard-Johnston (2011), 512.
126. Kaegi (1981), 225.
127. Howard-Johnston (2011), 462.
128. Brubaker (2012), 25.
129. Haldon (2016), 55.
130. Howard-Johnston (2011), 392; Borrut (2005), 329–378; that focus on religious policy within the Umayyad caliphate was also said to have affected that within the Roman Empire.
131. El-Cheikh (2004), 65–70; Brandes (2007), 65–91.
132. Howard-Johnston (2011), 510–512 on the changing Roman strategies and tactics under Leo III and others.

Chapter 7: Internal Enemies: The Rebellions Against Leo III

1. Theophanes, *Chron.* AM6211.
2. Theophanes, *Chron.* AM6207.

3. Theophanes, *Chron.* AM6209.
4. Nikephoros, *Brev.* 56.
5. cf. Theophanes, *Chron.* AM6209; Jones (1964), 304, 372.
6. Theophanes, *Chron.* AM6211.
7. Nikephoros, *Brev.* 58; Theophanes, *Chron.* AM6212 merely states that it took place on Easter Day, without giving a specific date.
8. Grumel (1958), 248.
9. Theophanes, *Chron.* AM6213 also has a rebellion in Syria in 720/721 under a certain Severus, who convinced some Jews that he was the Messiah.
10. Theophanes, *Chron.* AM6210; Nikephoros, *Brev.* 55.
11. Theophanes, *Chron.* AM6210.
12. Nikephoros, *Brev.* 55; Brown (1984), 65 on this being Paul, the later exarch of Ravenna.
13. While Theophanes, *Chron.* AM6210 suggests that becoming patrician was part of Paul's promotion at this point, Nikephoros, *Brev.* 55 seems to suggest that Paul was already a patrician.
14. Theophanes, *Chron.* AM6210.
15. Nikephoros, *Brev.* 55.
16. Theophanes, *Chron.* AM6210.
17. Theophanes, *Chron.* AM6211 dates it to 'the same year' as the baptism of the future Constantine V, which took place on Christmas Day 718, although this 'same year' is likely the Byzantine indiction year of 718/719, placing Anastasius' attempted return more likely at some point in 719 before 1 September.
18. Mango and Scott (1997), 553 n.8.
19. Nikephoros, *Brev.* 57; cf. Cankova-Petkova (1963), 41–53; Kaegi (1981), 211–212; Besevliev (1980), 201–202.
20. Ahrweiler (1966), 28–29.
21. Charanis (1970), 243–244.
22. There is some dispute over which walls Niketas Anthrax was commander of, with this being the first mention of the office. Croke (1982) rejects the suggestion of Bury (1911) 67–68 that it was the Anastasian Walls, while Oikonomides (1972) 336–337 and Haldon (1984) 265f. suggest that Anthrax commanded the walls of the imperial palace; cf. Mango and Scott (1997), 553 n.12.
23. Kaegi (1981), 212.
24. Canokova-Petkova (1963), 41–53.
25. Theophanes, *Chron.* AM6211.
26. Theophanes, *Chron.* AM6211.
27. Mango and Scott (1997), 553 n.8.
28. Grierson (1962), 52.
29. Theophanes, *Chron.* AM6218; cf. Nikephoros, *Brev.* 60.
30. Treadgold (1995), 26.
31. Treadgold (1995), 67–68 suggests 2,000 soldiers/marines to 6,500 oarsmen.
32. https://www.doaks.org/resources/seals/byzantine-seals/BZS.1958.106.667; https://harvardartmuseums.org/collections/object/72528; Nesbitt and Oikonomides (1994), 110–112.
33. cf. Zuckerman (2005), 111–119; Brubaker and Haldon (2011), 725–726 n.4.
34. Treadgold (1997), 352.
35. Theophanes, *Chron.* AM6187.
36. Theophanes, *Chron.* AM6218.
37. Nikephoros, *Brev.* 60.
38. Nikephoros, *Brev.* 60.
39. *Patria* III.133.

40. Theophanes, *Chron.* AM6218.
41. Theophanes, *Chron.* AM6229; Michael the Syrian II. 503–504; *Chr. 1234*, 242.22–243.21; Bar Hebraeus I.110.
42. Cook (1992); Cook in Motzki (2016), 217–241; Hoyland (1997), 333f.
43. Head (1972), 18.
44. There is some question as to how much initial say Justinian had in the naming of his son, for he was absent on his campaign to regain the throne in 704/705 when Theodora gave birth to Tiberios – the soon-to-be emperor again might have left instructions that should their child be male then he was to be named Tiberios, but it could also be that Theodora was showing some honour to the current emperor – Tiberius III Apsimar – to try to shield them from imperial attack in case Justinian was to fail in regaining the throne. It was certainly an unexpected bonus to be able to choose a name that had both Heraclian roots *and* honoured the usurper then sitting on the 'Heraclian throne'.
45. Theophanes, *Chron.* AM6171, 6161, 6159–6160.
46. Kaegi (1981), 168
47. Haldon (2016), 153.
48. Kaegi (1981), 204.
49. Herrin in Bryer and Herrin (1975) 17.
50. Theophanes, *Chron.* AM6233.
51. Kaegi (1981), 237.
52. Kaegi (1981), 213.
53. Kaegi (1981), 202, 203.
54. Kaegi (1981), 203.
55. Kaegi (1981), 201.
56. Kaegi (1981), 190; Theophanes, *Chron.* AM6203; Nikephoros, *Brev.* 47.
57. Kaegi (1981), 207.
58. Kaegi (1981), 207–208.

Chapter 8: Deliberate Destruction of Icons?: Leonid Religious Policies

1. Brubaker (2012), xv
2. Brubaker and Haldon (2011), 2.
3. Brubaker and Haldon (2011), 5.
4. Brubaker (2012), xv.
5. Humphreys (2015), 267.
6. Huxley (1980), 189.
7. Brubaker and Haldon (2011), 4.
8. Brubaker and Haldon (2011), 2.
9. cf. Ladner (1953).
10. Tempera is use of water, oil or eggs to bind a pigment into an emulsion, while encaustic is the fusing of the pigment and wax to the surface through the application of heat.
11. There are numerous other Greek words for images and statues that could be considered 'icons' – *andrias, bretas, hedos, hidruma, kolossos, xoanon* (Bremner (2008), 2 n.5), but many of them refer to specific mediums.
12. Brubaker (2012), 1.
13. Humphreys (2011), 152.
14. Noble (2011), 69.
15. Brubaker (2012), 6.
16. Cf. Noble (2011), 69 on complaints and evidence presented at the Second Council of Nicaea in 787.
17. Kitzinger (1977) 104–105.
18. Cicero, *de finibus* 5.1.3 on Epicureans worshiping representations of Epicurus.

19. Cf. Barnard in Bryer and Herrin (1975), 13
20. Mansi II.11.36; cf. Vasiliev (1964), I.254.
21. Eusebius, *HE* VII.18.4.
22. Maas (1929–1930).
23. Reynolds (2017).
24. *Little Iliad* 4 (West (2003), 123); cf. Virgil, *Aeneid* II.163.
25. Brubaker (2012), 13.
26. Cf. Brubaker (2012), 14.
27. Brubaker (2012), 9.
28. Re-enacting an edict of Theodosius II; Breckenridge (1959), 82.
29. Head (1972), 77.
30. *LP* I.372.
31. Brubaker (2012), 17.
32. Samuelson (2016), 84.
33. Breckenridge (1959), 2.
34. Breckenridge (1959), 2, 83–86; Head (1972), 77; Grabar (1936); Ladner (1940); (1953); Kitzinger (1954).
35. Barnard in Bryer and Herrin (1975), 12.
36. Wickham (2009), 268.
37. Head (1972), 77; Kitzinger (1954), 120.
38. Von Grunebaum (1962), 1–10.
39. Brock in Bryer and Herrin (1975), 55.
40. Brubaker (2012), 16.
41. Brubaker (2012), 17.
42. Brubaker (2012), 19.
43. Depending on the division or denomination, 'Thou shalt not make unto thee any graven image' is either the First (Catholicism, Lutheranism, Samaritan, Augustinian) or the Second (Septuagint, Talmudic, Reformed, Philonic) Commandment.
44. The recovery of Germanikeia by Constantine V in 746 likely aided the elevation of the idea of Leo's divinely laid out path to imperial power.
45. Theophanes, *Chron.* AM6218; Theophanes, *Chron.* AM6233 also uses this term for Besr; it is also used at the Second Council of Nicaea in 787, while John of Damascus was anathematised as κακωνυμω και σαρακηνοφρονι at the Council of Hieria in 754. This use of the term derisively against both sides of the iconoclastic divide could suggest 'that the term was simply one of abuse and did not refer to Muslim influence as a historical fact' (Barnard (1974), 27) or could it be an abusive term that also had a specific meaning? Other prominent individuals of the iconoclastic era are claimed to have similar geographical origins to Leo, with Eutychius of Alexandria having Leo's ally/son-in-law Artabasdos being from Mar'ash, while the Slavonic *Life of Stephen of Suroz* had the first iconoclastic patriarch, Anastasius, being of Syrian origin; Gero (1974b) 25.
46. Theophanes, *Chron.* AM6210.
47. Gero (1974b), 23–24.
48. Gero (1974b), 26.
49. Jeffery (1944), Gaudeul (1984); Kim (2017).
50. Kim (2017), 2.
51. Jeffery (1944), 269.
52. Theophanes, *Chron.* AM6215; Nikephoros, *Anti.* III *PG* 100 528f; Mansi XIII.196 E-200; Vasiliev (1956), 27.
53. The date of Yazid's iconoclastic edict is not the same in all sources; Vasiliev (1956), 47 considers July 721 the most likely, but as it is not thought to have lasted long, it was likely latter in Yazid's reign; Sahner (2017).

54. Theophanes, *Chron.* AM6215.
55. Sahner (2017), 56.
56. Barnard (1974), 18 n.23; Brubaker and Haldon (2011), 105–117; Grabar in Bryer and Herrin (1975), 46.
57. Sahner (2017), 55.
58. Cf. Vasiliev (1956), 37–39.
59. Vasiliev (1956), 27–29 n.12.
60. Gero (1974a), 59–84, 189–198.
61. Qur'an V.92; Gero (1974b), 36–37.
62. Reynolds (2017), 62.
63. Gero (1974b), 37–38.
64. Theophanes, *Chron.* AM6215.
65. Theophanes, *Chron.* AM6215, 6216.
66. Theophanes, *Chron.* AM6215.
67. Boyce (1975).
68. Shenkar (2015), 492.
69. Vasiliev (1964), I.255.
70. Gero (1974b), 32; Kitizinger (1954), 131.
71. cf. Brock in Bryer and Herrin (1975).
72. Leo's Isaurian successors, Constantine V and Leo IV, are claimed to have had some Monophysite sympathies, but it has been pointed out that Monophysite doctrine would allow for divine power permeating the matter of icons (cf. Gero (1974b), 33).
73. Alexander in Weitzmann (1955), 155–160; Alexander (1978), ch.7.
74. Garsoian (1971), 103; rejected by Gero (1974b), 34–35.
75. Brown (1973), 41.
76. Cf. Ladner (1940), 127–149.
77. Cf. Turner (1990), 421.
78. Vryonis (1971), 6–23 on the decline of Anatolian urbanism and Roman control being more an eleventh-century problem in the face of the Turks, rather than an eighth-century issue in the face of the Arabs.
79. Brown (1973), 31.
80. cf. Ahrweiler (1962), 27; (1966) 40–41.
81. Brown (1973), 41.
82. cf. Kaegi (1966), 48–70
83. Cheynet (2000) 281–322.
84. Mango in Bryer and Herrin (1975), 2.
85. Nikephoros, *Brev.* 59.
86. Theophanes, *Chron.* AM6210.
87. Nikephoros, *Brev.* 60.
88. Nikephoros, *Brev.* 59.
89. Theophanes, *Chron.* AM6218.
90. Theophanes, *Chron.* AM6217.
91. Theophanes, *Chron.* AM6218.
92. cf. Ostrogorsky (1930) and Ladner (1940).
93. Turtledove (1982), 95 n.187; cf. Anastos (1966), 61–104, 835–848; Anastos (1968) 5–41.
94. Anastos (1968) 8–10 on 'order'; Ostrogorsky (1930), I.235–255; (1969) 162–164 on 'discussion'.
95. *Vita Stephani iun.*, *PG* 100: 1084C.
96. *LP* 91.16–17.
97. Gouillard (1968), 260; Mango and Scott (1997), 559 n.3.
98. Mango (1959), 112.
99. Theophanes, *Chron.* AM6218.

100. Theophanes, *Chron.* AM6218; Nikephoros, *Brev.* 60.
101. Ostrogorsky (1930) supports their authenticity.
102. Mango (1959), 114.
103. Mango (1959), 119, 112ff.
104. Cf. Mango (1959), 119.
105. Mango (1959), 171.
106. Theophanes, *Chron.* AM6221.
107. Auzepy (1990), 445–492.
108. Theophanes, *Chron.* AM6218.
109. Nikephoros, *Brev.* 61.
110. Mango and Scott (1997), 562 n.11.
111. *Vita Willibaldi* 101.25.
112. Theophanes, *Chron.* AM6218.
113. Nikephoros, *Brev.* 64; Theophanes, *Chron.* AM6233; Brubaker and Haldon (2011), 80f/156–159; Baldwin (1990), 428.
114. Zonaras XIV.20.2–3.
115. Barnard (1973), 15; cf. Justinian, *Novel* 6.
116. Gregory II, *Ep.* 13 – spurious letter?
117. Barnard (1973), 28.
118. Barnard (1973), 18–19.
119. Theophanes, *Chron.* AM6218.
120. Brubaker and Haldon (2011), 94–105.
121. Theophanes, *Chron.* AM6215; Ostrogorsky (1930), 236–237 on Constantine of Nakoleia being the main instigator of iconoclasm.
122. Brubaker (2012), 23–24.
123. Cf. Theophanes, *Chron.* AM6218.
124. Elsner (2012), 386.
125. Huxley (1980), 192.
126. Mango in Bryer and Herrin (1975), 1.
127. Theophanes, *Chron.* AM6221.
128. Theophanes, *Chron.* AM6221.
129. *Synkellos* was originally the name of a monk who lived with his bishop – its literal meaning is 'one who shares a cell', to witness the purity of the bishop's life, but over time it developed into a position of patriarchal adviser with considerable power and influence, including seats and votes on church councils.
130. Theophanes, *Chron.* AM6221.
131. Theophanes, *Chron.* AM6235.
132. This could have been '17th' because '7th' was a Saturday.
133. Theophanes, *Chron.* AM6221; Gero (1975), 141–146 on it using Gregory Nazianus, *de seipso* PG37 1158 v.1838–1842, with Gregory willing to sacrifice himself for concord, even if he did not cause the storm.
134. Nikephoros, *Brev.* 62.
135. Theophanes, *Chron.* AM6221; Nikephoros, *Brev.* 62.
136. *LP* 91.24.
137. Theophanes, *Chron* AM6177.
138. *Synodicon vetus* c.147; cf. Lamza (1975), 178–179.
139. Ostrogorsky (1930), I.235–255; Ostrogorsky (1969), 162–164.
140. Mango and Scott (1997), 566 n.11; Constantine of Lyon, *Vita Germani* 27, 31; *Synodicon vetus* c.147.
141. Theophanes, *Chron.* AM6221; cf. Nikephoros, *Brev.* 62.
142. Auzepy (2001), 13–24.

143. Mango in Bryer and Herrin (1975), 6.
144. Wortley (1982), 253–279.
145. Turner (1990), 421.
146. Theophanes, *Chron.* AM6232.
147. Kaegi (1981), 264; Nikephoros, *Antirrhetici* 3.73.
148. Moorhead (1985), 179.
149. Ahrweiler in Bryer and Herrin (1975), 25.
150. cf. Vasiliev (1964), I.255.
151. Grumel (1952), 191–200; Ostrogorsky (1956), 170.
152. Anastos (1957); Runciman (1955); Turtledove (1982), 96 n.187.
153. Runciman (1955), 20.
154. Mauskopf Deliyannis (1996).
155. Riche (1993), 652ff.
156. Brubaker (2012), xv, 27.
157. Brubaker (2012), xv.
158. Turner (1990).
159. Herrin in Bryer and Herrin (1975), 19.
160. Turner (1990), 421; cf. Humphreys (2014), 267.
161. Brubaker (2012), 28.
162. 1 Samuel 22.18.
163. Brubaker (2012), 28.
164. Brubaker (2012), 29.
165. Brubaker (2012), 29.
166. Brubaker (2012), 24
167. Cf. Ahrweiler in Bryer and Herrin (1975), 22.
168. Ahrweiler in Bryer and Herrin (1975), 22; Gero (1973), 90–93.
169. Barnard in Bryer and Herrin (1975), 12.
170. Barnard in Bryer and Herrin (1975), 12.
171. Theophanes, *Chron.* AM6214.
172. *Chr. 1234*, 240.26–7; Elias Nis. 78; Michael the Syrian II.489–90; Agapios 244.
173. Olster (1994), 84–92; cf. Booth (2014), 170–171; Haldon (1997a), 345–348.
174. Theophanes, *Chron.* AM6213; Michael the Syrian II.490; *Chr. 1234*, 240.18–25; Agapios 244; *Chronicle of Zuqnin* 25–27.
175. *Ekloga* 17.52; cf. *CI* 1.5.16.
176. Theophanes, *Chron.* AM6214.
177. Procopius, *Secret History* 11.23.
178. Auzepy in Shepard (2019), 288–289.
179. cf. Starr (1936).
180. Peter of Sicily, *History of the Paulicians.*
181. Kelly (1978), 115–119.
182. Garsoian (1967), 13–26.
183. Dixon (2022), 50–51; Conybeare (1898), xxxvi.
184. Garsoian (1967), 231–233.
185. The date of this patriarchal interview is unknown, so it is uncertain if this patriarch was Germanos (715–730) or Anastasius (730–754).
186. Peter of Sicily, *History of the Paulicians* 113–22; cf. Dixon (2022), 33.
187. Cedrenus II.10 has Paulicians settled in Constantinople under Constantine, but this may be more out of need of repopulating the city after the plague outbreak of 746–747 rather than establishing Paulicians specifically in the city; that said, George Monachus 750–751 accused Constantine of being a Paulician. It is worth noting that Theophanes is the only source to specifically mention Paulicians amongst those transplanted to Thrace: George Monachus

752 refers to the transplanted as just 'heretics', while Michael the Syrian comments on them being Monophysites from around Melitene. Constantine's transplanting of Syrians and Armenians from around Theodosiopolis and Melitene to Thrace were repopulation moves, that may have had the side-effect of establishing some Paulicians in that area, as well as in Constantinople (Theophanes, *Chron.* AM6247).

188. Haldon (2016), 184, 185.
189. Humphreys (2011), 151; Herrin in Bryer and Herrin (1975), 17.
190. Prieto Dominguez (2020), 434.
191. Ahrweiler in Bryer and Herrin (1975), 25.
192. Prieto Dominguez (2020), 439.
193. Gero (1974a), 25.
194. Huxley (1980), 190.
195. Herrin in Bryer and Herrin (1975), 17.
196. Kaegi (1981), 221; cf. *Ekloga* praef.
197. Humphreys (2014), 268.
198. Prieto Dominguez (2020), 428; Brubaker and Haldon (2011), 5.

Chapter 9: Law and Order: The Administration of Leo III

1. The four sections were the *Codex Justinianus*, the *Digesta*, the *Institutiones* and the *Novellae*.
2. Humphreys (2017), 5.
3. Humphreys (2017), 2.
4. cf. Burgmann (1983), 10–12, 100–104.
5. Humphreys (2017), 14.
6. cf. *Ekloga* II.3, 9.
7. Humphreys (2017), 14.
8. *Ekloga*, praef.
9. Humphreys (2017), 15.
10. Code of Hammurabi (King, L.W. translation, https://avalon.law.yale.edu/ancient/hamframe.asp, 2008).
11. Sperati (2009); Mazzola (1987), 4 and Yalamanchili *et al.* (2008), 3.
12. Martial, *Epig.* II.83, III.85 has *rhinokopia* as a punishment for adultery in the first century AD.
13. Head (1972), 26.
14. Cf. *NJ* 134.
15. Stumpf (2017), 48.
16. Jovian's son Varronianus may have had his eye removed to prevent him being an imperial candidate, while Priscus Attalus had his hand mutilated by Honorius after his capture in 416 (John Chrysostom, *Hom. ad Philipp.* 15; *ad vid. iun.* 4; Orosius, *Hist. adv. Pag.* 7.42.9; Marcell. com. 412; Olympiodorus frag. 13; Procopius, *BV* III.3.9).
17. Suetonius, *Cla.* 3.2.
18. John of Nikiu, CXX.52, 54; Theophanes, *Chron.* AM6133.
19. Stumpf (2017), 46–54 on the frequency of mutilation and the changing of punishments like fashion.
20. Gregory of Tours, *HF* X.18; Qur'an 5:33, 38
21. Amos 2:6; *Ekloga* II.13.
22. Vasiliev (1964), 244.
23. Humphreys (2014), 268.
24. Humphreys (2014), 269.
25. Ahrweiler in Bryer and Herrin (1975), 26.
26. *Ekloga*, praef. 21–31; cf. Dagron (2003), 184; Rapp (2010); Haldon (1993b), 104–106; Haldon (2016), 122–123.
27. Haldon (2016), 132, 157; Meier (2012), 230–231; cf. Humphreys (2015), 73–80, 93–129, 255.

28. Humphreys (2015), 252.
29. Humphreys (2015), 253.
30. Head (1972), 26.
31. Humphreys (2015), 253.
32. *Nomos Mosaikos* 2.
33. Brown (1973), 1–34.
34. Humphreys (2014), 267.
35. Humphreys (2014), 267; cf. Anastos (1955).
36. Humphreys (2014), 270.
37. Humphreys (2017), 21.
38. It could be connected directly to section XIV.2 of the Justinianic *Digest*, the so-called 'Rhodian Law of Jettison'.
39. Ashburner (1909), cxii-cxiv; Humphreys (2017), 26.
40. cf. Humphreys (2015), 196–201.
41. Head (1972), 83; Ostrogorsky (1959), 45–47; (1968), 132–137; Cheynet (2006), 152.
42. Charanis (1963) surveys the arguments; Kaegi (1967), 40–43.
43. Head (1972), 84; Lemerle (1954), 265–308; (1958), 63–65 on the arguments on Slavic agricultural influence.
44. Humphreys (2017), 28.
45. Ostrogorsky (1953).
46. Vernadskij (1925), 172; Setton (1953), 233–234.
47. Vernadskij (1925), 172–173; Ostrogorsky (1968), 90–91; Jenkins (1966), 53 considered that the Farmer's Law was 'almost universally attributed' to Justinian II; *contra* Dolger (1944–1945), II.21–48; Lemerle (1958), 49–55; Karayannopulos (1958), 357–373; Ostrogorsky (1968), 90–91, while Medvedev (1984) considers it to be a composition of the sixth century.
48. Toševa-Nikolovska (2018), 217.
49. Humphreys (2017), 29.
50. Humphreys (2017), 29.
51. cf. *NG* 81; Mitchell (1993), II.133.
52. Breckenridge (1959), 18–27, 51, 63–68.
53. Humphreys (2013), 232; Head (1972), 56.
54. Humphreys (2013) questions the idea of these coin reforms fuelling a 'War of Images' between Justinian II and Abd al-Malik.
55. Humphreys (2013), 231.
56. Heidemann in Neuwirth *et al.* (2010), 157.
57. Heidemann in Neuwirth *et al.* (2010), 170.
58. Heidemann in Neuwirth *et al.* (2010), 184–185.
59. Grierson (1999), 13–14.
60. *Miliaresion* was also an alternative name given to the short-lived Heraclian *hexagram*.
61. Brubaker and Haldon (2001), 118.
62. Haldon (2016), 256.
63. Humphreys (2017), 9.
64. Humphreys (2015), 259.
65. Humphreys (2015), 259.
66. Hahn (1981), III.17.
67. Grierson (1965), 191.
68. Haldon (2016), 256.
69. Haldon (2016), 265; Brubaker and Haldon (2011), 695–717.
70. Humphreys (2015), 263.
71. Oikonides in Laiou (2002), 981
72. Haldon (2016), 257.

73. Teall (1971), 47–48 and Oikonomides (1975), 1–8 both support Heraclius being the thematic originator; Toynbee (1973), 224–238, Lilie (1976), 287–338, Haldon (1975), 81–82, 96–107, Pertusi (1958), 1–40 and Karayannopoulos (1959) all follow the gradual evolution approach
74. Humphreys (2015), 261.
75. Brooks (1901), 67–77 on Arab lists of Roman themes.
76. Runciman (1955), 20.
77. Anastos (1957) and Runciman (1955) vs Grumel (1952) and Ostrogorsky (1969), 170.
78. Theophanes, *Chron.* AM6224.
79. cf. Ahrweiler (1966), 31–35.
80. Ahrweiler (1966), 26–31; Pryor and Jeffreys (2006), 32.
81. Treadgold (1997), 352.
82. Theophanes, *Chron.* AM6224; Ahrweiler (1966), 26.
83. Theophanes, *Chron.* AM6190; Nikephoros, *Brev.* 41, with Nikephoros mentioning a contingent of Kibyrrhaeots from Korykos.
84. Herrin (1986), I.120–121.
85. Tsourgarakis (1988), 171.
86. Al-Maqrizi, *al-Khitat* 61.8.
87. Theophanes, *Chron.* AM6238; Nikephoros, *Brev.* 67–68; Pryor and Jeffreys (2006), 33.
88. Pryor and Jeffreys (2006), 33.
89. Bashear (1991).
90. Brubaker and Haldon (2011), 705–709.
91. Magdalino in Laiou and Simon (1994), 93–115; Brubaker and Haldon (2011), 676–677.
92. Haldon (2016), 165.
93. Winkelmann (1987).
94. Haldon (2016), 165.
95. Haldon (1999), 78; Haldon (1984), 228–235.
96. Haldon (2016), 152.
97. Cameron (1976).
98. Cameron (1976), 172–173; cf. *V. Steph. iun.* 1132f; Theophanes, *Chron.* AM6254 and Nikephoros. *Brev.* 76 on Constantine giving Bulgarian captives to the *demes* for execution.
99. Theophanes, *Chron.* AM6218
100. Nikephoros, *Brev.* 52.
101. Humphreys (2015), 260.
102. The lack of evidence that he did point to such a status during the civil war with Artabasdos would seem to show either his lack of need to rely on his status as a *Porphyrogenitus* over his older sister Anna or the lack of importance as yet placed in such a position.
103. Theophanes, *Chron.* AM6232; cf. Michael the Syrian II.504, 511; Agapios 249; Meg. *Chron.* c.15.
104. Theophanes, *Chron.* AM6232.
105. Nikephoros, *Brev.* 63.
106. Nikephoros, *Brev.* 63; George (1912), 5–6, 70 on upper part of building.
107. Theophanes, *Chron.* AM6232.
108. Theophanes, *Chron.* AM6232.
109. Theophanes, *Chron.* AM6232.
110. Ahrweiler in Bryer and Herrin (1975), 26.
111. Kaegi (1981), 221.

Chapter 10: From Constantinople to Akroinon: Romano-Arab Conflict 718–741

1. Tabari XXV.1395–1418; Theophanes, *Chron.* AM6212; *Chr. 1234*, 240.3–13; Michael the Syrian II.489; Elias of Nisibis 77–78.
2. Tabari XXV.1441–1449.

3. Theophanes, *Chron.* AM6218.
4. Theophanes, *Chron.* AM6218–6219; cf. *Chr. 819,* 11 AG1036, 12 AG1037; *Chr. 846,* 178; Michael the Syrian II.490–491; *Chr. 1234,* 241.18–24; Agapios 246; *Chronicle of Zuqnin* 24 all name 'Neocaesarea'; it is Caesarea in Elias of Nisibis 78 and Tabari XXV.29; Brooks (1898), 198–199; Leo Grammatikos 303; George Monachus *cont.* 889.
5. Blankinship (1994), 120.
6. Blankinship (1994), 119–120.
7. Blankinship (1994), 118–119.
8. These raids could be one and the same, with different leaders recorded by different sources; Theophanes, *Chron.* AM6216; Agapios 245; Tabari; Brooks (1898), 198.
9. Haldon (2016), 54.
10. Similar to his record of the revolt of Kosmas and Agallianos, Theophanes places the siege of Nicaea in his entry AM6218 – the year 725–726; however, he mentions that the siege took place in the 10th indiction, which places it in the summer of 727. This is backed by Nikephoros, *Brev.* 61, which states that the siege took place in the 'following summer' after the defeat of Kosmas and Agallianos.
11. Theophanes, *Chron.* AM6218; Nikephoros, *Brev.* 61; cf. Theophanes, *Chron.* AM6231; Mango and Scott (1997), 561–562 n.9.
12. Blankinship (1994), 314 n.20.
13. Blankinship (1994), 120–121.
14. Schneider and Karnapp (1938), 49, no.29, 150; cf. Mango (2005), 29–30.
15. Theophanes, *Chron.* AM6218.
16. Dunlop (1954), 51–54.
17. Noonan (1984), 182.
18. Blankinship (1994), 122.
19. Blankinship (1994), 124.
20. cf. *Chr. 1234,* 241.31–36; *Chr. 819* 12; *Chr. 846* 178; Michael the Syrian II.501 on two campaigns – flight of Arabs in AG1039 and a second in AG1042; Agapios 247; *Chronicle of Zuqnin* 21–23 (two Arab victories); Elias of Nisibis 79 (Maslamah in AH110 and 113).
21. cf. Theophanes, *Chron.* AM6224 *Chr.1234,* 241.25–30; *Elias of Nisibis 79; Michael the Syrian II.501 has the Khazars meeting Maslamah; Agapios 246; Chronicle of Zuqnin* 22–23.
22. Theophanes records many of these Arab and Khazar raids, although seemingly out of chronological sync with the Arab sources. He may also posit an extra Arab raid under Maslamah, which could be an example of Theophanes repeating information to fill a gap in his source material – a case of 'when in doubt posit an Arab raiding party'?
23. Dunlop (1954), 73–74; Blankinship (1994), 324 n.34.
24. This would be the last recorded command of Maslamah b. Abd al-Malik, one of the great Arab commanders of the era. While he played some role in the negotiations surrounding Hisham's accession, for the most part he lived out the rest of his life on his estates in Syria, dying on 24 December 738. Had he succeeded in taking Constantinople, there is no doubt that Maslamah would have been remembered as one of the great generals of the late antique/early medieval era.
25. Blankinship (1994), 153.
26. Theophanes, *Chron.* AM6224; Nikephoros, *Brev.* 63; Michael the Syrian II.501; *Chr. 1234,* 242.4–7, AG 1041; Agapios 247.
27. Constantine VII, *de caer.* I.1, line 19.
28. Erdal in Golden, Ben-Shammai and Roná-Tas (2007), 80 n.22.
29. Theophanes, *Chron.* AM6224.
30. Blankinship (1994), 170–171.
31. Blankinship (1994), 171.
32. Blankinship (1994), 172–173.

33. Blankinship (1994), 173 on how the text of al-Baladhuri, *Futuh* 245 suggests that the original source for this story of khagan conversion, Ibn A'tham, has been altered/misinterpreted with it being a Khazar noble, not the khagan who had accepted Islam and was taken south by Marwan where he became the leader of the Muslim Khazar settlement at al-Lakz.
34. Dunlop (1954), 86–87.
35. Blankinship (1994), 173.
36. Blankinship (1994), 121.
37. Blankinship (1994), 121.
38. Theophanes, *Chron.* AM6222 has the capture of Charsianon as an action of Maslamah.
39. Theophanes, *Chron.* AM6225; Michael the Syrian II.504; Agapios 248.
40. Theophanes, *Chron.* AM6226; cf. *Chr. 1234,* 242.15–16, AG 1043; Agapios 248.
41. Theophanes, *Chron.* AM6227; cf. *Chr. 1234,* 242.17–19, which has Suleiman invade Roman territory; cf. Agapios 248.
42. Theophanes, *Chron.* AM6229.
43. Theophanes, *Chron.* AM6228; cf. *Chr. 1234,* 242.20–21; Agapios 248; Elias of Nisibis 80 records Mu'awiyah's death in AH119.
44. Theophanes, *Chron.* AM6230; Agapios 248 records the capture of the fort Soudour in what would be AM6227, while Tabari XXV.167 calls it Sindirah and places its capture in 737/738.
45. Blankinship (1994), 169.
46. Theophanes, *Chron.* AM6231.
47. Theophanes, *Chron.* AM6231; there is no mention of the episode in Nikephoros.
48. MacDonald (1924), 81; Ramsay (1924), 2 on al-Battal's death at Akroinon becoming the basis for the story of the Turkish national hero Saiyid Battal Ghazi.
49. Theophanes, *Chron.* AM6231; there may be some translation issues here with the '6,800' number – it could actually mean that 800 Arabs escaped under pressure from 6,000 enemies (Mango and Scott (1997), 571 n.5).
50. Blankinship (1994), 212.
51. Lilie (1976), 152–154.
52. Blankinship (1994), 170 n.14.
53. Blankinship (1994), 200.
54. Haldon (2016), 54.
55. Blankinship (1994), 170.
56. *Chronicon ad 1234,* 244.6–13; cf. Theophanes, *Chron.* AM6232; Michael the Syrian II.501.
57. Theophanes, *Chron.* AM6218, 6226.
58. Haldon (2016), 54.
59. *Vita Willibaldi* 160; cf. Constantine VII, *de them.* 53–54 refers to the days of Constantine V as a time when 'the whole of the Peloponnesus became slavonized and barbarian.'
60. Theophanes, *Chron.* AM6275.

Chapter 11: Italian Afterthought: Papacy, Lombards and Franks

1. *LP* 87.1.
2. *LP* 90.2; Agnellus 366–371, with the latter claiming that the reason behind Justinian's attack on Ravenna was revenge for leading Ravennate citizens playing a part in his deposition and mutilation in 695. It is possible that Agnellus has a vested interest in plugging into this 'black legend' surrounding Justinian because the writer himself was a descendant from a man – Johannicus – who died during the imperial action against Ravenna.
3. *LP* 90.4.
4. It seems unlikely that Justinian II would order such a purge without papal knowledge or even acquiescence (Head (1972), 141). That the officials targeted were members of the papal treasury could suggest that there was some corruption involved (Richards (1979),

212). Might these officials have publicly opposed the rapprochement between the papacy and Constantinople (Ekonomou (2007), 271)? Or might Rizocopus have thrown his lot in with the Ravennate rebels and was targeting the papal consistory in the absence of he pope, who was *en route* to Constantinople?

5. Head (1972), 141.
6. Agnellus 142.
7. *LP* 90.11.
8. Noble (1984), 33 n.90.
9. Davis (2007), 14 n.67.
10. Paul the Deacon, *HL* VI.44, although the Cottian Alps would later be reconquered by Liutprand and then restored again.
11. *LP* 91.7; Davis (2007), 7 n.29.
12. *LP* 91.13; Paul the Deacon, *HL* VI.48.
13. It would not be returned by Liutprand until the tenure of Pope Zacharias, so between 741 and 744 (Noble (1984), 50).
14. Paul the Deacon, *HL* VI.44, 49.
15. *LP* 91.13; cf. Agnellus 151.
16. *LP* 84.2; cf. Noye (2015), 346–367.
17. *LP* 91.16.
18. *LP* 91.14.
19. Noble (1984), 29.
20. Brown (1984), 65.
21. *LP* 91.15.
22. *LP* 91.16; Davis (2007), 11 n.47.
23. *LP* 91.16.
24. Paul the Deacon, *HL* VI.49; Noble (1984), 34.
25. *LP* 91.17.
26. Brubaker and Haldon (2011), 69–155.
27. A duchy that made up part of the exarchate, with its *dux* appointed by the exarch. Named for the 'five cities' – πεντάπολις – it covered along the Adriatic coast between the Marecchia and Misco rivers: Ancona, Sinigaglia, Fano, Pesaro and Rimini, with the lattermost serving as the ducal capital.
28. *LP* 91.17.
29. Noble (1984), 30; cf. *LP* 91.17.
30. *LP* 91.20.
31. *LP* 91.18.
32. *LP* 91.18; cf. Agnellus 153.
33. Gasparri in Gelichi and Gasparri (2017), 12–18.
34. Not only did these Lombardo-Venetian confrontations sprout a semi-legendary origin story, they also provided the basis for a long-term geographical division. While again not cited until the *Pactum Lotharii*, an agreement signed between Venice and the Frankish king Lothar I on 23 February 840, Marcello and Paolo are mentioned in the sub-text called the *terminatio liutprandina*, which delineated the borders around what was Eraclea in the early-eighth century (Eraclea had been refounded as Cittanova by the time of the *Pactum*). This agreement would be reaffirmed between the Franks/Holy Roman Empire and the Venetians regularly until the late-tenth century.
35. *LP* 91.18; Paul the Deacon, *HL* VI.49 records Bologna falling to Liutprand at this point, but this appears to be an error, although Bologna did fall to the Lombards seemingly by 735; *contra* Noble (1984), 41.
36. Davis (2007), 12 n.56.
37. Noble (1984), 31.

38. *LP* 91.21.
39. *LP* 91.21.
40. Noble (1984), 32, 40.
41. *LP* 91.19.
42. *LP* 91.22.
43. *LP* 91.22.
44. cf. Procopius, *BG* I.19.28–29, II.1–2.
45. *LP* 91.22.
46. Davis (2007), 14 n.67.
47. *LP* 91.23.
48. Brown in Shepard (2019), 442.
49. Theophanes, *Chron.* AM6224; Ahrweiler (1966), 51 n.1, 81–83 on this being the earliest mention of the Kibyrrhaeot *strategos.*
50. Davis (2007), 17.
51. Theophanes, *Chron.* AM6224.
52. Bertolini (1968), 15–49 on Manes' expedition.
53. It has been argued that the transition of these territories to the patriarchal jurisdiction of Constantinople did not happen until the 750s (Grumel (1952), 191–200; Ostrogorsky (1969), 170 n.1).
54. Noble (1984), 40.
55. Cf. Mann (1914), 208.
56. Paul the Deacon, *HL* VI.54.
57. Liutprand had fallen ill in the mid-730s and the Lombard nobles had jumped the gun, thinking Liutprand was about to die, and elected Hildeprand, only for the king to recover; Liutprand himself had been elected before the death of his father Ansprand (Grierson (1941).
58. It was for his involvement in the reclaiming of Ravenna for the exarchate – the aforementioned '80 ships' – that Ursus was reputedly given the title of *hypatos* by Leo III, which came to be associated with his name.
59. *LP* 92.15.
60. *LP* 92.15.
61. Cf. Paul the Deacon, *HL* VI.55, who gets his dates wrong, placing this in 729 during the Lombard-exarchate march on Rome.
62. Duke Gregory died sometime in 739–740, with Godescalc being one of the dead duke's senior military commanders. As this succession came without royal assent and was against the likely plan of Liutprand for the now of age Gisulf II to take the dukedom, it was to be considered a usurpation.
63. Paul the Deacon, *HL* VI.54.
64. *LP* 93.2; the biography of Zacharias provides a useful round up of some events that took place in the last years of Gregory III's reign.
65. *LP* 93.2 refers to a blockade of Rome by Liutprand, resistance to which was helped by repairs done to the walls of Rome by both Gregory II and Gregory III; cf. *LP* 91.2, 92.15.
66. Cf. Davis (2007), 34 n.6.
67. This was not the first Frankish involvement in Italy, with an ill-advised Lombard raid into Provence in 584/585 provoking a furious counter-invasion by the Franks and almost a Romano-Frankish alliance.
68. Charles had had his son Pepin 'adopted' by Liutprand, having sent him to the Lombard court for a symbolic haircut (Paul the Deacon, *HL* VI.53).
69. *LP* 93.3.
70. Noble (1984), 45, but the chronology is uncertain.
71. Noble (1984), 47–48.
72. Noble (1984), 48.

73. Paul the Deacon, *HL* VI.56–57.
74. Noble (1984), 52.

Chapter 12: Leonid End and Isaurian Epilogue: Trouble with the In-Laws

1. Theophanes, *Chron.* AM6232; Nikephoros, *Brev.* 64.
2. Theophanes, *Chron.* AM6233.
3. Theophanes, *Chron.* AM6233.
4. Kaegi (1981), 224.
5. Nikephoros, *Brev.* 61; Theophanes, *Chron.* AM6234.
6. Theophanes, *Chron.* AM6235; Nikephoros, *Brev.* 62.
7. Kaegi (1981), 214.
8. Kaegi (1981), 213.
9. Kaegi (1981), 237
10. Theophanes, *Chron.* AM6211, 6218.
11. cf. Lampros (1886), III.729.
12. Haldon (2016), 55
13. Haldon (2016), 53.
14. Vasiliev (1964), 269.
15. Shepard in Shepard (2019), 30–31.
16. Theophanes, *Chron.* AM6232.

Appendix: A brief History of Greek Fire

1. Thucydides VII.53.4; Arrian, *Anabasis* II.19; Quintus Curtius, *History of Alexander* IV.3.3–7; Appian, *The Syrian Wars* V.27; Livy XXXVII.11, 30; Appian, *The Punic Wars* 99; Caesar, *Civil War* III.101; Dio L.34 on Octavian and Agrippa using fire missiles, pots and possibly even fireships at Actium; Procopius, *BV* I.6.20–21.
2. Leicester (1971), 75; Crosby (2002), 88–89.
3. Thucydides IV.100; Forbes (1959), 70–74; Partington (1999), 1–5.
4. Partington (1999), 6–10.
5. Julius Africanus, *Cestus*, D25, 116–117; Malalas XVI.16 has the philosopher Proclus giving Anastasius I advice on using sulphur to combat an enemy fleet, although there appears to be a chronological problem of Proclus dying before Anastasius came to the throne …
6. Roland (1992), 655.
7. Theophanes, *Chron.* AM6164–6165.
8. Partington (1999), 12–13.
9. Pryor and Jeffreys (2006), 32, 46, 61–62, 72–73, 86, 189.
10. Anna Komnene, *Alexiad* XI.10, XIII.3.
11. Haldon (2006), 316; Pryor and Jeffreys (2006), 630–631.
12. Roland (1992), 660–664.
13. Roland (1992), 660, 663–664; Pryor and Jeffreys (2006), 609–611; there is some suggestion that the Arab world had some form of 'Greek fire' by the time of the Seventh Crusade (1248–1254), although the eyewitness report of Jean de Joinville does not necessarily record the Roman version of Greek fire, merely a similar incendiary weapon.
14. Pryor and Jeffreys (2006), 608.
15. Constantine VII, *de adm. imp.* 13.
16. Anna Komnene, *Alexiad* XIII.3.
17. Leo VI, *Tactica*, XIX.59.
18. Cf. Haldon and Byrne (1977), 92.
19. A portable *siphon* – the χειροσίφων, *cheirosiphōn* – is recorded at least as early as the reign of Leo VI (886–912).

20. Anna Komnena, *Alexiad* XI.10.
21. Roland (1992), 657–658.
22. Roland (1992), 659.
23. Cf. Partington (1999), 6–10, 14; Ellis Davidson (1973), 70.
24. Leo VI, *Tactica* XIX.67, 63.
25. Haldon (2006), 310.
26. Haldon and Byrne (1977), 92.
27. cf. Haldon (2006), 297–315.

Bibliography

Abbreviations

ACO	*Acta Conciliorum Oecumenicorum*
CJ	*Codex Justinianus*
CTh	*Codex Theodosianus*
NJ	*Novels of Justinian*
PLRE	*Prosopography of the Late Roman Empire*
PmbZ	*Prosopographie der mittelbyzantinischen Zeit Online*

Primary Sources

Agapios, *Kitab al-Unvan* (Vasiliev, A.A. translation, 1910–1912)

Agathias, *De imperio et rebus gestis Iustiniani* (Frendo, J.D. translation, 1975)

Agathon the Deacon in Mansi XII.19E = *ACO* 2nd ser. ii/2 (1992), 900.

Agnellus, *Liber Pontificalis Ecclesiae Ravennatis* (Mauskopf, D. translation, 2004)

Al-Baladhuri, *Futūh al-buldān* (de Goeje, M.J. translation, 1866)

Al-Maqrīzī, *Book of Exhortations and Useful Lessons in Dealing with Topography and Historical Remains* (Stowasser, K. translation, 2022)

Al-Mubarrad, *Al-Kāmil* (Wright, W. translation, 1874)

Anna Komnena, *Alexiad* (Sewter, E.R.A. translation, Penguin, 2009)

Appian, *Roman History* (White, H. translation, Loeb Classical Library, 1913; Gabba, E. translation, 1958–1970)

Arrian, *Anabasis* (Brunt, P.A. translation, Loeb Classical Library, 1976)

Bar Hebraeus (Wallis Budge, E.A. translation, 1932)

Bede, *Ecclesiastical History of the English People* (Colgrave, B. and Mynors, R.A.B. edition, 1991 reprint)

Bede, *The Complete Works of Venerable Bede (Volume 6)* (Giles, J.A. edition, 1843)

Cassius Dio, *Historia Romana* (Cary, E. translation, Loeb Classical Library, 1914–1927)

Cedrenus, *Historiarium Compendium* (Bekker, I. edition, 1838)

Chronicon Altinate (Cessi, R. edition, 1933)

Chronicle of 741 (Hoyland, R. translation, 1997)

Chronicon ad annum Christi 1234 pertinens (Chabot, J-B. translation, 1920)

Chronicle of 846 (Brooks, E.W. translation, 1897)

Chronology of 354 (Mommsen, T. edition, *Chronica Minora* 1892)

Chronicle of Zuqnin/Pseudo-Dionysius of Tel-Mahre, *Chronicle* (Witakowski, W. translation, 1997)

Cicero, *de finibus* (Harris Rackham, H. translation, Loeb Classical Library, 1931)

Code of Hammurabi (King, L.W. translation, https://avalon.law.yale.edu/ancient/hamframe.asp, 2008).

Codex Gothanus (Hodgkin, T. translation, 1896)

Codex Iustinianus (Krueger, P. translation, 1914)

Codex Theodosianus (Pharr, C. translation, 1952)

Constantius of Lyon, *Vita S. Germani* (Noble, T. and Head, T. translation, 1994)

Constantine VII Porphyrogenitus, *De Administrando Imperio* (Jenkins, R.J.H. translation, 1967)

Constantine VII Porphyrogenitus, *De Caerimoniis* (Reiske, J.J. translation, 1828)
De Locis Sanctis (Macpherson J.R. translation, 1898)
Ekloga (Humphreys, M. translation, 2017)
Elias of Nisibis (Delaporte, L-J. edition, 1910)
Ennodius, *Panegyricus dictus Theoderico regi* (Vogel, F. edition, 1885)
Eusebius, *Historia Ecclesiastica* (McGiffert, A.C. translation, 2005)
Eutychius, *Annals* (Breydy, M. translation, 1985)
George Monachos, *Chronicon Breve* (de Boor, C. edition, 1905)
Gregory of Tours, *Historia Francorum* (Thorpe, L. translation, Penguin Classics, 1974)
Hsin-t'ang-shu (Hirth, F. edition, 1885)
Huneberz of Heidenheim, *Hodoeporicon of St Willibald* (Talbot, C.H. translation, 1954)
Ibn Sa'id al-Maghribi (Arberry, A.J. translation, 2001)
John Chrysostom, *In epistulam ad Philippenses argumentum et homiliae* (Allen, P. translation, 2013)
John Chrysostom, *On the Priesthood, Ascetic Treatises, Select Homilies and Letters* (Stephens, W.R.W., Brandram, T.P. and Blackburn, R. translation, 1889)
John of Antioch (Mariev, S. translation, 2008)
John of Nikiu, *Chronicle* (Charles, R.H. translation, 1916)
Jordanes, *Getica* (Mierow, C.C. translation, 1915)
Julius Africanus, *Cestus* (Adler, W. translation, 2012)
Julius Caesar, *The Civil Wars* (Carter, J. translation, 1997)
Kitab al Uyun (Brooks, E.W. translation, 1899)
Leo Grammatikos, *Chronographia* (Bekkeri, I edition, 1842)
Leo VI, *Tactica* (Dennis, G.T. translation, 2014)
Lewond, *History* (Arzoumanian, Z. translation, 1982)
Liber Pontificalis (Davis, R. translation, 1989, 2007)
Little Iliad 4 (West, M.L. translation, 2003)
Livy, *Ab Urbe Condita* (de Selincourt, A. translation, Penguin Classics, 1965)
Ma Tuan-lin, Wen-hsien-t'ung-k'ao (Hirth, F. edition, 1885)
Malalas, *Chronographia* (Jeffreys, E., Jeffreys, M. and Scott, R. translation, 1986)
Malchus, *Historia* (Blockley, R.C. translation, *The Fragmentary Classicising Historians of the Later Roman Empire*, 1981)
Marcellinus Comes, *Chronicon* (Croke, B. translation, 1995)
Martial, *Epigrams* (anonymous translation, Bohn Classical Library, 1897)
Mauricius, *Strategikon* (Dennis, G.T. translation, 1983)
Megas Chronographos (Whitby, M. and Whitby, M. translation, 1989)
Menander Protector, *Historia* (Blockley, R.C. translation, 1985)
Michael the Syrian, *Chronicle* (Palmer, A. translation, Translated Texts for Historians, 1993)
Moses Dasxuranci, *History of Albania* (Dowsett, C.J.F. translation, 1961)
Movses Khorenantsi, *History of Armenia* (Thomson, R.W. translation, 2006)
Nikephoros, *Breviarium* (Mango, C. translation, 1990)
Nomos Georgikos (Humphreys, M. translation, 2017)
Nomos Mosaikos (Humphreys, M. translation, 2017)
Novels of Justinian (Scott, S.P. translation, 1932)
Olympiodorus (Blockley, R.C. translation, *The Fragmentary Classicising Historians of the Later Roman Empire*, 1981)
Orosius, *Historiae adversum paganos* (Deferrari, R.J. translation, 1964)
Parastaseis syntomoi chronikai (Cameron, A. and Herrin, J. translation, 1984)
Patria of Constantinople (Preger, T. edition, 1907)
Paul the Deacon, *Historia Langobardorum* (Foulke, W.D. translation, 1906)
Paul the Deacon, *Historia Romana* (Crivellucci, A. translation, 1914)

Peter of Sicily, *Historia Manichaeorum* (Gieseler, D.J.C.L edition, 1846)
Pliny the Elder, *Natural History* (Bostock, J. and Riley, H.T. translation, 1855)
Procopius, *Anecdota* (Williamson, G.A. translation, Penguin Classics, 1967)
Procopius, *De Bello Gothico* (Dewing, H.B. translation, Loeb Classical Library,1919)
Procopius, *De Bello Persico* (Dewing, H.B. translation, Loeb Classical Library, 1914)
Procopius, *De Bello Vandalico* (Dewing, H.B. translation, Loeb Classical Library, 1916)
Ps-Zacharias Rhetor, *Historia ecclesiastica* (Hamilton, F.J. and Brooks, E.W. translation, 1899
Ptolemy, *Geographia* (Lennart Berggren, J. and Jones, A. translation, 2001)
Quintus Curtius, *History of Alexander* (Rolfe, J.C. translation, Loeb Classical Library, 1946)
Ravennatis Anonymi Cosmographia (Pinder, M. and Partheny, G. edition, 1860)
Sahih Bukhari (Musin Khan, M. translation, https://sunnah.com/bukhari)
Sebêos, *History* (Thomson, R.W. translation, 1999)
Severus of Al'Ashmunein, *History of the Patriarchs of the Coptic Church of Alexandria* (Evetts, B. translation, 1910)
Stephanos of Taron (Greenwood, T. translation, 2017)
Suda, *Lexicon* (Adler, A. translation, 1928–1938)
Suetonius, *Twelve Caesars* (Graves, R. and Grant, M. translation, Penguin Classics, 1979)
Synaxarium ecclesiae Constantinopolitanae (Delehaye, H. edition, 1902)
Synodicon Vetus (Duffy, J. and Parker, J. translation, 1979)
Tabari (Yar-Shater, E. translation, 1985–1999)
Tacitus, *Germania* (Mattingly, H. and Handford, S.A. translation, Penguin Classics, 1970)
Theodore Studite, *Oratio funebris in Platonem* (*PG* 99 804–849)
Theophanes, *Chronographia* (Turtledove, H. translation, 1982; Mango, C. and Scott, R. translation, 1997)
Theophylactus Simocatta, *Historiae* (Whitby, M. and Whitby, M. translation, 1986)
Thucydides (Warner, R. translation, Penguins Classics, 1954)
Velleius Paterculus, *Roman History* (Shipley, F.W. translation, Loeb Classical Library, 1924)
Virgil, *Aeneid* (Jackson Knight, W.F. translation, 1956)
Vita Romani (Peeters, P. translation, *AnBoll* 30 (1911)
Vita Stephani iunoris (*PG* 100 1069–1186)
Zacharias of Mytilene, *Historia ecclesiastica* (Brooks, E.W. translation, 1899)
Zonaras, *Epitome* (Banchich, T.M. and Lane, E.N. translation, 2009; Lindorf translation, 1868–1875)

Secondary Sources

Afinogenov, D. 'The Source of Theophanes' *Chronography* and Nikephoros' *Breviarium* for the Years 685–717,' *Hristiansky Vostok* 4 (2002) 11–22
Afinogenov, D. 'A Lost 8th Century Pamphlet against Leo III and Constantine V,' *Eranos* 100 (2002) 1–17
Ahrweiler, H. 'L'Asie mineure et les invasions arabes', *Revue Historique* 227 (1962) 1–32
Ahrweiler, H. *Byzance et la mer: La Marine de guerre, la politique et les institutions maritimes de Byzance aux VIIIe-XVe siecles.* Paris (1966)
Ahrweiler, H. 'The Geography of the Iconoclast World', in Bryer, A. and Herrin, J. *Iconoclasm: Papers given at the Ninth Spring Symposium of Byzantine Studies, University of Birmingham, March 1975.* Birmingham (1975) 21–27
Alexander, P.J. *The Patriarch Nicephorus of Constantinople: Ecclesiastical Policy and Image Worship in the Byzantine State.* Oxford (1958)
Alexander, P.J. *Religious and Political History and Thought in the Byzantine Empire.* London (1978)
Alexander, P.J. 'An Ascetic Sect of Iconoclasts in Seventh Century Armenia', in Weitzman, K. (ed.) *Late Classical and Medieval Studies in Honor of Albert M. Friend Jnr.* Princeton (1955) 155–160
Anastos, M.V. 'The Ethical Theory of Images Formulated by the Iconoclasts in 754 and 815', *DOP* 8 (1954) 151–160

Anastos, M.V. 'The argument for iconoclasm as presented to the Iconoclastic Council of 754', in Weitzman, K. (ed.) *Late Classical and Medieval Studies in Honor of Albert M. Friend Jnr.* Princeton (1955) 177–188

Anastos, M.V. 'The Transfer of Illyricum, Calabria and Sicily to the jurisdiction of the patriarch of Constantinople in 732–733,' *Studi Bizantini e Neoellenici in Onore di S.G.Mercati.* Rome (1957) 14–31

Anastos, M.V. 'Iconoclasm and the Imperial Rule 717–842,' in Hussey, J.M. (ed.) *Cambridge Medieval History IV.1: The Byzantine Empire.* Cambridge (1966) 61–104

Anastos, M.V. 'Leo III's Edict Against the Images in the Year 726–27 and Italo-Byzantine Relations Between 726 and 730,' *Polychordia: Festschrift Franz Dolger zum 75.* Amsterdam (1968) III.5–41

Artamonov, M. I. *The History of the Khazars.* St Petersburg (1962)

Ashburner, W. 'The Farmer's Law,' *JHS* 30 (1910) 85–108

Ashburner, W. 'The Farmer's Law Continued,' *JHS* 32 (1912) 68–95

Ashburner, W. 'The Byzantine Mutiny Act,' *JHS* 46 (1926) 80–109

Auzepy, M-F. 'La destruction de l'icone du Christ de la Chalce par Leon III: propaganda ou realite?', *Byzantion* 60 (1990) 445–492

Auzepy, M.-F. 'L'analyse litteraire et l'historien: l'exemple des vies de saints iconoclastes', *BS* 53 (1992) 57–67

Auzepy, M.-F. 'Les Isauriens et l'espace sacre: l'eglise et les reliques', in Kaplan, M. *Le sacre et son inscription dans l'espace a Byzance et en occident.* Byzantina Sorbonensia 18. Paris (2001) 13–24

Auzepy, M.-F. *L'histoire des iconoclastes.* Paris (2007)

Auzepy, M.-F. 'State of Emergency', in Shepard, J. (ed.) *The Cambridge History of the Byzantine Empire c.500–1492.* Cambridge (2019) 251–291

Baldwin, B. 'Theophanes and the Iconoclasm of Leo III,' *Byzantion* 60 (1990) 426–428

Barnard, L.W. 'The Emperor Cult and the Origins of the Iconoclastic Controversy', *Byzantion* 43 (1973) 13–29

Barnard, L.W. *The Graeco-Roman and Oriental Background of the Iconoclastic Controversy.* Leiden (1974)

Barnard, L.W. 'The Theology of Images', in Bryer, A. and Herrin, J. *Iconoclasm: Papers given at the Ninth Spring Symposium of Byzantine Studies, University of Birmingham, March 1975.* Birmingham (1975a) 7–13

Barnard, L.W. 'The Paulicians and Iconoclasm', in Bryer, A. and Herrin, J. *Iconoclasm: Papers given at the Ninth Spring Symposium of Byzantine Studies, University of Birmingham, March 1975.* Birmingham (1975b) 75–81

Bashear, S. 'Apocalyptic and other materials on early Muslim-Byzantine wars: A review of Arabic sources,' *JRAS* 1 (1991) 173–207

Bertolini, O. 'Quale ful il vero obbiettivo in Italia de Leone III 'Isaurio' all'armata di Manes, stratego dei Cibyrreoti?,' *ByzF* 2 (1968) 15–49

Besevliev, V. *Die protobulgarische Periode der bulgarischen Geschichte.* Amsterdam (1980)

Blankinship, K.Y. *The End of the Jihad State: The Reign of Hisham B. 'Abd Al-Malik and the Collapse of the Umayyads.* Albany (1994)

Booth, P. *Crisis of Empire: Doctrine and Dissent at the End of Late Antiquity.* London (2014)

Borrut, A. 'Entre tradition et histoire: genre et diffusion de l'image de Umar II,' *Melanges de L'Universite Saint-Joseph* 58 (2005) 329–378

Bosworth, C.E. *'Raja' Ibn Haywa al-Kindi and the Umayyad Caliphs,' Islamic Quarterly* 16 (1972*) 36–80*

Boyce, M. 'Iconoclasm amongst the Zoroastrians', in Neusner, J. (ed.) *Christianity, Judaism and Other Greco-Roman Cults: Studies for Morton Smith at Sixty.* Leiden (1975) 93–111

Brandes, W. *Die Staadt Kleinasiens in 7 un 8. Jahrhundert.* (*BBA* 56) Berlin (1989)

Brandes, W. 'Die Belagerung Konstantinopels 717/718 als apokalyptisches Ereignis. Zu einer Interpolation im griechischen Text der Pseudo-Methodios-Apokalypse,' in Belke, K. (ed.). Byzantina Mediterranea: Festschrift für Johannes Koder zum 65. Vienna (2007) 65–91

Brandes, W. and Haldon, J.F. 'Towns, Tax and Transformation: State, Cities and Their Hinterlands in the East Roman World, ca. 500–800,' in Gauthier, N. (ed.) *Towns and Their Hinterlands between Late Antiquity and the Early Middle Ages.* Leiden (2000) 141–172

Braudel, F. *La Mediterannee et le monde mediterraneen a l'epoque de Philippe II.* Paris (1976)

Breckenridge, J.D. *The Numismatic Iconography of Justinian II.* New York (1959)

Bremmer, J. 'Iconoclast, iconoclastic and iconoclasm: notes toward a genealogy,' *Church History and Religious Culture* 88 (2008) 1–17

Brock, S.P. 'Iconoclasm and the Monophysites', in Bryer, A. and Herrin, J. *Iconoclasm: Papers given at the Ninth Spring Symposium of Byzantine Studies, University of Birmingham, March 1975.* Birmingham (1975) 53–57

Brock, S.P. 'Syriac Sources for Seventh-Century History,' *BMGS* 2 (1976) 17–36

Brock, S.P. 'Jewish traditions in Syriac sources,' *Journal of Jewish Studies* 30 (1979) 210–232

Brook, K.A. *The Jews of Khazaria.* Lanham (2018)

Brooks, E.W. 'The Arabs in Asia Minor (641–750) from Arabic Sources,' *JHS* 18 (1898) 182–208

Brooks, E.W. 'The Campaign of 716–718, from Arabic sources,' *JHS* 19 (1899) 19–31

Brooks, E.W. 'Byzantines and Arabs in the time of the early Abbasids I', *EHR* 15 (1900) 728–747

Brooks, E.W. 'Byzantines and Arabs in the time of the early Abbasids II', *EHR* 16 (1901) 84–92

Brooks, E.W. 'Arabic Lists of the Byzantine Themes,' *JHS* 21 (1901) 67–77

Brooks, E.W. 'The sources of Theophanes and the Syriac chroniclers,' *BZ* 15 (1906) 578–587

Brooks, E.W. 'The Successors of Heraclius,' in Gwatkin, H.M. and Whitney, J.P. (eds.) *Cambridge Medieval History Vol. II: The Rise of the Saracens and the Foundation of the Western Empire.* Cambridge (1936) 391–417

Brown, P.R.L. 'A Dark-Age Crisis: Aspects of the Iconoclastic Controversy,' *EHR* 88 (1973) 1–34

Brown, T.S. *Gentleman and Officers: Imperial Administration and Aristocratic Power in Byzantine Italy AD 554–800.* London (1984)

Brown, T.S. 'Byzantine Italy (680–876)' in Shepard, J. (ed.) *Cambridge History of Byzantine Empire ca. 500–1492.* Cambridge (2019) 433–464

Brubaker, L. 'Icons before Iconoclasm?', *Morfologie sociali e culturali in europa fra tarda antichita e alto medioevo, Settimane di Studio del Centro Italiano di Studi aull'Alto Medioevo* 45 (1998) 1215–1254

Brubaker, L. 'The Chalke gate, the construction of the past, and the 'Trier ivory',' *BMGS* 23 (1999) 258–285

Brubaker, L. *Inventing Byzantine Iconoclasm.* London (2012)

Brubaker, L. and Haldon, J.F. *Byzantium in the Iconoclast Era (ca. 680–850): The Sources: An Annotated Survey.* Aldershot (2001)

Brubaker, L. and Haldon, J.F. *Byzantium in the Iconoclast Era, c. 680–850: A History.* Cambridge (2015)

Bruckner, W. *Die Sprache der Langobarden, Quellen und Forschungen zur Sprach- und Culturgeschichte der germanischen Völker.* Strassburg (1895)

Bryer, A. and Herrin, J. *Iconoclasm: Papers Given at the Ninth Spring Symposium of Byzantine Studies, University of Birmingham, March 1975.* Centre for Byzantine Studies. Birmingham (1977)

Bumazhnov, D. Grypeou, E. Sailors, T.B. and Toepel, A. (eds.) *Bibel, Byzanz und Christlicher Orient: Festschrift für Stephen Gerö zum 65. Geburtstag.* Orientalia Lovaniensia Analecta 187. Leuven/Paris/Walpole (2011)

Bury, J.B. *A History of the Later Roman Empire from Arcadius to Irene, 395 AD to 800 AD.* 2 Vols. London (1889)

Bury, J.B. 'A Greek Word in the Liber Pontificalis,' *BZ* 5 (1896) 570–571

Bury, J.B. *The Imperial Administration System in the Ninth Century.* London (1911)

Bury, J.B. 'The Great Palace,' *BZ* 21 (1912) 210–225

Calofonos, G.T. 'Dream Interpretation: A Byzantinist Superstition?', *BMGS* 9 (1985) 215–220
Cameron, Al. *Circus Factions: Blues and Greens at Rome and Constantinople.* Oxford (1976)
Cameron, Av. 'Images of Authority: Elites and Icons in Late Sixth-Century Constantinople,' *Past and Present* 84 (1979) 3–35
Cameron, Av. 'New Themes and Styles in Greek Literature: Seventh-Eighth Centuries,' in Cameron, A. and Conrad L.I. (eds.) *The Byzantine and Early Islamic Near East I: Problems in the Literary Source Material.* Princeton (1992) 81–105
Cameron, Av. 'The language of images: the rise of icons and Christian representation,' in Wood, D. (ed.) *The Church and the Arts.* Studies in Church History 28. Oxford (1992) 1–42
Cameron, Av. (ed.) *The Byzantine and Early Islamic Near East III: States, Resources and Armies.* Princeton (1995)
Cameron, Av. and Herrin, J. *Constantinople in the Early Eighth Century: The Parastaseis Syntomoi Chronikai: Introduction, Translation, and Commentary.* Leiden (1984)
Cameron, Av. and Conrad L.I. (eds.) *The Byzantine and Early Islamic Near East I: Problems in the Literary Source Material.* Princeton (1992)
Canard, M. 'L'aventure caucasienne du spathaire Léon, le futur empereur Léon III,' *RE Arm* NS 8 (1971) 353–357
Cankova-Petkova, G. 'Bulgarians and Byzantium during the First Decades after the foundation of the Bulgarian state,' *ByzSl* 24 (1963) 41–53
Charanis, P. 'Ethnic Changes in the Byzantine Empire in the Seventh Century,' *DOP* 13 (1959) 25–44
Charanis, P. 'The Transfer of Population as a Policy in the Byzantine Empire,' *Comparative Studies in Society and History* 3 (1960–1961) 140–154
Charanis, P. 'The Armenians in Byzantine Empire,' *ByzSl* 22 (1961a) 196–240
Charanis, P. 'The transfer of population as a policy in the Byzantine Empire,' *Vizantoloskog Instituta Zbornik radova* 8.1 (1961b) 71–76
Charanis, P. *The Armenians in the Byzantine Empire.* Lisbon (1963)
Charanis, P. 'Kouver, the Chronology of his Activities and their Ethnic Effects on the Regions around Thessalonica,' *Balkan Studies* 11 (1970) 229–247
Chen, S. *Multicultural China in the Early Middle Ages.* Philadelphia (2012)
Cheynet, J.-Cl. 'L'aristocratie byzantine (VIIIe-XIIIe siecle)', *Jsav* (2000) 281–322.
Cheynet, J.-Cl. 'The Byzantine aristocracy (8th-13th centuries)' in Cheynet, J-Cl. *The Byzantine Aristocracy and its Military Function.* Aldershot (2006) I.1–43
Cheynet, J.-Cl. *The Byzantine Aristocracy and Its Military Functions.* Aldershot (2006)
Christides, V. 'The Second Arab Siege of Constantinople (717–718?): Logistics and Naval Power,' in Bumazhnov, D. Grypeou, E. Sailors, T.B. and Toepel, A. (eds.) *Bibel, Byzanz und Christlicher Orient: Festschrift für Stephen Gerö zum 65. Geburtstag.* Orientalia Lovaniensia Analecta 187. Leuven/Paris/Walpole (2011) 511–534
Conrad, L.I. 'Theophanes and the Arabic historical tradition: some indications of intercultural transmission', *BF* 15 (1990) 1–44
Conrad, L.I. *History and Historiography in Early Islamic Times: Studies in Perspective.* Princeton (1994)
Constantelos, D.J. 'The Moslem Conquests of the Near East as Revealed in the Greek Sources of the Seventh and Eighth Centuries,' *Byzantion* 42 (1972) 325–357
Conterno, M. 'Theophilos, 'the more likely candidate'? Towards a reappraisal of the question of Theophanes' 'Oriental source(s)',' in Jankowiak, M. and Montinaro, F. (eds.) *Studies in Theophanes. Travaux et Memoires* 19. Paris (2015) 383–400
Conybeare, F.C. *The Key of Truth: A Manual of the Paulician Church of Armenia.* London (1896)
Cook, M. 'The Heraclian dynasty in Muslim eschatology', *Al-Qantara* 13 (1992) 3–24
Cook, M. 'Eschatology and the Dating of Traditions', in Motzki, H. *Hadith: Origins and Developments.* London and New York (2016) 217–241

Cosentino, S. 'Constans II and the Byzantine navy,' *BZ* 100 (2008) 577–603
Crawford, P. *Justinian II: The Roman Emperor Who Lost His Nose And His Throne… And Regained Both!* Barnsley (2021)
Croke, B. 'The Date of the 'Anastasian Long Walls' in Thrace,' *GRBS* 23 (1982) 59–78
Crone, P. 'Islam, Judaeo-Christianity and Byzantine iconoclasm,' in Bonner, M. (ed.) *Arab-Byzantine Relations in Early Islamic Times.* Aldershot (2005) 361–397
Crosby, A.W. *Throwing Fire: Projectile Technology Through History.* Cambridge (2002)
Curta, F. *Making an Early Medieval Ethnie: The Case of the Early Slavs (Sixth to Seventh Century AD)*, PhD thesis, Kalamazoo (1998)
Curta, F. *The Making of the Slavs: History and Archaeology of the Lower Danube Region, c. 500–700.* Cambridge (2001)
Curta, F. *Southeastern Europe in the Middle Ages 500–1200.* Cambridge (2006)
Dagron, G. *Emperor and Priest: The Imperial Office in Byzantium.* Cambridge (2003)
Debié, M. 'Theophanes' 'Oriental source': what can we learn from Syriac historiography?', in Jankowiak, M. and Montinaro, F. (eds.) *Studies in Theophanes. Travaux et Memoires* 19. Paris (2015) 365–382
Detschev, D. 'Der germanische Ursprung des bulgarischen Volksnamens,' *Zeitschr. f. Ortsnamenforschung* 2 (1927) 199–216
Dimitrov, D. *Prabylgarite po severnoto i zapadnoto Chernomorie.* Varna (1987)
Dixon, A.A. *The Umayyad Caliphate 65–86/684–705 (A Political Study)*. London (1971)
Dixon, C. *The Paulicians: Heresy, Persecution and Warfare on the Byzantine Frontier, c.750–880.* Leiden (2022).
Dolger, F. 'Ist der Nomos Georgikos ein Gesetz des Kaisers Justinian II?,' *Festschrift fur Leopold Wenger*. Munich. 2 vols (1944–1945)
Dols, M. W. 'Plague in Early Islamic History,' *JOAS* 94 (1974) 371–383
Donner, F.M. *Narratives of Islamic Origins: The Beginnings of Islamic Historical Writing.* Princeton (1998)
Dunlop, D.M. *The History of the Jewish Khazars.* Princeton (1954)
Ekonomou, A. *Byzantine Rome and the Greek Popes: Eastern Influences on Rome and the Papacy from Gregory the Great to Zacharias AD 590–752.* Lanham (2007)
El-Cheikh, N.M. *Byzantium Viewed by the Arabs.* Cambridge (2004)
Ellis Davidson, H.R. 'The Secret Weapon of Byzantium', *BZ* 66 (1973) 61–74
Elsner, J. 'Iconoclasm as Discourse from Antiquity to Byzantium,' *Art Bulletin* 94 (2012) 368–394
Erdal, M. 'The Khazar Language,' in Golden, P.B., Ben-Shammai, H. and Róna-Tas, A. (eds.) *The World of the Khazars: New Perspectives. Selected Papers from the Jerusalem 1999 International Khazar Colloquium* (Handbook of Oriental Studies. Section 8 Uralic & Central Asian Studies) Leiden (2007) 75–108
Ewig, E. 'The papacy's alienation from Byzantium and rapprochement with the Franks', in Kempf F. *et al. The Church in the Age of Feudalism.* New York (1969), 3–25.
Fiedler, U. 'Bulgars in the Lower Danube region: A survey of the archaeological evidence and of the state of current research,' in Curta, F. and Kovalev, R. (eds.). *The Other Europe in the Middle Ages: Avars, Bulgars, Khazars and Cumans.* Leiden (2008) 151–236
Fischer, F. *De patriarcharum Constantinopolitanorum catalogis.* Lipsiae (1884)
Forbes, R. J. *More Studies in Early Petroleum History 1860–1880.* Leiden (1959)
Forrest, S. 'Theophanes' Byzantine source for the late seventh and early eighth centuries, c. AD 668–716,' in Jankowiak, M. and Montinaro, F. (eds.) *Studies in Theophanes. Travaux et Memoires* 19. Paris (2015) 417–444
Fröhlich, H. 'Zur Herkunft der Langobarden,' *QFIAB* 55/56 (1976) 1–21
Fueg, F. *Corpus of the Nomismata from Anastatius II to John I in Constantinople 717–976: Structure of the Issues, Corpus of Coin Finds, Contribution to the Iconographic and Monetary History.* Lancaster (2007)

Garsoian, N.G. *The Paulician Heresy: A Study of the Origin and Development of Paulicianism in Armenia and the Eastern Provinces of the Byzantine Empire.* The Hague (1967)

Garsoian, N.G. 'Byzantine Heresy, a Reinterpretation', *DOP* 25 (1971) 85–113

Gasparri S. 'The first Dukes of Venice', in Gelichi S. and Gasparri S. (eds), *Venice and its Neighbours from the 8th to the 11th Century*. Leiden (2017)

Geary, P. *Myth of Nations: The Medieval Origins of Europe*. Princeton (2003)

George, W.S. *The Church of Saint Eirene at Constantinople*. Oxford (1912)

Gero, S. *Byzantine Iconoclasm during the Reign of Leo III.* Louvain (1973)

Gero, S. *Byzantine Iconoclasm during the Reign of Constantine V.* Louvain (1974a)

Gero, S. 'Notes on Byzantine Iconoclasm in the Eighth Century,' *Byzantion* 44 (1974b) 23–42

Gero. S. 'Jonah and the Patriarch', *Vigiliae Christianae* 29 (1975) 141–146

Golden, P.B. *An Introduction to the History of the Turkic Peoples: Ethnogenesis and State Formation in Medieval and Early Modern Eurasia and the Middle East.* Wiesbaden (1992)

Golden, P.B. 'The Khazar Sacral Kingship,' in Reyerson, K.V., Stavrou, T.G. and Tracy, J.D. (eds.) *Pre-modern Russia and its world: Essays in Honour of Thomas S. Noonan.* Wiesbaden (2006) 79–102

Golden, P.B. 'Khazar Studies: Achievements and Perspectives,' in Golden, P.B., Ben-Shammai, H. and Róna-Tas, A. (eds.) *The World of the Khazars: New Perspectives. Selected Papers from the Jerusalem 1999 International Khazar Colloquium* (Handbook of Oriental Studies. Section 8 Uralic & Central Asian Studies) Leiden (2007a) 7–57

Golden, P.B. 'Nomads of the western Eurasian steppes: Ogurs, Onogurs and Khazars,' in Golden, P.B. (ed.) *Studies on the Peoples and Cultures of the Eurasian Steppes.* Bucharest (2011) 135–162

Golden, P.B. (ed.) *Studies on the Peoples and Cultures of the Eurasian Steppes.* Bucharest (2011)

Golden, P.B. 'Oq and Oğur~Oğuz,' *Turkic Languages* 16 (2012) 155–199

Golden, P.B., Ben-Shammai, H. and Róna-Tas, A. (eds.) *The World of the Khazars: New Perspectives. Selected Papers from the Jerusalem 1999 International Khazar Colloquium* (Handbook of Oriental Studies. Section 8 Uralic & Central Asian Studies) Leiden (2007)

Gouillard, J. 'Aux origins de l'iconoclasme: le temoignage de Gregoire II,' *Travaux et Memories* 3 (1968) 243–307

Grabar, A., *L'empereur dans l'art Byzantin: recherches sur l'art officiel de l'empire d'Orient.* Paris (1936)

Grabar, A., *L'Iconoclasme Byzantin: dossier archéologique.* Paris (1957)

Grabar, O. 'Islam and Iconoclasm', in Bryer, A. and Herrin, J. *Iconoclasm: Papers given at the Ninth Spring Symposium of Byzantine Studies, University of Birmingham, March 1975.* Birmingham (1975) 45–51

Greenwood, J. 'Armenian Neighbours (600–1045)' in Shepard, J. (ed.) *Cambridge History of the Byzantine Empire ca 500–1492.* Cambridge (2019) 333–364

Gregory, T.E. 'The Ekloga of Leo III and the Concept of Philanthropia', *Byzantina* 7 (1975) 267–287

Grierson, P. 'Election and inheritance in Early Germanic kingship', *CHJ* 7 (1941) 1–22

Grierson, P. 'The Copper Coinage of Leo III (717–41) and Constantine V (720–75)', *The Numismatic Chronicle and Journal of the Royal Numismatic Society* 7.5 (1965) 183–196.

Grierson, P. *Catalogue of the Coins in the Dumbarton Oaks Collection and in the Whittemore Collection II: Phocas to Theodosius III, 602–717.* Washington DC (1968)

Grierson, P. *Catalogue of the Coins in the Dumbarton Oaks Collection and in the Whittemore Collection, Leo III to Nicephorus III, 717–1081.* Washington DC (1973)

Grierson, P. *Byzantine Coinage.* Washington DC (1999)

Grumel, V. 'L'annexion de l'Illyricum, de la Sicile et de la Calabre au patriarcat de Constantinople,' *Recherches de science religieuse* 40 (1952) 191–200

Grumel, V. 'Homelie de saint Germain sur la deliverance de Constantinople', *REB* 16 (1958) 183–205

Hahn, W. *Moneta Imperii Byzantini: Von Heraclius bis Leo III. Alleinregierung (610–720)* . Vol. III Vienna (1981)

Haldon, J.F. 'Aspects of Byzantine Military Administration: the Elite Corps, the Opsikion, and the Imperial Tagmata from the Sixth to the Ninth Century' Unpublish. diss. University of Birmingham (1975a)

Haldon, J.F. 'Some Aspects of Byzantine Military Technology from the Sixth to the Tenth Centuries,' *BMGS* 1 (1975b) 11–47

Haldon, J.F. 'Some Remarks on the Background to the Iconoclast Controversy,' *ByzSl* 38 (1977) 161–184

Haldon, J.F. *Recruitment and Conscription in the Byzantine Army c.550–950: A Study on the Origins of the Stratiotika Ktemata.* Vienna (1979)

Haldon, J.F. *Byzantine Praetorians: An Administrative, Institutional and Social Survey of the Opsikion and Tagmata c. 580–900.* Bonn (1984)

Haldon, J.F. *Byzantium in the Seventh Century: The Transformation of a Culture.* Cambridge (1990)

Haldon, J.F. 'Military service, military lands and the status of soldiers: Current problems and interpretations,' *DOP* 47 (1993) 1–67

Haldon, J.F. 'Seventh-Century Continuities: the *Ajnad* and the Thematic Myth," in Cameron, A. (ed.) *States, Resources and Armies: Papers of the Third Workshop on Antiquity and Early Islam.* Princeton (1995) 379–423

Haldon, J.F. *State, Army and Society in Byzantium: approaches to military, social and administrative history 6th-12th centuries.* Aldershot (1995)

Haldon, J.F. *Byzantium in the Seventh Century: The Transformation of a Culture.* Cambridge (1997)

Haldon, J.F. *Warfare, State and Society in the Byzantine World 565–1204.* London (1999)

Haldon, J.F. 'Greek Fire Revisited: Recent and Current Research,' in Jeffreys, E. (ed.) *Byzantine Style, Religion and Civilisation: In Honour of Sir Steven Runciman.* Cambridge (2006) 290–325

Haldon, J.F. (ed.) *Money, Power and Politics in Early Islamic Syria.* Farnham (2010)

Haldon, J.F. *The Empire That Would Not Die: The Paradox of Eastern Roman Survival, 640–740.* London (2016)

Haldon, J.F. and Byrne, M. 'A Possible Solution to the Problem of Greek Fire,' *BZ* 70 (1977) 91–99

Hasluck, F.W. 'The Mosques of the Arabs in Constantinople', *Christianity and Islam Under the Sultans, vol. 2. Oxford (1929) 717–735*

Hawting, G.R. *The First Dynasty of Islam: The Umayyad Caliphate AD 661–750.* London (2000)

Head, C. 'Who was the real Leo the Isaurian?,' *Byzantion* 4 (1971) 105–108

Head, C. *Justinian II of Byzantium.* London (1972)

Heather, P. *Empire and Barbarians: Migration, Development and the Birth of Europe.* London (2009)

Heidemann, S. 'The Evolving Representation in the Early Islamic Empire and its Religion on Coin Imagery,' in Neuwirth, A., Sinai, N. and Marx, M. (eds.) *The Qur'an in Context: Historical and Literacy Investigations into the Qur'anic Milieu.* Leiden (2010) 149–196

Herrin, J. 'The Geography of the Iconoclast World', in Bryer, A. and Herrin, J. *Iconoclasm: Papers given at the Ninth Spring Symposium of Byzantine Studies, University of Birmingham, March 1975.* Birmingham (1975) 15–19

Hirth, F. *China and the Roman Orient: Researches into their Ancient and Mediaeval Relations as Represented in Old Chinese Records.* Shanghai and Hong Kong (1885), 35–96

Howard-Johnston, J.D. 'The Rise of Islam and Byzantium's Response,' in Oddy, A. (ed.) *Coinage and History in the Seventh-Century Near East.* Oxford (2010) 1–9

Howard-Johnston, J.D. *Witnesses to a World Crisis: Historians and Histories of the Middle East in the Seventh Century.* Oxford (2010)

Hoyland, R.G. *Seeing Islam as Others Saw It: A Survey and Evaluation of Christian, Jewish and Zoroastrian Writing.* Princeton (1997)

Hoyland, R.G. 'Agapius, Theophilus and Muslim sources,' in Jankowiak, M. and Montinaro, F. (eds.) *Studies in Theophanes.* Travaux et Memoires 19. Paris (2015) 355–364

Humphreys, M. 'Images of Authority? Imperial Patronage of Icons from Justinian II and Leo III,' in Sarris, P., Dal Santo, M. and Booth, P. (eds.) *An Age of Saints? Power, Conflict and Dissent in Early Medieval Christianity.* Boston (2011) 150–168

Humphreys, M. 'The War of Images Revisited Justinian II's Coinage Reform and the Caliphate,' *NC* 173 (2013) 229–244

Humphreys, M. *Law, Power and Imperial Ideology in the Iconoclast Era c. 680–850.* Oxford (2015)

Hupchick, D.P. *The Bulgarian-Byzantine Wars for Early Medieval Balkan Hegemony: Silver-Lined Skulls and Blinded Armies.* London (2017)

Huxley, G.L. 'Hagiography and the First Byzantine Iconoclasm', *Proceedings of the Royal Irish Academy: Archaeology, Culture, History, Literature* 80 (1980) 187–196

Jankowiak, M. 'The First Arab siege of Constantinople,' in Zuckerman, C. (ed.) *Constructing the Seventh Century.* Travaux et Memoires 17. Paris (2013) 237–320

Jankowiak, M. and Montinaro, F. (eds.) *Studies in Theophanes. Travaux et Memoires* 19. Paris (2015)

Jeffery, A. 'Ghevond's Text of the Correspondence between Umar II and Leo III', *HTR* 37 (1944) 269–332

Jenkins, R.J.H. *Byzantium: The Imperial Centuries.* New York (1966)

Jones, A.H.M. *Later Roman Empire 284–602.* Oxford (1964)

Kaegi, W.E. 'The Byzantine Armies and Iconoclasm,' *Byzantioslavica* 22 (1966) 48–70

Kaegi, W.E. 'Some Reconsiderations on the Themes (Seventh-Ninth Centuries)' *JOB* 16 (1967) 39–53

Kaegi, W.E. 'Al-Baladhuri and the Armeniak theme,' *Byzantion* 38 (1968) 273–277

Kaegi, W.E. 'The First Arab Expedition against Amorium,' *BMGS* 3 (1977) 19–22

Kaegi, W.E. *Byzantine Military Unrest, 471–843: An Interpretation.* Amsterdam (1981)

Kaegi, W.E. *Byzantium and the Early Islamic Conquests.* Cambridge (1992)

Kaegi, W.E. 'Confronting Islam: Emperors vs Caliphs (641-c.850)' in Shepard, J. (ed.) *Cambridge History of Byzantine Empire ca. 500–1492.* Cambridge (2019) 365–394

Kaldellis, A. *Romanland: Ethnicity and Empire in Byzantium. Harvard (2019)*

Karayannopoulos, J. *Des Finanzwesen des fruhbyzantinischen Staates.* Munich (1958)

Karayannopoulos, J. *Die Entstehung der Byzantinischen Themeordnung.* Munich (1959)

Kelly, J.N.D. *Early Christian Doctrines.* San Francisco (1978)

Kennedy, H. *The Armies of the Caliphs: military and society in the early Islamic state.* London (2001)

Kennedy, H. *The Prophet and the Age of the Caliphates: The Islamic Near East from the Sixth to the Eleventh Century.* Harlow (2004)

Kennedy, H. *The Prophet and the Age of the Caliphates: The Islamic Near East from the 6th to the 11th Century.* Oxford and New York (2016)

Keramopoulos, A. Πρόσφορα εἰς Στ.Κυριαχίδην. Thessalonica (1953)

Kim, H.J. *The Huns, Rome and the Birth of Europe.* Cambridge (2013)

Kim, S. *The Arabic Letters of the Byzantine Emperor Leo III to the Caliph 'Umar Ibn 'Abd al-'Aziz: An Edition, Translation and Commentary.* (PhD thesis, Catholic University of America, 2017)

Kitzinger, E. 'The Cult of Images in the Age before Iconoclasm,' *DOP* 8 (1954) 83–150

Kitzinger, E. 'On Some Icons of the Seventh Century,' in *Late Classical and Mediaeval Studies in Honor of Albert Mathias Friend Jr.* Princeton (1955) 132–150

Koder, J. 'Fresh vegetables for the capital', in Mango, C. and Dagron, G. (eds.) *Constantinople and its Hinterlands: Papers from the Twenty-seventh Spring Symposium of Byzantine Studies, Oxford, April 1993.* Aldershot (1995) 49–56

Koestler, A. *The Thirteenth Tribe: The Khazar Empire and Its Heritage.* London (1977)

Kortlandt, F. 'The spread of the Indo-Europeans,' *Journal of Indo-European Studies* 18 (1990) 131–140

Kościelniak, K. *Greeks and Arabs. The History of the Melkite (Catholic) Church in the lands conquered by the Muslims (634–1516)*. Krakow (2004)

Kulakovskij, J. *Istorija Vizantii.* 3 vols. Kiev (1912–1915)

Ladner, G.B. 'Origin and Significance of the Byzantine Iconoclastic Controversy,' *Mediaeval Studies* 2 (1940) 127–149

Ladner, G.B. 'The Concept of the Image in the Greek Fathers and the Byzantine Iconoclastic Controversy,' *DOP* 7 (1953) 1–34

Lamza, L. *Patriarch Germanos I. von Konstantinopel.* Wurzburg (1975)

Leicester, H.M. *The Historical Background of Chemistry.* New York (1956)

Lemerle, P. 'Invasions et migrations dans les Balkans depuis la fin de l'epoque romaine jusqu'au VIIIe siècle,' *Revue historique* 211 (1954) 265–308

Lemerle, P. 'Esquisse pour une histoire agraire de Byzance,' *Revue historique* 219 (1958) 32–74, 254–284

Levcenko, M.V. 'Blues and Greens in Byzantium in the Fifth to Seventh Centuries,' *Vizantiiskii Vremenik* 1 (1947) 164–183

Lilie, R.J. *Die Byzantinische Reaktion auf die Ausbreitung der Araber.* Munich (1976)

Maas, P. 'Die ikonoclastiche Episode in dem Briefe des Epiphanios an Johannes', *BZ* 30 (1929–1930) 279–286.

MacDonald, D.B. 'The Earlier History of the Arabian Nights,' *JRAS* 56 (1924) 353–397

Madelung, W. *The Succession to Muhammad: A Study of the Early Caliphate.* Cambridge (1997)

Maenchen-Helfen, O.J. *The World of the Huns: Studies in Their History and Culture.* Berkeley (1973)

Magdalino, P. 'The Grain Supply of Constantinople' in Mango, C. and Dagron, G. (eds.) *Constantinople and its Hinterlands: Papers from the Twenty-seventh Spring Symposium of Byzantine Studies, Oxford, April 1993.* Aldershot (1995) 35–47

Mango, C. *The Brazen House: A study of the Vestibule of the Imperial Palace of Constantinople.* Copenhagen (1959)

Mango, C. 'Who wrote the Chronicle of Theophanes?' *ZRVI* 18 (1978) 9–17

Mango, C. 'The *Breviarium* of the Patriarch Nicephoros,' in *Byzantium: A Tribute to Andreas N. Stratos.* Athens (1986) II.539–552

Mango C. *Le développement urbain de Constantinople (IV–VII siècles).* Paris, 2nd edn. (1990)

Mango, C. 'Historical Introduction', in Bryer, A. and Herrin, J. *Iconoclasm: Papers given at the Ninth Spring Symposium of Byzantine Studies, University of Birmingham, March 1975.* Birmingham (1975) 1–5

Mango, C. 'The water supply of Constantinople,' in Mango, C. and Dagron, G. (eds.) *Constantinople and its Hinterlands: Papers from the Twenty-seventh Spring Symposium of Byzantine Studies, Oxford, April 1993.* Aldershot (1995) 9–18

Mango, C. (2005) *Byzantium: The Empire of New Rome.* London (2005)

Mango, C. and Dagron, G. (eds.) *Constantinople and its Hinterlands: Papers from the Twenty-seventh Spring Symposium of Byzantine Studies, Oxford, April 1993.* Aldershot (1995)

Mann, H. K. *The Lives of the Popes in the Early Middle Ages. Vol. I.* St Louis (1914)

Mansi, J.D. *Sacrorum Conciliorum nova et amplissima collection.* Florence (1759–1798)

Mauskopf Deliyannis, D. 'Agnellus of Ravenna and Iconoclasm: Theology and Politics in a Ninth-Century Historical Text', *Speculum* 71 (1996) 559–576

Mavroudi, M. *A Byzantine Book on Dream Interpretation: the Oneirocriticon of Achmet and Its Arabic Sources.* Leiden (2002)

Mazzola, R.F., 'History of Nasal Reconstruction. A Brief Survey,' *Handchirurgie – Mikrochirurgie – Plastische Chirurgie* 19 (1987) 4–6

McCormick, M. 'The Imperial Edge: Italo-Byzantine Identity, Movement and Integration AD 650–950,' in Ahrweiler, H. and Laiou, A.E. *Studies on the Internal Diaspora of the Byzantine Empire.* Washington (1998) 17–52

McKitterick, R. 'The Papacy and Byzantium in the Seventh and Early Eighth Century Sections of the Liber Pontificalis', *Papers of the British School at Rome* 84 (2016) 241–273

McKitterick, R. 'The Damnatio Memoriae of Pope Constantine II (767–768)', in Balzaretti, R., Barrow, J. and Skinner, P. (eds.) *Italy and Early Medieval Europe: Papers for Chris Wickham.* Oxford (2018) 231–248

Medvedev, I.P. *Vizantiĭskiĭ zemledel'cheskiĭ zakon*. Leningrad (1984)

Meier, M. 'Ostrom-Byzanz Spatantike-Mittelalter. Uberlegung zum 'Ende' der Antike im Osten des romischen Reiches,' *Millennium* 9 (2012) 187–253

Metzner, E.E. 'Textgestützte Nachträge zu Namen und Abkunft der 'Böhmer' und 'Mährer' und der zweierlei 'Baiern' des frühen Mittelalters – Die sprachliche, politische und religiöse Grenzerfahrung und Brückenfunktion alteuropäischer Gesellschaften nördlich und südlich der Donau,' in Fiala-Fürst, I. and Czmero, J. (eds.) *Amici amico III: Festschrift für Ludvík E. Václavek.* Olomouc (2011) 321–350

Mingazov, S. *Kubrat – the Ruler of Great Bulgaria and Qetrades – the character of John, Bishop of Nikiu.* Kazan (2012)

Mitchell, S. *Anatolia: Land, Men and Gods in Asia Minor*. 2 vols. Oxford (1993)

Moorhead, J. 'Iconoclasm, the Cross and the Imperial Image,' *Byzantion* 45 (1985) 165–179

Nesbitt, J.W. and Oikonomides, N. (eds.) *Catalogue of Byzantine Seals at Dumbarton Oaks and in the Fogg Museum of Art, Volume 2: South of the Balkans, the Islands, South of Asia Minor.* Washington, DC (1994)

Neuwirth, A., Sinai, N. and Marx, M. (eds.) *The Qur'an in Context: Historical and Literacy Investigations into the Qur'anic Milieu.* Leiden (2010)

Noble, T.F.X. *The Republic of St. Peter: the Birth of the Papal State 680–825*. Philadelphia (1984)

Noble, T.F.X. 'A new look at the Liber Pontificalis,' *Archivium Historiae Pontificae* 23 (1985) 347–358

Noble, T.F.X. *Images, Iconoclasm and the Carolingians*. Philadelphia (2009)

Noonan, T.S. 'The Khazar Qaghanate and its impact on the early Rus' state: the Translatio Imperii from Itil to Kiev,' in Khazanov, A.M. and Wink, A. (eds.). *Nomads in the Sedentary World.* London (2001) 76–102

Noonan, T.S. 'The Economy of the Khazar Khaganate,' in Golden, P.B., Ben-Shammai, H. and Róna-Tas, A. (eds.) *The World of the Khazars: New Perspectives. Selected Papers from the Jerusalem 1999 International Khazar Colloquium* (Handbook of Oriental Studies. Section 8 Uralic & Central Asian Studies) Leiden (2007) 207–244

Noth, A. and Conrad, L.I. *The Early Islamic Historical Traditions: A Source Critical Study.* Princeton (1994)

Noye, G. 'L'economie de la Calabre de la fin du Vie au VIIIe siècle,' in Cosentino, S. (ed.) *L'Italia Bizantina: una Prospettiva Economica. Cahiers de recherches medievales et humanistes* 28. Paris (2015) 323–388

Oberhelman, S.M. 'The oneirocritic literature of the late Roman and Byzantine eras of Greece: manuscript studies, translations and commentaries to the dream-books of Greece during the first millennium AD, with Greek and English catalogues of the dream-symbols and with a discussion of Greek oneiromancy from Homer to Manuel the Palaeologian', Unpublished diss., University of Minnesota (1981)

Oikonomides, N. *Les listes de préséance byzantines des IXe et Xe siècles*. Paris (1972)

Oikonomides, N. 'Les premieres mentions des themes dans la *Chronique* de Theophane,' *ZRVI* 16 (1975) 1–8

Olsen, R.J. 'The Last Arab Siege of Constantinople (717–718): A Neglected Source', *GRBS* 60 (2020) 425–443

Olsson, J.T. 'Coup d'état, Coronation and Conversion: Some Reflections on the Adoption of Judaism by the Khazar Khaganate,' *Journal of the Royal Asiatic Society 23* (2013) 495–526

Olster, D.M. *Roman Defeat, Christian Response and the Literary Construction of the Jew.* Philadelphia (1994)

Olster, D. 'Theodosius Grammaticus and the Arab Siege of 674–78,' *Byzantinoslavica* 56 (1995) 23–28

Orosz, L. *The London Manuscript of Nikephoros' 'Breviarium.'* Budapest (1948)
Ostrogorsky, G. 'Les debuts de la querelle des images,' *Melanges Charles Diehl*. Paris (1930) I.235–255
Ostrogorsky, G. 'Die *Chronologie* des Theophanes im 7. Und 8, Jahr-hundert,' *BNJ* 7 (1930) 1–56
Ostrogorsky, G. 'Sur la date de la composition du Livre des Themes et sur l'epoque de la constitution des premiers themes d'Asie mineure,' *Byzantion* 23 (1953) 31–66
Ostrogorsky, G. 'The Byzantine Empire in the World of the Seventh Century,' *DOP* 13 (1959a) 1–21
Ostrogorsky, G. 'Byzantine Cities in the Early Middle Ages,' *DOP* 13 (1959b) 45–66
Ostrogorsky, G. *History of the Byzantine State*. Oxford (1968)
Ostrogorsky, G. 'Observations on the Aristocracy in Byzantium,' *DOP* 25 (1972) 3–32
O'Sullivan, S. 'Sebeos' account of an Arab attack on Constantinople in 654,' *BMGS* 28 (2004) 67–88
Palmer, A. *The Seventh Century in the West-Syrian Chronicles*. Liverpool (1993)
Partington, J.R. *A History of Greek Fire and Gunpowder*. Baltimore (1999)
Pertusi, A. 'La formation des themes byzantins,' *Berichte zum XI Internationalen Byzantinisten-Kongress*. Munich (1958) 1–40
Petkov, K. *The Voices of Medieval Bulgaria, Seventh-Fifteenth Century: The Records of a Bygone Culture.* Leiden (2008)
Pizarro, J.M. *Writing Ravenna: The Liber Pontificalis of Andreas Agnellus*. Ann Arbor (1995)
Pohl, W. 'Conceptions of ethnicity in Early Medieval Studies,' in Rosenwein, B. and Little, L.K. (eds.) *Debating the Middle Ages: Issues and Readings*. Oxford (1998) 15–24
Priester, K. *Geschichte der Langobarden: Gesellschaft – Kultur – Altagsleben*. Stuttgart (2004)
Prieto Dominguez, O. *Literary Circles in Byzantine Iconoclasm: Patrons, Politics and Saints*. Cambridge (2021)
Proudfoot, A. 'The sources of Theophanes for the Heraclian dynasty,' *Byzantion* 44 (1974) 400–427
Pryor, J.H. and Jeffreys, E.M. *The Age of the ΔΡΟΜΩΝ: The Byzantine Navy ca. 500–1204*. Leiden and Boston (2006)
Rapp, C. 'Old Testament Models for Emperors in Early Byzantium,' in Magdalino, P. and Nelson, R. (eds.) *The Old Testament in Byzantium.* Washington DC (2010) 175–197
Remondon, R. *Papyrus grecs d'Appolonos Ano*. Cairo (1953)
Reynolds, D. 'Rethinking Palestinian Iconoclasm', *DOP* 71 (2017) 1–64
Richards, J. *The Popes and the Papacy in the Early Middle Ages, 476–752*. London (1979)
Riche, P. 'Le christianisme occidental,' in Dagron, G., Riche, P. and Vauchez, A. *Histoire du christianisme des origins a nos jours IV: Eveques, moines et empereurs (610–1054)* . Paris (1993) 607–866
Roland, A. 'Secrecy, Technology, and War: Greek Fire and the Defense of Byzantium, 678–1204,' *Technology and Culture* 33 (1992) 655–679
Rosenwein, B. and Little, L.K. (eds.) *Debating the Middle Ages: Issues and Readings*. Oxford (1998)
Runciman, S. *History of the First Bulgarian Empire.* London (1930)
Runciman, S. *The Eastern Schism: A Study of the Papacy and the Eastern Churches during the XIth and XIIth Centuries*. Oxford (1955)
Sahner, C.C. 'The First Iconoclasm in Islam: A New History of the Edict of Yazīd II (AH 104/ AD 723', *Der Islam* 94 (2017) 5–56
Samuelson, C. 'Iconography after the Quinisext Council (c. 680–720)' Unpublished diss. Darwin College, Cambridge (2016)
Schenk, K. 'Kaiser Leons III Walten im Innern,' *BZ* 5 (1896) 257–301
Schenker, A.M. *The Dawn of Slavic: An Introduction to Slavic Philology*. New Haven (1996)
Schneider, A.F. and Karnapp, W. *Die Stadtmauer von Iznik (Nicaea)* . Berlin (1938)
Setton, K.M. 'On the Importance of Land Tenure and Agrarian Taxation in the Byzantine Empire, from the Fourth Century to the Fourth Crusade,' *AJPh* 74 (1953) 225–259
Shaban, M.A. *Islamic History: A New Interpretation I: AD 600–750 (AHI32)* . Cambridge (1971)

Shenkar, M. 'Rethinking Sasanian Iconoclasm', *JOAS* 135 (2015) 471–498
Shepard, J. (ed.) *Cambridge History of the Byzantine Empire ca 500–1492*. Cambridge (2019)
Shepard, J. and Franklin, S. (eds.) *Byzantine Diplomacy*. Aldershot (1992)
Sheppard, S. *Constantinople AD 717–718: The Crucible of History*. Oxford (2020)
Shirota, S. 'The Chinese Chroniclers of the Khazars: Notes on Khazaria in Tang Period Texts,' *Archivum Eurasiae Medii Aevi* 14 (2005) 231–261
Simeonov, B. *Prabŭlgarska onomastika*. Plovdiv (2008)
Sinor, D. *Atour d'une migration des peuples au Ve siècle, Journal Asiatique* 1946–47. Paris (1948) 1–77
Sophoulis, P. *Byzantium and Bulgaria, 775–831*. Leiden (2011)
Spears, W.H. Jr. *Greek Fire: The Fabulous Secret Weapon That Saved Europe*. New York (1969)
Speck, P. *Das geteilte Dossier. Beobachtungen zu den Nachrichten über die Regierung des Kaisers Herakleios und die seiner Söhne bei Theophanes und Nikephoros*. Bonn (1988)
Sperati, G., 'Amputation of the Nose throughout History,' *Acta Otorhinolaryngol Italica* 29 (2009) 44–50
Starr, J. 'An Eastern Christian Sect: The Athinganoi', *HTR* 29 (1936) 93–106
Stewart, M.E. "A Furious Storm Fell Upon Them'; The Arab Siege of Constantinople, 717–18,' *Medieval Warfare Magazine* VIII.5 (2018) 24–33
Stumpf, J.A. 'On the Mutilation and Blinding of Byzantine Emperors from the Reign of Heraclius I until the Fall of Constantinople,' *Journal of Ancient History and Archaeology* 4 (2017) 46–54
Sumner, G.V. 'Philippicus, Anastasius II and Theodosius III,' *GRBS* 17 (1976) 287–294
Sussex, R. and Cubberley, P. *The Slavic Languages*. Cambridge (2011)
Teall, J.L. 'The Byzantine Agricultural Traditions,' *DOP* 25 (1971) 33–59
Toševa-Nikolovska, D. 'Some Observations on the *Nomos Georgikos*,' *Colloquia Humanistica* 7 (2018) 205–226
Toumanoff, C. *Studies in Christian Caucasian History*. Washington DC (1963)
Toumanoff, C. 'Caucasia and Byzantium,' *Traditio* 27 (1971) 111–158
Toynbee, A.J. *Constantine Porphyrogenitus*. Oxford (1973)
Treadgold, W. *The Byzantine State Finances in the Eighth and Ninth Centuries*. New York (1982)
Treadgold, W. 'Seven Byzantine Revolutions and the Chronology of Theophanes,' *GRBS* 31 (1990) 203–227
Treadgold, W. *Byzantium and its Army 284–1081*. Stanford (1995)
Treadgold, W. *A History of the Byzantine State and Society*. Stanford (1997)
Treadgold, W. 'Trajan the Patrician, Nicephorus, and Theophanes,' in Bumazhnov, D. Grypeou, E. Sailors, T.B. and Toepel, A. (eds.) *Bibel, Byzanz und Christlicher Orient: Festschrift für Stephen Gerö zum 65. Geburtstag*. Orientalia Lovaniensia Analecta 187. Leuven/Paris/Walpole (2011) 589–621
Treadgold, W. 'Opposition to Iconoclasm as Grounds for Civil War,' in Koder, J. and Stouraitis, I. (eds.) *Byzantine War Ideology Between Roman Imperial Concept and Christian Religion*. Vienna (2012) 17–26
Tsougarakis, D. *Byzantine Crete*. Athens (1988)
Turner, D. 'The Politics of Despair: The Plague of 746–747 and Iconoclasm in the Byzantine Empire,' *The Annual of the British School at Athens* 85 (1990) 419–434
Vasiliev, A.A. 'The Slavs in Greece', *Vizantiysky Vremennik* 5 (1898) 404–438, 626–670
Vasiliev, A.A. 'An Edict of the Emperor Justinian II, September 688,' *Speculum* 18 (1943) 1–13
Vasiliev, A.A. 'The Iconoclastic Edict of the Caliph Yazid II, AD 721', *DOP* 9/10 (1956), 23–47
Vasiliev, A.A. *History of the Byzantine Empire*. Madison (1964)
Velez Lopez, L.R. 'Las mutilaciones en los vasos antropomorfos del antiguo Peru,' *International Congress of Americanists. Proceedings of the XVIII session, Londres, 1912*, London (1913) 267–275
Vernadskij, G. 'Sur l'origine de la loi agraire,' *Byzantion* 2 (1925) 169–180
Von Grunebaum, G.E. 'Byzantine Iconoclasm and the Influence of the Islamic Environment', *History of Religions* 2 (1962) 1–10.

Vryonis, S. *The Decline of Medieval Hellenism in Asia Minor and the Process of Islamization from the Eleventh through the Fifteenth Century*. Berkeley (1971)

Wegewitz, W. 'Stand der Langobardenforschung im Gebeit der Niederelbe', in Tagliaferri, A. *Problemi della civilita e dell'economia Longobarda: Scritti in memoria di Gian Piero Bognetti* Milan (1964) 19–51

Wegewitz, W. *Das langobardische Brandgräberfeld von Putensen*. Hildesheim (1972)

Whitby, M. *The Emperor Maurice and his Historian: Theophylact Simocatta on Persian and Balkan Warfare*. Oxford (1988)

Wickham, C. *Framing the Early Middle Ages: Europe and the Mediterranean 400–800*. Oxford (2005)

Wickham, C. *The Inheritance of Rome: Illuminating the Dark Ages 400–1000*. London (2009)

Winkelmann, F. *Quellenstudien zur herrschenden Klasse von Byzanz im 8. Und 9. Jahrhundert*. Berlin (1987)

Wolfram, H. *History of the Goths*. Berkeley (1988)

Woods, D. 'Corruption and Mistranslation: The Common Syriac Source on the Origin of the Mardaites,' *American Foundation for Syriac Studies* (2011)

Woods, D. 'Maslama and the Alleged Construction of the First Mosque in Constantinople c.718,' in Crostini, B. and La Porta, S. (eds.) *Negotiating Co-Existence: Communities, Cultures and Convivencia in Byzantine Society*. Trier (2013) 19–30

Wortley, J. 'Iconoclasm and Leipsanoclasm: Leo III, Constantine V and the Relics', *BF* 8 (1982) 253–279

Yalamanchili, H., Sclafani, A.P., Schaefer, S. D. and Presti, P. 'The Path of Nasal Reconstruction: From Ancient India to the Present,' *Facial Plastic Surgery* 24 (2008) 3–10

Zacos, G. and Veglery, A. *Byzantine Lead Seals*. Basel (1972)

Zuckerman, C. 'Learning from the Enemy and More: Studies in 'Dark Centuries' Byzantium,' *Millennium* 2 (2005) 79–135

Zuckerman, C. 'The Khazars and Byzantium: the First Encounter,' in Golden, P.B., Ben-Shammai, H. and Rona-Tas, A. (eds.) *The World of the Khazars: New Perspectives – Selected Papers from the Jerusalem 1999 International Colloquium*. Leiden (2007) 399–432

Index